Flags of Convenience

An International Legal Study

Flags of Convenience

An International Legal Study

BOLESLAW ADAM BOCZEK

HARVARD UNIVERSITY PRESS
Cambridge · Massachusetts · 1962

Distributed in Great Britain
by Oxford University Press, London

Publication of this book has been aided
by a grant from the Ford Foundation

Library of Congress Catalog Card Number 62–13262

Printed in the United States of America

Preface

The issue of "flags of convenience" is, first of all, "a problem of the regulation of international competition in an important industry," and from that point of view it has been the subject of discussion in the daily press and the shipping periodicals of all the major maritime nations. But it has also an important international-law aspect which as yet has not been analyzed comprehensively by the literature on the subject. The primary purpose of this book is, then, to throw light upon this particular problem. However, to complete the picture it is necessary to carry out the purely legal analysis against the economic, social, and political background of the controversy surrounding the flags of Panama, Liberia, and Honduras.

After an introduction dealing with facts and statistics, the study proceeds to explain the reasons for the rise of the flags of convenience. The domestic legislations of the countries concerned and their shipping policies in relation to the issue in question are explored. Since reports have appeared on flag-of-convenience tendencies outside the so-called "Panlibhon" group, the veracity of these reports is checked after an analysis of the shipping legislations and statistics in various countries. Subsequently the social and political aspects of the Panlibhon phenomenon are discussed as well as the role played by pressure groups opposing the practice.

The discussion from the aspect of international law starts with the question whether flag-of-convenience countries have, under this law, the right to grant their flags to foreign-owned and -controlled vessels. Here the problem of the grant of nationality to merchant vessels and the conclusive test of this nationality are analyzed against the background of international practice and theory.

Anyone answering the question posed in the preceding paragraph must subsequently face the problems resulting from his answer, since nationality of ships is relevant in a great many situations covering practically the whole law of the sea and even going beyond it. Thus, it is appropriate to discuss the issues which actual developments have already brought to the attention of those following the flag-of-convenience problem.

The controversy over the membership of Liberia and Panama on the Maritime Safety Committee of the Inter-Governmental Maritime Consultative Organization (IMCO), a specialized agency of the United Nations, about which an advisory opinion has been rendered by the International Court of Justice, is discussed first. The opinion of the ICJ, though limiting itself to the interpretation of a provision in the convention establishing the IMCO, certainly will have some legal impact upon the question of the criteria of the nationality of ships in general and the nationality of the flag-of-convenience ships in particular.

Another problem is the result of the campaign of American and other seamen's unions to extend the application of United States laws to labor relations aboard American-owned Panlibhon vessels. Various jurisdictional aspects of this question are studied with particular reference to the decisions of the American courts. At the time when this book was in preparation the whole issue was still open and several cases were pending in United States courts, the Supreme Court included.

A separate chapter considers the international-law implications of the concept of "effective U.S. control" over American-owned Panlibhon shipping. The control of movement and the requisition of flag-of-convenience vessels in the case of war or any other emergency is discussed in this chapter.

Two chapters are devoted to a detailed critical analysis of the concept of "genuine link," followed in its evolution sine 1896 until the sessions, first, of the International Law Commission of the United Nations, and then, of the United Nations Conference on the

Law of the Sea in Geneva in 1958. An interpretation of article 5 of the Convention on the High Seas is suggested, and the results of the Geneva conference in relation to flags of convenience are assessed.

The final pages are devoted to the summary of the specific conclusions reached and to certain more general conclusions concerning the subject under inquiry. The bibliography, which does not purport to be exhaustive, includes the primary and secondary sources relied upon in the preparation of the book.

The book began with the author's Ph.D. thesis in political science, submitted to the Department of Government of Harvard University in May 1960. The present text has been revised and brought up-to-date by including—so far as possible—the most recent materials. For example, unlike the original thesis, it takes into account the decision of the ICJ of June 8, 1960, bearing upon the subject discussed in the book. It was gratifying for the author to find that the decision of the World Court did not differ in its argument and conclusions from the tentative opinion anticipated by the author in his thesis.

The author wishes to thank Professor Richard R. Baxter of the Harvard Law School and Professor Stanley H. Hoffmann of the Department of Government of Harvard University, directors of his thesis, for the encouragement they gave him to have this work published. The author is also grateful to Professor Myres S. McDougal of the Yale University Law School for his valuable criticism of the draft of the manuscript and for other kindnesses. Thanks are also due to Professor Milton Katz, Director of the International Legal Studies at Harvard Law School, and Mr. John A. King, Jr., Secretary of I.L.S., for making available to the author I.L.S. facilities, without which the preparation of this book would have been impossible. The author is equally grateful to the staff of the I.L.S. library for their assistance in his search for bibliographical material. Deep obligation must also be recorded to the staff of the Harvard University Press, especially to Miss Ann Orlov who bore the heavy burden of editing with skill and patience the manuscript of an author for whom English is not a native language.

Finally the author must add that the fellowships granted to him by the Ford Foundation and by Harvard University made it possible for him to write this book in the first place. To these institutions the author extends particular thanks.

B.A.B.

Cambridge, Massachusetts
April 1962

Table of Contents

Tables

Graphs

Foreword

In this definitive study of "Flags of Convenience" Dr. Boczek brings the skills of the disinterested scholar to bear, comprehensively and profoundly, upon a most important, and presently much controverted, chapter of the international law of the sea.

The international law of the sea, when viewed in broadest perspective, comprises three distinctive sets of principles. Certain basic constitutional principles express the general community preference for the freest possible access to, and the widest possible enjoyment by all peoples of, the great sharable resources of the oceans compatible with protecting the particular, exclusive interests common to all peoples. The second set of principles, sometimes described as jurisdictional, is designed to establish that shared competence over ships and events upon the oceans which is necessary to protect common interests in shared use. The third set of principles, most appropriately regarded as administrative in character, serves the function of facilitating the secure, economic, and harmonious application of the first two sets of principles in a highly decentralized arena, necessarily maintained as free from the comprehensive, exclusive authority of any particular state.

The more general principles of private international law, allocating competences among states with respect to events whose impacts transcend national boundaries, are of course, though it is sometimes forgotten, still different principles, designed for problems other than those directly affecting the shared enjoyment of the oceans and expressing very different policies. Though these principles of private international law may in many of their applications bear indirectly upon the shared use of the oceans, their compass extends beyond the shared domain of the oceans to events occurring within the most comprehensive, exclusive domains of particular states, and the policies of stability and comparative justice which they project depend, in their particular determinations, upon many factors other than the locale of events upon water or land, or in air space or outer space.

The outstanding merit of Dr. Boczek's book is that he has been able, even in the darkened light of contemporary controversy, to distinguish the very different general community policies at stake in the different principles of the law of the sea and of private international law and, hence, precisely to relate the problem of the nationality of ships to these policies in a way designed to promote overriding common interests.

The traditional principle of the international law of the sea establishing the conclusiveness of one state's attribution of national character to a ship against all other states Dr. Boczek correctly describes as an "organizing," or administrative, principle, having the function of making more secure the general community's basic constitutional policies about shared use and competence. "This subjection of the high seas to juridical order," he writes, "is organized and effected by means of a permanent legal relationship between ships flying a particular flag and the state whose flag they fly." A state attributing its national character to a ship is authorized to exercise certain controls over the ship and a certain competence over events occurring on board the ship; it is made responsible for the conduct of the ship; and it is accorded a competence to protect the ship against abuses of authority by other states. Because the "juridical order" of the oceans is, thus, so heavily "based upon the institution of the nationality of ships," Dr. Boczek finds it necessary that "this nationality be easily identifiable" and capable of being established with "certainty and clarity."

In his further efforts toward policy clarification, Dr. Boczek makes, however, a very careful distinction between two different types of problems: problems with respect to which continued acceptance of the conclusiveness of attributions of national character to ships is indispensable to the economic and secure maintenance of the public order of the oceans, and problems with respect to which the nationality of a ship is but one of many factors to be taken into account in reaching appropriate decision. The former problems embrace all controversies with respect to access to the high seas or to the territorial sea or internal waters of a particular state, all controversies relating to competence to prescribe and apply authority to activities upon the oceans, and all controversies with respect to competence to protect ships from abuses of authority. The latter problems include all the traditional controversies reflected in private international law, including the controversies about labor regulation and tax burdens so vexing in the contemporary world arena. With respect to these latter problems, Dr. Boczek very perceptively emphasizes that decisions minimizing the importance of the national character of ships in relation to other factors need not be regarded as denials of the conclusiveness of the national character of ships, with unfortunate consequences for the other type of problems.

It can scarcely be surprising, in view of his grasp of relevant community policies, that Dr. Boczek takes a strong stand against contemporary proposals to authorize states unilaterally to question each other's attributions of national character to ships because of the absence of "genuine link" or by other ill-defined criteria. He surveys past practice to demonstrate that international law has always regarded states' attributions of nationality by "whatever criteria of eligibility" they choose as conclusive and that the criteria which particular states have from time to time imposed upon themselves have never been regarded as requirements of international law. He examines the various recent proposals which would superimpose upon the competence of states a requirement of "genuine link" and finds that no clear or policy relevant criteria have yet been offered for ascribing empirical reference to this ill-born concept, derived by overextrapolation from the famous *Nottebohm* decision about individual human beings. He finds the proponents of the new concept in confusion both about recommended sanctions and about the potential consequences of different sanctions for the maintenance of public order upon the oceans. He notes that the 1958 Geneva Conference, though retaining the reference to "genuine link" in article 5 of the Convention on the High Seas, by specific vote eliminated the words "for purposes of recognition of the national character of the ship by other States." He concludes, therefore, with perhaps too much optimism, that article 5 of the Convention "cannot be interpreted to mean that if there is no link between the ship and the state the other state may refuse to recognize the ship's nationality, since this sanction is not laid down by the framers of the Convention, and, on the contrary, was explicitly rejected."

One who is concerned for the continued maintenance of even a minimum public order of the oceans, protecting freedom of access and shared competence for all peoples upon a basis of equality, can only hope that Dr. Boczek's book will be widely read and equally widely accepted as authoritative.

Myres S. McDougal

Abbreviations

ABS Bulletin: American Bureau of Shipping, *The Bulletin*
ACFN: American Committee for Flags of Necessity
AJIL: American Journal of International Law
Annuaire: Annuaire de l'Institut de Droit International
Ann. Dig.: Annual Digest and Reports of Public International Law Cases
B. & F. St. Pap.: British and Foreign State Papers 1917–1918
E.A.S.: *Executive Agreement Series*
Foreign Rel.: United States Department of State, *Papers Relating to the Foreign Relations of the United States*
Hearings (House) 1957: United States Congress, *Study of Vessel Transfer, Trade-in, and Reserve Fleet Policies, Hearings before the Subcommittee on Merchant Marine and Fisheries,* House of Representatives, 85th Congress, 1st Session, Pts. 1 and 2 (1957)
Hearings (Senate) 1957: United States Congress, *Ship Transfers to Foreign Flag, Hearings before the Merchant Marine and Fisheries Subcommittee of the Committee on Interstate and Foreign Commerce,* U.S. Senate, 85th Congress, 1st Session on S. 1488 (1957)
ICJ: International Court of Justice
ILC: International Law Commission
ILConf.: International Labor Conference
ILOffice: International Labor Office
ILO: International Labor Organization
IMCO: Inter-Governmental Maritime Consultative Organization
ITWF: International Transport Workers' Federation
LN.*OJ:* League of Nations, *Official Journal*
L.N.T.S.: *League of Nations Treaty Series*
N.L.R.B.: National Labor Relations Board Decisions
NMU: National Maritime Union
OEEC: Organization for European Economic Cooperation
OEEC.MTC "Study" (1958): Organization for European Economic Cooperation, Maritime Transport Committee, "Study on the Expansion of the Flags of Convenience Fleets and on Various Aspects Thereof" (1958)
RCADI: Recuil des Cours, Académie de Droit International de la Haye
Shipping Statistics: United States Department of Commerce, *Merchant Shipping Statistics Through 1958* (1959)
SIU: Seafarers' International Union

T.I.A.S.: *Treaties and Other International Acts Series*
T.S.: *Treaty Series*
UN.CLS.*OR:* United Nations Conference on the Law of the Sea (Geneva, 1958), *Official Records*
UN.GA.*OR:* United Nations, General Assembly, *Official Records*
UNLS or UNLS Supp.: United Nations Secretariat, *Laws Concerning the Nationality of Ships* (1955); *Supplement to Laws and Regulations on the Regime of the High Seas and Laws Concerning the Nationality of Ships* (1959) [United Nations Legislative Series]
U.N.T.S.: *United Nations Treaty Series*
YLJ: Yale Law Journal

Note: For other abbreviations used in the footnotes, in particular for those referring to the citations of judicial and statutory materials, consult *A Uniform System of Citation* 10th ed. (Cambridge, Mass., The Harvard Law Review Association, 1960)

Flags of Convenience

An International Legal Study

Mr. Lucky: Do you know what the international law is with regard to that, Mr. Brown?

Mr. Brown: I am not briefed fully on international law at all.

Chapter I. Introduction

The dialogue quoted on the facing page is a fragment from a congressional investigation into the transfer of United States ships to the flags of Panama, Liberia, and Honduras.[1] The question on which Mr. Brown, counsel for a major tanker-owning company, was not fully briefed referred to the status of American-owned vessels which, in this particular case, were flying the Panamanian flag. The congressional investigation itself was merely a small incident in the acute controversy that has developed in the international shipping industry over the last few years regarding the use of flags of convenience. This controversy has assumed a variety of forms; there have been strikes, boycotts, and picketing in ports all over the world — legal battles in municipal courts and international assemblies — and even an appeal before the International Court of Justice in The Hague.

It is hardly the first time that a problem relating to the use of the seas has been a source of international friction. Shipping is the most international of all industries and therefore the problems of the ocean have long been of particular interest for international law. A large body of "non-national or international law of an impressive maturity and universality"[2] regulating maritime matters has developed, first through custom and common practice, and sec-

1. *Ship Transfers to Foreign Flag, Hearings before the Merchant Marine and Fisheries Subcommittee of the Committee on Interstate and Foreign Commerce,* U.S. Sen. 85th Cong., 1st Sess. on S. 1488 (1957), p. 53. [Abbreviated hereafter as *Hearings* (Senate) 1957.]

2. Lauritzen v. Larsen, 345 U.S. 571, 578 (1953).

ond, through explicit agreements. Among the general principles of the law of the sea that of the "freedom of the seas" has gained undisputed recognition. This implies, among other rights, freedom to navigate on the high seas for ships of all nations, provided that these ships have a national character — that is, that they have been granted a nationality by their respective states, and that they ply the high seas under a recognized maritime flag.

However, with regard to the grant of nationality to merchant vessels, just as in the matter of the delimitation of the boundaries between the high seas and the territorial waters of any particular country, or as in the issue of nuclear tests conducted at sea, the general principle of the freedom of the seas is interpreted very differently by different nations. Some countries consider that they have the right to grant their flag as an unlimited prerogative; others, using the argument that every freedom must be limited in the interest of all, feel that they have the right to grant their flag to vessels only if they are owned by their nationals and that all other countries should adhere to this principle. Such differing positions reflect the conflicting economic interests of the nations concerned. For one group, under certain circumstances, a liberal interpretation is convenient; for another group, a restrictive interpretation better serves its interests.

Functionally, a "flag of convenience" can be defined as the flag of any country allowing the registration of foreign-owned and foreign-controlled vessels under conditions which, for whatever the reasons, are convenient and opportune for the persons who are registering the vessels. In common usage, particularly in the daily press, the term is applied to the flags of Panama, Liberia, and Honduras (frequently contracted as "Panlibhon"). The laws of these countries on the registration of merchant vessels are not only very liberal, but also — a decisive consideration — afford the shipowners who are registering their vessels under them very attractive financial advantages. These advantages are clearly what make the Panlibhon flags so convenient.

Statements made at the United Nations Conference on the Law of the Sea (Geneva, 1958) and acts adopted by the International Law Commission of the United Nations make it clear that in these circles "flags of convenience" refer to the flags of states which grant nationality to ships with which they have no genuine connection: the relation between them is merely the formality of the grant of the certificate of registry. Arguing *a contrario* from art. 5, para. 1 of the unratified Convention on the High Seas,[3] one can define the flags of convenience as such flags "under which there exists no genuine link between the state and the ships and, in particular, under which the state does not effectively exercise its jurisdiction and control in administrative, technical, and social matters over ships flying its flag." However, this definition is vague because the notion of "genuine link" is not clarified. And it can be applied also to flags other than those of the Panlibhon countries, since it does not emphasize the essential issue of the relation between the owner and the flag state. On the other hand, foreign-owned tonnage is registered sometimes under flags other than those of Panlibhon, for example, under the flag of Great Britain; but this ensign is not ever regarded as a flag of convenience.

In 1958 the Maritime Transport Committee of the Organization for European Economic Cooperation defined the flags of convenience as

> the flags of such countries as Panama, Liberia, Honduras and Costa Rica whose laws allow — and indeed make it easy for — ships owned by foreign nationals or companies to fly these flags . . . in contrast to the practice in the maritime countries (and in many others) where the right to fly the national flag is subject to stringent conditions and involves far-reaching obligations.[4]

The classic English textbook on the international law of the sea deals with flags of convenience in the section devoted to subsidies and flag discrimination. There the system of flags of convenience is quite rightly presented as a form of competition in international navigation "whereby some countries — chief amongst which are Panama, Honduras, Liberia, and Costa Rica (sometimes referred to as "Panhonlibco") — allow the use of their flags by foreign ship-

3. United Nations Conference on the Law of the Sea, *Official Records* 2:135 (1958) (Doc. A/CONF. 13/L. 53). [These *Records* are abbreviated hereafter as UN.CLS.*OR.*]

4. OEEC.MTC, "Study on the Expansion of the Flags of Convenience Fleets and on Various Aspects Thereof" (1958), p. 2 [mimeographed]. Printed in *Fairplay* 191:800–806 (1958). *The Norwegian Shipping News* 14:137–140 (1958) carries a detailed summary of this study; see also *The New York Times*, April 6, 1958, p. 78.

ping by a simple administrative formality, such as the mere registration or the grant of a certificate of registry."[5] The author of this textbook, Colombos, regards Panama, Liberia, Honduras, and Costa Rica only as the main flags of convenience, and he does so rightly, since — as will be seen — other countries, in particular, Lebanon, also have embarked upon a policy of the liberal registration of merchant vessels and offer other facilities similar to those offered by Panama and Liberia.

In this book the term "flags of convenience" or "Panlibhon" will be used to describe the flags of merchant vessels registered in Panama, Liberia, Honduras, and — to a certain extent still — in Costa Rica, with the understanding that the flags of some other countries may also be included in the description if the analysis of their laws and regulations about the grant of nationality to merchant vessels reveals possibilities similar or equivalent to those afforded by the classic flags of convenience.

The term itself is rendered in French as *pavillon de complaisance,* in German *billige Flagge,* in Italian *bandiera ombra* or *bandiera di convenienza,* in Spanish as *bandera de conveniencia,* in Dutch as *goedkope vlag.*[6] It apparently originated sometime in the early 1950's. In 1928 when the International Transport Workers' Federation raised the question of the transfer of ships to the "Panamanian, Honduran, and similar registries," the expression "flags of convenience" was not yet fashionable, and the resolution

5. Colombos, *The International Law of the Sea* (4th rev. ed. 1959), p. 336. The earlier editions co-authored by Higgins and Colombos do not mention flags of convenience.

6. See, *e.g.*, "La Conférence de Genève sur le droit de la mer," *Chronique de Politique Etrangère* 12:42 (1959); de Ferron, *Le Droit International de la Mer* (1958), I, 88–90. Patey translates the English term as "pavillon de convenance" in "La Conférence de Nations Unies sur le droit de la mer," *Revue Générale de Droit International Public* 29:454 (1958); Dahm, *Völkerrecht* (1958), I, 677; Fisser, "Konkurrenz der billigen Flaggen," *Hansa* 95:240 (1958); Conforti, "Le convenzioni di Ginevra sul diritto del mare," Istituto di Diritto Internazionale e Straniero della Università di Milano, *Comunicazioni e Studi* 9:230 (1958); Gabriele, "Le bandiere di convenienza e la NATO," *Rivista Marittima* 51 (1960); Standard, "Las convenciones marítimas y la paz mundial a través del derecho," *Inter-American Law Review* no. 2:401, 412 (1959); Vluchten, of Vechten, "De registratie van schepen onder goedkope vlag," *Marineblad* 68 no.1:60 (1958). In Russian the expression *deshevyi flag* ("cheap flag") is used, following the German and Dutch terminology. See, *e.g.*, Molodtsov, *Mezhdunarodno-pravovoi rezhim otkrytogo moria i kontinental'nogo shelfa* (1960), p. 140.

adopted by the ITWF mentioned only the practice of "spurious transfers." [7]

The term was used in 1954 in a report of the OEEC in relation to the flags of Panama, Honduras, Liberia, and "certain other countries some of which permit the operation of ships registered in [these] countries at a nominal level of taxation and where it is legally possible to apply lower standards of social security." [8] Since then the term has been almost universally used in English-language publications. However, the term is criticized both by the groups that take advantage of its possibilities and by those that oppose the existence of such flags. The governments of the major flag-of-convenience countries consider it to be an "unfortunate and improper" term. It is "derogatory" to the republics concerned. Addressing the Maritime Session of the International Labor Conference in 1958, the government delegate of Panama expressed his profound displeasure at the use of the term "flag of convenience," and called upon the International Labor Office to prohibit the use of the term with regard to the republics of Panama, Liberia, Honduras, and Costa Rica.[9] Furthermore, the official practice of the government of the United States, presumably for reasons of comity, is not to identify the use of the flags in question as flags of convenience but as Panlibhon flags.[10] The alternative term that was introduced and is favored by the American shipowners, who have registered their ships under the Panlibhon flags, is "flags of necessity." This term is meant to imply that in order for the shipowners to operate their ships competitively it has been necessary to reg-

7. For the text of the resolution see ILOffice, *Conditions in Ships Flying the Panama Flag: Report of the Committee of Enquiry of the International Labour Organization* [May-November 1949] (1950), p. 45. [Abbreviated hereafter as ILOffice, *Panama Conditions*.]

8. OEEC.MTC, *Maritime Transport*, Trends in Economic Sectors (Paris, December 1954), pp. 19, 65.

9. International Labor Conference, *Record of Proceedings*, 41st Session [Geneva, 1958] (1959), p. 115. [Abbreviated hereafter as ILConf.*RP*. 41 Sess. (Geneva, 1958).] See also the statement of the Liberian representative before the International Court of Justice in ICJ, *Pleadings*, Constitution of the Maritime Safety Committee of the IMCO (1960), p. 270.

10. Statement by Acting Secretary Dillon at the Washington conference of the U.S. and West European nations on their shipping policies, *DSB* 41:no. 1045 (1959). While the flag of Costa Rica was still playing some role as a flag of convenience, the form "Panlibhonco" was also in use. See, *e.g.*, a pamphlet issued in 1958 by the ITWF on the subject of the flags of convenience, *Panlibhonco: The Modern Shipping Problem* (1958).

ister them under such flags.[11] On the other hand, the American maritime unions, which vigorously oppose the practice, call the flags in question "runaway" flags, to imply that they have run away from the flag of the United States under which they should otherwise properly sail.[12] Several other phrases, such as "flags of refuge" or "tax-free flags," have also been used to describe the flags of convenience,[13] and opponents of the practice have coined such derogatory terms as "pirate flags," "bogus maritime flags," "freebooters" and "fictitious" or "nominal" flags.[14] Against all these pejorative nicknames Liberian sources have named their flag a "flag of attraction."[15]

History presents numerous cases that are analogous to the present-day practice of convenience flags. In the past, shipowners who deemed it advantageous did not hesitate to attach their vessels to foreign merchant fleets. For example, in the sixteenth century, many adventurous English merchants sailed under the Spanish flag in order to evade the monopolistic Spanish regulations governing the lucrative trade with the West Indies.[16] In the seventeenth cen-

11. *The New York Times,* April 11, 1958, p. 47; November 26, 1958, p. 46. See also the ACFN *Memorandum to the Department of State and to the General Counsel of the National Labor Relations Board* (n.p., n.d.), pp. 2–5 [submitted on October 30, 1959 by Donovan Leisure, Newton, and Irvine, counsel for the ACFN]. The term "flags of necessity" is also favored by the defense agencies of the United States since the flag-of-convenience ships play an essential part in the defense of the United States. See, *e.g.*, Schade, "The Strategic Importance of Control of the Seas," January 1960, p. 43 [mimeographed paper in the library of Center for International Affairs, Harvard University]. *Cf.* statement of Vice Admiral Wilson, Deputy Chief of Naval Operations, *The New York Times,* April 5, 1960, p. 62; statement of Rear Admiral D. V. Gallery in his talk before the Navy League on May 26, 1961, *id.*, June 21, 1961, p. 10. (The Rear Admiral speaks of "flags of survival" meaning that they are absolutely necessary for the defense purposes of the United States.)

12. See, *e.g.*, the statement of the executive secretary of the AFL-CIO Maritime Committee in *Study of Vessel Transfer, Trade-in and Reserve Fleet Policies: Hearings before the Subcommittee on Merchant Marine of the Committee on Merchant Marine and Fisheries,* H.R., 85th Cong., 1st Sess. (1957), pp. 685, 694, 710. [Abbreviated hereafter as *Hearings* (House) 1957.]

13. See, *e.g.*, Baker, "Flags of Refuge for Shipping Industry: Federal Income Tax Considerations," *Tax Law Review* 13:137 (1957–1958). See also *The New York Times,* March 28, 1958, p. 50. The expression "flags of refuge" was coined as an analogy to "countries of refuge," a term for countries where foreign-controlled companies are organized to avoid taxes.

14. Becu, "Fighting the pirate flags," *Free Labour World* no. 104:59 (February 1959); *The New York Times,* March 23, 1958, sec. 5, p. 11; *ILC Yearbook 1955,* I, 63 (statement by Scelle).

15. *Liberia Today,* March 1959, p. 12.

16. Williamson, *The Ocean in English History* (1941), p. 33.

tury, the Newfoundland "boat fisherman," who faced deportation by the authorities of their home country, England, which feared their competition in fishing, sailed under the French flag.[17] And at the end of the nineteenth century a similar subterfuge was resorted to by certain British trawler-owners who registered their vessels under the Norwegian flag in order to evade the British legislation that restricted trawling activities in Moray Firth. The fishermen in question assumed that, if they registered their vessels under a foreign flag, the British legislation could not apply to them.[18] It was stated in 1864 by Dr. Lushington, a British expert in maritime and prize law, with regard to British-owned vessels that "it is perfectly notorious that the merchants of Great Britain have repeatedly at various times been owners of foreign vessels sailing under foreign flags — a privilege of which they would be very sorry to be deprived — a privilege, which though it may subject them to difficulty in case of war, they are entitled to exercise, except so far as the rights of war interfere with it." [19]

The case of a Swiss-owned vessel, the *La Palme,* is a pertinent example of what American shipowners currently describe as a ship flying a "flag of necessity." It was registered under the flag of Hanover and subsequently under that of Germany (with a nominal German owner in order to comply with the German law), because its owners were refused by the Swiss Federal Council the use of the Swiss national flag as there was some doubt at that time whether a landlocked country had the right to grant nationality to ships. The vessel was captured in 1871 by the French as an enemy (German) vessel. However, the *Conseil d'Etat* which heard the appeal from the decision of the prize court in Bordeaux declared the prize unlawful, recognizing the need of the Swiss owners (a mission society) to sail under a foreign flag.[20]

17. *Id.,* p. 144.

18. These facts provided background for the case *Mortensen v. Peters* decided by the High Court of Justiciary of Scotland [1906] 14 S.L.T. 230. The vessels in question were owned, operated, and manned by the English, and a foreigner was nominally in charge of the vessel in order to satisfy the requirement of the registering state, Norway. The Norwegian actually often occupied a humble position, such as that of a cook. See comments in Briggs, *The Law of Nations* (2d ed. 1952), pp. 52–53. See also Fulton, *The Sovereignty of the Sea* (1911), p. 729.

19. Rienow, *The Test of the Nationality of a Merchant Vessel* (1937), p. 92. Rienow quotes *The Johanna Emilie,* Spinks, Reports of Cases Decided during the Present War (1854–1856) in the Admiralty Prize Court (1855–1858), p. 18.

20. Pradier-Fodéré, *Traité de droit international public européen et américain*

In addition, it has happened frequently that flags of other states have been employed during time of war when shipowners, who were nationals of a belligerent state, had to resort in great numbers to the use of a neutral flag in order to avoid capture. Thus, during Napoleon's continental blockade scores of English vessels were registered under the colors of such little German principalities as Knyphausen or Pappenburg. Their tiny or practically nonexistent merchant marines expanded overnight, as it were, by almost a hundredfold.[21] During the war of 1812 part of the Massachusetts fleet took out Portuguese papers as a protection against possible capture by the British.[22] The French flag granted to the subjects of the Sultan of Muscat, a British protectorate, was quite a typical flag of convenience. As is discussed later this particular case came to the attention of the Permanent Court of Arbitration.[23]

As capital was internationalized — largely the result of the development of corporate ownership — in an increasing number of cases the nationality of a ship came to be different from the nationality of its actual and ultimate owner, in spite of the apparently rigid municipal provisions that tried to regulate the problem. In 1911 the United States Commissioner of Navigation said: "The investment of American capital in ships under the British flag is not exceptional. Considerable amounts of British capital are understood to be invested in the shipping enterprises of Spain and Japan, and German capital has been invested in ships under the Brazilian flag and doubtless others." [24] Moreover, prior to the First World War, the United States Merchant Marine was in a state of almost complete disruption, largely because the bulk of Ameri-

(1906), VIII, 557–558; Colombos, p. 254; Fauchille, *Traité de droit international public* (1925), I, pt. 2, 904. *Cf.* also the grant of the Russian "flag of necessity" to Greek subjects of the Ottoman Empire described in Gidel, *Le droit international public de la mer* (1932), I, 90–91 n. 3.

21. Albion and Pope, *Sealanes in Wartime* (1942), p. 106.

22. Morison, *The Maritime History of Massachusetts 1783–1860* (1921), p. 205. One must add, however, that protection of this kind would be problematic in the case of a visit by an enemy man-of-war. Another instance of temporary protection by a foreign flag is the case of the ships of certain German cities that sailed on the Mediterranean under a Danish flag in order to avoid the attacks of the Barbary pirates, bound by treaty with Denmark to spare Danish ships. See Cantillon de Tramont, *De la nationalité des navires* (1907), pp. 113–114.

23. *The Muscat Dhows* case (France v. Great Britain) (1905), Scott ed., *Hague Court Reports* (1916), pp. 93–109. This case is discussed further in Ch. IV.

24. Rienow, p. 90, quoting the *Annual Report of the Commissioner of Navigation* (1911), pp. 24–25. See also ACFN *Memorandum*, p. 66.

can-owned ships were registered under various foreign flags.[25] Such foreign flags undoubtedly fulfilled, to a certain extent, the function of flags of convenience. Though in most cases the ultimate foreign ownership had to be hidden under a corporate veil, already in the period before the emergence of the Panlibhon flags there were various countries where the citizenship of the owner was of no consequence with respect to the registration of shipping. For example, a number of South American and Central American countries, interested in attracting foreign capital, have long allowed foreign-owned shipping into their merchant marines.[26] Thus, the practice of registering merchant vessels under a foreign flag is not of recent origin. The fact that registration under Panlibhon flags has become such a controversial issue in recent years is a result of the enormous dimensions which this practice has assumed — the result of the particular competitive conditions that have prevailed in the world shipping industry since the Second World War. The origin of the Panlibhon fleet, as such, however, can be traced to the years directly after the First World War.

In 1922 the United America Line, an American shipping company owned by W. Averill Harriman, was planning pleasure cruises for two of its liners, the SS *Resolute* and the SS *Reliance*, when, as a result of prohibition regulations, the Attorney General of the United States ruled that alcoholic beverages could not be sold or transported aboard American-owned vessels. To circumvent this rule the company decided to transfer their ships from American to Panamanian registry, "the most acceptable to American interests." On organizing a base company under the liberal corporation laws of Panama, the ownership of the vessels was subsequently transferred without difficulty to that company. On December 5, 1922, the Stars and Stripes were lowered aboard the two ships lying in New York harbor and the Panamanian colors

25. *Hearings* (House) 1957, p. 687; *Hearings* (Senate) 1957, p. 185. *Cf.* McFee, *The Law of the Sea* (1950), pp. 152–153.

26. For example: Argentina had no ownership requirement in 1854 when it was still known as Buenos Aires (Ortolan, *Règles internationales et diplomatie de la mer* [4th ed. 1864], I, 396–397; van Zijst, *De nationaliteit van Schepen beschouwd uit een internationaalrechtelijk oogpunt*, appendix A, xxii (1897); Colombia — when it was still named New Granada (Ortolan, I, 400; van Zijst, appendix A, xxiv); Guatemala and Honduras (van Zijst, appendix A, xxvi); Nicaragua and Paraguay (*id.*, p. xxvii); Uruguay (*id.*, pp. xxix–xxx).

were raised. The transferring company explained its action by pointing out that it could not compete otherwise with foreign companies whose governments did permit the sale of alcoholic beverages aboard their ships.[27]

Soon after this first experiment, when the operating costs of American-flag vessels began to rise under union pressure, other shipowners, in particular several oil companies, also shifted to the Panamanian colors in order to avoid being obliged to employ expensive American union crews and officers, and to be able to substitute for them the cheap labor of non-union foreign crews. By 1924, there were 15 ships recorded in *Lloyd's Register of Shipping* as flying the Panamanian flag. These early transfers were reflected in President Harding's report on the Merchant Marine in 1922, when he said that

> not so many months ago the head of a company operating a fleet of ships under our flag called at the Executive Offices to discuss a permit to transfer his fleet of cargo vessels to a foreign flag, though he meant to continue them in a distinctly American service. He based his request for transfer on the allegation that by such a transfer he could reduce his labor costs sufficiently to provide a profit on capital invested.[28]

The transfer of the United Fruit Co.'s fleet to Honduran registry was the origin of the Honduran flag of convenience. In a sense, this was a more natural arrangement than were the earlier transfers to the Panamanian flag, since the United Fruit Co., along with a few other American companies, already had interests in the Central American area. The United Fruit Co. used Honduran ports, carried Honduran bananas, and was partially manned by Honduran crews. However, Panama was especially favored as a country to whose flag ships might easily be transferred.

In the last years of the interwar period some transfers were dictated by reasons connected with the imminent outbreak of war. For example, in 1935 the Esso Shipping Co. had 25 ships sailing under the flag of the Free City of Danzig. These ships, formerly of German registry, were manned by German crews. The company, fearing imminent war, transferred the ships to the Panamanian flag. It was thus able to remove the German crews and replace

27. *The New York Times*, November 10, 1922, p. 2; December 6, p. 2.

28. Message of the President of the United States on the American Merchant Marine, November 2, 1922, H. R. Doc. No. 471, 67th Cong., 3d Sess. 6 (1921–1922).

them with American crews. The company operated the ships in this way until the Neutrality Act was passed which, among other things, prevented these ships from trading with the Allies in Europe because they carried United States passengers. Incidentally, the Panamanian laws favoring a flexible exchange of crews allowed the Esso Shipping Co. to remove the American crews and to substitute for them British crews, which then enabled the ships to trade with Great Britain.[29] By September 1, 1939, as a result of the transfer of merchant vessels from various foreign flags, but mostly from the American flag, 130 vessels of 719,041 gross tons (1,105,600 deadweight tons) were flying Panamanian colors, and 27 vessels of 82,068 gross tons (90,500 deadweight tons) Honduran colors.[30]

The next stage in the history of these convenience flags is connected with the neutrality laws and regulations enacted by the United States at the beginning of the Second World War and with various other war-control laws enacted by the belligerent countries. Previously, wars had often proved to be profitable for merchant shipping, but the United States Neutrality Act and the proclamations and regulations issued with it, in an attempt to keep American-flag vessels from entangling the United States in the conflict, barred American-flag vessels from the European war zone.[31] Consequently, numerous American-owned vessels, especially tankers, shifted to the neutral Panamanian flag and voyaged to Britain in 1939–1942, despite the United States neutrality laws. These transfers were approved by the United States Maritime Commission and in some cases were even requested by the United States government.[32] A number of European shipowners also found it expedient to transfer their vessels to a neutral flag in order to avoid the wartime requisitioning of their vessels. They chose the Panamanian flag because it already had a reputation as a flag of refuge. Thus the circumstances of the war gave a considerable boost to the Panamanian flag fleet. The heyday of the Panamanian ensign, however, was still to come. It was the specific competitive situation of the world shipping market after the Second World War that

29. Statement of president of Esso Shipping Co., *Hearings* (Senate) 1957, p. 79.
30. *Shipping Statistics* (1959), pp. 28–29.
31. Neutrality Act of 1939, ch. 2; 54 Stat. 4. For the Act and the related regulations see also *AJIL* 34 *Supp:* 21–74, 161–172 (1940).
32. Benedict, *Admiralty*, VI, 200; Carter, "The New Maritime Nations," *Journal of Business* 29:207–208 (1956). See also *Hearings* (Senate) 1957, p. 79.

gave rise to the tremendous increase of the Panamanian fleet as well as to the spectacular growth of the Liberian fleet. A large number of shipowners transferred their vessels to the country that offered them the most liberal registration possibilities and virtual freedom from taxation as well as other advantages. Panama, which in 1945 was already a well known convenience flag, offered the refuge of her registry to most of this tonnage[33] and by 1949 the number of vessels registered under her colors reached 462 (3,078,-000 gross tons). This made Panama the fourth largest maritime nation in the world, surpassed in number of ships only by the United States, the United Kingdom, and Norway.[34]

An ILO Committee of Enquiry reported in 1949 that the 644 vessels registered in 1948 under the Panamanian flag (owned by 384 different companies) were a motley assortment. They had been transferred from as many as 33 different countries to Panama — 306 had been transferred from the United States, 90 from the United Kingdom, 20 from Greece, 16 from Norway, 14 from Germany, the rest from other countries, such as Australia, France, Portugal, Italy, and Sweden.[35] The fleet registered under the flag of Honduras, though it had not grown by such enormous numbers as the Panamanian fleet, nonetheless had risen from 27 vessels in 1939 to 82 in 1949 (449,000 gross tons).[36] But, in a certain sense, the year 1949 is the turning point in the recent history of the flags of convenience. It was in this year that Liberia first joined the competition for registry and appeared in *Lloyd's Register of Shipping* as having under her flag vessels over 1000 gross tons, although the history of the Liberian flag actually goes back to 1947, when Liberia admitted to her registry the American-owned Far-

33. Thus, *e.g*, out of 1113 merchant vessels sold by the United States for foreign registry under the Merchant Ship Sales Act of 1946, 60 Stat. 41 (1946), as amended, 50 U.S.C. App. §§1735–1746 (1952), as amended, 50 U.S.C. App. §§1738 (b), (f), 1742 (c) (2) (Supp. V, 1958), as many as 152 vessels were registered in Panama. See *Shipping Statistics*, p. 107.

34. *Shipping Statistics*, p. 31. The number of ships grew from 268 in 1945 to 406 in 1946, and, as a result of wholesale transfers of the ships sold under the Ship Sales Act of 1946, doubled between 1946 and 1947. ILOffice, *Panama Conditions*, p. 83.

35. ILOffice, *Panama Conditions*, pp. 9, 74. There were nearly 100 ships for which no information as to the former nationality was given. One should point out that the former country of registration did not necessarily indicate the country of the shipowner at the time of the inquiry.

36. *Shipping Statistics*, p. 30.

rell line. This line started navigation along the Liberian coast employing Liberian crews. Therefore, it was not at this point a flag of convenience in the true sense of the term. The introduction of Liberia to the shipping world seems to have been due to the Stettinius Associates of New York (the Liberia Co.) who, having secured a flexible concession for the development of the Liberian economy, arranged the formalities for granting Liberian registration on terms still more liberal than those of Panama. Hundreds of vessels were soon flying the Liberian flag and it became the most attractive convenience flag.[37]

Table 1 shows that between the years 1949 and 1954 Panama was the leading flag-of-convenience nation and it was at the same time the fourth largest maritime country in the world. But in the same period the number of ships registered under the Liberian colors increased steadily; by 1955 the Liberian fleet overtook in volume of tonnage the fleets of such countries as the Netherlands, Italy, Japan, and Panama itself. This is shown by Graph 1. From 1955 on the volume of tonnage registered under the Liberian flag skyrocketed from 4,602,000 gross tons to as much as almost 12,000,000 gross tons at the end of 1959. In 1957 Liberia already stood third in the shipping statistics, behind only the United States and the United Kingdom. In comparison with this phenomenal increase, the Panamanian fleet has kept to more or less the same level of tonnage. It has grown somewhat since 1955 even though some of its former tonnage has been transferred to the more attractive Liberian flag. However, as Table 1 also shows, in the years 1960–1961 a decrease in the tonnage registered under the Panlibhon flags is noticeable. This is the result of the transfer of many Panlibhon vessels to the Greek flag and of the uncertainties that stem from the attempts of the American maritime unions to organize the crews of "runaway" vessels.[38]

The growth in tonnage of the other flag-of-convenience countries — Honduras and Costa Rica — has been more modest. The Honduran fleet, which in 1939 recorded 82,000 gross tons, reached its

37. See article by Albion on flags of convenience in *Grolier Encyclopedia* (1959). [The author wishes to thank Professor Albion for making available the manuscript of the article.] Before that, in 1948, only two small ships of 772 gross tons are recorded under the Liberian flag. *ABS Bulletin*, October 1958, pp. 40–41.

38. See *The New York Times*, March 27, 1961, p. 44. See also Chs. II and III.

peak in 1950 with 529,000 gross tons of shipping. Thereafter its popularity began to wane slowly, until at the end of 1957 it had 318,000 gross tons and in June 1961 only 94,000 gross tons (Table 1). In 1948, Costa Rica, like Liberia, did not have a merchant fleet that was worth mentioning in the shipping statistics. However, from a fleet that consisted of one vessel of 1000 gross tons in 1949, it grew steadily to 121 vessels of 516,000 gross tons recorded in 1958. This was the apogee of Costa Rica's career as a flag-of-convenience country.[39] After 1958 the tonnage registered under her flag fell by almost 50 per cent as a result of reforms carried out in her ship registration laws. Nonetheless, at the end of 1960 the tonnage of ships over 1000 gross tons registered under

TABLE 1. Number of ships (of 1000 gross tons and over) and tonnage (thousands of gross tons) of major merchant fleets in 1939 and yearly 1949–1961.

	1939		1949		1950	
Country	No.	Tonnage	No.	Tonnage	No.	Tonnage
Costa Rica	0	0	1	1	3	11
Denmark	379	1,042	298	1,045	307	1,116
France	555	2,678	494	2,733	519	2,889
Germany	854	3,916	47	103	174	476
Greece	436	1,698	223	1,263	218	1,212
Honduras	27	82	82	449	94	529
Italy	667	3,178	378	2,284	423	2,474
Japan	1,180	5,102	292	1,156	387	1,543
Liberia	0	0	15	221	39	431
Netherlands	537	2,670	492	2,731	500	2,820
Norway	1,072	4,499	912	4,728	955	5,135
Panama	130	719	462	3,078	495	3,414
Sweden	484	1,312	537	1,780	547	1,814
U.K.	2,850	16,027	2,571	16,387	2,605	16,766
U.S.A.	1,379	8,126	3,421	25,499	3,401	25,254
U.S.S.R.	354	1,136	432	1,331	432	1,325
	10,904	52,185	10,657	64,789	11,099	67,209
Other countries	1,894	6,085	2,211	8,851	1,183	8,509
Total (world fleet)	12,798	58,270	12,868	73,640	13,282	75,718

Sources: *Shipping Statistics; ABS Bulletin*, June 1960; June 1961; November 1961.

39. Costa Rica was not favored by the American shipowners. Only one American vessel was transferred to her flag. *Hearings* (House) 1957, p. 78.

the flag of this tiny Central American republic still amounted to 71,000 gross tons, and in June 1961 to 40,000 gross tons.

The spectacular growth and the present size of the Panlibhon fleets can be visualized better if it is compared with the increase in the world fleet as a whole. While in 1949 the total flag-of-convenience tonnage (3,749,000 gross tons) represented only a very small per cent of the entire world fleet (73,640,000 gross tons), ten years later, at the end of 1959, the combined fleets of Panama and Liberia and the relatively negligible amount of tonnage sailing under the Honduran and Costa Rican flags, aggregating 16,543,000 gross tons, accounted for 14 per cent of the world tonnage (117,640,000 gross tons). Of the total increase in world tonnage

TABLE 1. *(continued)*

	1951		1952		1953	
Country	No.	Tonnage	No.	Tonnage	No.	Tonnage
Costa Rica	15	79	20	97	36	179
Denmark	309	1,227	312	1,313	319	1,385
France	543	3,109	582	3,402	600	3,523
Germany	274	841	363	1,150	469	1,549
Greece	215	1,200	207	1,156	193	1,102
Honduras	79	414	81	435	66	383
Italy	488	2,862	537	3,184	556	3,342
Japan	465	2,087	521	2,578	567	2,973
Liberia	78	726	121	1,157	182	1,808
Netherlands	500	2,882	501	2,927	498	2,987
Norway	963	5,470	980	5,700	1,020	6,093
Panama	545	3,605	545	3,762	540	3,953
Sweden	576	2,032	599	2,225	598	2,419
U.K.	2,532	16,721	2,501	16,736	2,505	16,858
U.S.A.	3,373	25,181	3,349	25,124	3,348	25,290
U.S.S.R.	471	1,455	483	1,478	504	1,528
	11,426	69,891	11,702	72,424	12,001	75,372
Other countries	2,220	8,930	2,217	9,500	2,369	9,730
Total (world fleet)	13,646	78,821	14,019	81,924	14,370	85,102

since 1939 (excluding the United States reserve fleet in "moth balls"), 43 per cent is due to the Panlibhon fleets.

The type of vessels that compose the Panlibhon fleets is what one would expect under the circumstances (see Table 2). The number of passenger vessels is very small, although there are some such ships that sail under convenience flags. Some of these are reconditioned older ships and others are converted cargo ships or even aircraft carriers.[40] On the other hand it is interesting to note that 58 per cent of the Liberian fleet is composed of tankers as is 55 per cent of the Panamanian fleet.[41] In the world fleet generally the per cent of vessels flying convenience flags is much higher for tankers than it is for dry-cargo vessels (tankers — 25 per cent; dry-cargo ships — 14 per cent). Liberia, which in 1958 outstripped

TABLE 1. *(continued)*

	1954		1955		1956	
Country	No.	Tonnage	No.	Tonnage	No.	Tonnage
Costa Rica	62	254	112	463	123	506
Denmark	315	1,451	315	1,547	317	1,618
France	589	3,540	570	3,663	571	3,698
Germany	558	1,992	652	2,494	748	2,953
Greece	198	1,148	201	1,180	230	1,372
Honduras	67	401	58	353	56	335
Italy	581	3,634	589	3,811	647	4,135
Japan	598	3,242	622	3,436	651	3,740
Liberia	363	3,487	486	4,602	655	6,591
Netherlands	507	3,083	535	3,403	557	3,670
Norway	1,056	6,559	1,102	7,145	1,145	7,734
Panama	519	3,935	513	3,876	535	4,035
Sweden	576	2,492	571	2,586	577	2,747
U.K.	2,538	17,422	2,526	17,601	2,525	17,874
U.S.A.	3,255	24,938	3,215	24,711	3,108	24,013
U.S.S.R.	581	1,729	604	1,830	716	2,510
	12,363	79,327	12,671	82,701	13,161	87,531
Other countries	2,430	9,931	2,477	10,243	2,454	10,134
Total (world fleet)	14,793	89,258	15,148	92,944	15,615	97,665

40. *The Shipping World & World Shipbuilding,* March 5, 1958, pp. 263–264.

41. Costa Rica has never had more than four tankers registered. The number of 13 tankers registered in Honduras in 1950 has decreased to only one. *Shipping Statistics, passim.*

the United Kingdom, has the largest tanker fleet in the world, followed by the United Kingdom, Norway, the United States, and Panama (see Graph 2). It must also be noted that a very large proportion of the world tramp fleet (32.6 per cent) is sailing under flags of convenience.[42]

It is also interesting to note the age of the vessels sailing under the Panlibhon flags. Whereas in 1949 a considerable proportion of these were older vessels, a higher proportion than in most of the leading maritime countries,[43] the situation in the Panlibhon fleets since then has changed. As a result of scrappings and the registration of a large number of newly constructed vessels, mostly tankers, a lot of new ships are now flying the colors of Liberia and Panama. The total tonnage under construction for registration in

TABLE 1. *(continued)*

Country	1957		1958		1959	
	No.	Tonnage	No.	Tonnage	No.	Tonnage
Costa Rica	122	514	121	516	38	130
Denmark	330	1,782	357	1,924	356	2,002
France	594	3,871	624	4,212	631	4,399
Germany	818	3,383	866	3,866	892	4,170
Greece	250	1,492	289	1,776	409	2,834
Honduras	53	318	39	174	32	146
Italy	696	4,483	718	4,775	678	4,693
Japan	743	4,449	870	5,282	956	5,830
Liberia	894	9,396	1,020	11,253	1,015	11,945
Netherlands	587	4,003	580	4,040	555	4,163
Norway	1,212	8,519	1,288	9,503	1,332	10,398
Panama	560	4,277	546	4,340	542	4,322
Sweden	584	2,975	584	3,276	577	3,427
U.K.	2,517	18,192	2,522	18,655	2,466	19,092
U.S.A.	3,046	23,725	3,061	24,247	2,996	24,036
U.S.S.R.	737	2,625	774	2,789	858	3,331
	13,743	94,004	14,259	100,628	14,333	104,918
Other countries	2,550	10,766	2,707	11,686	2,852	12,722
Total (world fleet)	16,293	104,770	16,966	112,314	17,185	117,640

42. *Norwegian Shipping News* 15:789 (1959).
43. ILOffice, *Panama Conditions*, pp. 9–10.

Panama and Liberia showed a marked increase in 1957–1959. In particular this is true of Liberia, for whose registry the deliveries of new merchant vessels added a large amount of tonnage.[44] A comparison of the gross tonnage of Panama and Liberia, respectively, with the tonnage of ships delivered from new construction to these countries shows that 60 per cent of the Liberian and 30 per cent of the Panamanian tonnage has been registered in these countries from new construction (see Tables 1, 3, and 4). As a result of these new acquisitions, the Panlibhon fleets as a whole have a very favorable age distribution; over 35 per cent of the Panlibhon tonnage is less than five years old — in the United

TABLE 1. *(continued)*

	1960		1961 (June 30)	
Country	No.	Tonnage	No.	Tonnage
Costa Rica	21	71	12	40
Denmark	349	2,080	345	2,044
France	641	4,599	639	4,649
Germany	862	4,196	859	4,261
Greece	602	4,916	655	5,348
Honduras	27	122	21	94
Italy	656	4,808	648	4,832
Japan	1,036	6,431	1,074	6,663
Liberia	875	10,814	836	10,667
Netherlands	557	4,342	546	4,380
Norway	1,336	10,818	1,347	11,328
Panama	495	3,992	487	3,882
Sweden	564	3,581	563	3,647
U.K.	2,413	19,330	2,383	19,455
U.S.A.	2,926	23,754	2,810	23,081
U.S.S.R.	873	3,617	910	3,839
	14,233	107,471	14,135	108,210
Other countries	3,084	14,556	3,203	15,366
Total (world fleet)	17,317	122,027	17,338	123,576

44. OEEC.MTC, *Maritime Transport,* Trends in Economic Sectors (Paris, 1958), p. 22. However, after 1959 there followed a striking decrease in the tonnage being constructed for registration under the Liberian and Panamanian flags. See OEEC. MTC, *Maritime Transport,* Trends in Economic Sectors (Paris, May 1961), pp. 19, 57.

TABLE 2. The composition, by number of ships of 1000 gross tons and over, and tonnage (thousands of gross tons) of the merchant fleets of Panlibhonco as of December 31, 1959.

	Class													
	Passenger, cargo		Passenger, cargo, refrigerator		Freighter		Freighter, refrigerator		Bulk carrier		Tanker		Total	
Flag	No.	Tonnage	No.	Tonnage	No.	Tonnage	No.	Tonnage	No.	Tonnage	No.	Tonnage	No.	Tonnage
Liberia	8	76	1	2	461	3,204	3	11	122	1,301	420	7,351	1,015	11,945
Panama	17	113	0	0	282	1,410	7	22	45	299	191	2,478	542	4,322
Honduras	0	0	0	0	20	89	11	49	0	0	1	8	32	146
Costa Rica	0	0	0	0	36	126	0	0	2	4	0	0	38	130
Total	25	189	1	2	799	4,829	21	82	169	1,604	612	9,837	1,627	16,943

Source: *ABS Bulletin*, June 1960, pp. 38–39.

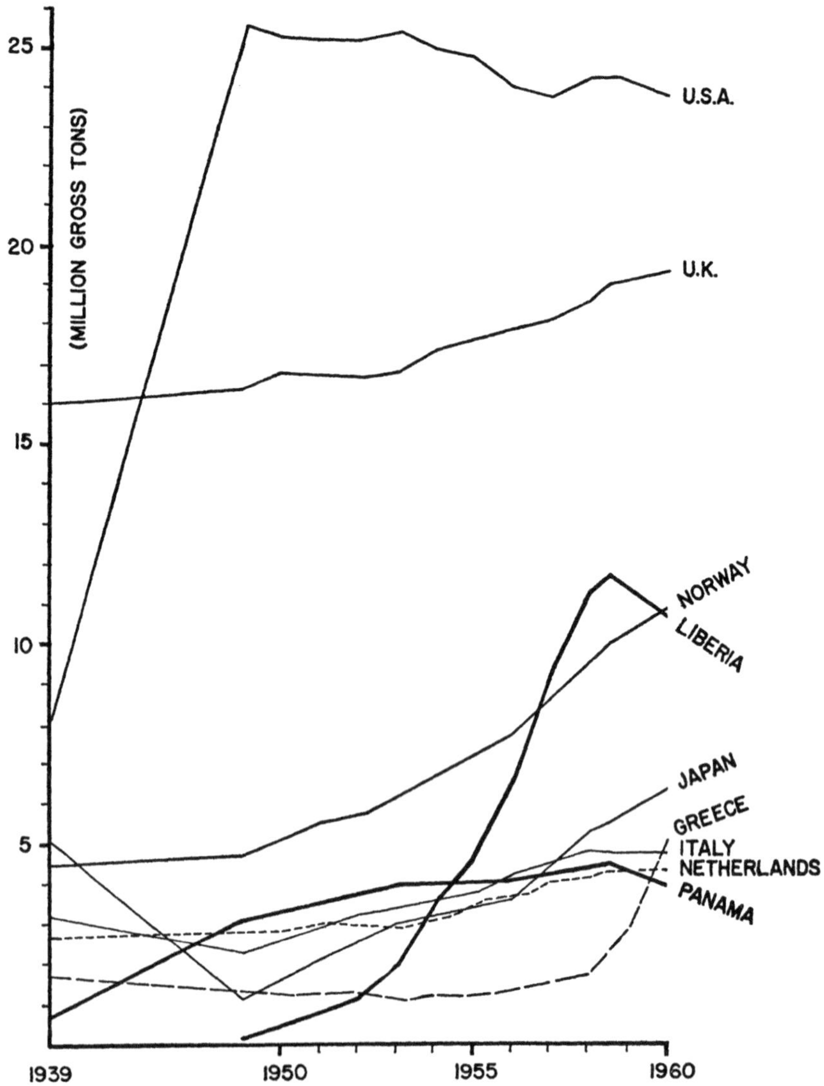

Graph 1. The growth of the major merchant fleets, 1939–1960.[a]

[a] As of June 30, 1961, the United States had the largest fleet, followed in order by the United Kingdom, Norway, Liberia, Japan, Greece, Italy, France, Netherlands, German Federal Republic, Panama, and the U.S.S.R. See Table 1.

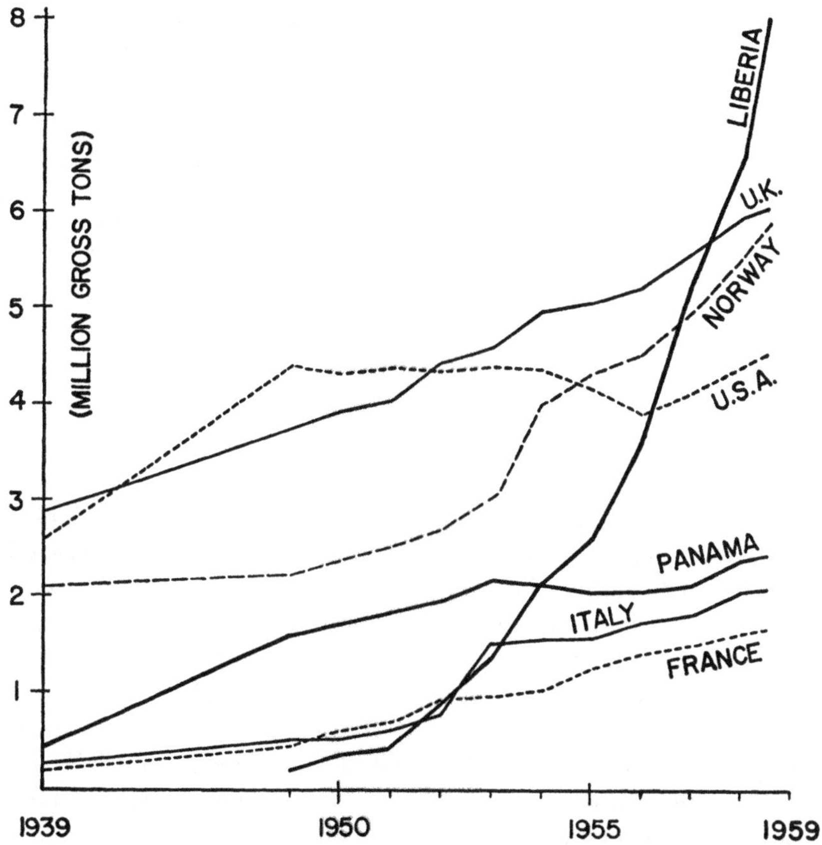

GRAPH 2. The growth of the major tanker fleets, 1939–1959.

TABLE 3. Number and tonnage (thousands) of new tankers and total new merchant ships delivered for the Liberian flag within the period 1956–1959.

	Tankers			Total		
Year	No.	Gross tons	Deadweight tons	No.	Gross tons	Deadweight tons
1956	37	764	1,208	93	1,329	2,126
1957	55	1,266	2,024	117	1,886	2,987
1958	47	1,109	1,823	83	1,496	2,449
1959	38	1,033	1,665	67	1,407	2,420
Total	177	4,172	6,720	360	6,018	9,982

Sources: *Shipping Statistics, passim; ABS Bulletin*, June 1960, p. 39.

TABLE 4. Number and tonnage (thousands) of dry-cargo ships and tankers delivered from new construction for Liberian and Panamanian flags within the period 1949–1958.

For flag of—	Dry-cargo ships No.	Dry-cargo ships Gross tons	Dry-cargo ships Dead-weight tons	Tankers No.	Tankers Gross tons	Tankers Dead-weight tons	Total No.	Total Gross tons	Total Dead-weight tons
Liberia	184	1,868	3,024	248	4,894	7,838	432	6,762	10,861
Panama	33	254	403	67	1,094	1,673	100	1,349	2,076
Total	217	2,122	3,427	315	5,988	9,511	532	8,111	12,937

Source: *Shipping Statistics, passim.*

Kingdom this figure is about 22 per cent.[45] The OEEC which follows with anxiety the rapid growth of the convenience fleets has not failed to notice the relative youth of the Panlibhon vessels.[46] Liberia and Panama operate tanker fleets made up primarily of big supertankers capable of attaining the highest speed possible (see Table 5). Actually, the average deadweight tonnage of the Liberian tankers is the highest in the world; their average speed is surpassed only by that of the United States' own tankers.[47]

It is difficult, if not impossible, to determine accurately the real beneficial ownership (that is, ownership yielding benefit or profit) of the tonnage registered under the convenience flags. In 1958 it was estimated that persons of Greek nationality or origin were operating approximately 50 per cent of the total Panlibhon ton-

45. *The Shipping World & World Shipbuilding*, February 26, 1958, p. 239.

46. It was noted by the OEEC, that 83 per cent of the tanker tonnage under the Liberian flag was under ten years old, as compared with 52 per cent for the rest of the world; OEEC.MTC, *Maritime Transport* (1958), p. 22. Out of 7 million gross tons of the Liberian ships classified by the American Bureau of Shipping, only 4 per cent were built prior to the Second World War. For the Panamanian vessels the corresponding figure is 13 per cent. See more statistical data in *ABS Bulletin*, February 1959, pp. 9–10. See also *The New York Times*, January 28, 1959, p. 49. For tables showing the age distribution of the major fleets at mid-1960 see OEEC.MTC, *Maritime Transport* (1961), pp. 51, 53.

47. As of December 31, 1958, only the 46,600 deadweight-ton Saudi Arabian tanker (the only ship registered under the Saudi Arabian flag) had higher speed than the average speed of the American or Liberian tankers; *ABS Bulletin*, November 1959, p. 35. *Cf.* also Table 5.

TABLE 5. Average tonnage and speed of vessels of 2000 gross tons and over in major tanker fleets as of December 31, 1958.[a]

Flag	Tonnage (deadweight)	Speed (knots)
Liberia	26,200	15.6
U.K.	15,700	13.8
Norway	18,000	14.2
U.S.A.	17,500	15.5
Panama	19,500	14.8
Italy	17,500	14.4
France	20,200	14.8
Sweden	18,200	16.6
Netherlands	15,100	14.1
Japan	19,300	14.7

Source: *ABS Bulletin,* November 1959, p. 35.

[a] The average deadweight tonnage of the United States-controlled Liberian-flag tankers is 28,900. The figure for the United States-controlled Panamanian-flag tankers is 20,100, and the average speed of both the Liberian and Panamanian tankers is 15.2 knots.

nage. Shipping titans of Greek descent owned the bulk of this tonnage.[48] The Greek contribution to the Panlibhon fleet in spite of recent transfers back to the Greek flag seems to be still about 40 per cent. With respect to the per cent of the fleet owned by American interests one must distinguish vessels owned by United States companies and their affiliates from vessels owned formally by foreign companies, the stock of which is owned and controlled by American individuals.[49] Statistical data show that American-owned convenience vessels total about 6.5 million out of 16.5 million gross

48. *The Shipping World & World Shipbuilding,* February 26, 1958, p. 239. In reality most of these Greeks are not of Greek nationality but only of Greek ancestry. They are internationally known owners of large fleets (Niarchos, Onassis, Goulandris, Kulukundis, Kivanos), mostly operating out of the United States and holding interests in many companies. Thus, *e.g.*, Onassis is a Greek, born in Turkey and holding Argentinian citizenship. His ships are registered under the names of 30 corporations and sail under at least 5 different flags; *Hearings* (House) 1957, p. 193 (statement of executive secretary of the AFL-CIO Maritime Committee); *cf. The New York Times,* August 3, 1959, p. 40; November 6, 1959, p. 49.

49. Letter from Clarence G. Morse, then Federal Maritime Administrator, to the *Yale Law Journal,* October 30, 1959, p. 2 [on file in Yale Law Library], cited in "The Effect of United States Labor Legislation on the Flag-of-Convenience Fleet: Regulation of Shipboard Labor Relations and Remedies against Shoreside Picketing," *YLJ* 69:499 n. 7 (1960).

TABLE 6. Number and tonnage of Liberian and Panamanian flag tankers of 2000 gross tons and over with those under United States-control as of December 31, 1958.

	No.	Gross tons	Deadweight tons
Liberia	417	6,784,600	10,940,500
under U.S. control	180	3,182,200	5,199,100
Panama	195	2,440,500	3,810,000
under U.S. control	131	1,680,300	2,630,900

Source: *ABS Bulletin*, November 1959, p. 35.

tons of Panlibhon shipping. This is about 40 per cent of the global flag-of-convenience fleet.[50]

The per cent of tankers under United States control flying Panamanian and Liberian flags is much higher than that of dry-cargo ships. It amounts to about 65 per cent for the Panamanian and 48 per cent for the Liberian fleet (see Table 6). In contrast to the United States-controlled vessels under these flags, those registered under Honduran colors are almost all dry-cargo vessels owned by the United Fruit Company. However, the Panlibhon countries are not the only ones under which American-owned shipping is registered. The United States companies also have ships registered in at least 13 other countries (see Table 7). It is striking to note that more than one million gross tons of American-owned tonnage sails under the British flag. In addition, although the bulk of American-controlled but foreign-registered ships is owned by United States companies and their affiliates rather than by individuals, independent American owners also have some control of ships under the British flag.[51] Over 80 per cent of the flag-of-convenience ships is thus owned ultimately either by United States interests, or by persons of Greek origin, supported to a certain extent by American capital. The ownership of the remainder

50. United States Maritime Administration, Statistics & Special Studies Office, Ship Data Branch, Dept. of Commerce, "Foreign Flag Vessels under Effective Control as of July 1, 1959," as quoted in *YLJ* 69:499 n. 7 (1960).

51. In the Anglo-American Shipping Company, Ltd., incorporated in Bermuda a few years ago, the majority of capital was supplied by United States investors, in particular by E. Naess, a member of the ACFN. Naess decided upon British participation in his venture because — as he said — operation under the British flag entirely on United States capital would invite the accusation that the British flag was being used as a flag of convenience; *The Times*, November 10, 1959, p. 17.

TABLE 7. Number and tonnage of ships owned by United States companies and their affiliates and registered under foreign flags as of December 31, 1958.

Flag	No.	Tonnage (gross tons)
Panama	109	1,250,432
Liberia	99	1,932,999
United Kingdom	89	1,033,169
Honduras	25	105,525
Netherlands	22	202,263
Venezuela	21	103,825
France	14	158,975
Norway	9	102,179
Germany	8	124,626
Belgium	6	73,650
Argentina	6	14,824
Canada	4	11,517
Italy	3	34,002
Denmark	3	38,876
Finland	1	1,025
Philippines	1	1,165
Other flags	2	12,851
Total	422	5,201,903

Source: *Shipping Statistics*, p. 27.

of the Panlibhon fleet lies with a variety of shipping companies and shipowners, among whom Italian and English nationals control a fairly substantial proportion of the tonnage.[52]

52. *Fairplay* 191:254 (1958); Carter, p. 213. On British ships transferred to Liberian registry, see *Hearings* (House) 1957, p. 39. On the European exile shipowners operating Panlibhon ships, see Mender, "Nationality of Ships — Politics and Law" *Arkiv for Sjørett* 5:265, 286 (1961) [Oslo], referring to Grönvold, *Panama and Greek Ships* (1959).

Chapter II. The Flight from National Flags

The prodigious growth of the Liberian and Panamanian flag-of-convenience fleets makes it necessary to examine carefully the reasons why these two small countries, with very little tradition in the shipping industry, are two of the largest maritime nations in the world today. It is necessary to distinguish 1) the circumstances which dissuade or perhaps by force even keep shipowners from registering their vessels under their respective national flags, and 2) the special circumstances that cause them to choose to register their vessels under the flags of Panama, Liberia, and Honduras (in some circumstances under other flags of convenience) rather than under the flag of any other foreign country It must be pointed out that, frequently, in discussions of this subject these two questions are confused. Here we will deal, first, with the reasons for the flight from national flags and, then, with the circumstances which have made the Panlibhon flags so especially attractive.

The reasons why so many United States shipowners have fled their national flag are somewhat different from the reasons that have motivated shipowners of other nationalities, but the same kind of economic and financial considerations are involved for both groups. The OEEC came to the conclusion that "there are two main motives actuating those shipowners who have adopted the practice of registering under flags of convenience, viz. opportunities for avoiding taxation on the earnings of ships registered under these flags and in some cases relief from high crew standards and consequent operating costs." [1] However, this OEEC conclusion, though in general true, confuses the two separate problems mentioned above. And since this aspect of the topic relates to the international law problems involved in the flag-of-convenience issue it will be discussed below, in particular with reference to American-owned Panlibhon shipping.

After the Second World War a substantial expansion of United States overseas trade took place in connection with the multiple increase of imports of petroleum products, metallic ores — and coal and grain exports. However, the United States merchant marine has not been able to keep pace with the growth of overseas trade, and the number of ships in foreign trade flying United States colors has declined to such an extent that, whereas in 1948 such ships carried 53 per cent of United States foreign trade, in 1960 they carried less than 12 per cent — a proportion lower than any recorded in the previous 40 years.[2] This is the result, first of all, of the high cost of ship construction in the United States and the ever-increasing expenses of operation. In fact, American shipowners have found it very difficult without government aid to compete with foreign-flag ships in foreign-trade operations. Actually most of the major shipping nations have had to grant some form of assistance, financial or otherwise, to maintain their fleets.[3] Government support of the merchant marine has been established national policy in the United States ever since 1817. Currently the chief form of government aid to shipping is the operating differential subsidy provided for by the Merchant Shipping Act of 1936, which is based on the difference between the cost of operating an American ship and the average costs incurred by foreign competitors. United States shipowners are also subsidized to en-

1. OEEC.MTC, "Study" (1958), p. 4.

2. *Shipping Statistics*, p. viii. *Cf.* the statement of Acting Secretary Dillon at the Washington conference in 1959, *DSB* 41:14 (1959). See also statement of Curran, president of the NMU, *The New York Times*, August 6, 1961, sec. 5, p. 11.

3. See Gorter, *United States Shipping Policy* (1956), pp. 67–105. For a historical outline of the subsidizing policies of various maritime countries up to the Second World War see Mance, *International Sea Transport* (1945), pp. 115–129. For a condensed summary of the principal direct and indirect aids granted today by the governments of ten major maritime nations (excluding Liberia and Panama!) to their shipbuilding and shipping see the table on foreign shipping and shipbuilding subsidies and aids in *Shipping Statistics*, p. 159. See also Colombos, pp. 335–336.

able them to compete with builders in countries where wages are lower.[4]

Nevertheless only about a third of the United States Merchant Marine, notably passenger-liner companies and dry-cargo vessels is subsidized. No subsidy is payable to the owners of tankers or of tramp ships. Hence, in the absence of a subsidy or of a flag-discrimination policy, many Americans who own tankers or other bulk-cargo vessels, in order not to destroy their ability to compete in international sea transportation, have transferred or directly registered their vessels under a Panlibhon flag. Unsubsidized American shipowners believe that, although they could obtain competitive parity through a subsidy, they can achieve the same results just as effectively by registering their vessels under what they call "flags of necessity." Moreover, by using this device, they avoid the increased taxation burden that is imposed upon the nation as a result of the government subsidy.[5]

In order to defend their particular interests, 19 American corporations holding interests in foreign corporations which own and operate bulk-cargo vessels flying the flags of Liberia, Panama, and Honduras, formed the American Committee for Flags of Necessity in November 1958. When it was founded the ACFN represented over 5 million deadweight tons of shipping (186 vessels) and in 1961 the committee, operating out of New York City, was composed of 20 American companies, owning beneficially 225 tankers

4. 49 Stat. 2001 (1936), as amended, 46 U.S.C. §§1171–1180, as amended, 46 U.S.C. §§1176, 1177 (a) (Supp. V, 1958); 49 Stat. 1955 (1936), as amended, 46 U.S.C. §§1151–1159 (1952), as amended, 46 U.S.C. §1152 (f) (Supp. V, 1958). For the data on the aids granted by the United States government to American shipbuilding and shipping see *Shipping Statistics*, pp. 157, 158, 160. *Cf.* Fridlund, *Tax Problems of the Shipping Industry*, Sixth Annual Tulane Tax Institute (1957), pp. 744, 767–768. See also Carter, pp. 209–210.

5. The subsidy necessary to equalize lower foreign-flag cost and to keep the required tonnage of bulk cargo carriers under the American flag would amount to $400 to $500 million yearly, which is about three times more than the sum now provided for this purpose. See ACFN, *Some Important Facts about Flags of Necessity Ships: A Fleet Vital to America's Defense and Economy, Summary* (2d ed. Selvage & Lee, Inc. [undated]), p. 9. The operating subsidy costs the United States government about $140 million annually. See statement of C. G. Morse, then Maritime Administrator, *The New York Times*, November 22, 1959, p. 88. The figure given by the ACFN is $130 million annually, out of which 87.5 per cent is devoured by labor and wages costs of 13,000 seamen who man the subsidized ships. The ACFN concludes that the American taxpayer is paying $8,673.08 a year for each U.S. seaman on a subsidized ship. See full-page advertisement of the ACFN entitled "Why 'Flags of Necessity'?" *The New York Times*, June 21, 1961, p. 10.

and other bulk carriers registered under the Panlibhon flags. This totals 6.7 million deadweight tons of shipping.[6]

The necessity to meet foreign competition by lowering operating costs was underscored by representatives of leading American oil companies in testimony before the Senate Committee on Interstate and Foreign Commerce in 1957. At that time the following statements were made:

> We feel that to be competitive, we have to have low cost transportation. Accordingly, it is necessary for us to construct and operate tankers under the foreign flag, where foreign trade is involved.[7]

> It is common knowledge that operating costs of tankers under the United States flag are substantially higher than the costs of tankers registered under foreign flags . . . [The American oil companies] are in competition with other companies in the countries in which they operate.[8]

> The fundamental reason for Gulf's operation of foreign-flag tankers is competition . . . We cannot remain competitive with [foreign-owned and controlled companies] by operating our tankers exclusively under the American flag, because our costs of operation under the United States flag would exceed their costs of operation under foreign flags by some 70 per cent. In any business which is as highly competitive as the international oil industry, it is impossible to absorb such increased costs if one is to continue in business.[9]

> [Our ships] were registered under the laws of Liberia in order to place them on a competitive basis with other foreign-flag vessels in the transportation of petroleum in world trade.[10]

The reduced cost of operation, particularly with respect to the wages that must be paid, is also recognized by the United States as an advantage that accrues to American shipowners from foreign registration. The Maritime Administrator, testifying before the Committee on Merchant Marine and Fisheries of the House of Representatives, listed seven advantages to be gained from the

6. ACFN *Memorandum*, pp. 2–5. For the names of the original 19 members see *id.*, p. 2 n. 1. See also *The New York Times*, June 21, 1961, p. 10. The seat of the committee is at 25 Broadway, New York, N.Y. Breck McAllister is chairman.

7. Statement of C. S. Teitsworth, vice-president and director of Socony Mobil Oil Co., *Hearings* (Senate) 1957, p. 48.

8. Statement of M. G. Gamble, president of Esso Shipping Co., *id.*, p. 64.

9. Statement of C. F. Van der Clute, general manager of Gulf Oil Corp., *id.*, p. 104.

10. Statement of A. E. Kihn, president of California Shipping Co., *id.*, p. 118. See also opinion of Vice Admiral Emory W. Land, U.S. Navy, Ret., former chairman of the United States Maritime Commission, *id.*, pp. 100–102.

transfer of United States ships to foreign flags: 1) Transfer to a foreign flag increases the market value of the ship. 2) Transfer reduces operating costs, particularly the wages and maintenance of good working conditions, due to lower standards permissible under foreign flags. 3) Transfer makes possible operating in world trade with easy currency conversion. 4) Transfer allows the owner to avoid United States Coast Guard requirements governing the condition of his vessel. 5) The owner may effect repairs aboard at less cost than the same repairs in the United States. 6) The owner can save money by avoiding United States income tax. 7) And ultimately, as a result of increased earnings, the owner's financial ability to acquire new tonnage is improved.[11]

According to authoritative sources, the annual operating costs of a bulk-cargo vessel under the United States flag are double the costs of a similar ship when operated under the Liberian or Panamanian flag.[12] The chief factor involved in these high operating costs under the United States flag is the extremely high wage scale of American-flag seamen as compared with seamen sailing under other flags. The American wage scale is the highest in the world and has increased about four times since 1918.[13] Furthermore, under United States law, all the officers and at least 75 per cent of the crew aboard a United States flag vessel must be American citizens.[14] If an American shipowner registers his vessel under the United States flag, he must pay the crew according to the American wage scale. By registering his ship under a foreign flag, an American shipowner may hire a foreign crew, thereby reducing the principal element in the differential cost of the vessel's operation.[15] This advantage is well illustrated by the following dia-

11. *Hearings* (House) 1957, p. 140.

12. See the schedules of comparative operating costs in *Hearings* (House) 1957, p. 142. *Cf.* the figures presented by the various oil companies, *Hearings* (Senate) 1957, pp. 9, 104–105, 118, 227.

13. For details see U.S. Maritime Administration records, Annual Report of Commission of Navigation, Dept. of Commerce, Collective Bargaining Agreements in *Shipping Statistics*, pp. 182–194. See also Gorter, *United States Shipping Policy*, p. 100, where a table shows comparative operating expenses of the U.S. and foreign-flag vessels in 1953. See also *The New York Times*, January 25, 1959, sec. 5, p. 12. American pay is 257 per cent higher than Swedish, 284 per cent higher than British, and 426 per cent higher than Dutch or German pay.

14. 49 Stat. 1935 (1936), 46 U.S.C. §672 (a) (b) (1952).

15. *Hearings* (House) 1957, pp. 51, 57 (tanker manning cost per calendar day of a T-2 type tanker of 16,500 deadweight tons equals $1200 under the U.S. flag, and

logue recorded at a congressional investigation:

Mr. Santangelo: There is a difference in wages between what the American crew would get and what the foreign crew would get?
Mr. Morse: There is quite a substantial difference.
Mr. Santangelo: The foreign crew is paid lower wages?
Mr. Morse: It is much lower for the foreign crews.[16]

One must, however, emphasize that the real effect of the registration of American-owned vessels under Panlibhon flags is "to bring the high operating costs incurred by ships registered in the United States down to a level nearer that of the general run in the countries of their foreign competitors. In a sense, therefore, it is the removal of a handicap rather than the gaining of an advantage," [17] since the wages aboard a Liberian or Panamanian vessel are not lower, and may even be higher, than those aboard the vessels of European nations.[18]

It is, therefore, common practice for American flag-of-convenience owners to man their vessels with alien crews. There are ships on which the entire unlicensed crew personnel are Indians, West Africans, or Italians, and the officers, British or German. The crews are recruited under local union contracts in Italy, India, or in West Africa. There are also ships where British, Dutch, Spanish, and Panamanian crews are employed.[19]

---

only $280 under a foreign flag). See also opinion of Vice Admiral Land, *id.*, pp. 65, 101. *Cf.* pp. 141–142.

16. *Id.*, p. 166.

17. OEEC.MTC, "Study," (1958), p. 5.

18. *The Economist*, November 22, 1958, p. 728; ACFN *Memorandum*, p. 5; Naess, a member of the ACFN claims, for example, that the wages aboard a Liberian vessel surpass by 50 per cent those paid aboard a Norwegian vessel (*The New York Times*, November 26, 1958, p. 46). Niarchos, one of the shipping titans of Greek origin, has stated that the wages aboard the flag-of-convenience vessels are in many cases higher than those aboard the vessels of the European countries (*The Times*, April 1, 1958, p. 11, "Why should the flag matter?" letter of Niarchos). *Cf.* the statement of the Acting Secretary Dillon at the Washington conference in 1959 (wages aboard the Panlibhon ships are often higher than those aboard the vessels of the traditional maritime countries of Europe), *DSB* 41:14 (1959). These data have not been questioned by the opponents of the flags of convenience.

19. *Hearings* (Senate) 1957, pp. 17, 19, 92, 106, 120. A study of the Maritime Administration covering only less than one-fourth of the American-controlled flag-of-convenience ships showed that 53 nationalities were represented there. Thirty-five ships had total crews of Dutch, Italian, or British nationality. Of more than 4000 unlicensed personnel, only 25 United States seamen were aboard, and out of the 1145 licensed personnel there were only 144 United States officers; *Hearings* (Senate) 1957, pp. 137–139. The members of the ACFN employ for the most part Italian nationals with some Norwegian, British, Dutch, West German, and others included as well. *The New York Times*, June 21, 1961, p. 10.

It has been estimated that wages represent 90 to 95 per cent of the economic disadvantage that the American shipowners suffer if they are not subsidized or not registered under a flag of convenience.[20] The remaining 5 to 10 per cent handicap consists largely of the cost of repairs; when made in the United States they are generally about twice as expensive as when made abroad.[21] And under United States law, United States flag ships must either be repaired in American shipyards or pay a tax amounting to 50 per cent of the cost of foreign-made repairs.[22] An American ship flying a flag of convenience is free of such a restriction. Moreover, such a ship does not, as do United States flag ships, need to undergo the periodic inspections of the United States Coast Guard, which imposes a very high standard of ship maintenance.[23]

Another factor which has contributed to the expansion of foreign-flag operation is the necessity of providing services and paying crews in currencies freely usable by the various subsidiaries of the American companies and by their customers under applicable governmental regulations. Foreign registration provides the advantage of operating with easy currency conversion.[24] Furthermore, apart from the benefits that accrue to the shipowners of foreign-registered vessels, the United States government itself has fostered the practice of registering American-controlled vessels abroad. It has done this as a means of ensuring an adequate and efficient tanker and tramp fleet under the effective control of the United States for trade and, if needed, for defense purposes. This aspect of the problem is connected with American shipping policy in general. To this a great deal of attention has been devoted in the last few decades by various congressional and governmental studies. The chief lines of United States policy are set forth in the Merchant Marine Act of 1936.[25] In the Declaration of Policy it is stated that:

20. *Hearings* (Senate) 1957, p. 101.

21. *Cf.* the data given in the letter from Maritime Administrator cited in "Flag-of-Convenience Fleet," *YLJ* 69:500 n. 15 (1960).

22. Rev. Stat. §3114 (1875), 19 U.S.C. §257 (1958). See also S. *Rep.* No. 2494, 81st Cong., 2d Sess. (1950), pp. 66, 73.

23. See *Hearings* (House) 1957, pp. 140, 142, where the problem of the savings that would accrue to the operator by avoiding American-class requirements is discussed by the Maritime Administrator.

24. *Hearings* (House) 1957, p. 140; *Hearings* (Senate) 1957, pp. 84, 105–106. See also Carter, p. 212.

25. 49 Stat. 1985 (1936), as amended, 46 U.S.C. §§1101–1294 (1952), as amended, 46 U.S.C. §§1111 (b)–1294 (Supp. V, 1958).

It is necessary for the national defense and development of its foreign and domestic commerce that the United States shall have a merchant marine (a) sufficient to carry its domestic water-borne commerce and a substantial portion of the water-borne export and import foreign commerce of the United States and to provide shipping service on all routes essential for maintaining the flow of such domestic and foreign water-borne commerce at all times, (b) capable of serving as a naval and military auxiliary in time of war or national emergency, (c) owned and operated under the United States flag by citizens of the United States, insofar as may be practicable, and (d) composed of the best-equipped, safest, and most suitable types of vessels, constructed in the United States and manned with a trained and efficient citizen personnel. It is declared to be the policy of the United States to foster the development and encourage the maintenance of such a merchant marine.[26]

The chief problem involved in the maintenance of the American merchant marine is the replacement of obsolescent tonnage. In order to prevent the "block obsolescence" of the American fleet, a program of extensive replacement must be followed. The earlier, post-Second World War policy of granting "trade-in" allowances on ships over 12 years old, against new construction, apparently failed, and a new way of fulfilling the replacement policy has gradually been adopted. This is the so-called "trade-out-and-build" program, under which transfer to foreign ownership and/or registry of a United States flag "war-built" vessel is approved only if the United States owner undertakes to replace the vessel to be transferred by the construction of a new vessel for United States flag documentation and operation — the acceptability of the size, design, speed, and carrying capacity of the vessel to be judged by the Maritime Administration. The owner of a vessel transferred to foreign registry and flag is to be either a United States citizen or a corporation organized under the laws of either the United States, Liberia, Panama, or Honduras. All or a majority of the stock in these companies must be owned by a citizen or citizens of the United States. The registry and flag of the vessel transferred is to be either Liberian, Panamanian, or Honduran.[27]

26. June 29, 1936, c. 858, §101, 49 Stat. 1985, 46 U.S.C. §1101 (Supp. V. 1958). For the defense aspects connected with the concept of "effective United States control" see Ch. VII.

27. Statement of Policy on Foreign Transfers, November 5, 1956; 21 Fed. Reg. 8588 (1956) as amended, 21 Fed. Reg. 8920 (1956); 22 Fed. Reg. 4289 (1957), 22 Fed. Reg. 4448 (1957), 22 Fed. Reg. 7397 (1957), 23 Fed. Reg. 5956 (1958). *Hear-*

As a result of these regulations, the transfer movement, which originated as described in Chapter I, has been given a great deal of impetus. Some American-controlled vessels in the flag-of-convenience fleets have been built and initially registered abroad, but most of them have been transferred from an initial United States registry.[28] The legal basis for these transfers has been the Shipping Act of 1916, one of many congressional attempts to encourage the growth of the United States Merchant Marine. Under this Act, the transfer of vessels from United States to foreign registry is unlawful without the consent of the Maritime Administration.[29] The conditions for the approval of transfer are laid down in rules made public by the Maritime Administrator. The statement of policy with respect to foreign transfer provides that each transfer application is to be considered on an individual basis and must be evaluated from the standpoint of national defense, the maintenance of an adequate merchant marine, foreign policy, and national interest. A shipowner, who transfers a ship "foreign," contracts to retain ultimate United States ownership for the stock of the transferred vessel. At the request of the United States these ships will be available to it on the same terms as vessels requisitioned in time of national emergency. However, if the transfer is to a flag of a signatory of the North Atlantic Treaty Organization, the condition shall be satisfied if the vessel is made available to a NATO country within the terms of the Pact. The vessel may not engage in trade

ings (House) 1957, pp. 70–72. For one new vessel of 46,000 deadweight tons built in the United States a shipowner is permitted to transfer to foreign registry two United States-flag T-2 tankers or three Victory-type vessels. The construction of larger vessels permits increased transfers according to a scale laid down by the regulations (*id.*, p. 69). The Maritime Administration also announced that Liberty-type vessels may be transferred to foreign registry without signing an agreement to build an American-flag replacement, *The New York Times,* January 26, 1960, p. 53.

28. See Table 4. According to the statement of the executive secretary of the AFL-CIO Maritime Committee, American companies built for foreign registry and in foreign yards 534 ships totaling 12,615,666 deadweight tons [*Hearings* (House) 1957, p. 698; *Hearings* (Senate) 1957, p. 196]. However, there were also ships built in the United States for registration in Liberia, Panama, and Honduras. For statistics see *Hearings* (House) 1957, p. 82. For the number and tonnage of the United States flag ships transferred to foreign flags in the years 1949–1958 see *Shipping Statistics,* pp. 108–113. For the statistics of ships transferred in the period July 1, 1951–June 30, 1956 see *Hearings* (House) 1957, p. 18.

29. Shipping Act of 1916, §§9, 37, 41; 39 Stat. 730, as amended, 46 U.S.C. §§808, 835, 839 (1952).

prohibited to United States-flag vessels under Department of Commerce transportation order T-1 and T-2 (that is to say, it may not trade with the communist countries except Yugoslavia), and in the case of breach of contract severe penalties will be imposed. The 1916 Act provides for similar conditions with respect to the approval of applications involving the construction in the United States of new vessels for foreign flag ownership and/or registry.[30]

Prior to 1950 there was no written transfer policy statement. The first formal statement of such a policy was issued in 1950 and modified in 1952. During this early period there were few transfers effected. In 1953 the construction of ships in American shipyards for foreign registry was allowed. And from 1954 on, when many Liberty ships were laid up, a new policy was adopted, which admitted a trade-out of one Liberty ship transferred "foreign" for the commitment to retain one for United States flag operation. In 1955 and 1956 the trade-out-and-build program assumed even greater importance because of the growing danger of the block obsolescence of the merchant marine.[31]

This government policy has not been popular with the maritime unions but they have so far failed in their endeavor to achieve the enactment of legislation that would virtually eliminate transfers from United States to foreign registry as well as subsidies for United States flag owners or operators, operating foreign-flag vessels in competition with essential United States shipping service.[32] The policy has been popular, however, with United States shipowning companies and with the shipbuilding industry; it has also

30. See 46 C.F.R., §221.13 (1958).

31. For an exhaustive survey of vessel transfers, see United States Department of Commerce, Maritime Administration, "Review of Vessel Transfer Activities — History & Policies Relating to Transfer of United States Merchant Ships to Foreign Ownership and/or Registry," reprinted in *Hearings* (House) 1957, pp. 53–100. Many interesting details can also be found in *Hearings* (Senate) 1957, *passim.* Quite revealing are *Hearings on Trade-out and Build Activities of Onassis Companies before the Special Subcommittee on Merchant Marine and Fisheries of the House of Representatives,* 85th Cong., 2d Sess. (1958). The penalties imposed for breach of contract are those provided by the Shipping Act of 1916, §41, added by 40 Stat. 902 (1918), as amended, 46 U.S.C. §839 (1952).

32. See *Hearings on S. 3823 before a Subcommittee of the Senate Committee on Interstate and Foreign Commerce,* 81st Cong., 2d Sess., 31, 56, 59–61 (1950); *Hearings* (House) 1957, pp. 684–685, 715; *Hearings* (Senate) 1957, pp. 183–184, 235; *Hearings on H.R. 6601, 7601, before the Subcommittee on Merchant Marine and Fisheries,* 86th Cong., 1st Sess., 211–215 (1959).

been supported by the United States Department of State and the United States Department of the Navy.[33]

Now to turn to the advantages that accrue for Europeans who operate ships under Panlibhon flags, we must indicate first that the primary motive for Europeans is not to save on operating costs since these are not lower for them under the convenience flags. In Greece, for example, in the years immediately after the Second World War, it was the unstable political conditions which aroused fears of nationalization among Greek shipowners and prospective investors in Greek shipping ventures. Also Greek shipowners were subject to heavy taxation as were owners in most of the maritime countries. In addition, obsolete shipping laws were a further reason why Greek shipowners fled the Greek flag. Investors, reluctant to lay out funds for shipping under the Greek flag, were far more willing to provide credits for foreign-flag operations. They considered suitable the Panamanian, Honduran, Costa Rican, and later, the Liberian flag, all flags of countries offering liberal registration and virtual tax immunity. As a result of generous credits a large Greek-owned merchant fleet was launched under the flags of Panama and Liberia, but with business seats in New York or London.

The Greek Merchant Marine Ministry in a recent review of the history of Greek merchant shipping just after the Second World War described the flags of convenience as flags of necessity because they had provided the means for the survival and expansion of the Greek shipping enterprise.[34] Nonetheless, the Greek govern-

33. Representatives of leading American oil companies stated that they would not build new ships for American-flag operation unless they transferred the older ones to a foreign flag. See, *e.g.*, *Hearings* (Senate) 1957, pp. 14, 23, 25, 63, 99, 109, 121–123, 142, 144. On the position of the United States State and Navy departments see *id.*, pp. 214–220, 223–226. See also statement by Acting Secretary Dillon, *DSB* 41:14 (1959); the statements by Vice Admiral R. E. Wilson in *The New York Times*, October 17, 1959, p. 46; April 5, 1960, p. 62; the statement of then Secretary of the Navy Gates on behalf of the defense agencies, *Hearings* (House) 1957, pp. 630–635. Gates' letter of October 26, 1960 to the Attorney General was quoted in *The New York Times*, June 21, 1961, p. 10.

34. Greek Ministry of Mercantile Marine, "Greek Shipping Policy" in *Greek Shipping News*, quoted in "Greek Shipping Policy and the Flags of Convenience," *Norwegian Shipping News* 15:383 (1959); *Cf.*, "Greek Shipping Policy," *The Shipping World & World Shipbuilding*, February 4, 1959, p. 271. On the Greek exile shipowners in general see Mender, pp. 283–285.

ment has always taken the position that the flag-of-convenience ships, or, as they were in fact for the Greeks, flag-of-necessity ships, were prejudicial to the Greek shipping economy and that to retrieve the Greek-owned tonnage under the flags of convenience for national registration had to be a major objective of Greek economic policy. This position was expressed in the law passed in 1953, the main purpose of which was to minimize the advantages offered by the flags of convenience. The principal feature of this law was that vessels of 1,500 gross tons and over, admitted under its provision, were to be considered as imported capital, and that an owner was able to change registration or to sell the vessels to foreigners. The fixed taxation rates that may not be increased, tax exemption for vessels up to two years of age, tax reduction for vessels up to 20 years old, preferred mortgage lien for creditors, liberal formalities of registry, and a guarantee that the vessel is not liable to requisition by the government, except in the event of a general international conflict in which Greece should be involved, are additional features of the 1953 law.[35]

This orientation of Greek shipping policies has already brought good results. Statistics show a steady and considerable rise in the number of ships registered under the Greek flag. This reached an unprecedented high in December 1958 when 450,000 gross tons joined the Greek flag.[36] The influx of new tonnage continued in the years from 1959 to 1961, a direct result of further legislative measures initiated by the Greek government.[37] These measures as well as more stable political and economic conditions prevailing in Greece, and, to a certain extent, the threat of the boycott of the Panlibhon vessels by the seamen's unions, brought a huge amount of tonnage owned by Greece's truant shipowners back to the Greek flag. It reached 5,983,652 gross tons in the middle of 1961 — triple what it was in 1958. This "maritime miracle in Greece" has un-

35. See the Legislative Decrees No. 2687/1953 and No. 2958/1954 on foreign capital investment and its protection; see *Norwegian Shipping News* 15:383 (1959); *The Shipping World & World Shipbuilding*, February 4, 1959, p. 171. See also *Fairplay* 194:37 (1960).

36. This fact is also attributed to the world-wide boycott of the flag-of-convenience ships organized by the ITWF; *The New York Times*, January 7, 1959, p. 65. The boycott is discussed in Ch. III.

37. In particular the Legislative Decree No. 3899/1958 dealing with preferred mortgage. See Potamianos, "L'hypothèque de préférence (mortgage) sur les navires," *Le Droit Maritime Français* 13:566, 633 (1961).

doubtedly given a great impetus to Greek economic development. There has been a considerable increase in the earnings from the shipping industry, which has helped to bridge the foreign exchange gap between the limited exports of Greece and its soaring imports, and there has been a reduction in the unemployment of Greek seamen.[38]

It seems clear that the success of Greek government policy in encouraging Greek owners to transfer their ships back to the Greek flag has come about because, first of all, the government has been able to offer significant advantages to shipowners, advantages that have diminished considerably the competitive disparity of operating under the Greek flag as compared with operating under a convenience flag. However, the question of operating costs is not a salient feature of the situation in Greece whereas, in the United States, for United States shipowners who operate under the flags of convenience, it continues to be the principal element in their calculations.

The high costs of operating a ship and the desire and necessity of reducing these have impelled many unsubsidized United States shipowners to transfer from their flag, and this might have been expected even if there were no Panlibhon flags under which they could register their ships. In fact United States-owned vessels had been registered under foreign flags before the emergence of the flags of convenience. Moreover, operating under Panlibhon flags is not less expensive than operating under the flags of most European countries. What has made Panlibhon flags especially attractive is the fact that Panama, Liberia, and Honduras have provided certain additional advantages such as very liberal corporation and shipping registration laws, and — what has been even more important — extremely liberal taxation laws favoring foreign investment, in particular, foreign-owned shipping, and providing virtual tax immunity for such enterprises. This tax immunity has, in turn, given Americans an immense competitive advantage over their European rivals, and it is mainly the relief from taxation re-

38. *Norwegian Shipping News* 15:930 (1959); *The New York Times*, September 8, 1959, p. 56; August 5, 1961, p. 30; *The Times*, October 6, 1960, p. 15 (leading article "Maritime Miracle in Greece"). In 1961 income from shipping rose in Greece 33 per cent and amounted to $102 millions. It was the largest single source of foreign currency for Greece: *The New York Times*, March 1, 1962, p. 52.

sulting from registration under Panlibhon flags that has caused grave concern among European shipowners.

The existence of large flag-of-convenience fleets sailing under the Panlibhon ensigns is an accomplished fact whose main features have been described above. Now it is necessary to examine the legal nature of the advantages granted by the Panlibhon to foreign shipowners — to look at the shipping registration laws of those countries and the other legal provisions which make their flags so attractive. It is a general principle of international law that the conditions a state imposes in order for a merchant ship to be eligible to obtain its nationality are municipal prerequisites and are not standards imposed by international law. Each state has "the undisputed right . . . to set up such prerequisites for the assumption of its nationality as its concept of national welfare dictates."[39] It has, furthermore, long been recognized that the contents of the municipal laws concerning the grant of nationality to merchant vessels are shaped on the basis of the particular economic, political, and military interests of the respective countries.[40] Therefore, these laws undergo changes according to the actual needs of the states and also to the actual conditions in the international shipping industry. The gradual elimination of the national build requirement from the municipal statutes and the changes in the scope of the national crew or national ownership requirements are evidence of this fact.[41]

39. Rienow, p. 215.

40. See, *e.g.*, Ortolan, I, 167: "Les nations, dans l'établissement de ces conditions, seront évidemment plus ou moin faciles, plus ou moins rigoureuses, selon ce qu'elles croiront le plus de leur interêt, selon l'état de prospérité, de développement, d'enfance, ou de décadence où se trouvera leur marine, suivant de degré de leurs resources maritimes en matériel et en personnel." See also Calvo, *Le droit international théorique et pratique* (3d ed. 1880), II, 102; Fauchille, I, pt. 2, 899–902. Higgins, "Le régime juridique des navires de commerce," *RCADI* 30:22 (1929, pt. V); Ripert, *Droit maritime* (4th ed. 1950), I, 300, 318; Müller, "Das Flaggenrecht von Schiffen und Luftfahrzeugen nach Völkerrecht und Landesrecht," *Zeitschrift für Völkerrecht* 13:355, 360–361 (1926); Rienow, pp. 16–17; Scerni, *Il diritto internazionale privato marittimo ed aeronautico* (1936), p. 36; Florio, *Nazionalità della nave e legge della bandiera* (1957), pp. 116–117; Colombos, pp. 251–252. See also ILC *Yearbook 1951*, II, 75–77 (Doc. A/CN.4/42). In this second report on the high seas François quotes Higgins and Colombos, *The Freedom of the Seas* (1943), p. 190.

41. In 1937 Rienow saw a trend away from the requirement of total ownership toward partial ownership (Rienow, pp. 25, 88, 215). This is even more true today.

If, for example, we analyze the requirement of national ownership, we can see that a small or new country, wishing to offer opportunities for foreign capital, provides liberal registration laws that allow foreign-owned vessels into its merchant marine. This was what took place in some Latin American nations in the nineteenth century, and the same is true of Panama and Liberia today. The national interest of Panama was stressed by the Panamanian delegate at the 1958 United Nations Conference on the Law of the Sea in Geneva. In his words: "Panama being an underdeveloped country which needed to attract foreign capital and benefit from foreign technical experience, followed an open door policy in regard to foreign capital." [42]

The Liberians claim that their maritime law was devised not as a deliberate attempt to establish a special system of easy registration designed to subvert the existing system of national registration or primarily intended to create a source of national revenue, but that the Liberian maritime system was established in the exercise of Liberian sovereign desire to promote a national marine. The Liberians also contend that their liberal shipping registration was designed primarily to employ Liberian nationals scattered down the African coast acting as sailors, and to develop a Liberian merchant marine which would eventually be available for the carriage of raw materials exported by Liberia. The eventual development of huge tanker and bulk-carrier fleets flying the Liberian flag is presented by the Liberians as "an almost incidental consequence of legislation designed primarily for another purpose." On the other hand, the Liberian government openly pursues the policy of open door and free trade in the shipping matters and takes the position that Liberia is entitled to develop its merchant marine even if that development takes place with foreign capital.[43] According to the Liberian delegate at the 1958 law of the sea conference, the purpose of the prerequisites for granting nationality to a ship laid down by a state was not to secure compliance with the rules governing the high seas; registration policy was

42. UN.CLS.*OR* 4:29 (1958).

43. ICJ *Pleadings*, Constitution (1960), pp. 276–277 (statement of the Liberian representative).

based merely on the state's domestic, economic, and social policies.[44]

The extent to which the laws of the Panlibhon countries are liberal with respect to the registration of vessels is more easily seen when these are compared with the registration requirements of other states.

The material prerequisites stipulated by the municipal laws of most countries as conditions under which nationality may be granted to ships can usually be classified as they refer to national ownership, operation, crew, or — of historical importance — national build.[45] Among these, the requirement of national ownership is the one most frequently met in the laws of the various states. This prerequisite originated earlier at a time when ships were a precious and jealously guarded asset of the national economy. This prerequisite was almost universal as late as 1870, when total ownership was the rule.[46] Actually in the municipal laws of

44. UN.CLS.*OR* 4:22 (1958).

45. A collection of extracts from the municipal laws concerning the nationality of ships in 69 countries has been prepared by the United Nations Secretariat and published in the United Nations Legislative Series as *Laws concerning the Nationality of Ships* (Doc. St/Leg./Ser. B/5) (1955) [abbreviated hereafter as UNLS]. Additional materials are included in the *Supplement to Laws and Regulations on the Regime of the High Sea and Laws concerning the Nationality of Ships* (1959) [abbreviated hereafter as UNLS Supp.]. In spite of some gaps and omissions (*e.g.* no mention of the laws of Albania, Indonesia, Iraq, Iran, Saudi Arabia and some other countries; no mention of the important changes in the laws of Lebanon, Morocco, Tunisia, Viet-Nam) the two collections are the best source on the subject. For information on the requisites concerning nationality of ships in various countries see also Florio, *La nazionalità della nave e legge della bandiera* (1957) pp. 207–224; Brajkovic & Pallua, "Les conditions dans lesquelles les Etats accordent aux navires le droit d'arborer le pavillon national" (Académie Internationale de Droit Comparé–Le Congrès International de Droit Comparé 1958) [mimeographed]. For material mostly of historical interest, see Ortolan, I, 383–404; *Annuaire* 15:54–67 (1896); Van Zijst, pp. 164–165 and appendix A; Cantillon de Tramont, pp. 201–202. See also LN.*OJ*. 12:1631–1671 (1931) ("The Comparative Study of National Laws Governing the Granting of the Right to Fly a Merchant Flag.") and "Tableau des conditions imposées par les principales puissances maritimes pour le droit au pavillon national," *Recueil Général Périodique et Critique des Décisions, Conventions et Lois Relatives au Droit International Public et Privé* (1936, pt VI) pp. 1–6. For a Soviet presentation see Kolodkin, "Predostavlenie sudam natsional'nosti po morskomu pravu kapitalisticheskikh stran," *Morskoe Pravo i Praktika* (1960, no. 8), pp. 10–27.

46. Van Eik, "Aperçu de la législation néerlandaise récente sur la nationalité des navires," *Revue de Droit International et de Législation Comparée* 2:579 (1870). Van Eik noted there that only France, the Netherlands, Denmark, Greece, Buenos Aires [now Argentina], New Granada [now Colombia], and Paraguay did not require exclusive national ownership.

nearly half of the maritime states of the world the prerequisite of total national ownership is still preserved.[47] In other states only partial national ownership of vessels is required, varying from 75 per cent to less than 50 per cent.[48] In addition, in some states it is possible to make exceptions even to these regulations to reduce per cent of national ownership or to grant nationality to foreign-owned ships. These exceptions are usually motivated by the desire to benefit the national merchant marine or to promote the national economy.[49] There are, however, states which will grant their nationality to ships even if the total ownership thereof is vested in aliens. These states are Argentina, Guatemala, Ecuador, Nicaragua, Uruguay, Costa Rica, Honduras, and Liberia.[50]

Most municipal legislations, particularly modern ones, deal with the problem of the ownership of vessels by all types of commercial associations. Some of them deal both with associations in which a personal element predominates (such as partnerships, *sociétés en nom collectif*, or *sociétés en commandite*) and with associations of capital, endowed with juridical personality (such as corporations, *sociétés anonymes*, or limited liability companies). In the former case, the nationality of the partners or the amount of capital owned by nationals is the test of the grant of nationality to the vessels owned by the partnership, there being, in some cases, the additional stipulation of the national location of the head office. The required per cent of national partners and, in particular, of

47. The United Kingdom and the countries of the British Commonwealth, Burma, Brazil, Cuba, Dominican Republic, Mexico, Peru, the United States, German Federal Republic, Denmark, Bulgaria, Czechoslovakia, Finland, Norway, Portugal, Roumania, Switzerland, the U.S.S.R., Vatican City, China, Egypt, Israel, Japan, Korea, Thailand, Turkey (UNLS and UNLS Supp., *passim*); Yugoslavia (Decree of May 12, 1951, art. 2: in *Official Journal of the Federal People's Republic of Yugoslavia*, No. 25/1951). In some states aliens may be treated as nationals provided certain conditions are fulfilled, *e.g.*, domicile, as it is the case in Chile, Colombia, Iceland, Ireland, and the Philippines (UNLS *passim*).

48. Seventy-five per cent: Austria, UNLS Supp., p. 113; Morocco, UNLS, p. 58. Two-thirds: The Netherlands, UNLS, p. 111 (the remainder must be owned by resident aliens); Italy (*Codice della Navigazione 1942*, art. 143); Sweden, UNLS, p. 162. 50 per cent: Belgium, France, Hungary, Monaco, Vietnam, Cambodia, Syria, Lebanon (but on Lebanon see more below), Venezuela, Haiti, Libya; UNLS *passim*. Less than 50 per cent: Ethiopia 35 per cent; *Id.*, p. 47. On Tunisia see below.

49. See, *e.g.*, Austria, UNLS Supp., p. 113; Czechoslovakia and Libya, UNLS pp. 37, 99; Vietnam, *Ordonnance du 2 avril 1956*, art. 3. For the text see *Le Droit Maritime Français* 8:376 (1956).

50. UNLS, pp. 1, 72, 42, 123, 195–197, 28, 75, 98. It may be of historical interest that Latvia did not know any ownership prerequisite; LN.*OJ* 12:1656 (1931).

national capital varies from total to 50 per cent. In the case of juridical persons (who own a large per cent of the world's merchant fleet) various tests are applicable by the different municipal laws, and, as in the case of individuals and partnerships, there is no uniformity among the various municipal definitions of a "national" owner of vessels. Separately or in combination, the factors of incorporation under the law of the flag, national control in the sense of the management (total or partial) of the corporate body by nationals, national control in the sense of national capital and principal place of business (head office, seat of business, or *siège social*) are usually taken into account.

Thus, for example, the British type of legislation, adopted in the countries of the British Commonwealth of Nations and a few other countries, determines the eligibility of a body corporate to own a national ship by the combined elements of the local principal place of business and national incorporation.[51] The element of national incorporation is stressed in Brazil, Czechoslovakia, and Finland.[52] The legislations of France and of countries that have modelled their laws on the French system, start from the proposition that if foreign capital is managed by nationals it will be used for the national advantage, and apply the criterion of citizen management. France, Monaco, Morocco, and Tunisia, as well as Denmark, have this type of legislation.[53] In other countries the criterion of citizen management is strengthened by the requirement of the national location of the seat of business.[54] Most stringent are the states that require not only national management of the corporation and location of its head office in the flag state and/or national incorporation, but also stipulate that the capital of the corporation owning the ships be owned wholly or — more frequently — partially by nationals. The most exacting seem to be Switzerland, requiring all the criteria in the highest degree, with nominative shares included,[55] Sweden, the U.S.S.R.[56] and Yugoslavia.[57] The

51. Merchant Shipping Act of August 25, 1894 (57 & 58 Vict. c. 60) §1 (d); (UNLS, p. 181). *Cf.* the laws of Canada, Ceylon, New Zealand, Pakistan, Union of South Africa, Burma, Mexico, Ethiopia; (UNLS, *passim*), Ireland (UNLS Supp., p. 125).
52. UNLS, pp. 6, 50, 36.
53. *Id.*, pp. 54, 58, 165, 62; UNLS Supp. pp. 118–119.
54. Germany, Korea, Iceland (UNLS, pp. 64, 93, 79).
55. Loi Fédérale sur la navigation maritime sous pavillon suisse du 23 séptembre

laws of other countries provide for partial national ownership of the shares, the various requirements being 75 per cent, 70 per cent, two-thirds, 51 per cent, more than 50 per cent, 50 per cent or one-third.[58] In the United States the present legal situation is governed not only by the factors of local incorporation and local seat of business, but also by controlling American interest in the management and capital of the corporation.[59]

Even from this very cursory review of the requirements relating to the ownership of national vessels it can be seen clearly that it is impossible to give a uniform definition of a "national owner" because the requirements laid down by the states vary a great deal according to their exclusive national interests. In addition, a number of national laws provide for exceptions admitting, in the interests of national economy, foreign-owned vessels to their merchant marines, and, even in the states where the requirement of national ownership seems to be strict, a ship may be ultimately owned by aliens if it is formally owned by a nationally incorporated juridical person and, of course, if the law does not bar aliens from having interest in nationally incorporated bodies. As a result of this situation a large number of merchant ships, interest in which is held by United States companies and their affiliates, can be registered under the flag of the United Kingdom.[60]

1953, arts. 19–23; *Feuille Fédérale,* Vol. III, No. 39 (1953). On the nationality of Swiss vessels see Demaurex, *La nationalité des navires de mer — Etude de droit suisse* (1958).

56. UNLS, pp. 162, 177.

57. Decree concerning the registration of merchant ships of 1951, art. 2(1); *Official Journal of the Federal People's Republic of Yugoslavia,* No. 25/1951. However, any ship may be registered if this is in the interest of the state. See the same decree, art. 2 (2). See also Pallua, "La nationalité des navires," *Jugoslovenska Revija za Medunarodno Pravo* 3:71, 73 (1956).

58. 75 per cent: Italy, Peru, the Philippines, Chile, Spain; UNLS, *passim.* India; the Merchant Shipping Act 1958, art. 21(b). For the text of this Act see, *e.g.* ILOffice, *Legislative Series* (July-August 1958) (1959) p. 11. 70 per cent: Thailand; UNLS, pp. 167–168. Two thirds: China, the Netherlands, Norway, Poland; *Id., passim.* 51 per cent: Cambodia, *id.,* p. 10. More than 50 per cent: Belgium, *id.,* p. 3, 50 per cent: Libya, Hungary, Roumania, Venezuela; *id., passim.* One third: Portugal, *id.,* pp. 146–147.

59. For details see 46 U.S.C. §§11, 802.

60. See Table 7. *Cf.* the opinion of Higgins: "Lorsque, comme c'est souvent le cas, le navire est la propriété d'une société, il n'est pas toujours aisé de déterminer la nationalité de cette société"; (*RCADI* 30: 21, 1929, pt. V). H. A. Smith: "English law requires the complete legal ownership to be vested in British subjects, but this requirement is of less value than might appear, since it does not exclude ownership

Compared with the requirements of the great majority of municipal legislations, the attribution of nationality to merchant vessels under the laws of the Panlibhon countries is effected on particularly easy terms. However, as has been pointed out previously, the registration law itself is not enough to make a flag attractive to a foreign shipowner; it must be accompanied by easy incorporation rules and a liberal fiscal policy on the part of the flag-of-convenience country.

Before we discuss the shipping registration laws of the flag-of-convenience countries, we should distinguish between the legislation of Panama and those of the other countries. Although it has virtually no practical significance, the Panamanian law does pose some ownership requirements. The relevant article of the Commercial Code of Panama of 22 August 1916 states:

> Merchant vessels which are wholly or partly the property of Panamanian citizens or of foreigners domiciled in the Republic with more than five years of residence therein, or of commercial societies having their headquarters in Panama shall be deemed to be Panamanian, provided that they are registered and enrolled as such and that the owners thereof submit expressly to the laws of the Republic concerning navigation.[61]

This means that an individual alien may be in fact the total owner of a Panamanian ship if he is domiciled in Panama and if he has had more than five years residence therein.[62] Honduras, Costa Rica, and Liberia, however, impose no ownership qualifications whatsoever. Article 5 of the Honduran Organic Act of the National Merchant Marine No. 55 of 2 March 1943 expressly states:

> Any person, whether a Honduran national or an alien, who owns a merchant ship and wishes to register it as a Honduran ship under the Honduran flag shall apply in writing to the Executive through the Department of War, Marine and Aviation. . . .[63]

---

by a British company, in which the controlling interest is held by foreigners" [Smith, *The Law and Custom of the Sea* (3d ed. 1959), p. 64]. *Cf.* also the decision in *Continental Tyre & Rubber Company v. Daimler Company Ltd.* [1915] 1 K.B. 904; Hackworth, *Digest of International Law* (1941), II, 249–250.

61. UNLS, p. 129.

62. One can add that this provision is not less stringent than, *e.g.*, the law of Iceland. See Shipping Registration Act of Iceland, No. 17 of March 18, 1948, art. 1(1); UNLS, p. 79. This law admits to the ownership of national vessels aliens domiciled in Iceland for at least five preceding years.

63. UNLS, p. 76. It results from the wording of art. 41 of the Honduran law that

Article 6 makes the issuance of the final registry certificate dependent on the application and accompanying documents (the title to the ship and survey certificate) and payment of the registration fee.

The Liberian law is most liberal of all. The following vessels are eligible to be documented under the laws of Liberia:

(a) sea-going vessels, regardless of tonnage, wherever built, owned by a citizen or national of Liberia or of any foreign country. The terms "citizen" and "national" shall include corporations, partnerships, and associations of individuals.

(b) any vessel of twenty net tons or over engaged in trading on the inland waters of Liberia or between ports in Liberia.[64]

The only restriction as to the ownership seems to be that the person desiring to register his vessel under the Liberian flag may not be stateless.

The legal position of Costa Rica in this situation cannot be stated as easily and must be clarified in connection with the reported withdrawal of facilities for shipping registration by that country.[65] The law of October 22, 1941, governing the operation of national ships, which does not lay down any ownership requirements, is still in force. Here, as in the Honduran and Liberian laws, the grant of the flag (*abanderamiento*) is effected by mere registration without any prerequisite of ownership. Article 43 of the law only prescribes that every individual or juridical person domiciled outside Costa Rica and owning one or more Costa Rican ships shall appoint and maintain in Costa Rica an agent or legal representative with whom the authorities may settle all matters relating to the ships. The Costa Rican law also provides for conferring

---

two types of vessels are to be distinguished: vessels to which the Honduran nationality is attributed obligatorily (vessels belonging to individuals or bodies corporate resident in Honduras, whether of Honduran or alien nationality, if they ply regularly in Honduran waters or if they have their home port in Honduras), and vessels which may be granted Honduran nationality at the request of the owners (*id.*, p. 75).

64. *Liberian Code of Laws of 1956*, vol. II, tit. 22, *Maritime Law*, Ch. 2, "Documentation and Identification of Vessels," §51 (1957).

65. See, *e.g.*, *The New York Times*, October 31, 1958, p. 57; November 16, 1958, sec. 1, p. 3.

Costa Rican nationality upon a ship chartered but not owned by the operator.[66]

The Costa Rican law of 1941 was enacted by Costa Rica with the open intention of profiting from registration fees in the same way as Panama. Since, however, in later years many shipowners became in arrears of the fees due to Costa Rica, and since some of the ships, particularly those of smaller tonnage, engaged in illegal activities and smuggling, the Costa Rican Congress began action to curb the registry of foreign vessels. In 1956 a special committee of inquiry was set up to examine the whole problem of issuing registration certificates to merchant vessels.[67] In October 1958 a memorandum presented to the Costa Rican Legislative Assembly revealed complete absence of Costa Rican control and jurisdiction in administrative, financial, social, or technical matters over vessels flying the Costa Rican flag and suggested certain amendments to be effected in the Costa Rican shipping-registration law of 1941.[68]

As a result of public pressure the Legislative Assembly passed a law on November 22, 1958, the main points of which are: 1) Some articles of the law of 1941 were repealed. In particular the institution of consular registration, which was a major cause of abuses, was abolished. 2) The law ordered the cancellation at the end of the current fiscal year of all registrations effected under the law of 1941, and immediate cancellation of the registration of the vessels in arrears of the annual duties. 3) An investigation of the activities of Costa Rican consuls was ordered.[69] Pursuant to the

66. Costa Rica, Republica de, *Colección de Leyes, Decretos, Acuerdos y Resoluciones* (1941), Segundo Semestre, pp. 556–564: Ley No. 12 de octubre 1941 que regirá en el servicio de naves nacionales (La Ley de Matrícula Naviera Mercante, arts. 4 & 43).

67. *The New York Times,* June 23, 1956, p. 26. *Cf.*, statement of the Costa Rican government observer at the session of the committee on flag transfer: ILOffice, ILConf., 41 sess. (Geneva 1958), *Report IV. Flag Transfer in Relation to Social Conditions and Safety* (1957) p. 6 [abbreviated hereafter as ILOffice, *Report IV* (1957)].

68. For this interesting document see Asamblea Legislativa, Fernando Fournier, *Proyecto,* San José, octubre de 1958; *La Gaceta, Diario Oficial* 80:3771–3772, Segundo Semestre, 7 de noviembre de 1958.

69. Ley No. 2295 de 22 de noviembre 1958 in *La Gaceta, Diario Oficial* 80:4009, Segundo Semestre, No. 269. See also Costa Rica, *Colección de Leyes* (1958), Segundo Semestre, p. 343. Also, a special law was passed on June 21, 1958, under which coastwise shipping was restricted to Costa Rican citizens or companies organized in Costa Rica with 60 per cent of their shares owned by Costa Ricans. See Costa Rica, *Colección de Leyes* (1958), Primero Semestre.

law of November 22, 1958, the Ministry of Economy ordered the cancellation from the shipping register of 153 vessels whose owners had not paid the annual duties by the time of the promulgation of the law of November 22, 1958.[70] In consequence, the number of Costa Rican vessels of 1000 gross tons and over, which as of December 31, 1958 amounted to 121 (516,000 gross tons), was cut down to 21 vessels (71,000 gross tons) at the end of 1960.[71] If the law of 1958 were to be fully implemented, this tonnage, too, should be reduced. At any rate, one can say that Costa Rica has clearly initiated measures to terminate her career as a flag-of-convenience country.[72]

On the other hand, and in another part of the world — in Lebanon — both legislative measures recently enacted and statistics point to a development very much along the lines of flags of convenience. Lebanon is a country of free enterprise — in the last decade it has made great strides toward the simplification and the liberalization of its business laws in an effort to encourage foreign investment and to attract foreign capital.[73] In 1954 Lebanon also revised its laws concerning the grant of nationality to merchant vessels. The relevant provisions of the new law added the following two new and extremely liberal clauses to the second article of the Maritime Code of February 18, 1947, which requires a Lebanese *port d'attache,* 50 per cent national ownership, a Lebanese president, and a Lebanese majority on the admininstrative board:

All the ships of more than 500 net tons employed in long distance navigation, having a Lebanese port as their *port d'attache,* are also Lebanese, whatever be the nationality of their owners. The registration of these

70. Costa Rica, *Colección de Leyes* (1958), Segundo Semestre, p. 373: Resolución No. 662 de 28 de noviembre de 1958 del Ministro de Economía y Hacienda. The resolution gives the names of the vessels cancelled from the Costa Rican registry, but it does not give their tonnage. The ships in question must have been mostly vessels of small tonnage.

71. *Shipping Statistics,* p. 48; *ABS Bulletin,* June 1961, p. 32.

72. The report of the committee on Latin American law of the Section of International and Comparative Law of the American Bar Association states, not quite strictly, that "at the end of May 1959 steps had not yet been taken to revoke any of the outstanding registration nor had the January 1 deadline been officially extended." American Bar Association, Section of International and Comparative Law, *Proceedings* (1960), p. 193.

73. See American University of Beirut, Economic Research Institute, "Business Legislation in Lebanon" (1955) [mimeographed].

ships is subject to preliminary approval of the Minister of Public Works.
The ships provided for in clause 2 of the present article are subject to an annual duty of 25 piastres for net ton.

What is more, the law of 1954 even lays down in art. 2 that the presence of the ship in one of the Lebanese ports is not obligatory for the fulfillment of the formalities of registration. Another interesting amendment to the original law, enacted in 1954, is the reduction of the requirement of a two-thirds national crew to one-fifth. If a shipowner takes advantage of this provision he must train for ocean navigation an equivalent number of seamen.[74]

It can be readily seen that the 1954 Lebanese law has some of the characteristic features of flag-of-convenience legislation: there is no property requirement whatsoever; the ship does not even have to put in at a Lebanese harbor for registration; and a very low annual tax is imposed, amounting to about eight cents per net ton, which is a 20 per cent discount on the Liberian or Panamanian rate of 10 cents per net ton.[75] As a result, in the last few years, a number of shipowners have been attracted to the Lebanese flag by its liberal registration facilities in combination with the advantages offered by its corporation and taxation laws.[76] In the period from 1959 to 1960 the increase of the Lebanese fleet was especially rapid. Table 8 indicates that as many as 78 ships registered under the Lebanese ensign in this period. It must be left to the future to demonstrate how far the Lebanese flag, having already overtaken the flag of Honduras, will advance in its career as a flag of convenience.

Morocco has also demonstrated its ambition to develop a merchant fleet.[77] This has found legal expression in an interesting provision enacted in 1957 by the "Empire chérifien," as Morocco is officially known in French. The general law on the nationality of

74. Law of December 21, 1954, amending some articles of the Maritime Code. For the text see *Le Droit Maritime Français* 8:120–123 (1956).

75. In 1955 the exchange rate was: U.S. $1 = 3.20–3.25 Lebanese pounds. One Lebanese pound has 25 piastres. American University of Beirut, Economic Research Institute, "Business Legislation in Lebanon" (1955), p. 9.

76. *Id.*, pp. 8, 57. See also Gibbons, p. 3, n. 1. The rise of the Lebanese ensign as a flag of convenience has been noted by the OEEC. See OEEC.MTC, *Maritime Transport* (1961), p. 37.

77. See statement of the Moroccan government delegate, IL.Conf.*RP*. 41 Sess. (Geneva, 1958), pp. 79–80.

TABLE 8. Number of ships and tonnage (thousands) of the merchant fleet of Lebanon as of December 31 of each year (1953–1960).

Year	No.	Gross tons	Deadweight tons
1953	0	0	0
1954	2	4	5
1955	4	11	16
1956	6	20	29
1957	8	25	39
1958	15	43	68
1959	51	186	289
1960	93	402	616

Sources. *Shipping Statistics*, pp. 38–48. *ABS Bulletin*, June 1960, p. 38; June 1961, p. 32.

the ocean-going ships of Morocco has the following requirements: 1) Moroccan *port d'attache*, 2) Three-fourth national or French ownership (national or French majority on the administrative board), 3) National captain, officers, and half of the crew. In addition, the ship must be engaged in navigation which in a direct and principal way is of interest to Morocco.[78] However, after the International Zone of Tangier was abolished on October 29, 1956, and Tangier was declared an integral part of Morocco[79] the law, extending to Tangier the provisions relating to maritime navigation, provided for exceptional and liberal provisions in registering ships in Tangier.[80] Under these rules, an ocean ship choosing Tangier as its *port d'attache* may be granted Moroccan nationality if it belongs to individuals domiciled in Morocco or to a corporation having its *siège social* in Tangier, or whose affiliate has its *siège* in this port, and if it puts into Tangier at least once in six months.[81]

78. Code de Commerce Maritime 1914–1953, art. 3 (UNLS, p. 58). The crew requirement was recently laid down by Decree No. 2-57-0193 of March 23, 1957; see *Le Droit Maritime Français* 9:387 (1957).

79. *Dahir* no. 1-56-301, Empire chérifien, *Bulletin Officiel*, 28 décembre, 1956, p. 1474.

80. *Dahir* no. 1-57-215 du 6 *moharrem* [3 August, 1957] rendant applicables à la province de Tanger les dispositions du Code de Commerce Maritime Marocain promulgué par le *dahir* du 28 *joumada* II 1337 (31 March, 1919); Empire chérifien, *Bulletin Officiel*, 23 August, 1957, pp. 1112–1113.

81. *Id.*, art. 2.

This solution continues the tradition of the International Zone of Tangier as a paradise for international commercial operations, where, in the years following the end of the Second World War, the virtual absence of any governmental restrictions, taxes, or exchange controls created very favorable conditions for establishing base companies by nonresident corporations.[82] Now shipping corporations can also take advantage of the Tangier laws, since the *dahir* of August 3, 1957, allows the registration, under the Moroccan flag, of ships owned by companies which have their *siège social* in Tangier, a condition analogous to that obtaining in Panama. The conditions relating to the composition of the crew are even more favorable than in Panama, since no definite per cent of Moroccan nationals is required. There is, however, the one condition that attempts a kind of "genuine link" between Morocco and the ship, namely, the condition that the ship must once in six months visit the port of Tangier. This rule seems to have been motivated by the need to exercise a degree of direct jurisdiction and control over the ships flying the Moroccan flag. Perhaps as a result of this provision, the number of Moroccan vessels has not increased since the enactment of the liberal 1957 *dahir.*[83]

Tunisia, also, has been referred to as a country that wants to attract flag-of-convenience shipping.[84] In 1958 a liberal law modifying the rules concerning the nationality of ships was enacted by the Tunisian legislature. This law reduced the ownership requirement to one-third ownership by a Tunisian individual or juridical person, adding the prerequisite of a Tunisian *port d'attache.* A national crew requirement was not mentioned.[85] This new Tuni-

82. See Gibbons, pp. 151–156.

83. The statistics show that in 1957 and 1958 there were seven Moroccan ships over 1000 gross tons and that in December 1959 and December 1960 there were six; *Shipping Statistics*, pp. 47, 49; *ABS Bulletin*, June 30, 1960, p. 39; *id.* June 30, 1961, p. 32. There are, however, many more smaller vessels (over 34 in 1958). See statement of the government delegate of Morocco, ILConf.*RP*. 41 Sess. (Geneva, 1958), p. 79.

84. *The New York Times*, October 30, 1958, p. 61. See also "Flag-of-Convenience Fleet." *YLJ* 69:498 n. 2 (1960) and Mender, p. 288 n. 38, referring to *The New York Times* but not investigating the subject.

85. *Loi* no. 58–50 du 24 avril 1958 (*chaoual* 4:1377) relative à la nationalité des navires, *Journal Officiel de la République Tunisienne* 101:438 (1958).

sian law — although it may have violated the provisions of the agreement with France that was concluded in 1955 [86] — cannot as yet be regarded as the beginning of a Tunisian flag of convenience. However, the reduction of the ownership requirement to one-third is significant — it represents the policy followed by the new ex-colonial countries desirous of attracting foreign capital in order to promote the development of their merchant marines.

The requirement of national crew, like the requirement of national ownership, is not imposed by international law. However, for various reasons of national self-interest, a number of states impose the condition that a fixed proportion of or even all the members of the crews of their flag vessels must be nationals.[87] Although many states are not concerned with the nationality of the crew,[88] others have explicit requirements. In some, only the captain (that is, the master) must be a national; in others, the captain and officers; in still others, the captain and the crew in varying proportions.[89] There are some countries in which not only the captain and officers must be nationals but so must all[90] or a goodly per cent of the crew.[91] However, in most countries, in ex-

86. On December 28, 1955, Tunisia and France signed an agreement concerning maritime navigation, under which the two contracting parties bound themselves, in case of modification of their respective laws concerning the grant of nationality to ships, to observe the rule of 50 per cent national ownership of the vessels (the Tunisian law in force provided for 51 per cent Tunisian or French ownership). Under the same agreement, the crews aboard the vessels of either party were to be either French or Tunisian, but the flag state might grant exceptions to that rule. The agreement contained other provisions establishing reciprocal privileges of the contracting parties. For the text see the French *Journal Officiel*, December 30, 1955; reprinted in *Le Droit Maritime Français* 8:124–125 (1956).

87. One of the reasons is, *e.g.*, the protection of local labor practiced by capital-importing countries. See *Legal Aspects of Foreign Investment* (Friedmann & Pugh eds.) (1959), pp. 744–745.

88. The United Kingdom and the other members of the Commonwealth, Burma, Ireland, Denmark, Iceland, Norway, Sweden, Germany, Bulgaria, Roumania, Turkey, Vatican, Israel, Syria, China, Japan, Korea, Cuba, Dominican Republic, Ecuador, Guatemala, Honduras, Nicaragua, and Liberia (UNLS and UNLS Supp. *passim*).

89. Captain only: Tunisia, Finland, the Netherlands (UNLS, pp. 50, 62, 112). Captain and officers: Belgium, Hungary (*id.*, pp. 5, 78). Captain and crew: Brazil — two-thirds, Venezuela — 50 per cent (*id.*, pp. 6, 20). Colombia — also 50 per cent (Florio, *Nazionalità della nave e legge della bandiera*, p. 211).

90. Italy, Libya, Mexico, Peru, U.S.S.R. (UNLS, pp. 88, 101, 109, 135.) Poland (the Law of April 28, 1952, concerning work aboard the Polish merchant vessels in international navigation, *Dziennik Ustaw* [Journal of Laws], No. 25/171 [1952]).

91. *E.g.*, three-fourths of the crew in France. See Ripert, I, 313, 315, where the

ceptional cases provided for by the law, aliens may also be employed aboard national vessels.

In the Panlibhon countries, the absence of provisions making the registration of vessels dependent on the prerequisite of a national crew is an additional attraction of their shipping laws. However, it must be noted that there are provisions in the Panamanian and Costa Rican laws requiring that 10 per cent of the ship's personnel be nationals (formerly this was 25 per cent), but this is not a prerequisite for the granting of nationality, only the consequence thereof — the crew's nationality does not govern the ship's nationality. The escape clauses providing temporal exemption from this provision in case of the unavailability of national seamen make these provisions still more illusory.[92]

The requirement of national build — never a requirement of international law[93] — has become now for all practical purposes an anachronism in municipal shipping legislations. Only in the United States is the requirement of national build of some, though not essential, consequence.[94] In France, Monaco, Tunisia, and Portugal, this requirement is preserved only for fiscal reasons, since foreign-built ships may be registered only after paying the prescribed duties.[95] In Ethiopia and Greece the mere fact that a ship has been built in a home shipyard gives it the right to be registered in the home country.[96] In the flag-of-convenience countries there is no such thing as the requirement of national build.

Above and beyond all the above-mentioned requirements or lack thereof foreign shipowners are interested also in the ad-

---

difficulties of the interpretation of the French laws in this respect are mentioned. For Monaco and Greece see UNLS, pp. 69, 110. For the United States, 46 U.S.C. §672a. In Portugal two-thirds, UNLS, pp. 146, 150. For Syria, *id.*, p. 167. On Lebanon see note 74 above. 50 per cent in Cambodia (UNLS, p. 10), in Vietnam, *Le Droit Maritime Français* 8:376 (1956), in Morocco (*id.*, 9.387), in Argentina, UNLS, p. 1.

92. The respective laws are: for Panama, the Merchant Marine Act No. 7 of 1950, §7; for Costa Rica, Ley No. 12 de 21 de octubre 1941, art. 41 (2). The nonobservance of this provision was stated in the memorandum submitted to the Costa Rican Legislative Assembly, referred to in note 68 above. For Tunisia, see note 86 above.

93. Rienow, pp. 24–49.

94. 46 U.S.C. §11 (1952). Foreign-built vessels may be registered but may not engage in the coastwise trade; *ibid.*

95. UNLS, pp. 53, 63, 109–110, 146.

96. *Id.*, pp. 48, 68–69.

vantages of liberal and favorable corporation laws as well as those providing virtual tax immunity. Panama and Liberia afford ideal conditions for foreign corporations that wish to establish bases for conducting business abroad. In this sense, they are referred to as "foreign bases of incorporation" or "base countries."[97] A base country is defined as "a country which imposes only negligible income or capital taxes at all, on income of its domestic corporations derived from sources ouside the base country."[98] For a long time Panama has been particularly favored by American business as a country in which to establish base companies, and, for example, by 1955, more than 10,000 base companies had been organized in Panama.[99] The Panamanian government has even established special services to handle the problems connected with the incorporation of these companies. Many of them have been organized by foreign shipowners, in particular by oil companies. The usual method involved is for the parent company to establish under the Panamanian law a directly controlled operating subsidiary, which is the formal owner of the ships. As a rule, however, all shares are owned by the parent company. In this sense a Panamanian company is a "wholly owned subsidiary" of its parent company. The device of the subsidiary is employed because under Panamanian law a foreign-incorporated company may not operate ships under the Panamanian flag.[100]

97. See Gibbons, *Tax Factors in Basing International Business Abroad* (1957), where the use of the base countries and base companies for doing business abroad is comprehensively covered. Among the 13 base countries whose tax and corporation laws are described by Gibbons are Panama and Liberia, regarded by American businessmen as the most suitable bases of incorporation for the "tax haven" operations. See also, in general, Barlow & Wender, *Foreign Investment and Taxation* (1955); Friedmann, "Legal Problems in Foreign Investments," *Business Law* 14:746 (1959); *Legal Aspects of Foreign Investment*, p. 72; *Legal Problems of International Trade* (Proehl, ed.) (1959).

98. Gibbons, p. 3.

99. *Business Week*, October 1, 1955 (quoted in Gibbons, p. 125, n. 1).

100. Thus, *e.g.*, the United States-incorporated Socony Mobil Oil Co. has established in Panama a wholly owned subsidiary named Mobil Tankers Co., S.A. ("sociedad anónima" since it is incorporated under the Panamanian law), which formally owns and/or operates tankers under the Panamanian flag. See *Hearings* (House) 1957, p. 7. Similarly Esso Shipping Co., Standard Oil of New Jersey, a United States-incorporated company, has established under the Panamanian law the Panama Transport Co., S.A., as its subsidiary, all the shares of the Panamanian company being owned by its American parent; *Hearings* (House) 1957, pp. 59, 71. The Committee of Enquiry of the ILO found that in 1948 644 Panamian vessels were owned by 384 different companies, the majority of the ships belonging to

Liberia at one time was unfavorable toward direct investment, but has subsequently remodelled her laws in order to be attractive to foreign-owned corporations.[101] Special facilities have been afforded for foreign shipping. Since ships owned by foreign companies may be registered in Liberia the device of a base company for purposes of owning and operating a vessel under the national flag is not necessary. Even so, about 65 per cent of Liberia's registered tonnage is formally owned by Liberian corporations,[102] controlled primarily by American companies that, of course, may have other international connections.[103] It is interesting to note that many "Panamanian" corporations are owners of "Liberian" ships.[104]

The corporation laws of Panama and Liberia are extremely liberal. In both countries, incorporation is a mere formality and simplified to a minimum. Incorporation is effected upon the filing of the necessary papers. The fees attendant upon the formality are minimal in Liberia; the time required is only 48 hours.[105] Almost any type of corporate charter will be approved under Panamanian law. There are no requirements with respect to the nationality or residence of the incorporators or the directors or the officers. All kinds of shares are authorized; shareholders' meetings may be held outside Panama; and no director is required to be a shareholder.[106]

---

companies with only one ship registered in Panama. Only four companies had more than ten ships each, ILOffice, *Panama Conditions*, pp. 8–9.

101. Gibbons, p. 89.

102. *The New York Times*, January 11, 1959, p. 11. See also the statement of Weeks, representing the government of Liberia before the ICJ. See ICJ *Pleadings*, Constitution (1960), p. 272.

103. Thus, *e.g.*, the United States-incorporated Gulf Oil Corp., in addition to its United States-flag fleet, through its subsidiaries owned and operated in 1957 a total of 26 vessels registered under the flags of three foreign countries. Liberian-incorporated were Afran Transport Co., a 100 per cent directly owned subsidiary, and Kupran Transport Co. (capital stock issued to Kuwait Tankers, Inc., a Delaware corporation whose capital stock is 50 per cent owned by Gulf Oil Corp. and 50 per cent by the Atlantic Refining Co.). Another wholly owned subsidiary was established in Belgium. Standard Oil Co. of California organized a Liberian corporation, California Transport Corp., and all its issued capital stock was subscribed for and issued to the parent company, *Hearings* (Senate) 1957, pp. 103, 108, 119.

104. See *Hearings* (House) 1957, pp. 26–36.

105. For details see Gibbons, pp. 36, 93, 130–131.

106. Law No. 32 of February 26, 1927, as amended by Law No. 9 of July 3, 1946, cited in Gibbons, p. 130, n. 21. See also *Hearings* (Senate) 1957, pp. 13–14, 21–22, 32–34, 71–72, 94–95, where representatives of American oil companies initiate the senators into the technicalities of incorporating base companies in Panama.

The corporation law in Liberia also gives wide latitude to the Liberian corporations in respect to issuance, payment, and transfer of stock. Again there are no requirements as to the nationality or residence of directors, and meetings of the board of directors or stockholders may be held anywhere in the world. However, every corporation must have a place of business in Liberia and a qualified resident business agent. If a corporation has no operating office in Liberia, the resident business agent must be an incorporated bank or trust company with a paid-in capital of not less than fifty thousand dollars authorized by the Liberian legislature to act as resident agent for the corporation.[107]

The shipping registration formalities in Panama and Liberia are also very simple. In both countries permanent registration of ships is granted — in the case of Liberia — by the Commissioner of Maritime Affairs or by one of his deputies[108] (one of them has an office in New York) — in the case of Panama — by the Inspector of a Panamanian port,[109] Provisional registration is issued under Liberian law for one year by the Commissioner or by the Deputy Commissioner of Maritime Affairs, by a Liberian consular or diplomatic officer or agent, or even by any other person designated by the President of Liberia.[110] Under Panamanian law provisional registration has effect for six months (or even more) and can be granted by Panamanian consuls abroad.[111] The Honduran law does not have any provisions for consular or provisional registration and in Costa Rica this kind of registration was abolished in 1958.

The Panlibhon flags are made further attractive to foreign shipowners by the low registration fees and taxes that these coun-

107. For the details of the Liberian corporation law see *Liberian Code of Laws of 1956*, vol. I, tit. 4, ch. 1 (Liberian Corporation Law of 1948) (1957), pp. 123–148. See also *Hearings* (Senate) 1957, pp. 116, 119, where representatives of American oil companies testify on their subsidiary companies in Liberia.

International Trust Co. of Liberia takes care of all the formalities of incorporation and acts as resident agent. Registration of vessels may be settled through Liberian Services, Inc., which is a correspondent for the International Trust Co. and has its seat in New York; Gibbons, p. 89, n. 1.

108. *Liberian Code of Laws of 1956*, vol. II, tit. 22, Maritime Law, ch. 2 "Documentation and Identification of Vessels," §56.

109. Law No. 8 of January 12, 1925, art. 2; UNLS, p. 130.

110. *Liberian Code of Laws of 1956*, vol. II, tit. 22, ch. 2, §65.

111. Law No. 8 of January 12, 1925, art. 18 (UNLS, p. 132). For details relating to the Panamanian registration procedure see ILOffice, *Panama Conditions*, pp. 65–73.

tries impose upon ships registered under their respective flags. Table 9 indicates how very low these fees and taxes are:

TABLE 9. Registration fees and annual taxes on shipping in Panlibhonco.

Country	Fees	Tax
Liberia	$1.20 per net ton ("initial registration fee and Administrator's fee")	$0.10 per net ton
	The two kinds of charges shall not be increased during the term of 20 years counted from the date of initial registration	
Panama	1 balboa ($1.00 U.S.) per net ton or fraction of a ton (2 per cent as fees for consul) Permanent permit, 25 balboas; provisional permit, 20 balboas (50 per cent as fees to honorary consuls only)	10 centésimos ($0.10) per net ton (10 per cent as fees for consul)
Honduras	50 centavos ($0.25 U.S.) per net registered ton	10 centavos ($0.05 U.S.) This tax may not be increased during the term of 30 years from the date of the registration of the vessel
Costa Rica	$1.00 per net ton or fraction of a ton; $25.00 for registration certificate; $25.00 for radio license; $5.00 for the issue of certificate of competence for each navigation book of the ship	$0.10 per net ton This tax (duty) may not be increased during a period of 25 years from the date the license is issued

Sources: *Liberian Code of Laws of 1956* Vol. II tit. 22, ch. 2, §53. ILOffice, *Panama Conditions*, p. 66; *Hearings* (Senate) 1957, p. 93. OEEC "Study," p. 4. Ley No. 12 de 21 de octubre de 1941, art. 24, *Colección de Leyes* [Costa Rica] (1941, Segundo Semestre), p. 660, as amended by Ley No. 2295 de 22 de noviembre de 1958, *Colección de Leyes* (1958, Segundo Semestre), p. 343; Ley No. 12 de 21 de octubre de 1941, art. 26.

In contrast to this situation such a maritime country as, for example, the United Kingdom taxes all vessels on an average of something over two shillings for every ton of cargo carried.[112] The charges in the Panlibhon countries, negligible for the ship-

112. *The Shipping World & World Shipbuilding*, February 26, 1958, p. 263.

owners,[113] represent an easy source of revenue for these states. In Costa Rica, both the liberal law of 1941 and the subsequent withdrawal of flag-of-convenience facilities in 1958 were actuated by fiscal reasons.[114] The income that Liberia receives from the registration of ships in its flag-of-convenience fleet constitutes about one-seventh of the total revenue of the Liberian government.[115] Thus, it is obviously in the interest of the Panlibhon countries to maintain the practice of flags-of-convenience and to compete with each other in offering more attractive terms of registration.[116]

A further advantage, and perhaps the greatest of all, offered by the flag-of-convenience countries to foreign shipowners, is that, besides the registration fees and annual taxes (and a few other negligible administrative dues), no other taxes are payable by shipowners in these countries. In Panama the law expressly exempts from taxation any income derived from vessels registered in Panama and engaged in international maritime commerce, even if transportation contracts are signed within Panama.[117] Moreover, in 1941, by executive agreement, the Panamanian and the United States governments agreed to exempt the revenues of shipping companies incorporated under each other's laws from income taxation.[118] In Liberia, income derived by a Liberian corporation

113. Thus, *e.g.*, the owner of 38,000 deadweight-ton tanker (which would have a net tonnage of about 14,000) would pay in Liberia an initial registration fee of $16,800, plus an annual tax of only $1400.

114. Between 1950 and 1955 the revenue from registration fee and taxes brought one million colons to Costa Rica annually.

115. *Petroleum Press Service*, January 1959, p. 14. Largely because of this increase in revenue, Liberia was experiencing an era of economic prosperity (according to the Liberian daily newspaper, *The Listener*); *The New York Times*, April 6, 1958, p. 78. See, however, the statement of the Liberian representative before the ICJ, saying that "the net revenue now derived by the Government from Liberian flag vessels forms a comparatively small part of the national budget." ICJ *Pleadings*, Constitution (1960), p. 276. For Panama the registration fees and taxes represent only about one per cent of her total revenue; *The New York Times*, April 6, 1958, p. 78.

116. Similarly the Lebanese government, presenting the draft of the law of 1954 to Parliament, openly stated that one of the motives of the amendments provided by the draft was the increase of the revenue of the Lebanese treasury by registration fees and annual duties and also by consular fees. See *Le Droit Maritime Français* 8:122–123 (1956).

117. Fiscal Code, art. 708 (e); *Gaceta Official*, June 29, 1956.

118. See arrangements providing for relief from double income tax on shipping profits, January 15, February 8, and March 28, 1941; 55 Stat. 1363; E.A.S. 221; 103 U.N.T.S.: 163. About reciprocal exemptions see Baker, pp. 137, 138–140. See also *Hearings* (House) 1957, p. 142. The matter is also regulated by the United States Internal Revenue Code; I.R.C. §872 (a) (1954) for non-resident alien indi-

from the operation of vessels registered in Liberia and not engaged exclusively in coastwise Liberian trade is exempt from income tax.[119] These tax immunities decisively swing the competitive balance to the favor of United States Panlibhon operators as compared with their European competitors.

The question of whether American owners operating under Panlibhon flags are subject to United States taxation in any form gives the following answer: First of all, the transfer of the ownership of the vessels from the parent company to the foreign subsidiary is tax-free if the transferor receives 80 per cent or more of the stock of the foreign corporation to which the assets are transferred.[120] Since the shipowning subsidiaries are, as a rule, wholly owned by the transferor, this provision covers the case of the flag-of-convenience shipowners. The income of corporations established under the law of the United States is, in general, subject to United States tax no matter where it has been earned. Therefore, if a United States-incorporated company operates a ship under Liberian or Panamanian colors, the earnings of that ship must be reported by the company for United States tax purposes. On the other hand, the income of a foreign corporation is taxed only if it is derived from the United States sources. A subsidiary company organized by its American parent under Liberian or Panamanian law is recognized as a separate, foreign entity by United States tax law, and its profits are not taxed until they are distributed to its domestic parent in the form of dividends.[121] From this point of

viduals, I.R.C. §883 (1) (1954) for foreign corporations. See also *Hearings* (Senate) 1957, p. 94.

119. *Liberian Code of Laws of 1956*, vol. III, tit. 35, pt. II, ch. 6, §140 (c). About the exemption from the fiscal obligations of the ships operating under the flags of Liberia and Panama see also testimony of the Maritime Administrator, *Hearings* (House) 1957, pp. 139, 142–143; testimony of various oil company executives, *Hearings* (Senate) 1957, pp. 10, 50, 58, 65, 93–94, 107, 227. *Cf.* the statement of Alfaro (Panama) at the 3d session of the ILC, about the "extremely liberal" fiscal laws of his country; ILC *Yearbook 1951* I, 328. About the conveniences offered bv Honduras see Diamond, "Tax Advantages of Incorporating in Liberia and Honduras," *P-H Tax Ideas* §8022 (1956).

120. IRC, §351 (1954). See also *Hearings* (House) 1957, p. 143.

121. About the taxation of foreign income in general see Barlow & Wender, pp. 231–246. On the methods of taxation of American shipowners when their earnings are repatriated to the United States see the interesting testimony of various representatives of American oil companies in *Hearings* (Senate) 1957, pp. 10–11, 65–66, 88–89, 96, 107, 118–119, 136. See also the statement of the Maritime Administrator in *Hearings* (House) 1957, p. 143, and the statement of then Acting Secretary Dillon in *DSB* 41:14 (1959).

view the statement made by E.D. Naess, a major Panlibhon operator, before the House Ways and Means Committee, was substantially correct when he said that the tax on earnings from Panlibhon shipping must be paid sooner or later. This statement was challenged by Jorgen Jahre, president of the Norwegian Shipowners' Association, and his comments were in turn rebutted by the ACFN. This committee stated in a letter that "any correct comparison of tax burdens [of the United States and Norwegian shipowners] must take into account the total tax which must be paid sooner or later." [122]

Nonetheless, American shipowners receive tremendous financial and economic benefits from the deferral of taxation. First of all, the Liberian or Panamanian subsidiary corporation does not have to distribute dividends to the domestic corporation, and if it does distribute them, it may defer the distribution until the tax rate (which is variable) seems most advantageous.[123] Moreover, the tax-free accumulation of foreign earnings permits the parent corporation to use for new investment or for the maintenance of its fleet that portion of the foreign income which would have been paid to the United States in the form of taxes, and which their competitors in other countries must set aside to meet tax requirements.[124] This advantage, of course, tends to be cumulative, since increased fleets earn increased profits which in turn provide for further increases. It is for this reason that the flag-of-convenience fleets have grown so rapidly. Their development is given further impetus by the fact that, because of their high profit-earning potentialities due to freedom from taxation, finance houses, especially in the United States, are very willing to lend them money for fleet expansion.[125]

122. *The New York Times,* June 30, 1961, p. 54; *News of Norway,* June 22, 1961, p. 94.

123. *Hearings* (Senate) 1957, pp. 88–89, 101, 136. Thus, *e.g.,* Panamanian Transport Co., a Panamanian subsidiary of Esso Shipping Co., Standard Oil of New Jersey, did not declare any dividends between 1935 and 1949 (*id.,* p. 88).

124. In the case of Socony Mobil Oil Co. its Panamanian subsidiary declared in 1955 and 1956 only 20 per cent of its earnings to the parent company as dividends, and 80 per cent of its earnings were used for new construction and capital outlay to implement and supplement the Panamanian company's fleet; see testimony of Teitsworth, vice-president and director of Socony Mobil Oil Co., *Hearings* (Senate) pp. 10–11. See also *Hearings* (House) 1957, p. 143. The tax rate on dividends averages 50 per cent.

125. OEEC.MTC, "Study," p. 8. See also *Hearings* (Senate) 1957, p. 11.

The overwhelming advantage of this tax immunity is the object of resentment in European maritime countries, and is regarded as unfair competition. In the eyes of American maritime unions, the avoidance of taxation is the primary reason why American businessmen operate ships under flags of convenience, high seamen's wages being, according to the unions, only a minor reason.[126] This statement is true, but only in the sense that American owners prefer to operate their vessels specifically under the Panlibhon flags, and not others, because others do not give them tax immunity, and if they do, they are perhaps inconvenient for other reasons.[127]

The factor of tax avoidance is well known to the Congress and government of the United States. Senator Magnuson, Chairman of the Senate Committee on Interstate and Foreign Commerce, put it bluntly: "Most of those who fly the Panamanian, Liberian, or Honduran flag, which are the three biggest, do it because it lends itself to a subtly legal bit of tax evasion." [128] Also to the point is the dialogue between Representative Bonner, Chairman of the House Committee on Merchant Marine, and Mr. Morse, then Maritime Administrator and Chairman of the (then existing) Federal Maritime Board, at the hearings of the said committee:

Mr. Morse: It is my understanding that there is no income tax on earnings of vessels under Liberian flag.
The Chairman: There would be under American flag.
Mr. Morse: Certainly.
The Chairman: What would be the fair estimate of that savings?
Mr. Morse: Assuming that they made the same earnings, it would be 100 per cent of the American income tax which would be saved.
The Chairman: Another thing interested me. Why do not any of these ships go under the Cuban flag? I see that they all go under Panama and Liberia.
Mr. Morse: I do not know what the laws are in Cuba.

126. *Hearings* (House) 1957, pp. 698–700; *Hearings* (Senate) 1957, pp. 196–198.

127. More than 40 countries grant preferential treatment to foreign income earned by companies incorporated in their territories or levy no income tax at all on foreign or domestic income; Gibbons, p. 3. However, various other elements contribute to the choice of a particular country as a foreign base of incorporation for a given industry, in this case for the shipping industry.

128. *Hearings* (Senate) 1957, p. 136.

The Chairman: Is it to avoid tax?
Mr. Morse: Undoubtedly it is in part to avoid tax.[129]

The representatives of the American oil companies whose ships are registered in Panama are reluctant to admit that tax avoidance is the true reason for their preference of Panama and Liberia to other flags. The reasons adduced by certain of these representatives of the oil interests cannot, however, be treated very seriously. Thus, for example, one of them said: "The main reason for preferring, when practicable, to maintain ships under the flag of Panama in preference to flags of other foreign nations, is because of the close, cordial relationship between Panama and the United States." [!] Another reason for registering under the Panamanian flag, given by the same oil company executive, was the flexibility of crews.[130] This has some bearing upon the problem, but is only a minor reason, since such flexibility can also be taken advantage of under other flags.

The Statement of Policy on Foreign Transfers of November 5, 1956, provided legal sanction for these two main economic reasons — the high operating costs under the American flag and tax saving or virtual tax immunity under the flags of Panama, Liberia, and Honduras. The statement provided, *inter alia,* that the owner of a vessel transferred to foreign registry and flag under the trade-out-and-build program must be a United States citizen or a United States, Liberian, Panamanian, or Honduran corporation, in which all or the majority of the stock must be owned by a citizen or citizens of the United States, and that "the registry and flag of the vessel transferred shall be either Liberian, Panamanian, or Honduran."[131] This 1956 regulation only confirmed the practice of registering ships in Liberia and Panama, which, by the time it was promulgated, had already been well established. The legal techniques and practical problems of the incorporation of companies

129. *Hearings* (House) 1957, p. 139. This tax avoidance or deferral is, of course, not limited to shipping. It is true of any other type of foreign investment, which, in addition, in the case of the United States is favored by the policy of encouraging foreign investment and not taxing income derived from foreign corporations. See the statement of Acting Secretary Dillon, *DSB* 41:14 (1959).

130. *Hearings* (House) 1957, p. 74. But see the reasons given by Alfaro (Panama) at the 3d sess. of the ILC in 1951, who realistically gave fiscal privileges as the main reason for registering ships under his country's flag; ILC *Yearbook 1951* I, 328.

131. 21 F.R. 8588. See also *Hearings* (House) 1957, pp. 71–72.

and the registration of ships in Panama and Liberia have been well explored and have a long tradition already.

As for the reasons for preferring Liberia to Panama the dialogue which took place between the Chairman of the Senate Committee on Interstate and Foreign Commerce and an oil company executive is worth quoting:

The Chairman: Incidentally, I am curious, and there must be a reason, why did you go to Liberia instead of Panama?

Mr. Vander Clute: I can tell you that very easily. Liberia we look upon as the godson of the United States. The flag is the nearest thing to the United States flag, and Uncle Sam certainly would have control over Liberian ships . . .[132]

This statement does not reveal much, and can be complemented by the explanation that Liberia has dethroned Panama as the leading flag-of-convenience country as a result — in addition to its more liberal laws — of further inducements offered by Liberia, particularly for Americans. Liberia is an English-speaking country, the United States dollar is official currency, and the legal systems of the two countries are related to each other.[133]

132. *Hearings* (Senate) 1957, p. 115.

133. See Benedict, VI, 220. See also the statement of the Liberian representative before the ICJ; ICJ *Pleadings*, Constitution (1960), p. 274. *Cf.* Gibbons, p. 89. About the reasons connected with the "effective United States control" see Ch. VII.

Chapter III. The Opposition to Flags of Convenience

Inevitably the rise of the flag-of-convenience fleets provoked a storm of protest at both national and international levels from the groups which, for one reason or another, were harmed by their existence. The anti-Panlibhon camp consists of two main groups, equally resolute in their condemnation of the practice, but, although their reasons overlap to a certain extent, their protest stems from different aspects of the problem. The seamen's unions are concerned about the allegedly lower labor standards aboard the Panlibhon ships and — particularly the American unions — about the loss of job opportunities for American seamen that results from the flight from the American flag. The shipowners of the traditional maritime countries in Europe, supported by their governments, find that the vessels operating under the virtually tax-free flags of convenience present very serious competition.

Initially opposition to the flags of convenience came only from the seamen's labor organizations, grappling with the problem "in the face of apparent indifference on the part of governments and shipowners in the traditional maritime countries.[1] It was only after the rapidly growing Panlibhon fleets had became a real menace to European shipping interests, for whom competition — not shipboard labor conditions — was the vital question, that the European shipowners joined the campaign against Panlibhon in an unholy alliance with labor.

As early as the years following the First World War,[2] the

1. ILOffice, *Report IV* (1957), p. 3. See also Becu, p. 59.
2. Not as late as after the Second World War, as is noted by Sørensen, p. 203.

ITWF raised the question of the effect on seafarers' employment conditions of certain transfers of ships from one flag to another for purposes of evading safety regulations and labor standards.[3] In 1933, at the request of the ITWF, the question was discussed by the Joint Maritime Commission of the ILO. The seafarers' group of this commission complained that shipowners of important maritime nations transferred to and operated their ships under the flags of certain small countries of no previous maritime standing, and that considerably lower social standards prevailed on those ships, without any effective change having taken place in ownership. It was held by the seafarers' group that those "spurious transfers" endangered the conditions of work and employment of the seafarers, and created unfair competition with other shipowners in the country.[4] However, no agreement was reached with the Joint Maritime Commission on the exact nature of the problem.

With the rapid expansion of the Panamanian fleet in the postwar period, the question of flag transfers came into greater prominence. In 1946 the ITWF asked the ILO to carry out an investigation of flag transfers, and the matter was again discussed by the commission in 1947. However, as in 1933, no positive action was taken, though both the shipowners' and seafarers' groups agreed that transfers made purely for the purpose of reducing seafarers' standards should be condemned.[5]

In July 1948 at its Oslo congress, the ITWF adopted a resolution threatening to boycott certain ships that had been transferred to the Panamanian flag on the ground that conditions on these ships were unsatisfactory. A similar resolution was adopted by the seafarers' section of the ITWF, meeting in Geneva in the same year; and in February 1949 in London, an international boycott committee of eight members was appointed by the conference of dockers' and seafarers' representatives affiliated with ITWF. The conference also adopted two resolutions — one condemning the transfers of obsolete and uneconomic tonnage from Britain, Holland, Norway, and Sweden to the Panamanian registry as "menac-

3. ILOffice, *Panama Conditions*, p. 45.
4. *Ibid.* See also "Seven Maritime Sessions of the International Labour Conference," *International Labour Review* 78:446–447 (1958).
5. *Id.*, p. 447.

ing the established standards of the shipping industry and calculated to place the traditional maritime countries at a serious disadvantage" — the other calling upon the European Recovery Program administrative authorities not to carry its cargoes in ships "placed on registers such as the Panamanian, Honduran and the like."[6] The government of Panama, threatened by the boycott, rejected the conference's allegations as to the safety and labor standards of the transferred ships, and asked the ILO to appoint an independent tripartite committee of investigation to examine and report on the accusations. The Governing Body of the ILO appointed a committee consisting of three members, one nominated by each group of the Governing Body. Thereupon, the government of Panama convened a merchant marine conference in order to discuss the boycott. It adopted 14 resolutions proposing a number of reforms in Panamanian maritime legislation and administration.[7]

The Committee of Enquiry of the ILO studied the nature and composition of the Panamanian merchant marine, the laws and regulations of Panama concerning maritime questions, especially seafarers' conditions of employment, and the application of the legislation in practice, more particularly as revealed by the committee's visits of inspection of 30 Panamanian flag ships in different ports of six countries on three continents. The ILO inquiry found a number of defects in the legislation of Panama on maritime questions and in the application thereof by the consular service of Panama and by the owners and captains of the ships. A large per cent of obsolete tonnage was found, and some evasion of safety standards was clearly demonstrated. Social and labor standards were also found to be very low in a number of cases. However, the committee expressed the belief that the conditions on many ships under the Panamanian flag were good, that the Panamanian authorities seemed to be cognizant of the situation

6. ILOffice, *Panama Conditions*, pp. 45–46.

7. The ILO committee consisted of government group: Senator Herman Vos (Belgium), former minister of education; employers' group: A. G. Fennema (Netherlands), employers' deputy member of the Governing Body; workers' group: A. Dalgleish (United Kingdom), former trade union official. The conference was attended by delegates of the government, shipping firms, Panamanian seamen's unions, and three classification societies. For the text of the resolutions see *id.*, pp. 50–55.

and to realize the responsibilities which a large merchant fleet entailed.[8]

The Governing Body, to which the report was submitted, asked the government of Panama for its reactions to it, and in 1950 decided to publish the report, together with the Panamanian government commentary and a statement by the Governing Body. The ILO investigation has acquired historical rather than immediate importance now, since conditions in the Panamanian fleet have changed since 1949. One must also bear in mind that the conclusions of the report were accepted by the Governing Body of the ILO as valid only with respect to the ships inspected, and they expressly stated that they did not feel justified in drawing any conclusions from it concerning the merchant marine of Panama as a whole. Further, they commended Panama for the serious efforts made to improve seafarers' conditions and they suggested certain problems toward which efforts especially might be directed to provide better protection for seamen sailing under the Panamanian flag. Modifying the finding of the Committee of Enquiry, the Governing Body noted that, with the rapid expansion of tonnage in the postwar period, an increasing proportion of the Panamanian fleet consisted of new and safe vessels. They thanked the government of Panama for its cooperation throughout the inquiry, and declared that nothing in the report was to be construed as an intrusion into the sovereign rights of the Republic of Panama or as a breach of the full respect due to its institutions.[9]

In addition, the general secretary of the ITWF, Mr. Oldenbroek, who represented his organization at the first meeting of the Committee of Enquiry, for unknown reasons would not submit specific evidence of the charges brought against Panama. Repeatedly urged by the committee to supply it with more specific and detailed information, with evidence in support of the charges and with a list of the ships involved, he submitted only one or two "vague and meagre" documents. For this reason the inquiry was carried out only on the basis of the extremely general charges listed in the ITWF resolutions and did not give an exhaustive picture of the Panamanian fleet in 1949. Thus, Panama came out of

8. For the details of the findings see *id.*, pp. 8–40.
9. *Id.*, pp. 80–85, 86–87.

the whole affair quite well, both the Committee of Enquiry and the Governing Body feeling that she deserved commendation for the courtesy and helpfulness of her officials.[10]

Following the publication of the committee's report, the government of Panama set up a new organization to oversee the working conditions of her seamen, and a number of collective agreements were signed between the owners of the Panamanian ships and the seafarers' section of the ITWF.[11] However, the seafarers' unions continued to complain about the flag transfers, and in 1954 requested that the question be taken up by the proposed Preparatory Maritime Conference and by the Maritime Session of the ILO to be held thereafter.[12] At the same time, on certain occasions some seamen's unions would refuse to despatch flag-of-convenience vessels where the working conditions were, in their opinion, unsatisfactory.[13]

As a result of the pressure exercised by the unions, the item "Flag Transfer in Relation to Social Conditions and Safety" was placed on the agenda of the 41st (Maritime) Session of the International Labor Conference. The types of flag transfer meant by the Joint Maritime Commission were transfers to flags outside the "traditional maritime" countries.[14]

The matter was first discussed by the Preparatory Technical Maritime Conference of the ILO which met in London in September and October 1956, on the basis of a prepared report that contained a historical review of the action previously taken by the ILO on the flag-transfer question, a summary of the replies received from 24 governments of "traditional maritime" countries, the replies received to letters addressed to the governments of Costa Rica and Honduras, and certain conclusions.[15] The proceedings of this conference, in particular of its Committee on Flag

10. *Id.*, pp. 27, 87. See also ILOffice, ILConf., 41 Sess. 1958, *Report I: Report of the Director General* (1957), p. 41 [abbreviated hereafter as ILOffice, *Report I* (1957)]. The helpful attitude of Panama *vis à vis* the ILO was one of the arguments used by the Panamanian government delegate at the 41st Sess. of the ILConf. in Geneva in 1958; See ILConf. *RP.* 41 Sess. (Geneva 1958), pp. 115–116 (1959).

11. ILOffice, *Report I* (1957), p. 41.

12. "Seven Maritime Sessions," *International Labour Review* 78:429 (1958).

13. OEEC.MTC. "Study," p. 14.

14. ILOffice, *Report IV* (1957), p. 1.

15. ILO Preparatory Technical Maritime Conference, *Reports III/1 & III/2*, "Flag Transfer in Relation to Social Conditions and Safety" (1956).

Transfer composed of 20 government members, 10 shipowners' and 10 seafarers' members, were important for several reasons.

The 1956 conference noted a new development in the flag-of-convenience fleets, namely, the fact that, in addition to the tremendous increase in their tonnage, "since 1949 a fundamental change had occurred in the situation through the vast increase in modernization of ships registered in the flag of convenience countries," and that "the emphasis had shifted to some extent from attacking the substandard conditions *formerly* prevailing on ships under flags of convenience . . . to economic competition from new and efficient vessels free from the burden of taxation and social charges applying to ships belonging to the traditional maritime countries." [16] The spokesman of the shipowners' group also pointed out that "the problem of bad social conditions had diminished." [17]

Because of this "shift of emphasis" and the increasing danger to their economic interests, the shipowners of the traditional maritime countries joined the seamen in an unusual alliance against a common enemy. However, the shipowners' attitude was not uniform. The Greek shipowners' representative urged the London conference not to exaggerate, and even to devise some rules which would obviate arbitrary action by the seafarers' organizations. He also emphasized the altered conditions prevailing in the flag-of-convenience fleet in consequence of its modernization. His position is understandable in view of the large tonnage of Greek shipping registered under flags of convenience. Similarly, the United States government delegate warned against subjecting ship transfers to specific conditions or imposing prohibitions against a particular country or group of countries. This attitude also reflected the United States government policy on ship transfers, discussed in Chapter II. The member of the United Kingdom

16. See the statement of a member of the seafarers' group; *id.*, pp. 3–4. *Cf.* similar formulation of the change by Sørensen two years later: "Because of improved conditions in the many modern ships registered under flags of convenience, the emphasis has shifted since then. The problem is now also viewed as one of economic competition between the merchant fleets of traditionally maritime countries and the new and efficient vessels operating with lower costs under the flags of countries to which they are attached only by administrative formality of registration." Sørensen, p. 203.

17. ILOffice, *Report IV* (1957) p. 7.

government group took a moderate stand stating that any restrictions on transfer would not only run counter to his government's declared policy of promoting the maximum possible freedom in international shipping and commerce, but also would not afford a solution of the problem.[18]

Finally, and most important, the London Preparatory Technical Maritime Conference of 1956 revealed the close connection between the various labor facets of the flag-of-convenience issue and its international legal aspect, which had been discussed just previously by the International Law Commission. The principle of genuine link that — as the International Law Commission had ruled — must exist as a condition of the recognition of national character by other states, was readily taken up in 1956 by the seamen's unions as a panacea for the allegedly substandard social conditions aboard Panlibhon ships. "If this principle [that is, the principle of genuine link] could be implemented there might be a possible solution to one aspect of the problem," the seafarers' delegate stated in his opening speech, expressly referring to the ILC ruling.[19] What was meant by "one aspect," and what he hoped would be achieved by the implementation of the genuine link concept is presented in the "Proposals Made by the Seafarers' Members," submitted to the Committee on Flag Transfer of the Preparatory Technical Maritime Conference. This document reads as follows:

> The Seafarers' group has considered points in relation to flag transfers and submits that the following points should be considered in relation to any form of instrument which is finally adopted:
>
> 1. Notice to be taken of the declaration made by the International Law Commission of the United Nations on the subject of merchant ships having a broader link with the country of registration than merely the formality of registration.
>
> 2. The country of registration to have greater and more intimate jurisdiction over ships flying its flag, possibly by requiring that a) ships should be owned by companies having their principal place of business in the country of registration; b) each company shall have nationals of the registering country on its board of directors; c) meetings of the board of directors shall be held within the territory of the registering country.

18. *Id.*, p. 4.
19. *Ibid.* The ILC's discussion of the "genuine link" is analyzed in Ch. VIII.

3. To make and adopt regulations designed to insure that all ships flying its flag observe internationally accepted safety standards.
4. To establish and operate a government-controlled ship inspection service within its territory adequate to the requirements of the tonnage on its register and to ensure that all ships flying its flag are regularly inspected within its territory to ensure conformity with regulations issued under 3 above.
5. To lay down regulations governing the recruitment, engagement and discharge of seafarers serving in its ships according to internationally accepted standards and establish the requisite government-controlled agencies to give effect to such regulations.
6. To lay down regulations or legislation providing that no less than 25 per cent of seafarers in any one ship are nationals of the country of registration.
7. To make and adopt regulations or legislation, if such do not already exist in the country, providing for the freedom of association of its seafarers.
8. To ensure by regulation that proper repatriation for its seafarers be provided.
9. To provide that seafarers will be covered by social security arrangements which in any case shall not be less than those provided for workers in other countries.
10. To ensure that proper and satisfactory arrangements are made within the country concerned for the examination of candidates for certificates of competency and for the issuing of such certificates.[20]

A resolution of similar content, submitted by the government members' group, expressly referred in its preamble to the provisions of arts. 29 and 34 and the relevant commentaries adopted by the ILC on the subject of the nationality of ships. The shipowners' group agreed to the resolution with the exception of the first paragraph of the preamble, referring to the work of the ILC.[21] The final resolution, therefore, does not mention the ILC work, but contains a new paragraph in the preamble indicating expressly that "the problems involved have been brought into special prominence by the large volume of tonnage registered in countries not hitherto regarded as being traditionally maritime."[22]

After preliminary consideration by the Preparatory Technical

20. *Id.*, p. 5. *Cf.* similar requirements demanded by the ITWF in *Panlibhonco: The Modern Shipping Problem* (1958).
21. ILOffice, *Report IV* (1957), pp. 6, 7.
22. *Id.*, p. 9. The Greek shipowners recorded their opposition to the resolution; *id.*, p. 8.

Maritime Conference in 1956, the question of flags of convenience was examined by the 41st Maritime Session of the International Labor Conference in Geneva. It is interesting to note that the proceedings of this conference began on exactly the same day as the signing of the final act of the United Nations Conference on the Law of the Sea, that is, on April 29, 1958, and were held in the same building. The conference was attended by 370 delegates, advisers, and observers, representing the governments, shipowners, and seafarers of 46 member states and international organizations.[23]

The text of the resolution concerning flag transfer as it had been adopted in London in 1956 was the basis of discussion for the Committee on Flag Transfer.[24] The committee did not make many changes in it — the most significant was the insertion of a new paragraph in the preamble taking into account the results of the UN Conference on the Law of the Sea. This was done at the instigation of the government delegates from the Netherlands and Belgium.[25] At the UN conference, as at the ILO conference the Netherlands' delegates were in the forefront of opposition to the flags of convenience.[26]

There is no doubt that the adoption of the genuine-link clause by the UN Conference on the Law of the Sea was influenced by the pressure of both the seamen's unions and shipowning interests.

23. ILConf.*RP.* 41 Sess. (Geneva, 1958), pp. xv–xxiv. The 41st Session of the International Labor Conference was the seventh session since 1919 devoted entirely to maritime questions. See "Seven Maritime Sessions," *International Labour Review* 78:429–460 (1958). The records of the conference are printed in ILConf.*RP.* 41 Sess. (Geneva, 1958).

24. The Committee on Flag Transfer was composed of 50 members (25 government members, 10 employers' members, and 15 workers' members). See *id.*, pp. xxxii–xxxiii. The government member of Norway was chairman. The two vice-chairmen were from the Netherlands; *id.*, p. 237.

25. *Ibid.*

26. Support for the proposed text of the resolution on flag transfer was expressed by the government member of the Netherlands and by the workers' members, in particular the workers' member of the U.S.S.R. (*ibid*). In Soviet comments the practice of using flags of convenience is presented as a "new form of exploitation of seamen's masses by shipowners of capitalist countries." See Bulushev, "Bluzhdaiushchie flagi," *Morskoi Flot* (1956, no. 12), p. 26. See also, *e.g.*, Vereshchetin, *Svoboda sudokhodstva v otkrytom more* (1958), pp. 32–40. In general, the Soviet commentators emphasize the economic background of the flag-of-convenience problem. See Molodtsov, pp. 139–142; Vereshchetin, pp. 32–40; Burmistrov, "V tiskakh rastushchikh protivorechii," *Morskoi Flot* (1959, no. 11), pp. 23–26.

But the influence was reciprocal.[27] The spirit of the genuine link adopted by the Conference on the Law of the Sea perhaps still haunted the meeting hall at the International Labor Conference, since it was reinstated in the final text of the document. It took the form of a recommendation concerning the social conditions and the safety of seafarers in relation to the registration of ships. This recommendation was adopted by 144 votes in favor, 0 against, with three very characteristic abstentions — by the Greek employers' delegate and by the two United States government delegates.[28] The instrument notes that the problems involved have been brought into special prominence by the large volume of tonnage registered in countries not hitherto regarded as being traditionally maritime,[29] and then refers to the provisions of the Convention on the High Seas regarding 1) the right of every state to sail ships under its flag;[30] 2) the nationality of the ship, that "there must exist a genuine link between the state and the ship, in particular, the state must effectively exercise its jurisdiction and control in administrative, technical and social matters over ships flying its flag";[31] and 3) the obligation that every state shall take such measures for ships under its flags as are necessary to ensure safety at sea with regard, *inter alia,* to the manning of ships and labor conditions for crews, taking into account applicable labor instruments.[32] Reference is also made there to such related instruments as the Seafarers' Engagement (Foreign Vessels) Recommendation, adopted at the same International Labor Con-

27. The general secretary of the ITWF stated expressly that the action of the unions stimulated various parliaments. He said: "It is certainly no exaggeration to claim that this largely contributed to the unanimous adoption at the Law of the Sea Conference of a resolution calling for the establishment of a 'genuine link' between a merchant vessel and the country whose flag it flies" (Becu, p. 60). Incidentally it was not a "resolution" but art. 5 of the Convention on the High Seas.

28. For the text of this recommendation, as submitted by the Committee on Flag Transfer, see ILConf. *RP.* 41 Sess. (Geneva, 1958), pp. 238–239. For the authentic text see *id.,* appendix XII, pp. 270–272. The recommendation is also reprinted in the ILOffice, *Official Bulletin* 41:11–12 (1958). For the results of the voting see ILConf.*RP.* 41 Sess. (Geneva, 1958), pp. 187–188.

29. This clause had been originally inserted at the London conference in 1956 at the proposal of the shipowners' group; ILOffice, *Report IV* (1957) p. 7.

30. The Convention on the High Seas (U.N. Doc. A/CONF. 13/L.53), art. 5; UN.CLS.*OR* 2:135, 136 (1958).

31. The Convention on the High Seas, art. 5.

32. The Convention on the High Seas, art. 10(b).

ference in 1958, and the Social Security (Seafarers') Convention of 1946. The recommendation expresses "serious concern at the tendency of nationals of certain maritime countries to serve in vessels of other countries without properly negotiated collective agreements ensuring them the protection and standards applicable to vessels of their own countries," and urges each member

> to do everything in its power to discourage seafarers within its territory from joining or agreeing to join vessels registered in a foreign country unless the conditions under which such seafarers are to be engaged are generally equivalent to those applicable under collective agreements and social standards accepted by *bona fide* organizations of shipowners and seafarers of maritime countries where such agreements and standards are traditionally observed.

The recommendation goes on to state that the country of registration "should accept the full obligations implied by registration and exercise effective jurisdiction and control for the purpose of the safety and welfare of seafarers in its seagoing merchant ships."[33]

The measures which should be taken to give effect to this include those provided for by the seafarers' proposal at the London Conference of 1956, such as proper ship-inspection service, government-controlled agencies to supervise the signing-on and signing-off of seamen at home and abroad,[34] regulations to ensure freedom of association for seafarers, proper repatriation, and examination for — and granting of — certificates of competency.

On the whole, the proceedings of the 41st (Maritime) Session of the International Labor Conference, in particular the resolutions adopted there, revealed strong anti-flag-of-convenience feel-

33. ILConf.*RP*. 41 Sess. (Geneva, 1958), pp. 268–270; also, in ILOffice, *Official Bulletin* 41:10–11 (1958). The recommendation was intended to make the manning of the Panlibhon ships difficult; it was opposed by the Greek delegates; ILConf.*RP*. 41 Sess. (Geneva, 1958), pp. 112–113. The recommendation was adopted by 138 votes in favor, no votes opposed, and 11 abstentions which were characteristic: two government members and one employers' member from Greece, all the delegates of Liberia and Panama (government, workers' and employers' members), and the employers' member of the United States (*id.*, p. 162).

34. The establishment of these agencies abroad also was proposed by Belgium and the Netherlands (*id.*, p. 238). It is interesting to note that the conference rejected a proposal by the United States government member that the clause be amended to provide for the establishment of government-controlled "procedures" (not "agencies") to supervise the signing-on and signing-off of seafarers "as required by national laws or regulations."

ings of international labor — feelings supported by the governments and shipowners of the traditional European maritime countries.[35] In the formulation of the demands of these groups, the provisions of the previously held Geneva Conference on the Law of the Sea, in particular those relating to the nationality of ships, became the legal basis for arguments against the practice of registering under Panlibhon flags.

The next stage in the fight of the seamen's unions against flags of convenience was the organization by the ITWF of a world-wide "selective" boycott of ships flying flags of convenience not signing collective agreements with an ITWF affiliate. The boycott decided upon at the ITWF Amsterdam Congress in July 1958[36] had two main objectives; first, to prod the governments of the traditional European maritime countries to take measures against Panlibhon ships; and second, to bring as many Panlibhon ships as possible under agreements sponsored by the ITWF. The decision in favor of the boycott was also taken in view of the fact that — as the general secretary of the ITWF said — "there was no overall move by governments or shipowners to end the Panlibhon scandal" and "a more dramatic gesture was therefore needed.[37]

It was decided that the boycott should last four days, from midnight, November 30, to midnight, December 4, 1958. It proved to be a half-success. In United States ports it was much more successful than in Europe, where some non-affiliated unions (in France, Holland, and Italy) refused to collaborate with the ITWF. In some other countries (for example, Germany) even ITWF members did not take part in the boycott.[38] In the United States

35. The problem of the flags of convenience was also touched by some delegates in the discussion of the report of the Director-General. The workers' adviser of the United Kingdom attacked the flags of convenience as the main cause of the shipping recession and warned that "unless some very definite steps are taken — and we can take some at this conference — the genuine maritime countries may well be wrecked on the rocks of 'Panlibhonco,'" (ILConf.*RP.* 41 Sess. (Geneva, 1958), p. 23). The flags of convenience were also denounced by the workers' delegate of Cuba (*id.*, pp. 20–21). The government delegates of Liberia and Panama in their statements defended the policies of their governments (*id.*, pp. 73–74, 115–116).

36. *The New York Times,* October 27, 1958, p. 53; August 7, 1958, p. 48.

37. Becu, p. 60.

38. *Id.*, pp. 60–61. Panama had sent notes to all the governments of the traditional maritime nations protesting the boycott (*The New York Times,* November 27, 1958, p. 59).

129 ships were picketed by 16 unions, primarily by the National Maritime Union (NMU) and the Seafarers' International Union (SIU).[39] The temporary injunction sought against the unions' picketing in the United States District Court for the Southern District of New York by 15 foreign subsidiaries of the members of the ACFN had been denied by the court.[40]

The success of the boycott in the United States is explained by the fact that a large per cent of the flag-of-convenience fleet is owned by United States interests. The stand of the unions is also clarified in the statements of their representatives testifying before the Congress.[41] American unions put forward the argument that in consequence of the transfers and foreign registration of United States ships seafaring employment aboard American-flag ships had decreased considerably, because on flag-of-convenience ships American seamen had been replaced by aliens,[42] that a large number of seamen were unemployed,[43] and that the lower wage scales and poor working conditions aboard flag-of-convenience ships could negatively affect the labor conditions of the seamen employed aboard American-flag vessels.[44] The unions

39. *Id.*, December 5, 1958, p. 62. About the outcome of the boycott see also *The New York Times*, December 2, 1958, p. 1; December 3, 1958, p. 73; December 4, 1958, p. 78; January 4, 1959, p. 18. About earlier instances of picketing Panlibhon vessels see November 15, 1958, p. 40; and see also NMU *Pilot*, November 20, 1958, p. 3.

40. Afran Transport Co. v. National Maritime Union, 169 F. Supp. 416 (S.D.N.Y. 1958). But see 175 F. Supp. 285 (S.D.N.Y. 1959).

41. The statement of Hoyt S. Haddock, executive secretary of the AFL-CIO Maritime Committee, submitted before the Subcommittee on Merchant Marine of the House Committee on Merchant Marine and Fisheries on July 23, 1957 is an exhaustive denouncement of the flags of convenience; *Hearings* (House) 1957, pp. 684–714. Haddock also testified before the Merchant Marine and Fisheries Subcommittee of the Senate Committee on Interstate and Foreign Commerce on August 21, 1957; *Hearings* (Senate) 1957, pp. 182–212. See also the statement of Harry E. O'Reilly, executive secretary-treasurer of the Maritime Trades Dept., AFL-CIO; *Hearings* (House) 1957, pp. 714–720; *Hearings* (Senate) 1957, pp. 234–240.

42. Statistics show that this argument is correct. The number of seamen employed aboard the United States-flag vessels fell from 97,630 on December 31, 1951 (during the Korean War) to 70,850 on December 31, 1952 and to 51,640 on December 31, 1958; *Shipping Statistics*, p. 177. Detailed data on seafaring employment are also available *id.*, pp. 169–196. The unions claim that at least 16,000 jobs have been lost for American seamen through the Panlibhon operations. See, *e.g.*, *The New York Times*, October 22, 1959, p. 66.

43. "Flag-of-Convenience Fleet," *YLJ* 69:502 n. 32 (1960).

44. See, *e.g.*, Afran Transport Co. v. National Maritime Union, 169 F. Supp. 416, 429 (S.D.N.Y. 1958).

also supported, but without success, the legislation directed against foreign tranfers.[45]

The subsequent development in the unions' anti-Panlibhon campaign represented a change in policy *vis-à-vis* the Panlibhon shipowners. Previously, the ITWF policy had been to demand collective bargaining between shipowners and unions of the country where a crew had been signed on. The Panlibhon ships, from the union's point of view, were classified according to the nationality of their crew members.[46] The new policy adopted by the ITWF at its London meeting early in 1959 was to classify the flag-of-convenience ships according to the ultimate owner's nationality. This change in policy, made at the instigation of the United States member unions, had the objective of forcing American Panlibhon operators to accept contracts with American unions.[47] The resolution adopted on January 22, 1959 by the joint conference of the dockers' and seafarers' section of the ITWF in London decided:

a) to call again upon the appropriate governments to get together for the purpose of finding a solution to this problem;
b) to continue the fight against any shipowner using a flag for the purpose of avoiding the proper wages and working conditions and normal taxation; and
c) to seek to have established the appropriate collective agreements covering wages and working conditions and, where lacking, social security; such agreements to be concluded through affiliated unions of the country in which *actual* control of the shipping operation is vested and, where necessary, by the ITF Seafarers' Section through its Fair Practices Committee.[48]

According to the decision of the Fair Practices Committee of the ITWF, each union affiliated with the ITWF was to list all the shipping companies it regarded as within its jurisdiction. This meant the shipping companies whose control was vested in the union's home country. The unions were then to demand collective

45. See in general "Panlibhon Registration of American-owned Merchant Ships: Government Policy and the Problem of the Courts," *Columbia Law Review* 60:711, 715–718 (1960).
46. See *Hearings* (Senate) 1957, pp. 81, 91–92.
47. *The New York Times*: January 23, 1959, p. 41; January 24, 1959, p. 38; April 15, 1959, p. 53; *Fairplay* 192:947 (1959).
48. *The Baltic & International Maritime Conference Monthly Circular*, no. 181, February 1959, pp. 7687–7688. See also *The New York Times*, January 24, 1959, p. 38.

bargaining by the ship operators within their jurisdiction, no matter what flags the ships were flying. Thus, for example, under such jurisdictional directives a ship formally owned by a Liberian subsidiary of an American parent corporation was within the jurisdiction of one of the American unions. As a spokesman for the United States delegation at the ITWF London conference in January 1959 said: "The nationality of the parent company proves the nationality of the subsidiary." [49] However, the ITWF made one concession regarding United States shipowners operating ships under flags of convenience, namely, American unions were to get for the crews of these ships only "the best possible conditions," since, as the ITWF spokesman explained, high wages and good conditions prevailed aboard American ships, whereas those of other nationalities were generally not so good, and the United States had several unions with varying standards.[50]

The assignment of jurisdiction by the ITWF to national unions has not, however, in practice proved to be easy. The difficulties of localizing and identifying the country in which the actual control of a shipping operation is vested are well known. Hence, a jurisdictional dispute arose in 1959 between American and Greek unions. The Americans pointed out that many of the Greek-owned ships were financed by American capital or traded primarily from United States ports, and therefore they claimed bargaining jurisdiction for the majority of these vessels. This was challenged by the Greek Pan-Hellenic Federation, which insisted on the right to make contracts covering any ship carrying a Greek crew, regardless of the operation of the ship. The Greek owners of more than 300 Panlibhon ships began to sign contracts with the Greek unions, which, incidentally, are more advantageous for the seamen than, for example, British contracts.[51] In spite of efforts to reach an agreement with the Greek unions,[52] the latter persisted in their schism, and attempted to reestablish their jurisdictional rights on the basis of the nationality of the crew — risking the charge of

49. *The New York Times,* January 24, 1959, p. 38.
50. *Id.,* April 15, 1959, p. 53.
51. *Id.,* August 3, 1959, p. 40.
52. *Id.,* November 6, 1959, p. 49. The dispute was to be settled by the ITWF economists who were to ascertain the proper jurisdiction over the vessels on the basis of "vested control."

"union busting" (put forward by their American colleagues) and even expulsion from the ITWF.[53] It is instructive that the unions advocating the concept of genuine link as a weapon against Panlibhon shipowners have, in a sense, been victims of this selfsame concept; it was specifically a dispute as to the nature of genuine link that caused a jurisdictional rift between the Greek unions and the ITWF, in particular its American affiliates.[54]

As can be easily understood, the main targets of the ITWF policy have been the American shipowners of the Panlibhon fleets. The two major American unions, the NMU and the SIU, having even signed a truce after 20 years of maritime strife and established a united front in order to better fight the "runaway" ships,[55] began to organize the alien crews of about 800 American-controlled Panlibhon ships and to gain recognition as their bargaining representatives.[56] To carry out this campaign, in 1959 the NMU and SIU formed a new union, the International Maritime Workers Union, to represent all the "exploited" seamen who sail on ships flying the flags of Panama, Liberia, and Honduras. The union is defined as the organization "of all seamen employed aboard vessels whose flags are foreign to the United States and whose ultimate ownership or control has no substantial connection with the country of registry, in order to assure those seamen just and fair treatment and to improve and protect their wages, their hours of labor and their working conditions." [57]

Although the partnership of these two rival unions was eventually dissolved, each of them has continued independently their struggle for the right to organize seamen aboard American-owned ships flying flags of convenience, an issue about which both the

53. *The New York Times,* December 19, 1959, p. 42.

54. To back their position in the dispute over the allocation of jurisdiction, the American unions turned to the Navy to supply them a list of merchant vessels flying one of the Panlibhon flags and considered to be under effective United States control for national emergency purposes; *The New York Times,* December 7, 1959, p. 53.

55. *Id.,* January 9, 1959, p. 45; September 24, 1959, p. 61.

56. This has caused grave concern among American corporations. They see in the organizing drive of the maritime unions a future challenge for other foreign investments. (*The New York Times,* December 22, 1959, p. 62; March 18, 1959, p. 61; January 24, 1959, p. 38.)

57. *The New York Times,* November 26, 1959, p. 74. See also the ACFN *Memorandum,* p. 6 n. 4. Curran, president of the NMU, and Hall, president of the SIU were designated co-chairmen of the organization.

NMU and SIU are agreed. This right was the chief demand of the five American maritime unions which started a strike on June 15, 1961, idling about 250 vessels of the United States merchant marine fleet.[58] The strike was halted after 18 days by the 80-day injunction under the Taft-Hartley Law, invoked by President Kennedy for the first time in his administration. During this "cooling off" period temporary settlements were reached with the striking seamen and several shipping companies signed agreements permitting the unions to organize seamen aboard their vessels.[59]

The American seamen's strike found support with the Seafarers' section of the ITWF, which at its Geneva meeting in September 1961 adopted a resolution emphasizing that the flag-of-convenience registration was not limited to ships registered in Panama, Liberia, or Honduras. As the Seafarers' section put it, the term also covers the use of "any flag to evade wage and working standards of the country in which the actual control of the shipping operation is vested and to evade organizing by unions of that country."[60] This new approach to the definition of a flag of convenience, which might under certain circumstances also include the flag of a traditional maritime country, resulted from the fact that several American shipowners, seeing the danger inherent in the unions' action against the "runaway" ships, began to think seriously of transferring their ships from the Panlibhon flags to some European flags.[61] In fact, as statistics show, this movement from the Panlibhon has already started, and in particular Panama has lost a considerable amount of tonnage (see Table 1).

58. The unions on strike were: the NMU, 37,000 members; the SIU (Atlantic Gulf and Lake Section), 22,000 members [these two groups representing unlicensed seamen]; the Marine Engineers Beneficial Associations, 11,000 members; the Masters, Mates and Pilots, 11,000 members; and the American Radio Association (*The New York Times*, June 26, 1961, p. 42). For the complex collective bargaining structure in the American maritime industry see the report of the Board of Inquiry in the maritime dispute, presented to President Kennedy; *id.*, July 4, 1961, p. 8. (On the injunction, see pp. 1 and 8.)

59. Thus, *e.g.*, by the beginning of August 1961 more than 5,000 pledge cards had been signed by seamen employed on about 250 American-owned Panlibhon ships. The SIU and NMU won the right to seek representation on such vessels operated by more than 50 companies, and negotiations looking to similar arrangements were under way in several other companies; *The New York Times*, August 6, 1961, sec. 5, p. 11. See also *id.*, September 22, 1961, p. 64.

60. *The New York Times*, September 26, 1961, p. 77.

61. *Id.*, September 13, 1961, pp. 74, 75.

Thus the unions' efforts to fight the flags of convenience have brought some visible results. Of decisive, legal impact may be the decisions of the National Labor Relations Board which in several cases has upheld the right of the American unions to organize the crews of the American-owned Panlibhon vessels. This relates to an important question of international law—whether a state is entitled to control labor relations on board ships which are beneficially owned by its nationals but are registered under foreign flags—an issue discussed further in Chapter VI.

Turning now to the opposition of the traditional European maritime nations to the flags of convenience, we can say that this results from the fear of competition in the world shipping market, engendered by the virtually tax-free modern fleets sailing under Panlibhon flags, but beneficially owned by American and Greek capital. It is characteristic that the battle against the flags of convenience was at first fought by the unions alone, and that the business circles of the traditional European maritime countries did not join the campaign initiated by the unions until the practice had assumed menacing proportions. The emphasis in the campaign has shifted now more to the economic competition created by the flags of convenience, not only — as Sørenson says — "because of improved conditions in the many modern ships registered under flags of convenience," but — first of all — because of the menacing growth of these flags, so dangerous for European shipowners.[62]

The campaign launched by European business circles reached its first climax in the spring of 1958 when the Geneva Conference on the Law of the Sea discussed the concept of "genuine link" which afforded the anti-Panlibhon camp a theoretical basis for their attack on the flags of convenience. Other peaks in the campaign were the inaugural session of the Inter-Governmental Maritime Consultative Organization in London in January 1959 and the conference in Washington in June 1959, at which the representatives of the European maritime nations and the United States discussed their shipping policies. The issue also attracted interest in the summer of 1961 during the maritime strike in the United States.

62. ILOffice, *Report IV* (1957), p. 3; Sørensen, p. 203.

The OEEC, which, through its Maritime Transport Committee, follows trends in the field of maritime transport, has since the first report of the committee in 1954 devoted its attention to the rise of the flags of convenience. The 1954 report, besides noting the rapid growth of the Panlibhon fleets and the participation of American capital in their operation, saw flag discrimination as the worst enemy of international shipping, and flags of convenience were considered the second factor worsening the situation in international maritime transport.[63] In the years that followed, the problem of registration of vessels under flags of convenience was given close attention by the OEEC. In the 1957 OEEC report flags of convenience were treated among the "basic problems confronting shipping," but were still second to flag discrimination and delays to turn-round of shipping in ports.[64] In the meantime, the tonnage of the flags of convenience had been growing rapidly, and when the next maritime report of the OEEC appeared in 1958, the registration of vessels under the flags of convenience was placed as the first of the "basic problems confronting shipping," more important even than flag discrimination.[65]

The OEEC Study, prepared after the eighth session of the International Law Commission, but before the Geneva Conference on the Law of the Sea, devotes some attention to the requirement of genuine link between the ship and the state of registry, but in conclusion states that "no specific action [against the flags of convenience] on an international level can be advocated." [66]

Among the European maritime nations, England and Norway, two countries whose economic viability depends to a great degree on their earnings from shipping, stand in the forefront of the opposition to the flags of convenience. The role of the Netherlands, in this respect, has also been important, particularly in the legal aspect of the controversy, the idea of genuine link

63. OEEC.MTC, *Maritime Transport* (1954), pp. 14–20, 65.
64. OEEC.MTC, *Maritime Transport* (1957), p. 58.
65. OEEC.MTC, *Maritime Transport* (1958), p. 57.
66. OEEC.MTC, "Study," p. 12. More recently, the OEEC, though noting an over-all decrease in 1960 of 1.3 million gross tons in the total fleets registered under flags of convenience, emphasized the fact that "the basic problems inherent in the use of flags of convenience, which the [Maritime Transport] Committee referred to in its report submitted to the Council early in 1958, still remain." *See* OEEC.MTC, *Maritime Transport* (1961), p. 37.

having originated in the proposal of the Netherlands government. Although concern about the growth of the flag-of-convenience fleet had been voiced earlier by the European governments,[67] feeling intensified early in 1958 and reached its climax at the time of the Geneva Conference on the Law of the Sea, which, as it was hoped, would — by the genuine link requirement — curtail the Panlibhon.

"Is it too much to hope that the international lawyers who are now considering this question can devise a wide enough acceptance of this principle [*i.e.*, the genuine link] to enable the maritime countries to refuse entry to ships which cannot produce proof that there is a genuine link with the State whose flag it flies [*sic*]?" wrote the commentator of a British shipping periodical on the eve of the Geneva Conference.[68] Early in 1958 the question of the flags of convenience was described in England as "the greatest menace by which British shipping is threatened to day," and the Panlibhon ships as ships which "threaten the livelihood of shipowners and seafarers and in some cases the very economy of the truly maritime countries." [69] Many other alarms, which reveal the truly economic basis of the problem, were sounded. The following statements, made by representatives of British industry, speak for themselves:

> The growth of flag-of-convenience fleets has reached menacing proportions. Some means of meeting this tax-free competition must be found. So far, a resolution has eluded governments, international organisations and the shipowners whose future depends on one being forthcoming [here the Geneva Conference on the Law of the Sea is meant]. . . . What must be sought is a solution which will provide an effective means

67. See, *e.g.*, the *Annual Report* of the United Kingdom Chamber of Shipping for 1955, where concern was expressed that the Panlibhon countries could exert or be used to exert undue influence upon international shipping affairs, in particular in international organizations (*The New York Times*, February 20, 1956, p. 46). Again, Sir William Currie, chairman of the Pacific and Orient Shipping line, remarked that "the flags of convenience have become such a serious matter that they can no longer be regarded lightly." *The New York Times*, May 10, 1956, p. 62.

68. "The Link between Ship and Flag," *The Shipping World & World Shipbuilding*, February 12, 1958, p. 195.

69. Statement of Sir Richard Snedden, director of the Shipping Federation; *ibid.* Mender notes that the shipping earnings of the traditional maritime nations of Europe rank in foreign currency, as a per cent of their total earnings, from about 11 per cent in the case of Italy, Netherlands, and the United Kingdom to about 45 per cent in the case of Norway. He states that "the outgrowth of the P-H-L [Panlibhon] fleets has disturbed and will continue to disturb the balance of payments in the traditional maritime countries." Mender, p. 287 & n. 37.

of adjusting the competitive balance between Panhonlib operators and those of other countries. The present disparity is such as to give Panhonlib operators overwhelming advantages over their competitors . . .[70]

Some may think that the most important is taxation. I beg to differ. Our Public Enemy No. 1 is the flag of convenience.[71]

In the discussion at the 1958 general meeting of the United Kingdom Chamber of Shipping, the rise of the flags of convenience was found to be "a development which threatens our very existence as the leading maritime power in the world," a problem so profound that it must be faced by the shipping industry "free of inhibitions." It was also stated that "This is an all-in struggle. If we can't win it one way, we have got to win it another." [72] The danger of the flags of convenience was also discussed by the British Parliament, both in the House of Commons and the House of Lords. Thus, in 1958, 86 M.P.'s tabled a motion in the Commons calling for measures to strengthen the competitive power of the British shipping industry in its struggle with the flags of convenience. A motion was also made to establish a special committee to study the problem. The Prime Minister, however, did not think new machinery was necessary, feeling that the Ministry of Transport, which was in close touch with the General Council of British Shipping, was sufficient for the purpose of tackling the problems of the flags of convenience.[73] More recently, in July 1961, Conservative and Labor members of the House of Commons joined in the attack against the American shipping policy during a debate in

70. "Chamber of Shipping *Annual Report*, The British Shipping Industry in 1957," *The Shipping World & World Shipbuilding*, February 26, 1958, pp. 239–240.

71. From the address of Robert Ropner, president of the Chamber of Shipping of the United Kingdom at the annual general meeting of the Chamber on February 27, 1958 (*The Shipping World & World Shipbuilding*, March 5, 1958, p. 261). *Cf.* the resolution adopted at the 1958 meeting, and noting profound concern "at the serious implications for British shipping of the rapid expansion of the [Panlibhon] tonnage," and stressing "the urgency of establishing conditions under which British shipping can compete on terms of parity with ships flying these flags of convenience" (*Id.*, p. 263).

72. *The Shipping World & World Shipbuilding*, March 5, 1958, p. 263. See also statement by Lord Simon, *id.*, p. 255. *Cf.* the tone of alarm in the annual report of the Liverpool Steamship Owners' Association (*The Times*, March 17, 1958, p. 4).

73. *Id.*, March 17, 1958, p. 4; May 2, 1958, p. 4. See also statement by Harold Watkinson, British Minister of Transport, about bringing under "proper responsibility" ships flying flags of convenience. *The New York Times*, June 20, 1958, p. 46.

which the shortcomings of the British shipbuilding industry were catalogued by the Minister of Transport. Both the flag discrimination, that is, the requirement that at least half of United States-aid cargoes must be carried in American ships, and the practice of registering under flags of convenience were condemned by the members of the House as unfair. Regret was also voiced that the United States had ignored repeated British protests against its shipping policies.[74] In the House of Lords as well the flags of convenience were listed among the evils affecting the British shipping industry.[75]

Norway found itself in no less danger, being dependent, to the largest extent, on the income flowing from her large merchant marine. The anxiety of the Norwegian shipowners is evident from the many articles in the *Norwegian Shipping News* discussing the flag-of-convenience problem.[76] Recently, the president of the Norwegian Shipowners Association has taken sharp issue with the statements made by a member of the ACFN before a United States congressional committee and challenged the American shipowners' claim that the American-owned Panlibhon shipping was liable to just as high taxation as shipping in Norway and other European maritime countries, and that registration of ships under Panlibhon flags only meant tax deferment.[77] Deep concern at the growing use of flags of convenience was also expressed at the conference of the Scandinavian foreign ministers, who hoped that the international attention which the problem was attracting would facilitate measures to limit the practice.[78] The resentment of the Norwegian shipping circles, deepened by the large number of laid-up ships, was so great that at one time attempts were even made to come to an agreement with the British Chamber of Shipping on imposing discriminatory harbor dues against Panlibhon vessels.

74. *The New York Times*, July 15, 1961, p. 42.
75. House of Lords *Parliamentary Debates*, 208:323–330 (March 20, 1958); *The Times*, March 20, 1958, p. 14. The undiplomatic language of Lord Winster, who "did not think a Liberian existed who knew the stem of a ship from a stern" since "they mostly lived in a bush" [!], immediately provoked a diplomatic protest of Liberia at the Foreign Office. *The Times*, March 22, 1958, p. 5.
76. See. *e.g.*, "A Serious Warning by the Oslo Shipowners Association," *Norwegian Shipping News* 14:137–140 (1958). See also Mender, pp. 286–287.
77. *The New York Times*, June 30, 1961, p. 54; *News of Norway*, June 22, 1961, p. 94.
78. *The Times*, March 20, 1958, p. 9.

The British shipowners, however, were rather cool to the idea of any sanctions or discriminatory practices.[79]

The Geneva Conference on the Law of the Sea revealed the rift between the European shipping circles and the American capital using Panlibhon ships, but did not solve the problem of the flags of convenience. The genuine-link concept failed to fulfill the hopes of shipowners in the European maritime countries, and in a more realistic appraisal of the situation the opinion has been voiced generally that, since the advantage of the flag-of-convenience operators lay in their virtual tax immunity, the solution to the problem must be found in taxation. Thus, for example, the president of the British Chamber of Shipping, answering a letter addressed to him by Niarchos, agreed with him that "taxation is the kernel of the immediate problem, and it must be fairly and squarely faced by our Government." [80] Similarly in a major British shipping periodical it was stated that: "The crux of the problem is undoubtedly the heavy burden of postwar taxation which has made it difficult even in profitable times for British shipowners to finance replacement of obsolescent tonnage and severely curtailed the possibility of expansion." [81] Examining the problem "on a rational, and not an emotional, level" the commentator of the same periodical came to the conclusion that there is no need for any discriminatory action: "The matter can be simply remedied, since the root of the problem is taxation. The Americans cannot be blamed for taking advantage of the tax position under flags of convenience." [82] Similar views can be found in many other enunciations which, recommending a cautious and realistic approach, warn against discrimination and boycotts, and point to the necessity of liberalization of national tax policy as the only way of restoring the competitive balance of the British shipping.[83]

79. *The New York Times*, April 13, 1958, sec. 5, p. 11. However, two Norwegian insurance societies refused to continue insuring ships registered in Liberia.

80. *The Times*, April 3, 1958, p. 9.

81. *The Shipping World & World Shipbuilding*, May 14, 1958, p. 467.

82. *Id.*, July 16, 1958, p. 47.

83. See, *e.g.*, the letter of Geddes to *The Times*, April 11, 1958, p. 11: "Such proposals [*i.e.*, discriminatory measures] merely deflect thinking from the root cause — our laws. . . . The only thing to be done is to sweep away government restriction and taxation." Peyton, M.P., stated in the House of Commons that, although the trend in shipping matters was "disastrous" for England, flag discrimination would not be wise (*id.*, May 13, 1958, p. 13). *Cf.* also the following comment

The situation on the eve of the December 1958 boycott was soberly put by the chairman of the Court Line Limited in the following words:

> Some critics of operators under the so-called flags of convenience take the narrow view that it is merely a matter of unfair wages and working conditions, and suggest the traditional maritime nations should join together and impose sanctions. According to my information, the conditions on most flags of convenience vessels so far as they affect the crew are in no way inferior to those existing in the best conducted fleets. We must face the fact that people cannot be blamed for taking advantage of circumstances which place them in a superior position to that of their competitors. It must be recognized that they are not doing anything which is illegal except when it is done by English owners. There is no doubt, under present conditions, our industry is facing a deadly menace which can only have one ending, that is the accelerated decline and final elimination of our Merchant Fleet, more especially the Tramp section. There is only one way to remedy the situation and the government need look no further than a revision of its taxation policy as it affects the Shipping Industry . . . It is simply a matter of ships or taxes.[84]

The controversy surrounding the flags of convenience flared up anew with the boycott of December 1958. The stand taken by the shipowning circles and governments of European maritime countries on the question of the boycott was — as the general secretary of the ITWF put it — "in the worst possible tradition and gave evidence of a chronic short-sightedness that reveals once again the tremendous gulf which separates the two sides of industry [*i.e.*, the shipowners and the seamen] when matters of

---

in a British periodical: "Minimal taxation is the only real 'Panhonlib' advantage at present. The balance can be reversed by measures designed to relieve the 'traditional' shipowner of the burden of taxation to a considerable extent, but the rights and wrongs of such a course are matter of economics and politics, not law." *Business Law Review* 5:63 (1958).

There were some unconfirmed reports of discriminatory measures against flag-of-convenience ships, by the Soviet Union, in the form of greatly increased harbor charges. The Soviet embassy in Washington and the Soviet delegation at the United Nations declined to confirm the reports (*The New York Times*, August 31, 1958, sec. 5, p. 11). However, even if this were true, the measures would not have practical importance since the Panlibhon ships are, under their national laws, barred from the Soviet ports.

84. *The Economist*, November 22, 1958, p. 734. *Cf.* the opinion of the British commentator in *The Shipping World & World Shipbuilding*, July 16, 1958, p. 47. See also similar concession of Viscount Runciman in the House of Lords in *Parliamentary Debates*, 208:341 (March 20, 1958).

principle are involved."[85] Although the boycott was in the interest of the European shipowners, they provided no real support, and the International Shipping Federation, representing the shipowners, disassociated itself completely from the action.[86]

The battle over the flag-of-convenience ships took a new and more bitter turn after the January 1959 session of IMCO, when, an unfortunate atmosphere of mutual recrimination between American and European shipping circles gathered new intensity. There were even attempts by American shipowners to have the United States Congress take retaliatory measures against certain European vessels.[87] In spite of this, shipping circles in Europe have continued, for the most part, to be opposed to reckless discriminatory measures, and the most frequently voiced opinion is that the individual governments should take steps to remove the disability under which their nationals labor if they register vessels under their own flags. In practice, this means tax concessions, which are now generally considered as the measures by which the challenge of the Panlibhon fleets will have to be met.[88] Thus, Birger Krogius, then president of the Baltic and International Maritime Conference stated at the biennial meeting of the conference in London, May 1959, that

> If these deplorable conditions are to continue I cannot see but that there is only one course to pursue for countries wishing to maintain their position on the high seas. Their shipowners must ultimately be given the same facilities and advantages as those who operate vessels under "flags of convenience" and, I dare hardly say so, the same liberties when it comes to manning their vessels.[89]

British shipowners, in fact, are free to register in and operate their ships from certain parts of the British Commonwealth, such as Bermuda or the Bahamas, which, because of their favorable tax legislation can play the same role for the British shipping industry as the Panlibhon countries play for the United States. Corporations established in Bermuda or the Bahamas, which derive income from

85. Becu, p. 62.
86. *The Economist*, November 22, 1958, p. 728.
87. *The New York Times*, January 19, 1959, p. 42; January 25, 1959, p. 12.
88. See, *e.g.*, *Petroleum Press Service*, January 1959, p. 15.
89. *The Baltic & International Maritime Conference Monthly Circular*, no. 183, June 1959, p. 7863.

operations carried on outside the islands, are virtually free from taxation and for this reason these crown colonies, in particular Bermuda, have attracted a goodly number of shipowners to register their vessels there.[90]

In general, flags of convenience are regarded as one of three principal threats to the European shipping industry, standing second only to the problem of flag discrimination, which is believed to be "the root of most of the evil," and excessive subsidies by foreign governments.[91] The governments of nine European nations, the United Kingdom, Sweden, Norway, Denmark, Belgium, France, German Federal Republic, the Netherlands, and Italy, proposed a conference with the United States, which was held in Washington, June 8–11, 1959 as "informal intergovernmental talks" purporting "to explore whether the shipping policies of the West European countries and of the United States could be brought into closer harmony without impairing either the legitimate needs of the United States in shipping matters or the common economic strength of the West."[92] The talks brought no solution. The American position on the flag-of-convenience issue presented by the Acting Secretary Dillon, remained the same. Mr. Dillon stated explicitly: "My final thought on this subject is that until such time as it may prove feasible for these American shipowners to operate competitively under the United States flag, my government retains its interest in the continued operation of ships under foreign flags, including the 'Panlibhon' registries. From our viewpoint there are important and valid defense requirements which support this position."[93] It is interesting to note that the solution to the problem, at least in the short run, as it was envisaged by the American side, was analogous to that generally proposed by the

90. See Gibbons, pp. 41–54. See also *The New York Times*, September 8, 1959, p. 56; *Hearings* (Senate) 1957, pp. 29–30; *The Shipping World & World Shipbuilding*, April 16, 1958, p. 387; July 16, 1958, p. 47; August 13, 1958, p. 129; *The Times*, November 10, 1959, p. 17.

91. See the resolution adopted at the 82d annual meeting of the Chamber of Shipping of the United Kingdom in 1959 (*The Shipping World & World Shipbuilding*, March 4, 1959, p. 256). See also the discussion in the House of Commons in *The New York Times*, July 15, 1961, p. 42. About the problems and shortcomings of British shipping, see the pamphlet "The British Shipping Industry," published by Political and Economic Planning (1959).

92. *DSB* 41:10 (1959).

93. *Id.*, p. 14.

British shipping circles. The individual countries which consider that their shipowners are operating at a competitive disadvantage should themselves take measures to remove this disadvantage. The final communiqué of the conference stated: "The complex problems arising from the rapid growth of tonnage registered under so-called flags of convenience were considered, and it was recognized that there was a need for further study and discussion."[94]

The flag-of-convenience controversy between the United States and its European allies remains a serious problem in the relations between the members of the Atlantic alliance and, although it has economic sources, it may provoke dangerous repercussions in the political and even military sphere. Evidence of this might be the statement in the British House of Commons, made by Paul Williams, a Conservative member for Sunderland. Britain, according to him, should tell the United States: "If you persist in promoting your shipping interests in this way and damaging our economy and national defense, then we will promote policies which conflict with your aims in other fields."[95] For instance, he said, Britain might review its policy toward American bases and discriminate against Americans in other ways. "Unless we talk to them in this way, we will never get them to change their ways," Mr. Williams declared.[96]

Thus, there is no doubt that the Panlibhon issue is a source of political and even strategic difficulties within the Western bloc of nations. This imposes the necessity of a settlement acceptable to all the parties directly or indirectly involved in the complexities of the flags of convenience.

94. *Id.*, p. 16. On the Washington conference see also *The New York Times*, June 9, 1959, p. 62; June 10, 1959, p. 54; June 11, 1959, p. 56; June 12, 1959, p. 44; June 14, 1959, sec. 1, p. 88. The Liberian government protested its exclusion from the Washington conference (*id.*, June 11, 1959, p. 56).
95. *Id.*, July 15, 1961, p. 42.
96. *Ibid.*

Chapter IV. The Basic Issue for International Law

For the topic to be considered in this chapter it is of essential importance to answer the questions whether the Panlibhon states have, under international law, the unlimited right to confer nationality upon merchant vessels, paying regard only to such criteria as they deem proper under their respective municipal legislations, and what test of the attribution of nationality is valid under international law.

As with many other questions relating to the law of the sea, the inquiry must start from the cardinal and undisputed principle of this law, the freedom of the high seas implying that "no state may validly purport to subject any part of them to its sovereignty." [1] Ships of all nations, coastal or not, have an equal right to navigate the high seas, and utilize their resources, and — except for extraordinary cases, irrelevant here — no state is authorized to interfere with the navigation of other states on the high seas. All nations, large and small, equally assert their right to the enjoyment of the high seas and openly declare their aspirations in the matter of the development of their merchant fleets. "Liberia makes no apology for her ambition to attain eminence as a maritime nation. . . . The Liberian is not deterred by the argument that Liberia cannot claim to be a "true" maritime nation. It is "the home of one of the greatest seafaring tribes in Africa — the Krus,"

1. UN.CLS.*OR* 2:135, 136 (1958), The Convention on the High Seas (Doc. A/CONF. 13/L.53), art. 2.

proclaimed the official organ of this oldest Negro republic in Africa.[2]

But the high seas are subject to law, and this idea lies at the basis of regulations for their utilization. This subjection of the high seas to juridical order is organized and effected by means of a permanent legal relation between ships flying a particular flag and the state whose flag they fly. This was appropriately put by Rienow: "The entire legal system which states have evolved for the regulation of the use of the high seas is predicated on the possession by each vessel of a connection with a State having a recognized maritime flag. This connection has been commonly called nationality."[3]

In this relation the personal nationality of the operator gives way to that of the ship which is considered as an entity and as a distinct unit subject, as a general rule, only to the jurisdiction of the flag state. In the peaceful utilization of the oceans the institution of the nationality of ships is of primary importance. Owing to it ships can be subject to the control and authority of the state which has ascribed its national character to them.[4] This state takes responsibility for the lawful conduct of its ships and the use they make of maritime areas. This state is also their protector against any deprivations the ship may suffer on the part of other states.[5]

For these reasons the use of the high seas is granted only to ships which can prove possession of nationality, and in suspicious circumstances a ship which is not able to identify its national character is liable to seizure.[6] This principle is regarded as self-

2. *Liberia Today,* March 19, 1959, p. 12. The word "Kru" is simply the transliteration of the English word "crew"; see the explanation given by the Liberian representative in ICJ *Pleadings,* Constitution (1960), p. 276.

3. Rienow, pp. 13–14.

4. This does not exclude the possibility of concurrent jurisdiction, *e.g.,* in the territorial waters. See in general Jessup, *The Law of Territorial Waters and Maritime Jurisdiction* (1927).

5. About nationality of ships in general and its significance see, *e.g.,* Higgins, *RCADI* (1929, pt. V) p. 20; Gidel, I, 73–77, 230; Hyde, *International Law Chiefly As Interpreted and Applied by the United States* (2d rev. ed. 1947), I, 809–810; Hackworth, II, 724–728; Briggs, p. 330; Colombos, pp. 249–250; Dahm, I, 674–679; United Nations Secretariat, "Memorandum on the Regime of the High Seas," ILC *Yearbook* 1950, II, 67, 74–75 (Doc. A/CN.4/32) [prepared by Gidel]; Rienow, pp. 3–23.

6. See Molvan v. Attorney General for Palestine [1948] A.C. 351; [1948] *Ann. Dig.* (1953), p. 115 (no. 37).

evident in international law and the discussion of the question of stateless ships is of purely academic value.[7] Nationality of a ship, subjecting it to the law of the country to which it belongs ("the law of the flag") is, of course, relevant in many situations, both under municipal and international law, although in some circumstances it may be only one of the factors taken into account at the assertion of a state's authority to the persons and things aboard the ship.[8]

Since the juridical order of the maritime spaces is based on the institution of the nationality of ships, it is necessary that this nationality be easily identifiable, that, in case of disputing claims or other situations requiring the identification of the ship, its nationality may be with certainty and clarity established. This has been achieved by a combination of the rules of municipal law and international law. As to the way in which ships are conferred the national character of a given state, the traditional rule of international law is that the municipal law of each particular country determines which vessels should be considered as endowed with its national character, and that this act of the state conferring its nationality upon a vessel, motivated by whatever reasons and establishing whatever criteria of eligibility, is conclusive for all purposes that may arise, and must be honored and recognized by other states.

The principle of international law that the states have conclusive unilateral competence to grant nationality to merchant vessels, recognized in the first sentence of art. 5 of the Convention on the High Seas of 1958, has a wide background in international practice, manifested in treaties, judicial decisions, diplomatic correspondence, and other sources of international law. It is also documented by the municipal laws and practice of the particular states. So far as the theory of international law is concerned, there has also been universal agreement as to the principle of the states' competence to fix the conditions of the granting of nationality to

7. From the practical point of view this is due to the fact that access to ports is granted only to the ships which have some nationality. "It is by this control of their ports that states, in practice, clear the seas of nondescript vessels." Rienow, p. 15.

8. See Chapter VI. For the different types of claims in which the conclusiveness of the national character of a vessel is relevant, see the elaborate scheme worked out by McDougal, Burke & Vlasic in "The Maintenance of Public Order at Sea and the Nationality of Ships," *AJIL* 54:25, 46–49, 56–114 (1960).

vessels. However, the scope of this competence and the implications of the principle have given rise to disagreement among authorities of international law, particularly in recent years, as a result of the growth of the flags of convenience.

The analysis that follows attempts to give a background of theory and practice to substantiate the thesis that states themselves are authorized to decide under what conditions they will grant nationality to merchant vessels, and that this grant of nationality must be recognized by other states. To avoid confusion, it should be borne in mind that there is distinction between the denial by state *A* of the competence of state *B* to grant its nationality to ships and the application of the authority of state *A* to ships endowed with the nationality (national character) of state *B*, which latter case may be, and often is, justified and lawful under particular circumstances, for example, in the territorial waters of state *A*.[9]

The principle of modern international law, that it is the municipal law of each particular country that determines which vessels should be recognized as possessing its nationality, did not originate until modern times, namely at the beginning of the nineteenth century.[10] Roughly three periods can be distinguished in the evolution of this principle:

1) Until about the end of the eighteenth century, the notion of the nationality of ships was not yet fully developed, and merchant vessels were referred to as belonging to the subjects of the state, not to the state itself. This state of things led to great arbitrariness on the part of the stronger powers, in particular in connection with neutrality in naval warfare. The question, decided by each state according to its needs, was, what criteria should be applied in recognizing or not recognizing the flag under which the given ship was sailing. The principles in this matter evolved slowly, in connection with specific questions, first in naval warfare at the

9. See the pertinent argument in McDougal, Burke & Vlasic, pp. 54–55, that ends with this sentence: "The confusion of saying the 'national character is irrelevant' with saying that the 'competence of a state to attribute national character is denied' arises from simple failure to distinguish different types of problems and uniquely relevant policies." See also Chapter VI.

10. Müller, p. 355; Neumeyer, *Internationales Verwaltungsrecht* (1926), III, 87–89.

determination of the neutral goods not subject to capture as prize, then for the purposes of enjoying various trade privileges.[11]

At first the great naval powers determined by themselves which vessels they would regard as neutral. Thus, for example, the French "Ordonnance de la Marine" of 1681, modified by the prize laws of 1704, 1744, and 1788, arbitrarily fixed stringent rules (referring to the composition of the crew) as to which vessels would be regarded as lawful prize. If a neutral vessel did not satisfy that prerequisite and was not manned by a crew of the national percentage required by the French law, it was liable to capture. The English Navigation Act of 1651 simply held such ships neutral as fulfilled the requirements of nationality that were set for the English ships.[12] This procedure was sometimes clad in pretexts of legality by a treaty forced upon the weaker state by a stronger power.[13]

2) With the development of the institution of the nationality of ships the precarious state of affairs began to change. There followed a series of bilateral treaties of commerce and navigation, concluded as early as the 1820's, in which the maritime states which were parties to the treaty expressly stipulated particular conditions under which they would recognize the nationality of each other's merchant vessels.[14] Not all of those treaties satisfied the conditions of the equality of the contracting parties. In some of them the stronger power demanded the recognition of its vessels' nationality after its own municipal law, whereas the conditions of the recognition of the nationality of the weaker party's vessels were fixed in the treaty itself, in conditions convenient to the stronger power. The Treaty of Friendship, Navigation and Commerce between France and Brazil, signed in Rio de Janeiro on June 8, 1826, is usually given as an example of this kind of approach to the problem of the recognition of the ship's nationality. Article XII of the treaty read as follows: "Les Hautes parties contractantes conviennent de déclarer que seront considérés navires

11. Neumeyer, III, 88.
12. Van Zijst, pp. 147–148.
13. See, *e.g.*, arts. XXVII–XXX of the Treaty of Commerce between France and Mecklemburg-Schwerin, September 18, 1779; Martens, *Recueil des Traités* (1817), II, 709.
14. Van Zijst, pp. 149–150; Müller, p. 356; Neumeyer, III, 89.

brésiliens, ceux qui seront construits ou possédés par des sujets brésiliens, et dont le capitaine et les trois quart de l'équipage seront brésiliens . . . De la même manière seront considérés navires françois ceux qui navigueront et seront possédés conformément aux règlemens en vigueur en France." [15] As the contents of the conditions show, they referred to national build, national ownership, and a percentage of national crew.

3) The next stage is the period beginning in the 1830's and continuing until the present day. It was then that various states made bilateral treaties in which they recognized mutually that the nationality of a vessel was to be decided in accordance with the laws of the country under whose flag it was sailing, and that the other state was obliged to recognize that nationality.[16] The first treaty of this kind was the Treaty of Commerce and Navigation concluded between Sweden-Norway and Denmark on November 2, 1826, providing in art. viii that "Les bâtimens et embarcations suédois et norvégiens, ainsi que les bâtimens et embarcations danois, ne pouvront profiter des immunités et avantages, que leur accorde le présent traité qu'autant qu'ils se trouveront munis des papiers et certificats, voulus par les règlemens existens des deux côtés pour constater leur port et leur nationalités." [17] Since that time hundreds of treaties of friendship, commerce, and navigation have reiterated, in various phrasings, the principle of the mutual recognition of the nationality of ships as it was granted by the municipal law of the respective party. Provisions embodying this rule have come to be so basic and regularly inserted in treaties of this kind that their absence would cause surprise and their omission would necessarily be deliberate and legally meaningful. The flag-recognition clause is also embodied in the treaties of friendship, commerce, and navigation concluded by the United States.[18]

15. Martens, *Nouveau Recueil des Traités* (1828), VI, 872.

16. Van Zijst, pp. 150–151; Müller, pp. 356–357; Neumeyer, III, 89; Heyck, *Die Staatszugehörigkeit der Schiffe und Luftfahrzeuge* (1935), p. 42.

17. Martens, *Nouveau Recueil des Traités,* VI, 1075.

18. For a list of the early treaties of this kind see van Zijst, appendix C, pp. xxiv–xxvi; see also Rienow, pp. 19–21, notes 50–52 and pp. 165–170, notes 50–59. This excellent monograph gives the most thorough analysis of the flag-recognition clause in the bilateral treaties up to 1937. It is also the best study of the problem of nationality of ships, and it has remained as fundamental as it was at the time of its publication in 1937.

For the relevant extracts from the early treaties of friendship, commerce, and

In some treaties the contracting parties even stipulate that information be given to each other on the changes in the provisions concerning the documentation of the ships.[19] The German-Turkish Agreement of 1890 is an interesting case. It provided that a ship might be regarded in the territorial waters of either party as national by either party, if it was German according to the German law and Turkish according to the Turkish law.[20]

Around the mid-nineteenth century, however, flag-recognition clauses became more abstract and read, for instance, like art. VII of the friendship, commerce, and navigation treaty, concluded February 4, 1859, between the United States and Paraguay: "All vessels which, according to the laws of the United States of America, are to be deemed vessels of the United States of America, and all vessels which according to the laws of Paraguay, are to be deemed Paraguayan vessels, shall, for the purposes of this treaty, be deemed vessels of the United States of America and Paraguayan vessels, respectively." [21] In the clauses worded like this, flag recognition is still limited by the phrase "for the purposes of this treaty." The next stage in the metamorphosis of the clause was the provision that the ship's documents are the test of its nationality. The intermediate stage was the clause which, though providing for the documentary test of nationality, still contained the phrase "for the purposes of this treaty." [22]

At present, the clause in almost every case provides for recipro-

navigation concluded between the United States and various nations, see Wharton, *A Digest of the International Law of the United States* (1888), III, 691. The flag-recognition provisions found in the treaties of the United States are also discussed in the ACFN *Memorandum*, p. 104, notes 4, 5, and pp. 110–111, notes 9–17. The FCN (friendship, commerce, and navigation) treaties signed by the United States after the Second World War are specified in Walker, "Provisions on Companies in United States Commercial Treaties," *AJIL* 50:373 n.1 (1956) and in Walker, "Modern Treaties of Friendship, Commerce and Navigation," *Minn. L. Rev.* 42:85 (1958). See also Friedman & Pugh [eds.] p. 705 n. 18, where the FCN treaties concluded by the United States since 1949 are specified. For the FCN treaties that are in force at present see the latest edition of the Department of State annual publication, *Treaties in Force.*

19. Such was the treaty of commerce between the Kingdom of Sardinia and the German *Zollverein* of 1865 (Florio, *Nazionalità della nave*, p. 150 n. 23).

20. *Ibid.*

21. Malloy (1910), II, 1366. For other examples of this type of clause see Rienow, p. 19, n. 50. See also ACFN *Memorandum*, p. 104 n. 4.

22. Article XV of the Treaty of Friendship, Commerce and Consular Rights with Finland, signed February 13, 1934 and still in force, is an example of this (49 Stat. 2659; T.S. 868; 152 L.N.T.S. 45).

cal flag recognition, based on the test of the ship's documents. In the case of the treaties recently concluded by the United States, the flag-recognition clause usually reads as follows: "Vessels under the flag of either party, and carrying the papers required by its law in proof of nationality, shall be deemed to be vessels of that Party both on the high seas and within its ports, places and waters of the other party." [23]

In some treaties the clause is even simpler, omitting the reference to the place where the vessel may be found: "Vessels under the flag of either party and carrying the papers required by its law in proof of nationality, shall be deemed to be vessels of that Party." [24] or "The nationality of vessels shall be reciprocally recognized in accordance with the law and enactments of the two contracting Parties on the basis of the documents and certificates on board the vessel issued by the proper authorities of either of the contracting Parties." [25]

In these treaties a vessel is regarded to have the nationality of the state whose flag it lawfully flies, without any reference to the question of who owns it or by which country's nationals it is manned or where it was built. This principle is declared in the second sentence of art. 5, para. 1 of the Geneva Convention on the High Seas: "Ships have the nationality of the State whose flag they are entitled to fly."

It is important that flag-recognition provisions bind the United

23. See, *e.g.*, treaties of FCN: With China, November 4, 1946, art. XXI, 63 Stat. (2) 1299; T.I.A.S. 1871; 25 U.N.T.S. 69. With Italy, February 2, 1947, art. XIX; 63 Stat. (2) 2255; T.I.A.S. 1965; 79 U.N.T.S. 171. With Ireland, January 21, 1950, art. XVIII (2); 1 U.S.T. 785; T.I.A.S. 2155. With Japan, April 2, 1953, art. XIX; 4 U.S.T. 2063; T.I.A.S. 2863. With Israel, August 23, 1951, art. XIX; 5 U.S.T. 550; T.I.A.S. 2948. With Greece, August 3, 1951, art. XXI; 5 U.S.T. 1829; T.I.A.S. 3059. Treaty with Iran, August 15, 1955, art. X(2); T.I.A.S. 3853. Treaty with the Netherlands, March 27, 1956, art. XIX; 8 U.S.T. 2043; T.I.A.S. 3942.

24. Treaty of FCN with the Federal Republic of Germany, October 29, 1954, art. XIX(1); 7(2) U.S.T. 1839; T.I.A.S. 3593.

25. Treaty of Commerce and Navigation between Denmark and the U.S.S.R., August 17, 1946; 8 U.N.T.S. 124. For recent British practice see, *e.g.*, the treaty of FCN with the Sultan of Muscat and Oman, December 20, 1951; United Kingdom T.S. No. 44 of 1952. Article I(3) states that "For the purposes of the present Treaty the term 'British vessels' . . . means all ships registered at a port of the U.K. or in any territory to which the present Treaty applies . . . and the term 'Omani vessels' . . . means all ships registered under the law of the Sultan's Government." *Cf.* "Convention Franco-Allemande d'établissement et de navigation" (art. XIII) of October 27, 1956, promulgated in the French *Journal Officiel* (1959), p. 8850. For the text see also *Le Droit Maritime Français* 11:701 (1959).

States under its treaties with two of the Panlibhon countries, namely Honduras and Liberia.[26] There is no treaty with Panama. It is appropriate to mention here, also, that a recognition clause is binding between Costa Rica and Denmark. The two countries concluded in 1956 — at the height of Costa Rica's career as a flag of convenience — a treaty of commerce and navigation.[27]

The above-mentioned flag-recognition provisions of the bilateral treaties were one of the main arguments put forward by some members of the International Law Commission against making the recognition of a vessel's nationality dependent upon some specific ownership requirement, and, later, upon the existence of a "genuine link" between the vessel and the state of registration.[28]

From the reciprocal recognition of the national character of vessels as granted by the municipal laws of either party important commercial advantages and privileges result for the contracting parties. Thus, access to the ports, stipulated in the bilateral treaties of friendship, commerce, and navigation, is granted to vessels of either party, but here again even if there is no commercial agreement, access is not denied on the ground that the flag state had no competence to confer its national character on the given ship using criteria of its own choice.[29]

There are also numerous multilateral international agreements from which it results that the contracting parties by the ship's nationality mean the national character as it has been conferred upon the ship by each of them. Thus treaty practice shows that the states do not hold that international law imposes any other

26. Treaty of Friendship, Commerce and Consular Rights with Honduras, December 7, 1927, art. X; 45 Stat. 2618; T.S. 764; 87 L.N.T.S. 421. Treaty of FCN with Liberia, August 8, 1938, art. XV; 54 Stat. 1739; T.S. 956; 201 L.N.T.S. 163.

27. Tratado de Comercio y Navegación entre Costa Rica y Dinamarca, *Colección de Leyes* [Costa Rica] (1958, Segundo Semestre), pp. 171, 172. *Cf.* the Convention concluded by Costa Rica with the Netherlands in June 1957, stipulating reciprocal equal treatment of the parties and including the most favored nation clause. For the text see *id.*, p. 174–177.

28. See, *e.g.*, the statements of Padilla Nervo from Mexico and Faris Bey el-Khouri from Syria in ILC *Yearbook 1956,* I, 70. See also Ch. VIII.

29. The prevailing opinion is that each state has the right to decide whether or not to admit foreign vessels to its ports (Sørensen, p. 200). In this sense the relevant treaty provisions are consequential. Another problem arises if the flag state is not recognized as a state. See McDougal, Burke & Vlasic (p. 69), where the authors refer to the case of the Manchukuo vessel whose documents had no validity for the United States since Manchukuo was not recognized by this country as a state. For this case see Hackworth, II, 207–208.

conditions upon themselves, besides registration, in order that the ships flying their flag be recognized by other states as possessing their respective nationality. This, of course, does not prevent a state from enforcing any requirement it chooses upon its vessels, which is the domestic jurisdiction of each state. The same conclusion can be drawn also from other manifestations of the states' practice, such as diplomatic correspondence, custom regulations, and naval instructions.

In connection with the rise of the flags of convenience, it is interesting to note that none of the states whose interests are affected by the Panlibhon practice have taken recourse, as a result of the liberal registration laws enacted by the flag-of-convenience countries, to the means of redress provided by international law. This "negative" aspect of the states' practice confirms the principle that the matter of fixing the conditions of the registration of ships lies within each state's exclusive competence.[30]

This principle also found substantiation in the opinion of the Permanent Court of Arbitration at The Hague, expressed in the arbitral award of August 8, 1905 in the *Muscat Dhows* case between France and Great Britain.[31] The Court decided in this award upon the lawfulness of the grant of the French flag to certain "dhows" owned by the subjects of the Sultan of Muscat.[32] By using the French flag "of convenience," the subjects of the Sultan could evade the regulations and inspection of Muscat, and were even suspected of engaging in slave trade. Great Britain contended that France's rights were restricted by certain treaty provisions, and that the dhows, being owned by the subjects of

30. *Cf.* Pallua, "La nationalité des navires de commerce en droit international public et privé," *Jugoslovenska Revija za Medunarodno Pravo* 5:81, 84–85 (1958), where the author finds it difficult to explain whether juridical scruples as to the freedom of the states in this sphere or economic considerations have prevented the maritime states from reacting to the practice of the flags of convenience. One can certainly answer that it has been due to juridical scruples. The United States did not react because of both economic reasons (but of quite the opposite nature) and juridical reasons (presented above). An example of one country's challenging another's legislation was afforded by the United States' challenge of the Honduran law in 1909. See note 51 below.

31. Scott ed., *Hague Court Reports* (1916), pp. 93–109.

32. The "dhows" (in French, "boutres") are vessels of Arab build, 200–500 tons, which ply the Indian Ocean and the Red Sea. They are owned and operated mainly by the subjects of the Sultan of Muscat, a British protectorate; Westlake, "The Muscat Dhows," *Law Quarterly Review* 23:83 (1907).

Muscat, should fly the British flag. For the matter under discussion it is relevant that the Court, before dealing with the question of whether France's rights were limited by treaty provisions, proclaimed the right of a state to grant its nationality to such ships as were entitled thereto under its laws:

> Whereas, generally speaking, it belongs to every sovereign to decide to whom he will accord the right to fly his flag and to prescribe the rules governing such grants, and whereas therefore, the granting of the French flag to subjects of His Highness the Sultan of Muscat in itself constitutes no attack on the independence of the Sultan . . . for these reasons [the Court] decides and pronounces as follows: 1. Before the second of January 1892, France was entitled to authorize vessels belonging to subjects of His Highness the Sultan of Muscat to fly the French flag, only bound by own legislation and administrative rules.[33]

The Court's opinion was that the execution of the State's right in the matter of granting nationality to ships, could be restricted only by a treaty, which, in this particular case, we found applicable *vis-à-vis* France after January 2, 1892, when she acceded to the treaty provisions in question.[34] The *Muscat Dhows* case is the leading precedent usually adduced to support the principle of international law that each state decides what conditions it will impose for the registration of its vessels under its flag.

The view was restated and reaffirmed by the United States Supreme Court in its opinion given on May 25, 1953 in the well-known case *Lauritzen v. Larsen.* Justice Jackson, speaking for the majority, stressed the importance of the law of the flag principle and stated that

> Each state under international law may determine for itself the conditions on which it will grant its nationality to a merchant ship, thereby accepting responsibility for it and acquiring authority over it. Nationality is evidenced to the world by the ship's papers and its flag. The United

33. Scott ed., *Hague Court Reports* (1916), p. 96.

34. The treaty in question was the General Act for the Repression of the African Slave Trade, signed at Brussels on July 2, 1890; 27 Stat. 886; T.S. 383; Malloy (1910), II, 1366.

One who is not familiar with the case would, after reading the presentation of McDougal, Burke, and Vlasic (p. 27), draw the erroneous conclusion that even a treaty cannot limit the state in its right to grant the flag. Such a conclusion would be, of course, contrary to the Court's opinion.

States has firmly and successfully maintained that the regularity and validity of a registration can be questioned only by the registering state.[35]

There are a number of cases in the lower courts which deal with the problem of the law applicable to the labor relations aboard ships registered in the Panlibhon countries. One view repeats the above-mentioned opinion of *Lauritzen v. Larsen.* It is the decision in *McQuade v. Compañía de Vapores San Antonio, S. A.,* given by the United States District Court, Southern District of New York, February 1, 1955. After referring to the decision in *Lauritzen v. Larsen,* the judge stated:

> Since a State may grant its nationality to a merchant ship and the flag evidences nationality, the authority given by a State for a ship to fly its flag ought to be construed as constituting a grant of its nationality by the State to the ship. But States are permitted under international law to authorize vessels which are the property of foreigners to fly its flag. I Oppenheim, *International Law* 3 ed. 422, sec. 261. It would seem to follow that a State, under international law, may be permitted to grant its nationality to a ship owned by foreigners and is considered to have done so when it authorizes the use of its maritime flag.[36]

Against the background of this international practice, it is no wonder that the doctrine of international law unanimously indorses the general principle expressed in the first sentence of art. 5 of the Convention on the High Seas, that "each State shall fix the conditions for the grant of its nationality to ships, for the registration of ships in its territory and for the right to fly its flag." [37]

There is general agreement, then, first, that international law requires a merchant ship on the high seas to possess a nationality and to be able to prove its existence.[38] Second, there are no rules in international law that lay down the specific conditions of the acquisition of nationality by merchant vessels. These conditions are determined by each state for itself, according to its exclusive

35. 345 U.S. 571, 584 (1953). This is the leading American case on the "law of the flag." See Ch. VI.

36. 131 F. Supp. 365 (S.D.N.Y. 1955).

37. The differences of view arise, however, concerning the scope of the states' freedom to lay down the conditions governing the grant of nationality to merchant vessels.

38. See, *e.g.*, Ortolan, I, 178; Calvo (5th ed. 1896), II, 521; Colombos, p. 270; Müller, p. 252; Rienow, p. 15, and many others.

national policies; but each state having a merchant marine is bound to regulate by its law the conditions under which vessels can claim to sail under its flag. This rule is recognized both by the traditional liberal school of thought,[39] and by those authors who, though in general recognize the principle, attempt to find limits to the states' discretionary power of granting the right to fly the flag.[40]

39. The following are statements of the more important authorities:

Briggs, p. 330: "The right of each State to fix the conditions upon which vessels can acquire its national character and fly its flag finds frequent confirmation in treaties of commerce and navigation."

Calvo, II, 522; "Chaque Etat est libre de fixer les conditions auxquelles il confère sa nationalité aux navires, leur donne le droit de porter son pavillon et leur accorde sa protection."

Dahm, I, 676: "Die Voraussetzungen für die Gewährung und Entziehung des Flaggenrechts werden im allgemeinen nicht vom Völkerrecht, sondern von den einzelnen Staaten bestimmt, die entsprechende Gesetze erlassen."

Diena, "Principes du droit international privé maritime," *RCADI* 51:424 (1935 pt. I): "Chaque État en vertu de sa souveraineté a la faculté de fixer à son gré — en l'absence de conventions internationales limitant sa liberté d'action — les conditions pour qu'un navire privé puisse être considéré comme un navire national."

Fauchille, I, pt. II 899; "C'est au droit public de chaque pays à fixer les conditions auxquelles il accorde aux navires son indigénat maritime. Il y a là une question de droit interne. . . ."

Hyde, I, 810: "It is probably a sound proposition that a vessel registered under the laws of a State and possessed of a certificate of registry may be deemed in an international sense to belong to that State, and to justify it in giving it the privilege of flying its flag regardless of the nationality of the owners of the ship. . . ."

Oppenheim, *International Law* (8th ed. 1955, Lauterpacht ed.), I, 595: "The Law of Nations does not contain any rules regarding the claims of vessels to sail under a certain maritime flag, but imposes a duty upon every State having a maritime flag, to provide by its own municipal laws the conditions to be fulfilled by those vessels which wish to sail under its flag . . . But a State is absolutely independent in framing the rules concerning the claim of vessels to its flag. . . ."

Rousseau, *Droit international public* (1953), pp. 416–417: "C'est la législation de chaque Etat qui détermine pour son propre compte et qui est seule à pouvoir le faire — les conditions d'acquisition de la nationalité des navires ou du droit au pavillon."

Cf. also: Fedozzi, "La condition juridique des navires de commerce," *RCADI* 10:49–50 (1925, pt. V); Fenwick, *International Law* (2d ed. 1934), p. 190; Giuliano, *I diritti e gli obblighi degli Stati* (1956), I, 366–367 (where the problem of nationality of ships is extensively treated); Higgins, *RCADI* (1929, pt. V) p. 20; Liszt, *Das Völkerrecht* (11th ed. 1918), p. 190; Müller, p. 353; Ortolan, I, 163; Westlake, *International Law* (1910), I, 169 (where, however, the states' rights are modified by the duty of the ships to render periodic visits to their home ports for purposes of the exercise of criminal jurisdiction). Last but not least, see the fundamental work of Rienow, *passim*, where a thorough analysis of the subject leaves little to be added. About the interesting modification in the latest edition (1959) of Colombos' work, see Ch. IX note 165.

40. Asser and Reay, "Rapport, Règles relatives à l'usage du pavillon national pour les navires de commerce," *Annuaire* 15:52 (1896); Gidel, I, 81; Kauffmann, "Règles

It is also interesting to note that the "Memorandum on the High Seas" published by the Secretariat of the United Nations and included among the documents of the International Law Commission does not find any limitations in the states' rights in this respect, since its says that "international law confines itself to requiring the compulsory attribution of a nationality to a ship, all other matters being left to the flag State. The conditions governing the grant of nationality and penalties to be applied in the event of their nonfulfillment are determined by the domestic law of the State concerned." [41] The traditional doctrine proclaims that a "State is absolutely independent in framing the rules concerning the claim of vessels to its flag," [42] that each state has "the undisputed right . . . to set up such prerequisites for the assumption of its nationality as its concept of national welfare dictates." [43] This right is presented as a corollary of the sovereignty of the states, entitling them to pass such legislation as best will serve their national interests.[44] For some authors, this rule has become an "international blank provision" which, as to its content, must be referred to municipal law and whose content is not incorporated into international law.[45]

The latitude granted to the states in the matter under discussion is wide, both in restricting, and in admitting ships to their registry. As to the restrictions, Rienow concludes that "there are apparently no limits on the positive exactions of States," and that "theoretically a State may, by the harshness of its rules prevent any vessel from sailing under its flag." [46] On the other hand, a state may enact liberal rules in order to attract vessels to its registry.[47] The right of a state to grant its nationality to foreign-owned vessels

générales du droit de la paix," *RCADI* 54:376 (1935, pt. IV); Neumeyer, III, 89–90; Verdross, *Völkerrecht* (4th rev. ed. 1959), p. 247; Watts, "The Protection of Merchant Ships," *British Yearbook of International Law* 33:52, 53 (1957); Sørensen, p. 202. *Cf.* also the ILC reports on the high seas by François, *e.g.*, his second report; ILC *Yearbook 1951*, II, 75–77 (UN. Doc. A/CN.4/42).

41. ILC *Yearbook 1950*, II, 74 (Doc. A/CN.4/32).

42. Oppenheim, I, 595.

43. Rienow, p. 215.

44. Müller, p. 353; Diena, p. 424.

45. Triepel, *Völkerrecht und Landesrecht* (1899), pp. 162, 232. Triepel called such rules "nicht recipierende Blankettrechtsätze."

46. Rienow, p. 21 n. 53 and p. 214.

47. Rienow notes here that "a State's efforts in this direction are partially counteracted by the pressure of labor and shipbuilding interests"; *id.*, p. 219 n. 34.

has not been denied by any authority; on the contrary, it has been expressly recognized by a number of authors.[48] This is also confirmed by the practice of the states, which does not show any cases of the denial of the nationality of a vessel because of the fact that the owners are not nationals of the flag state.

The question might be raised whether, even accepting the traditional "liberal" point of view, there are, under international law, any limits to the states' right of granting their flags to the merchant vessels. The limitations arise in the following cases:

1) A state may be limited by express treaty provisions. Besides the earlier treaties provided with such a clause,[49] an interesting example of the more recent state practice is the Agreement between France and Tunisia of December 28, 1955, under which the parties bind themselves that in case of any changes in legislation the grant of nationality to ships, they will not reduce the ownership requisite below 50 per cent.[50]

2) A state comes short of this right at the point where it impinges upon the prior rights of other states. In particular, a state is not allowed to impose its nationality upon such vessels as already have the nationality of another state.[51] Of course, a state may enact a new ship registration law, prohibiting its nationals to own foreign-registered vessels, and thus bring about a transfer

48. See, *e.g.*, Oppenheim, I, 595: "[A state] can . . . authorize such vessels to sail under its flag as are the property of foreign subjects." [This passage was quoted by the U.S. District Court S.D.N.Y. in *McQuade v. Compañía de Vapores San Antonio, S.A.;* 131 F. Supp. 365 (S.D.N.Y. 1955)]. See also Hyde, I, 811: "A State enjoys latitude in exercising the right to register ships. It is not obliged to abstain from registering those of foreign ownership."

49. See, *e.g.*, art. 32 of the General Act for the Repression of the Slave Trade, July 2, 1890 (27 Stat. 886; T.S. 383; Malloy, II, 1366) mentioned in connection with the *Muscat Dhows* case. Similar provisions were stipulated in the Treaty of St. Germain, September 10, 1919, and some other international acts; Dahm, I, 677 n. 16.

50. See Chapter II, note 86.

51. Oppenheim, I, 595; Hyde, I, 811; Rienow, pp. 10, 21, 219. An incident of this kind occurred in 1909 when the United States protested against the Honduran law providing that all the vessels in the service of any individual residing in Honduras would be considered as Honduran. Application of this law would have meant imposing the Honduran nationality on vessels holding American or other foreign registry. The American protest did not question the right of Honduras to enact such rules as it deemed proper for itself; the protest concerned the fact that the decree would have imposed the Honduran nationality upon vessels that were already registered in other countries and thereby would have been violative of international law. As a result of the protest the respective provisions of the decree were not enforced by the executive authority of Honduras; [1909] Foreign Rel. (1914), pp. 367, 368, 375. Briggs, p. 332; Rienow, pp. 106–107.

(or re-transfer) of foreign-registered but national-owned vessels to its flag and registry.[52] Cases of double nationality, which might arise in such and similar transfers, are dealt with in art. 6 of the Geneva Convention on the High Seas.

3) A state is not allowed to grant its nationality to a ship if there is reasonable ground for suspicion that the ship will be used for purposes violative of international law.[53]

One must add to the foregoing considerations, however, that the outcomes authorized in time of war are authorized irrespective of the nationality of ships.

The question remains how the act of attributing a state's national character to a ship is proved under international law, what is its evidence and test, because "to impress effectively its nationality and to be assured that such nationality will be respected, a state must have certain established steps intended to make other states cognizant of certain particulars: that the vessel has met to the satisfaction of the state all the statutory conditions; that the state considers the vessel one of its own." [54]

The universal practice of states, both on international and national levels, shows that registration, usually accompanied by appropriate documents issued by the competent authority, is the only test of a ship's nationality. The test of registration is independent of any requirements which may be, and in most cases are, imposed by national laws before a vessel is admitted to a particular merchant marine, and are dictated by exclusive national policies of the states. However,

> international law does not require that a vessel, in order to be considered of the nationality of a certain State, be built in such State, be navigated by a crew who are nationals of such State, be owned in whole or in part by its nationals . . . Conversely, it is apparent that international practice will not sustain a State in an attempt to assert the rights of nationality over a vessel on the grounds of national build, of national crew, of national ownership. . . .[55]

52. Rienow, p. 219 n.31.
53. *Cf.* Dahm, I, 678.
54. Rienow, p. 116.
55. *Id.*, p. 154.

This point was thoroughly analyzed and proved by Rienow on the basis of the historic practice of states, and little can be added to his convincing analysis. So far as treaty practice is concerned, it shows that no state can deny that a vessel belongs to another state just because the vessel is not owned by nationals of the latter states.[56]

Conclusions similar to those of Rienow were more recently reached by another scholar who examined the provisions of commercial treaties. He found that

> While national laws do commonly limit national registry to vessels owned by the nationals of the country concerned, it is not this requirement but the fact that the vessel has been admitted to national registry that is significant from the treaty standpoint. . . . Under such treaty provisions, nationality of the vessel is determined solely by the state of registry irrespective of the nationality of the owner.[57]

After examining the other manifestations of the states' practice, Rienow comes to the conclusion that

> There is actually no correlation between ownership and nationality; the treaties and correspondence of States do not indicate the need for national ownership; and although some States refuse to consider as of their own respective nationalities, vessels, the titles to which are not held by nationals, their practice indicates that they do not deny other States the privilege of dispensing with this requirement. Moreover, the bare fact of national ownership does not impress upon a vessel a closer connection with the State of the owner's nationality than with any other State.[58]

56. One single treaty, namely the Treaty of Amity, Commerce, and Navigation between the United States and the Congo (January 24, 1891) offers but negligible evidence. Article VI of that treaty stated: "It is agreed that every vessel belonging to one of the High Contracting Parties or to a citizen or inhabitant of one of them, having the right to bear the flag of that country and having the right to its protection, both according to the laws of that country, shall be considered as vessel of that nationality" (Malloy, I, 331, as cited by Rienow, p. 99 n. 75).

57. Hawkins, *Commercial Treaties and Agreements* (1951), p. 6 as cited by McDougal, Burke, & Vlasic (p. 111 n. 268). *Cf.* also the conclusion of Walker: "A vessel, by definition, is deemed to have the nationality of the country whose flag it flies, without reference to such question as who owns it or where it was built. . . ." Walker, "Provisions on Companies in United States Commercial Treaties," *AJIL* 50:373, 382 (1956).

58. Rienow, p. 116. However, there have been decisions, in particular, of British courts, stressing the decisive importance of ownership for the determination of nationality in particular cases. See, *e.g.*, Chartered Mercantile Bank of India v. Netherlands Steam Navigation Co., (1883) L.R. 10 Q.B.D. 521, 535; The Assunzione,

Even less than national ownership can national crew be considered as essential under international law as a test of a ship's nationality. There is lack of treaty evidence pointing to the conclusion that national crews are indispensable to a state's claim that a vessel has its nationality. The decision in *The Montijo* dispute between the United States and Colombia, in which the umpire, Robert Bunch, British Minister Resident in Bogotá, rejected the Colombian contention that *The Montijo* could not claim American nationality since the composition of the crew did not comply with the relevant American prerequisite, ruled that:

> There remains to be noticed the allegation of the Colombian arbitrator that *The Montijo* was not entitled to be reputed as an American vessel because only a third of her crew were American citizens, and that this is a violation of the Law of the United States. The undersigned must remark, first, that this is rather a question for the Government of the United States than for this tribunal of arbitration, and, secondly, that it constantly happens that the requirements of such a law can not be carried out, owing to the impossibility of procuring such citizens . . . The undersigned can not go behind the undoubted fact that the Government of the United States considers *The Montijo* as an American ship. On this point it is the sole judge.[59]

The problem of crew was also considered by the Institute of International Law at its Venice session in 1896. However, the attempts to limit the states' competence in this respect were rejected by a great majority, and a recommendation was adopted that "the nationality of the captain and the other members of the crew shall not be a condition of acquiring or forfeiting the right to fly the flag."[60] The question of captain's nationality as a condition of recognizing the national character of a merchant ship was revived again at the sessions of the International Law Commission, but the sober reasoning of several of the delegates prevailed and the

---

[1954] P. 150 (C.A.) 190, as cited by Singh, "The Indian Merchant Shipping Act, 1958, and International Law," *The Indian Journal of International Law* 1:10, 15–17 (1960). Nevertheless, as is noted also by Singh, the ownership factor comes into play only for particular spheres and aspects of shipping, and the proper law to be applied depends upon the subject matter under consideration. *Cf.* Ch. VI.

59. The Montijo, Moore, *Arbitrations* (1898), II, 1421, 1433–1434 (decision of Robert Bunch, umpire, of July 25, 1875).

60. *Annuaire* 15:202 (1896). The work of the Institute is discussed in Chapter VIII.

extravagant motion was twice rejected, first in 1951 and, by a very low margin, in 1955.[61]

As to the anachronistic requirement of national build there is no correlation between the construction and the nationality of a vessel, and it has never been a requirement of international law. The fact that a ship has been built in a particular country does not necessarily establish that it has the nationality of this country from the point of view of international law.[62]

Unlike the above-considered factors of national ownership, crew or build which may — from the municipal point of view — be conditions of attribution of nationality, the flag is an evidence thereof, not always conclusive, though most conspicuous, and usually symbolizing nationality of ships in international practice. Thus, it seems appropriate at this juncture to clarify briefly the mutual relation of flag to nationality and registry of a merchant vessel.

A study of the municipal shipping legislations shows that a large number of states speak of granting the right to fly the flag, instead of granting nationality to a ship, although in both cases the same thing is meant, the act of attributing national character to the ship, and in both cases registration of the ships is compulsory.[63] Others identify the right to fly the national flag with nationality (or "national character").[64] There is no doubt that registration within a state gives a ship the right and even duty to fly that state's flag,[65] but sometimes another flag may be flown along with the flag of the state of registry to indicate some interest in the vessel.[66] There

61. ILC *Yearbook 1951,* I, 333; ILC *Yearbook 1955,* I, 63.

62. See Rienow, pp. 24–49.

63. See, *e.g.*, the legislations of: Argentine, UNLS, p. 1; Belgium, *id.*, p. 3; Bulgaria, *id.*, p. 8; Czechoslovakia, *id.*, p. 36; German Federal Republic, *id.*, p. 64; Austria, UNLS Supp., p. 113.

64. See, *e.g.*, the legislation of Ireland; UNLS Supp., p. 125.

65. But some vessels which are exempt from registration (usually small craft) are also permitted to fly the national flag. See, *e.g.*, The New Zealand Shipping and Seamen Act No. 49 of October 23, 1952, art. 440(2) in UNLS, p. 122.

66. See, *e.g.*, the case of the Chinese vessels chartered to United States companies. The Department of State did not object to the flying of the United States flag at the masthead of the ships, provided that it was intended that the vessels would continue to fly the Chinese flag aft and to operate under Chinese registry; Secretary Hughes to the U.S. Consul at Canton, China, May 31, 1921 (MS. Department of State, file 195.2/2701); see Hackworth, II, 732. There is no United States prohibition of the display of the American flag on foreign vessels owned by citizens of the United States; Moore, *Digest* (1906), II, 1002–1003; Hackworth, II, 731.

have also been cases of temporary and conditional grants of a national flag which did not impress upon the ship the nationality of the flag or serve as an indication thereof.[67] That the flag cannot by itself be considered sufficient token of a vessel's nationality is further substantiated by the ease with which it can be falsified and abusively displayed, and by the fact that in time of war the hoisting of a false flag has international legal sanction.[68] Because of all these factors, the flag a vessel flies can be regarded only as "prima facie evidence, on the high seas, that the nationality of the vessel carrying it corresponds to that of the flag." [69] A flag is only a symbol of the fact that the ship is able to give evidence of its being endowed with the national character of a given state. The real proof of a ship's nationality lies in its registration in the flag state, which fact is recorded in the documents carried on board the ship.

Registration of ships, which is said to have been practiced even in ancient Rome,[70] was known to the Italian city states in the Middle Ages, and became accepted practice in the modern era. In England, registration was introduced in connection with the Navigation Acts furthering English commercial policies, as a means of preventing unauthorized ships from sailing under the English flag and taking advantage of the Navigation Acts.[71] In the United States the registration of vessels was ordered as early as in 1792 by the Registry Act, which provides for registration, enrolment or license of the "regularly documented" vessels of the United States. "The purpose of a register is to declare the nationality of a vessel engaged in trade with foreign nations, and to enable her to assert that nationality wherever found. The purpose of an enrolment is to evidence the national character of a

67. See, *e.g.*, the case of Dutch vessels that were requisitioned by the United States in the First World War and subsequently were operated under the United States flag; Rienow, pp. 146–149. Rienow discusses also other cases of this kind.

68. For discussion of the false flags, see Rienow, pp. 149–151. In many municipal legislations the abuse or unauthorized use of the national flag is treated as a criminal offense for which severe penalties are provided. See, *e.g.*, the Danish Shipping Registration Act No. 93 of March 29, 1957, art. 57, cl. 4 (UNLS Supp., pp. 122–123).

69. Moore, *Digest*, II, 1002. See also The Chiquita, Hartwig v. United States, 19 F. 2d 417, 418 (C.C.A. 5th, 1927), cited in Hackworth, II, 728.

70. Williams, "Function of Evidence in Roman Law," *Law Magazine and Review* 20:73 (4th ser.), quoted in Rienow, p. 155 n. 4.

71. See, *e.g.*, Navigation Act, 1660; 12 Car. II c. 18. Navigation Act, 1698; 7 and 8 Will. III, c. 22.

vessel engaged in the coasting trade or home traffic, and to enable such vessel to procure a coasting license." [72]

The practice of registering ships has become universal and it is an established rule of international law that all maritime states make registration a formal condition of their nationality, the only exception being small craft which are not intended for long-distance navigation. The practice of issuing a document indicating and evidencing that a vessel is registered in accordance with the national law is also universal, and it is not necessary to quote the hundreds of specific municipal provisions dealing with this problem.[73] The legislations of the flag-of-convenience states do not differ in this respect from those of traditional maritime countries.[74] That the practice of registering and documenting national vessels has become obligatory under international law can best be evidenced by the already discussed treaties, both bilateral and multilateral. In some of these treaties, already in the first half of the 19th century, it was common for states to call for the documentation of each other's vessels as the test of their nationality. The unanimous acceptance of documentation as evidence of a ship's nationality is also corroborated by customs regulations, naval instructions, and statements of diplomatic officials.[75] A vessel without documents may be refused permission to enter foreign ports and engage in commercial activities. The case of *The Merritt,* an Ameri-

72. The Mohawk, 70 U.S. 566, 571 (1865). About the peculiar circumstances of the United States registration practice, which reflects a distinction between "registered or enrolled ships" and "certified ships," see Hackworth, II, 735; Rienow, pp. 161–164; Briggs, pp. 331–332.

73. See UNLS and UNLS Supp., *passim.* It can be seen that all shipping laws provide for registration of ships, and many laws expressly consider the certificate of nationality (or registry) as evidence of a ship's nationality. The number and type of ship's papers are not specified by international law and the regulations vary in different countries. See Gidel, I, 83–86; Colombos, pp. 255–256; Oppenheim, I, 596–597; Fedozzi, pp. 49–50.

74. See, *e.g.,* the following: Honduras — Organic Act of the National Merchant Marine No. 55 of March 2, 1943, art. 1 ". . . Only ships duly registered in the shipping register and carrying a proper certificate of registry may use and wear the Honduran flag and sail under its protection. . ." UNLS, p. 75. Panama — Law No. 8 of January 12, 1925, arts. 1(1) and 9. Liberia — *Liberian Code of Laws of 1956,* vol. II, tit. 22, ch. 2, §50 ". . . No vessel engaged in foreign trade shall fly the flag of the Republic of Liberia or be accorded the rights and privileges of a Liberian vessel unless such vessel shall be registered. . . . The home port of every vessel so registered shall be Monrovia, and the name of the home port shall be shown on the Certificate of Registry."

75. See Rienow, pp. 170–174.

can-owned, foreign-built ship without any documents, shows the disadvantages of an undocumented vessel. It had been importing coal and iron from Canada to the United States in violation of the provisions of the Act of March 1, 1817, which required the ship either to be a United States vessel or a vessel of the nationality of the state whose goods were imported.[76] Deciding the issue of whether *The Merritt*, having no documents at all, could establish either British or Canadian nationality, Mr. Justice Hunt said:

> The case does not show that *The Merritt* has any of the evidences of being a British ship. She produces no register, or certificate, or document of any kind to entitle her to make that claim. The fact that she is foreign-built does not prove it . . . Proof even that she was built in Great Britain would not establish it. Pirates and rovers may issue from the most peaceful and most friendly ports. The documents a vessel carries furnish the only evidence of her nationality. Of these *the Merritt* is entirely destitute, so far as the case shows. . . .[77]

The documents issued by a state certifying the nationality of a ship must be regarded as a reliable proof of the true national character of a ship and the question whether a ship carries proper papers and is entitled to the flag it is flying must be finally decided by the courts of the flag state only. The famous case of *The Virginius* is the leading case on this point.[78] A United States registered vessel, it was captured in 1873 on the high seas by a Spanish warship and great part of the crew and passengers were tried by a Spanish court martial and put to death, under the charge of aiding the Cuban insurgents. To the Spanish charges that *The Virginius* was not eligible for American registration because she was owned by Cubans (a fact which had been concealed by the owners), the American side replied that even if the ship had fraudulently obtained her registry, the offense was committed against the American laws, and only American tribunals were competent to decide the question.[79] This was also supported by the opinion of the Secretary of State, supported by the Attorney-General who categorically affirmed that "[Spain] has no jurisdiction whatever over the question as to whether [a] vessel

76. 3 Stat. 351.
77. 17 Wall. (81 U.S.) 582, 586–587 (1873).
78. Moore, *Digest*, II, 895; [1874] Foreign Rel. (1874), pp. 1035–1074.
79. Special Message by President Grant, January 5, 1874; Moore, *Digest*, II, 901.

is on the high seas in violation of any law of the United States." [80] Eventually, Spain restored the ship to the United States government.

The validity of documents and certificates as a mode of establishing the nationality of vessels has found its confirmation not only in countless bilateral treaties, but also in multilateral conventions in which the test of the ship's nationality is laid down. Of these, one should mention the major Pan-American convention, the famous Bustamante Code of Private International Law, signed at Havana on February 20, 1928, which, making an attempt to unify private international law, deals also with the question of nationality of vessels. Under this convention, nationality of ships "is proved by the navigation license and the certificate of registration and has the flag as an apparent distinctive symbol." [81] Another example is provided by the Treaty on International Commercial Navigation Law, signed at Montevideo, March 19, 1940, which determines and regulates the nationality of vessels "by the law of the State which permitted the use of the flag. Proof of this nationality is afforded in the appropriate certificate, lawfully issued by the competent authorities of the said State." [82]

The conventions dealing with safety at sea, being ratified by almost all maritime states, carry great weight as evidence of the recognition of the principle that it is registration that invests the vessel with a national character without any additional criteria to be satisfied. In these conventions the states seem to want to confine their treaty obligations only to the ships with which they have established a connection by registration. "[A] ship is regarded as belonging to a country if it is registered by the government of that country," states art. 3(a) of the Loadline Convention, signed in London July 5, 1930,[83] and the Convention on Safety of Life at Sea, signed in London, June 10, 1948, lays down in art. II that

80. 14 Op. Atty. Gen. (December 17, 1873) 340, 343; quoted in Rienow, pp. 177–178 n. 87.

81. Article 274 of the Code of Private International Law, tit. III. Maritime and Air Commerce [86 L.N.T.S. 254, 326 (1929); Hudson, *International Legislation* IV (1931), 2283, 2320].

82. Hudson, VIII, 460.

83. T.S. 858; 47 Stat. 2228; 135 L.N.T.S. 301. *Cf.* similar formulation in art. 2(3)(a) of the Convention on Safety of Life at Sea, London, May 31, 1929; T.S. 910; 50 Stat. 1121; 136 L.N.T.S. 81.

the "ships to which the present convention applies are ships registered in countries the governments of which are contracting governments. . . ." [84] Similar phrasing is used also in art. 2 of the Agreement on the Financial Support of the North Atlantic Ice Patrol signed in Washington on January 4, 1956.[85]

The principle of registration as test of the ship's nationality is perhaps best illustrated by the language used in the conventions concluded under the auspices of the International Labor Conference. The conventions adopted at Geneva in 1926 made registry the criterion for the jurisdiction over a ship. Although the Convention on the Simplification of the Inspection of Emigrants on Board Ships (1926) mentioned in art. 3 "the country whose flag the vessel flies," [86] art. 1 of both the Convention on the Repatriation of Seamen (1926) and the Convention on Seamen's Articles of Agreement (1926) state that "this Convention shall apply to all sea-going vessels registered in the country of any member ratifying this Convention, and to the owners, masters and seamen of such vessels." [87]

Discussing the standards adopted by the labor conventions one must mention the 21st session of the International Labor Conference at Geneva, 1936, which dealt with the issue of the most appropriate criterion to be adopted in international labor conventions in the matter of the demarcation of the scope of these conventions as regards the vessels. The coordination committee, appointed to find a uniform formula for all the conventions which were under consideration, found registration to be the most appropriate criterion for demarcating the scope of the maritime conventions adopted at the session. The phrase "all (any) vessels registered in a territory for which this Convention is in force" can be found in art. 1 of each of the conventions adopted in 1936.[88]

84. 3 U.S.T. 3450; T.I.A.S. 2495; 164 U.N.T.S. 113.
85. T.I.A.S. 3597; 7 U.S.T. 1969.
86. Hudson, III, 1899.
87. *Id.*, pp. 1981–1982, 1987–1988.
88. ILConf.*RP*. 21 and 22 Sessions (1937), pp. 210–211, 317, 322, 327–328, 334, 340. The conventions in question are: draft convention concerning the minimum requirement of professional capacity for masters and officers on board merchant ships (Hudson, VII, 440, 441), draft convention concerning annual holidays with pay for seamen (*id.*, pp. 446, 447–448), draft convention concerning liability of the shipowner in case of sickness, injury, or death of seamen (*id.*, pp. 453, 454–455), draft convention concerning sickness insurance for seamen (*id.* pp. 462, 463) and

Discussing the results of the work of the conference, Mr. C. W. Jenks, then a delegate to the conference from Great Britain, and now assistant director general and legal advisor to the International Labor Office, noted that "nationality" as a criterion had been rejected, since it might be thought to refer to

> the nationality of the ownership and control of the vessel, and perhaps even to the nationality of the real as distinct from the apparent ownership and control . . . Nationality, understood in this sense, is not the criterion which determines the jurisdictional rights of States over conditions of employment on board, and . . . the criterion defining the obligations to be assumed by states must necessarily correspond with that which, under general rules of international law, delimits the extent of their powers of control.[89]

Mr. Jenks' conclusion was that "registration will perhaps commend itself as the most satisfactory criterion." [90]

The postwar conventions adopted under the auspices of the International Labor Office, which attempted to set international labor standards in maritime labor, have consistently adhered to the formulation of registry as criterion of the ship's nationality, adopted in 1936.[91] International practice as evidenced by the multi- and bilateral treaties was one of the arguments of the Panlibhon group in the pleadings before the International Court of Justice in the case of the Constitution of the Maritime Safety Committee of IMCO decided by the Court in 1960 (see Chapter V). There the Liberian government submitted to the Court extracts from 25 multilateral and 39 bilateral treaties and conventions illustrating the use of registration as a connecting factor in maritime matters.[92]

---

draft convention concerning hours of work on board ship and manning (*id.*, pp. 470, 471).

89. Jenks, "Nationality, the Flag, and Registration as Criteria for Demarcating the Scope of Maritime Conventions, *Journal of Comparative Legislation and International Law* 19:245, 249 (3d Ser. 1937). Jenks represented the International Labor Organization at the Geneva Conference on the Law of the Sea in 1958.

90. *Id.*, p. 252.

91. For these conventions see ILOffice, *The International Labor Code 1951*, I, 748, 787, 789, 852, 878, 889, 909 (1952). For the state of ratifications of the maritime labor conventions, see ILOffice, *Report I* (1957), pp. 54, 55 (Appendix I: Chart of Ratifications of Maritime Conventions as of August 1, 1957). The postwar conventions have not, as yet, received the requisite number of ratifications.

92. ICJ *Pleadings*, Constitution (1960), pp. 86–99. See also discussion of these treaties in the written statement of the government of Liberia (*id.*, pp. 48–54).

The principle in question is also confirmed by the doctrine of international law, from which the succinct statement by Hyde is worth quoting: "[A] vessel registered under the laws of a State and possessed of a certificate of registry may be deemed in an international sense to belong to that State, and to justify it in giving it the privilege of flying its flag, regardless of the nationality of the owners of the ship."[93] Similarly comprehensive is the conclusion of Rienow, that "a state, having issued in accordance with accepted maritime usage a certificate of registry or other certificate of nationality . . . may, under international law, expect to have the relationship of nationality, thus established and affirmed, respected by other States."[94]

There is one more issue which is worthwhile exploring when speaking about the concept of the nationality of ships in international law. It is the relation between the nationality of ships and that of individuals, a problem to which special attention has been given, particularly in connection with the decision of the International Court of Justice in the famous *Nottebohm* case.[95] The followers of the genuine-link concept and adversaries of the flags of convenience find it a favorite argument to transfer the principle of real and effective nationality, as enunciated by the International Court of Justice in the *Nottebohm* case, to the relation that should exist between a ship and the source of its nationality.

The contention of this part of the doctrine, derived from *Nottebohm,* is that just as the grant of nationality to an individual need not be respected by other states if there is no genuine connection between the state and the individual, so in the case of ships a state has the right to refuse recognition of a registration because

93. Hyde, I, 810. See also, *Annuaire* 15:191 (1896), "Voici le principe fondamental de ce que nous proposons: c'est l'enrigistrement du bâtiment marchand que nous rendons obligatoire. . . ."; Fenwick, p. 217, ". . . all that international law has prescribed is that some one state must authorize the vessel to use its flag, provide it with the proper 'ship's papers', and thereupon exercise in respect to the vessel the degree of jurisdiction permitted by the law"; Higgins, *RCADI* (1929, pt. V), p. 21, "La seule condition qui soit généralement exigée dans tous les pays, c'est l'inscription du navire sur le registre tenu par les autorités désignées à cet effet et la délivrance à son propriétaire d'un certificat établissant que les formalités nécessaires ont été remplies." See also, *e.g.*, Oppenheim, I, 590; Wilson, *International Law* (3d ed. 1939), p. 123; Diena, p. 426.

94. Rienow, p. 187.

95. [1955] I.C.J. Rep. 4.

a genuine link does not exist between the ship and the state of registration.[96] It is thus appropriate to examine whether the *Nottebohm* decision can be projected into the relations between a ship and the state of its nationality.

First, the more general question of the analogy between the nationality of individuals and the nationality of ships must be discussed. This analogy was underlying the views of Neumeyer and Verdross. Neumeyer, referring to the grant of nationality to individuals, admitted the possibility that the transgression of the competence to grant the right to fly the flag might entail the loss of protection of international law.[97] Similarly, Verdross speaks of a "factual domestic link between the ship and the state of registry" which must exist in the case of nationality of ships, as in that of individuals.[98] These authors, however, do not give any substantiation to their views.

Ever since the initial discussion of the subject of nationality of ships in the International Law Commission, the advocates of the limitation of the states' right to grant nationality to merchant vessels have made references in their arguments to an analogy between the nationality of the ships and the nationality of individuals. In particular, they refer to the provisions concerning

96. See, *e.g.*, Watts, "The Protection of Merchant Ships", p. 52; Sørensen, p. 204; Verzijl, "The United Nations Conference on the Law of the Sea, Geneva 1958 (II)," *Nederlands Tijdschrift voor Internationaal Recht* 6:115, 116 (1959); Mouton, "De Conferentie betreffende het Recht van de Zee, gehouden te Genève van 24 februari tot 29 april 1958," *Marineblad* 69:7, 84 (No. 1, 1959); Mender, pp. 362–366: Johnson, "The Geneva Conference on the Law of the Sea," *Yearbook of World Affairs* 13:68, 87 (1959): Johnson even states that "The International Law Commission had recommended that the principle of the *Nottebohm* case should be applied to ships." His statement is not strictly accurate because the ILC did not make such recommendation explicitly. See also statements of Riphagen (Netherlands), Seyersted (Norway), and Vallat (U.K.) in ICJ *Pleadings*, Constitution (1960), pp. 357–359, 365–366, 374. *Contra*, McDougal, Burke, & Vlasic, pp. 36–40; Kunz, "The Nottebohm Judgment," *AJIL* 54:536, 568–571 (1960); Pinto, "Flags of Convenience" [in English and in French] *Journal du Droit International* 87:344 (1960); statement of Weeks (Liberia), ICJ *Pleadings*, Constitution (1960), pp. 404–405. Van Panhuis, as a delegate of the Netherlands to the Geneva Conference on the Law of the Sea in 1958, spoke for the application of the genuine link principle to the nationality of ships. But in his book, which was published later, Van Panhuis sharply criticizes the *Nottebohm* judgment. See Van Panhuis, *The Role of Nationality in International Law* (1959).

97. Neumeyer, III, 90. Neumeyer refers in particular to Triepel, *Virtuelle Staatsangehörigkeit* (1921), p. 30.

98. Verdross, p. 247.

nationality laid down by the Hague Conference for the Codification of International Law — saying that although it is for each state to determine under its own law who are its nationals, "this law shall be recognized by other States in so far as it is consistent with international conventions, international custom, and the principles of Law generally recognized with regard to nationality." [99] It was claimed by the ILC that the same rule should be applied when dealing with the attribution of nationality to a ship.[100]

The concept of the "effective nationality" of natural persons was first evolved in cases of dual nationality, with regard to the exercise of protection, by international arbitrators, who were to decide whether the nationality invoked by the applicant state could be invoked as against the respondent state, that is, whether the respondent state was obliged to recognize the effects of that nationality. The tendency was — also in treaties on the subject — that for the nationality to be invoked against another state, it must be real and effective and corresponding with the factual situation. The tendency found its climax in the *Nottebohm* judgment, which extended it to the cases of single nationality.[101]

The *Nottebohm* judgment dealt with the question whether the unilateral act of Liechtenstein granting nationality to a natural person (Nottebohm) entailed the obligation, on the part of Guatemala, to recognize its effects, namely, Liechtenstein's right to exercise protection over the person naturalized by it. In other words, the question was whether "the naturalization conferred on Nottebohm can be successfully invoked against Guatemala, whether . . . it can be relied upon as against that State, so that Liechtenstein is thereby entitled to exercise its protection in favour of Nottebohm against Guatemala." [102] It should be emphasized that the Court did not question the right of each state to determine the

99. Convention concerning Certain Questions relating to the Conflict of Nationality Laws, signed at The Hague, April 12, 1930, art. 1; 179 L.N.T.S. 89; Hudson, V, 364.

100. ILC *Yearbook 1951*, II, 76 (François). See also *id.*, I, 331, and the comment by the Netherlands government on the 1955 Provisional Articles of the ILC; ILC *Yearbook 1956*, II, 62–63.

101. The Court stated, however, that the cases in which the real and effective nationality was given preference were the cases of dual nationality; [1955] ICJ Rep. 22.

102. *Id.*, p. 21.

rules granting nationality to individuals other than in relation to the capacity of a state to present an international claim against another, in particular with the admissibility of diplomatic protection of individuals. It was held by the Court that (also in cases of only one nationality) for the grant of nationality by state *A* to an individual to be effective *vis-à-vis* state *B*, and to be recognized by state *B* in the sense that it could give state *A* the right to protect that individual, the nationality must be real and effective, reinforced by the existence of a genuine connection between the individual and state *A*. If the nationality granted is not based upon a genuine connection (link) and thereby does not constitute "a translation into juridical terms of the individual's connection with the state which made him its national," [103] it need not be recognized by other states, and cannot be invoked against those other states as an effective and valid act on the plane of international law. By this "severance of diplomatic protection from the question of nationality" [104] the Court laid down the rule limiting the right to exercise protection in the international sphere.

Assuming for the time being that the *Nottebohm* judgment expresses a general rule of international law in the case of individuals, we must consider the question as to its extension by analogy to the cases dealing with the recognition of the nationality of ships.

At the eighth session of the ILC, this analogy was affirmed by Scelle without any express reference to the *Nottebohm* case. He stated then, against the doubts of Padilla Nervo, that "it would be for their States to decide whether a genuine link existed between the ship and the State of new registration and consequently whether the ship was entitled to fly its flag. The situation was analogous to a disagreement between the States over the nationality of an individual." [105] The *Nottebohm* case, although not mentioned explicitly at the ILC's sessions devoted to the nationality of ships, very probably influenced that body in adopting the principle of genuine link for the matters connected with the recognition of the nationality of ships, particularly since the genuine-link principle was proposed by the government of the Netherlands,

103. *Id.*, p. 23.
104. *Id.*, p. 30 (dissenting opinion of Judge Klaestad).
105. ILC *Yearbook 1956,* I, 71.

which in its comment on the provisional articles referred to the *Nottebohm* judgment.[106] This is also substantiated by the fact that the *Nottebohm* judgment was mentioned in the "Reference Guide to the Law of the Sea" adopted by the ILC, prepared by the United Nations Secretariat, where it was stated:

> In connexion with the question of the nationality of ships, it may be noted that, in the *Nottebohm case,* the International Court of Justice enunciated certain principles concerning the duty of one State to recognize the nationality legislation of another State. Although this case concerned the nationality of individuals . . . the Court considered the matter of nationality in general terms. It is possible, therefore, that some of the principles laid down by the Court may be relevant to the question of the nationality of ships, in particular, to the question of the circumstances under which one State may or may not be obliged to recognize the national character of ships of other States.[107]

The Netherlands government, which had proposed the genuine-link clause, discussing in their comment on art. 29 of the Law of the Sea, prepared by the ILC, the legal consequences of the non-recognition clause, expressly referred to the *Nottebohm* case and proposed that, on the analogy with that decision it should be explicitly stated that a state need not recognize claims by states whose flags are "unlawfully" flown, insofar as those claims were based on the use of the flag, for example, the right to exercise jurisdiction.[108] At the conference itself, three references were made to the *Nottebohm* case. In the first, the opinion was expressed that an analogy could be drawn from that decision and that the principle of genuine link embodied a parallel rule in regard to the nationality of ships.[109] The second quoted the "genuine connection" of the *Nottebohm* judgment to support the sometimes necessary use of vague terms.[110] The third reference was made by the delegate of Guatemala (which was the respondent party in the *Nottebohm* case). The Guatemalan delegate agreed with the opinion of Pinto, the French delegate at the Sixth Committee of the General Assembly's eleventh session,[111] and stated that the

106. *Id.*, II, 62.
107. A/C.6/L.378 (1956) [mimeographed].
108. UN.CLS.*OR* 1:108.
109. New Zealand; *id.*, 4:65.
110. Norway; *id.*, p. 62.
111. A/CONF.13/19 (1957), pp. 272–275 [mimeographed].

"principles laid down in the *Nottebohm* case did not apply to ships."[112]

In view of the above-mentioned discussions the following remarks can be made on the problem of the extension, by analogy, of the principles of the *Nottebohm* case to merchant vessels:

First of all, when using the well-established term "nationality" in relation to ships, one should not forget that this so-called "nationality of ships" is not and cannot be, in its nature, the same as nationality of individuals. It is a "pseudo-nationality,"[113] which, although being a term convenient and helpful in some instances, should not be made the premise from which conclusions of law are drawn.[114] At any rate, the differences between nationality of persons and nationality of ships must be taken into account when dealing with the various legal problems in which this nationality is relevant.[115]

For the above-mentioned reasons, the introduction of the concept of "nationality" of ships into the ILC's draft seemed unnecessary and even dangerous to Pinto, the delegate of France at the Sixth Committee of the General Assembly's eleventh session. He rightly pointed out that the legislation of some 37 countries did not know the term "nationality" of ship (but "the right to fly the flag" or "registration"),[116] but, on the other hand, his fears seem to be exaggerated. This is only a problem of terminology and — as Ripert said — "La comparaison est pittoresque; elle n'est point inexacte si on ne la force point."[117]

One should not forget that the *Nottebohm* decision limits its

112. UN.CLS.*OR* 4:4. See also Pinto, p. 350.

113. Lapradelle and Niboyet, *Répertoire de droit international* (1931), X, 9–10; Ripert, I, 274–275. *Accord,* Hudson (in the ILC), ILC *Yearbook 1950,* I, 190. For the various theories relating to the legal nature of the ship see Florio, *Nazionalità della nave e legge della bandiera,* pp. 11–40.

114. This was stressed by François himself; UN.GA.*OR,* 11th sess., 6th Com, 500th meeting, p. 113. (1956) [also as Doc. A/C.6/L.395 (1956)].

115. *Cf.* Watts' review of Florio's *Nazionalità della nave* in which Watts criticizes Florio for too readily assuming that the nationality of a ship is of the same quality as the nationality of an individual; *International and Comparative Law Quarterly,* 7:399,401 (1958). But see Watts, "The Protection of Merchant Ships" pp. 52, 55, where this British author, strangely enough, applies the rule of the *Nottebohm* case to the protection of merchant ships.

116. *Cf.* Pinto, p. 350.

117. Ripert, I, 275. In German, nationality of persons is usually referred to as "Staatsangehörigkeit," whereas nationality of ships and aircraft is referred to as "Staatszugehörigkeit." See Heyck, p. 16 n. 74.

scope to individuals, and does not make any reference to corporations or ships. What is more, the Court confines this scope within narrow limits, even with respect to individuals. The following formulation shows the Court's cautiousness:

> In the first place, what is involved is not recognition for all purposes but merely for the purposes of the admissibility of the Application, and secondly, that what is involved is not recognition by all States but only by Guatemala.[118]

Then, in the *Nottebohm* case, the Court defined the effective and real nationality of an individual as the juridical expression of the social fact of the individual's connection with his country by his behavior, his activities, his family ties, his tradition, his interests, sentiments, and establishment. All these are criteria characteristic of human beings, but quite irrelevant for an inanimate object.[119] It would also hardly be possible, in many cases, to link by analogy a ship with a state by the factors of the ship's operations across the world.[120] The identification — via analogy with an individual — of the genuine link in the case of a merchant vessel would, of course, be much more difficult than in the case of an individual, taking into account the international character of sea transportation.[121]

Trying to find a genuine connection between the owner of the ship and the state is also, in many cases, unworkable, in particular in the case of juristic persons. For similar reasons, the authors of the draft convention on the international responsibility of states prepared by the Harvard Law School found it difficult to extend

118. [1955] ICJ Rep. 17.

119. This aspect of the application of the *Nottebohm* decision to ships is emphasized by McDougal, Burke, & Vlasic (p. 39).

120. *Cf.* the remarks of Pinto at a meeting of the Sixth Committee of the 11th Session of the General Assembly. This French delegate, proving that the attempt to find an analogy between *Nottebohm* and the problem of nationality of ships was not the right way to regulate the issue in question, said that at all events "it does not seem likely to help to solve the very real and vexatious problem of the flags of convenience." (A/CONF.13/19 (1957), p. 275). See also Pinto, p. 352.

121. *Cf.* the letter of Stavros Niarchos published in *The Times,* April 1, 1958, p. 11. This owner of a large flag-of-convenience fleet stresses the fact that a vessel owned by a national of one country may be discharged in another country for marketing in still another country. Niarchos does not see any reason founded on principle for maintaining that such a vessel should fly one flag rather than another, nor why the owner of the vessel should be of any particular nationality. See also McDougal, Burke, & Vlasic, p. 41 n. 17 where the authors speak of the "peripatetic activities of the representatives of business."

the *Nottebohm* case by analogy to corporations.[122] On the other hand, Jessup, without entering into this complex problem, believes that the link theory, as found in the *Nottebohm* case, "could easily be utilized internationally to determine the national character of corporations and ships" and that "in the light of the court's opinion in the *Nottebohm* case, it is probable that if the issue were presented to it, that tribunal would sustain the link theory in its application to the nationality of ships." [123] This reliance placed on the *Nottebohm* case is perhaps too bold, since it is not quite sure how the case can be extended, even with respect to individuals. The *Nottebohm* decision was also criticized because of uncertainty which it introduced into the relations of nationality.[124]

One should emphasize that the requirement of certainty is much more important with respect to ships than with respect to individuals. This factor also speaks against the applicability of the *Nottebohm* theory to the nationality of ships, and once more confirms the thesis that registry is the test of the ship's nationality.[125]

For all the above reasons, the *Nottebohm* principle cannot rationally be applied to the relations between the ship and the state of its nationality. Indeed, even the solution adopted by the Geneva Conference, in spite of its mentioning the concept of genuine link and stressing the element of effectiveness, does not follow the *Nottebohm* case.[126] This is so because, first, art. 5 in its formulation shifts the emphasis from the ship and shipowner to the flag state. It is up to the state to maintain the link of proper legislation and effective organization of its enforcement, and, second, the essen-

122. Harvard Law School, "Convention on the International Responsibility of States for Injuries to Aliens," (May 1, 1959), Preliminary Draft with Explanatory Notes, pp. 110–112, 124.

123. Jessup, "The United Nations Conference on the Law of the Sea," *Colum. L. Rev.* 59:234,256 (1959). As the advisory opinion of the ICJ has shown, the Court found the genuine link theory irrelevant, at least for the case in question. See Ch. V.

124. See the dissenting opinion of Judge Read [1955], ICJ Rep. 46. *Cf.* also Jones, "The Nottebohm Case," *International and Comparative Law Quarterly*, 5:230, 244 (1956).

125. See McDougal, Burke & Vlasic, p. 40. This is also admitted by Charles de Visscher who, discussing the *Nottebohm* decision and its application to merchant vessels, notes that "l'éxigence de la certitude (spécialement de la sécurité du tiers) l'emporte sur l'éxigence du rattachement effectif," and adds that for this reason the 1944 Chicago Convention on International Civil Aviation adopts the easily verifiable test of registry as the test of the aircraft's nationality (61 Stat. 1160; T.I.A.S. 1591; 15 U.N.T.S. 295); de Visscher, p. 607 & n. 11.

126. See Chapter IX.

tial idea of *Nottebohm,* that is the non-recognition of nationality in case of absence of genuine link was in the final text of the Convention dropped by the plenary session of the conference. Neither was there any mention of the possible applicability of the *Nottebohm* principle to nationality of ships in the advisory opinion of the International Court of Justice of June 8, 1960, on the Constitution of the Maritime Safety Committee of the IMCO.[127]

Applying to flag-of-convenience shipping the discussion of nationality of ships in international law and registration and documents as the only conclusive evidence of this nationality, one must reach the conclusion that, in the light of international law, Panama, Liberia, and Honduras have, with limitations also binding on other maritime states, the competence to confer nationality upon merchant vessels no matter by whom the ships are owned, operated, manned, or where they were built. The only criterion for determining the nationality of a Panlibhon ship is its registry, as recorded by the ship's documents. The nationality thus conferred should be recognized and respected by other states.

The argument here presented found its confirmation in the advisory opinion on the Constitution of the Maritime Safety Committee of the IMCO where the Court, after a thorough discussion of the question, found that "the criterion of registered tonnage is practical, certain and capable of easy application. Moreover, the test of registered tonnage is that which is most consonant with international practice and with maritime usage." [128]

The above-mentioned advisory opinion of the International Court of Justice, because of its importance for the subject in question, is analyzed in Chapter V.

127. Neither was this issue explored in the individual opinions as Jessup had hoped. See Jessup, "The United Nations Conference on the Law of the Sea," *Colum. L. Rev.* 59:257 (1959). The remarks of Judge Moreno Quintana certainly do not explore the whole problem which was also only touched on in the statements of the parties.

128. [1960] ICJ Rep. 169.

Chapter V. The IMCO Dispute: The Case before the World Court

The advisory opinion of the International Court of Justice, June 8, 1960, was the result of a controversy involving flags of convenience, which almost disrupted the inaugural meeting of a new specialized agency of the United Nations, the Inter-Governmental Maritime Consultative Organization (IMCO), in London, January 1959. The problem in relation to IMCO arose in 1948, when the organization was still in a formative stage — at the United Nations Maritime Conference which met in Geneva, February 19–March 6, 1948 by invitation of the United Nations Economic and Social Council.[1] This conference concluded the convention which established IMCO. It was the culmination of a long effort toward the establishment of a permanent world organization to deal with maritime questions.[2]

The controversy of 1948 was caused by the position of Panama, which at that time was the only major flag-of-convenience nation — in terms of tonnage ranking sixth among the maritime nations of the world. The Panamanian delegate was aware of the quasi-maritime status of his country and, at the discussion of the purposes

1. For the documents relating to this conference, see UN.EcoSoc Documents, E/CONF. 4 (1947–1948), pp. 1–63. Doc. E/CONF. 4/SR. (1948), pp. 1–6, contain the summary records of the meetings of this United Nations Maritime Conference.

2. For the history of the long effort to establish such an organization see McDonald & Cates, *Toward a World Maritime Organization* (1948), a publication of the Department of State, which also discusses the United Nations Maritime Conference of 1948; reprinted from *DSB*, 18:99–107, 115, 131–137, 495–499 (1948). See also Padwa, "The Curriculum of IMCO," *International Organization* 14:524 (1960).

of the organization, expressed his consent to its establishment, but with the reservation that "his government was opposed in principle to any measure which might limit its registered tonnage or interfere with freedom of maritime trade." [3]

Because she ranked sixth in registered tonnage, Panama asserted her right to play an important part in the maritime conference. In particular, Panama wanted to be a member of the "Main Working Party" of the conference — set up to develop the proposals which were to become the basis of the final IMCO convention;[4] but in addition, her ambition was to be an original member of the IMCO Council under the terms of arts. 17 and 18 of the IMCO convention.[5] However, these expectations were not fulfilled — Panama was neither included among the 13 members of the main working party[6] nor elected to the IMCO Council.

The composition of the Council was one of the three basic issues discussed at the conference of 1948. The other two issues were whether shipping problems should be handled by an independent maritime organization or by a commission of the United Nations (the conference assumed, even without voting, that there should be a separate organization), and whether the scope of the organization should be limited only to technical matters or whether it should be broadened to include also economic and commercial matters of shipping, such as discrimination, unfair practices, subsidies, etc. (The present art. 1 of the convention shows that the latter tendency prevailed.) As for the Council, the 1948 conference agreed to divide the 16 members of the Council into groups of 6, 6, and 4. This was a substantial departure from the make up of the Council as it had been set up in the so-called "Washington Draft" proposed by the United Maritime Consultative Council (UMCC) in 1946 and which served as the working basis for

3. Doc. E/CONF. 4/SR. 4 Rev. (1948), p. 33.

4. Doc. E/CONF. 4/SR. Rev. (1948), pp. 30–32.

5. Doc. E/CONF. 4/61 (1948). The text of the convention establishing the IMCO is reprinted, *e.g.*, in T.I.A.S. No. 4044; in *DSB* 18:499–505 (1948); in McDonald & Cates, pp. 22–27; in *AJIL* 53:516–531 (1959). On IMCO in general see Magrassi de Sá, "A Organização Intergovernamental Consultiva de Navegação Marítima," *Revista Brasileira de Política Internacional* 1:76–97 (1958). See also Padwa.

6. Doc. E/CONF. 4/SR. Rev. (1948), pp. 31–32. The Main Working Party was comprised of Argentia, Australia, Belgium, Brazil, China, France, India, Ireland, Norway, Poland, Sweden, the United Kingdom, and the United States of America.

the 1948 Maritime Conference.[7] The Argentine proposal, as finally adopted in art. 17 of the convention, provided that six members should be governments of the nations "with the *largest* interest in providing international shipping services," and six "with the *largest* interest in international seaborne trade," and that of the four remaining two should be governments "having a *substantial* interest in international seaborne trade." Only the first 12 of these places were designated in 1948. Having no definite formula before it, the working party agreed that tonnage statistics were not the only criterion for the determination of the six nations with the largest interest in providing international shipping services. Ownership, however, is not mentioned as a criterion. The "ship-using" nations to be represented in the original Council were chosen on the basis of 1938 statistics.[8] In order to maintain a balance between ship-providing nations and ship-using nations, art. 18 provides for changes in the future composition of the Council.

Panama — despite the large tonnage registered under her flag — was practically ignored as an important maritime nation, and was not proposed by the Main Working Party as a member of the Council. Objecting to this, the Panamanian delegate, Dr. Amado, stated that

> he had greatest respect for all nations, especially those listed in E/CONF. 4/22 [i.e., the proposed members of the Council] but some statesmen forgot the importance of his country in the shipping field. Though admittedly small, Panama ranked fifth or sixth in terms of tonnage, was situated at a meeting point of world shipping lines, and had long been interested in international trade. If Panama was not added to the countries listed in E/CONF. 4/22, it had no part to play at the present Conference.[9]

7. For this prototype of the IMCO convention, see Doc. E/CONF. 4/1 (1947), pp. 3–17 ("Draft Convention for a Permanent Intergovernmental Maritime Consultative Organization as Agreed by the 2d Session of the United Maritime Consultative Council of the United Nations"); reprinted in *DSB* 15:1094–1098 (1946). Extracts from the documents of the UMCC are found in ICJ *Pleadings*, Constitution (1960), pp. 151–160. Article VI, §1 of the UMCC Draft of 1946 provided for a council composed of representatives of the eight nations with the largest interest in the provision of shipping services — four nations with the largest interest in international trade and four elected with regard to the desirability of adequate geographical representation.

8. Doc. E/CONF. 4/SR. Rev. (1948), pp. 57–58, 60.

9. *Id.*, p. 59.

But despite this threat, Panama was not chosen among the 12 original members of the Council,[10] and it consequently withdrew from the conference. In the letter to the president of the conference, the delegate of Panama gave as the reasons of the Panamanian withdrawal "systematic failure to recognize the maritime rights and interests of Panama" by excluding Panama from the working party and from the twelve seats in the Council

> as figured out on the basis of world tonnage, geographical situation and participation of small nations. . . . The maritime rights and interests of Panama, which result from international economic developments, are self evident because of . . . our exceptional geographical situation and the importance of our merchant marine, which today measures approximately two and a half million tons, and thus occupies fifth or sixth place in world tonnage. Such a prominent position would, in any international organization on shipping, deserve recognition.[11]

To ignore Panama as a maritime nation, the Panamanian delegate argued, was a deviation from the international law and practice embodied in the Bustamante Code.[12] Because of her withdrawal from the conference, Panama's designation to the working party on maritime safety questions[13] was of no practical importance.

Thus, the most difficult problem that the new United Nations agency was to face at its first session in 1959 was already presented at the conference establishing IMCO. To put it in most general terms, this problem was whether the mere fact of having a very large amount of tonnage registered under its flag entitled a nation to be considered eligible for privileges reserved for the largest maritime nations, and in particular to seats in the various organs provided for by the constitution of IMCO.

The convention establishing IMCO in 1948 did not come into effect until ten years later, on March 17, 1958, when Japan ratified it, thereby fulfilling the requirement that 21 states, of which seven should each have a total tonnage of not less than 1,000,000 g.t.

10. The six largest ship-providing nations — as elected by the conference — were: Greece, the Netherlands, Norway, Sweden, the United Kingdom, the United States. As the six largest ship-using nations, Argentina, Australia, Belgium, Canada, France, and India were elected. See Appendix I, IMCO convention.

11. Doc. E/CONF. 4/29 (1948), p. 1.

12. Article 274; Hudson, IV, 2282, 2320.

13. Doc. E/CONF. 4/SR. Rev. (1948), pp. 69–70. This working party consisted of the delegations of 16 countries.

of shipping, must become parties to it before the convention was to enter into force.[14] In the meantime, the distribution of the world shipping tonnage had undergone further changes, of which the emergence of Liberia as the greatest flag-of-convenience nation and the third largest nation in terms of tonnage was the most notable. The Panamanian fleet had also continued its growth, although not at such a spectacular speed as that of Liberia. At any rate, at the end of 1958 Panama was placed eighth in *Lloyd's Register of Shipping*.[15] The rapidly increasing tonnage registered under the flags of Liberia and Panama caused understandable concern in the traditional European maritime countries that Panama and Liberia would be able to exert or would be used to exert a "disproportionate" influence on international shipping. In 1956, the European shipping circles, in particular British shipowners, had expressed their fear that "by virtue of this technical ownership they [Panama and Liberia] may be able to participate in international discussions and to affect by their vote both maritime law and maritime safety regulations through for instance the (proposed Intergovernmental Maritime Consultative Organization." [16]

Just at the time when the IMCO convention came into effect, the warning was voiced again that "the increasing tonnage registered under the Panlibhon flags gives those countries a potential voting power in intergovernmental shipping discussions out of all proportion to the authority they exercise and the responsibility they bear." [17]

When the first Assembly of the IMCO convened in London on January 6, 1959, it was a foregone conclusion that the European maritime nations would block the election of Panama and Liberia

14. IMCO convention, art. 60. For the information about how the convention came into effect, see ICJ *Pleadings*, Constitution (1960), pp. 161–162. See also UN Press Release IMCO/20, April 4, 1958. See also *International Organization* 12:380 (1958).

15. *Cf.* Table 1. Panama was seventh so far as ships of 1000 gross tons and over were concerned. Subsequently Panama's tonnage decreased to 11th place.

16. This warning is voiced by the United Kingdom Chamber of Shipping in its *Annual Report* (1955). See *The New York Times*, February 20, 1956, p. 46.

17. Robert D. Ropner, chairman of the General Council of British Shipping in a letter to *The Times*, April 3, 1958, p. 13. *Cf.* also the statement of Fábrega of Panama pleading before the ICJ in the case of the Constitution of the Maritime Safety Committee of the IMCO. The Panamanian representative spoke of the anxiety in the European maritime circles because of the increase in tonnage carried in ships flying the Panamanian flag; ICJ *Pleadings*, Constitution (1960), pp. 416–417.

to organs of the new United Nations agency, manifesting thereby their non-recognition of Panama and Liberia as "true" maritime nations. On the other hand, Panama and Liberia, having just ratified the IMCO convention on January 6, 1959, were equally determined to play major roles as maritime nations in the deliberations of the Assembly.

To judge by the 1948 maritime conference, one might suppose that Panama and Liberia would press for representation in the Council, the governing body of the agency, in the periods between the biennial sessions of the Assembly. This supposition had even been confirmed, before IMCO started its session, by Panama's acting permanent delegate to the United Nations, who declared that "Panama looks forward to having a seat on the Council, to which it is entitled under terms of the convention." [18] However, the question of electing Liberia or Panama to the Council was not discussed, since these countries deposited instruments of ratification after the candidatures to the Council had been proposed, and the four vacant places were therefore filled in harmony. Japan and Italy were elected as the "nations having a substantial interest in providing international shipping." They had been proposed by the six members of the Council, elected in 1948 under art. 17(a), because they "clearly surpassed the others in the size of their tonnage." [19] The Soviet Union and the Federal Republic of Germany filled the two remaining seats in the Council reserved for the nations "having a substantial interest in international seaborne trade." [20] The harmonious election of the six members of the Council was only a short lull before the storm, which raged over the election of the Maritime Safety Committee, a major organ of IMCO.[21]

18. *The New York Times,* January 3, 1959, p. 30. The Panamanian spokesman, Jorge E. Illueca, refers to the six-member inner group of "the nations with the largest interest in providing international shipping services" as laid down in art. 17(a) of the IMCO convention.

19. IMCO/A.I/SR. 3 (1959), p. 3. In reply to Weeks of Liberia Sir Gilmour Jenkins, who presided over the committee of six, stated that "it had not been possible to consider the case of Liberia as that country was not a member [of IMCO] at the time of the meeting."

20. IMCO/A.I/SR. 4 (1959), pp. 2–3.

21. The functions and duties of the Maritime Safety Committee are laid down in arts. 29–32 of the IMCO convention.

The legal aspect of the whole controversy is summed up in art. 28 of the convention on IMCO which reads:

(a) The Maritime Safety Committee shall consist of fourteen Members elected by the Assembly from the Members, governments of those nations *having an important interest in maritime safety, of which not less than eight shall be the largest shipowning nations* [emphasis added by the author], and the remainder shall be elected so as to ensure adequate representation of Members, governments of other nations with an important interest in maritime safety, such as nations interested in the supply of large numbers of crews or in the carriage of large numbers of berthed and unberthed passengers, and of major geographical areas.

(b) Members shall be elected for a term of four years and shall be eligible for re-election.

The battle that resulted between the traditional maritime countries and the Panlibhon camp took first of all the form of a dispute over the interpretation of the phrase "the largest shipowning nations." In general terms, the issue was how the size of a nation's shipping fleet was to be estimated—by its registered tonnage or by the amount actually and beneficially owned by the nationals of that state. Panama and Liberia, supported by the United States and a few other non-European nations, contended that the phrase "the [eight] largest shipowning nations" should be interpreted as the eight nations having the largest tonnage registered under their respective national flags, as they were listed in *Lloyd's Register of Shipping*. This would have assured both Liberia and Panama membership in the Maritime Safety Committee, for the tables in *Lloyd's Register of Shipping* (1958) placed Liberia as third and Panama as eighth among the merchant fleets of the world.[22] The opponents of Panlibhon, among whom were virtually all the European members of the IMCO, maintained that the phrase "the [eight] largest shipowning nations" did not necessarily mean the eight nations which had the largest tonnage registered under their respective flags, but rather the nations to whose nationals the vessels really and actually belonged. By forcing such an interpretation the opponents of the flag-of-convenience countries were

22. See IMCO/A.I/Working Paper 5 (1959). (Merchant Fleets of the IMCO members according to the statistics in *Lloyd's Register of Shipping*, 1958.)

attempting to block Liberia and Panama from membership in the Maritime Safety Committee. As a result neither Liberia nor Panama were elected to the Maritime Safety Committee, but the matter was referred by the IMCO Assembly to the International Court of Justice, whose opinion of June 8, 1960, confirming the old established rule of international law that registry is the test of a ship's nationality, constituted a victory for the countries representing the flag-of-convenience point of view.[23]

Even before the election of members of the Maritime Safety Committee began the atmosphere in the lobbies of the Assembly was full of tension, and it was generally expected that an all-out fight would develop for the seats in the committee.[24] The United States delegation put the matter rather mildly in its proposal for the establishment of a "Provisional Maritime Safety Committee," stating that "informal conversations have developed the fact that there is considerable difference in certain interpretations of art. 28 "crystallized in two draft resolutions proposed before the discussion of the matter by the two sides in the dispute — the anti-flag-of-convenience camp represented by the United Kingdom, the other camp by Liberia. The draft resolution of the United Kingdom, noting the list prepared by the Secretary General,[25] which reproduced the registered tonnage of each member of

23. The legal issue argued at the IMCO Assembly touches the problems discussed in the preceding chapter and therefore, for reasons of systematic and logical arrangement, is dealt with in this chapter. On the other hand, the proceedings at the IMCO session, held almost one year after the Geneva Conference on the Law of the Sea, clearly showed the influence of the new concept of genuine link and might as well be included within the discussion of the new trends tending to limit the states' competence to grant nationality to merchant vessels. Here, as was mentioned above, the problem is approached as one connected with registry as the test of a vessel's nationality.

It seems worthwhile to present the sequence of events relating to the flag-of-convenience conflict within the IMCO. This sequence eventually led to an advisory opinion of the World Court on the matter directly bearing on the essential issues of nationality of ships in general and of the Panlibhon countries in particular.

24. Interviews with the Panamanian and Liberian delegates on the prospects of electing Panama and Liberia to the Maritime Safety Committee; *The New York Times,* January 11, 1959, sec. 5, p. 11. The delegates felt very strongly on the issue, and they deemed it impossible to believe that there could be a movement to exclude their countries from the committee.

25. IMCO/A.I/Working Paper 5 (1959). There was no challenge to the effect that the figures in this paper were identical with the figures shown in *Lloyd's Register of Shipping* (1958).

IMCO after *Lloyd's* tables, proposed to take a separate vote for each of the eight places covered by the phrase "the largest shipowning nations," and to declare as elected those eight nations that attained a majority. Voting, under the draft resolution, was to be in the order in which the nations appeared in the Secretary General's list.[26] Obviously, the purpose of the resolution was to bar Liberia and Panama from the Maritime Safety Committee. Neither of these countries had much chance to be elected if the seats were voted for separately, virtually all the European nations being determined to vote against them.

The Liberian counterresolution proposed to determine the eight largest shipowning nations by reference to the issue of *Lloyd's Register of Shipping* current on the date of election. The Liberian proposal was based on the consideration that the criterion of tonnage was used in art. 60 for the purpose of bringing the convention into force ("The present Convention shall enter into force on the date when 21 States, of which 7 shall each have a total tonnage of not less than 1,000,000 gross tons of shipping, have become parties to the Convention in accordance with Article 57."), and that questions might be raised as to the interpretation of the expression "shipowning nations." Questions might be raised as well about the nature of the evidence by reference to which the size of a shipowning nation should be determined and Liberia asserted that no uniform rule prevailed in the maritime laws of the members of IMCO as to the nature of the connection between a vessel and the state under whose flag it sailed. The draft resolution also referred to the great difficulties of identifying the nationality of the beneficial owners of vessels owned by corporations, which precluded the Assembly from adopting ownership by nationals as the criterion of a shipowning nation. As the procedural basis of her resolution, Liberia put forward art. 55 of the convention providing that questions concerning the interpretation of the convention should be referred for settlement to the Assembly.[27]

In an attempt at the first session of the Assembly to avert the defeat of Liberia and Panama in their applications as candidates to the Maritime Safety Committee, the United States offered a

26. IMCO/A.I/Working Paper 6 (1959).
27. IMCO/A.I/Working Paper 8 (1959).

resolution suggesting that the election of a permanent Maritime Safety Committee be deferred until the second session of the Assembly in 1961, and proposed that, since under art. 16(c), the Assembly was competent "to establish any temporary . . . subsidiary bodies it may consider to be necessary," the Assembly should establish at the first session a Provisional Maritime Safety Committee. This provisional committee would be open to all members of the organization desiring to participate and willing to send technically qualified representatives to its meetings. This, of course, would have permitted the membership of Panama, Liberia, and even Honduras. The American proposal suggested that when in 1961, at the second assembly, the Maritime Safety Committee was elected, its members would be those which had demonstrated great interest in the work of the provisional committee. The proposal pointed out that during the first Assembly meeting the degree of interest provided for in art. 28(a) as the basic criterion for the election to the Maritime Safety Committee was impossible to ascertain accurately. Taking account of the "considerable differences" in the interpretation of art. 28(a), the proposal expressed the hope that by electing a provisional committee time would be given to work out agreement on the differing interpretations, and also to examine the matter thoroughly from the legal standpoint. "Attempt to resolve these differences at this first meeting of the Assembly could produce very undesirable results which might injure the Organization and the cause of maritime safety generally," the proposal of the United States warned.[28] However, the American resolution was defeated by fourteen votes to twelve, with two abstentions.[29]

28. IMCO/A.I/Working Paper 7 (1959). The proposal also gave other reasons for the establishment of a provisional Maritime Safety Committee, but these other reasons are not directly relevant to the issue of flags of convenience.

29. Those voting in favor were: Panama, the United States, Argentina, China (Nationalist), Dominican Republic, Ecuador, Haiti, Honduras, Iran, Israel, Japan, Liberia. Those voting against were: Switzerland, Turkey, the United Kingdom, Australia, Belgium, Canada, Federal Republic of Germany, France, Greece, Ireland, Italy, the Netherlands, Norway, Pakistan. The U.S.S.R. and the United Arab Republic abstained. India was barred from voting because she had made certain reservations regarding her membership, and other members of IMCO had not yet accepted these reservations. See IMCO/A.I/3 Rev. 1/Add. 1 (1959). It is very possible that, if India had been voting, the United States resolution would have obtained the majority, because India was in favor of the resolution and would probably have been joined by other nations — *e.g.*, the United Arab Republic. See IMCO/A.I/SR. 7

After the defeat of the American proposal, the delegate of the United Kingdom submitted his draft resolution, but, before it was voted upon, the Assembly examined the consolidated text of the amendments thereto, proposed by Liberia and the United States.[30] Under the consolidated American-Liberian amendment to the draft resolution of the United Kingdom, the eight largest shipowning nations for purposes of art. 28(a) were those appearing first in *Lloyd's Register of Shipping*, namely the United States of America, the United Kingdom, Liberia, Norway, Japan, Italy, the Netherlands, and Panama, which therefore should be automatically elected to the Maritime Safety Committee.

The consolidated text of the Liberian and United States amendment was rejected after two separate votes were taken on para. I and on paras. II and III, respectively.[31] After this second defeat for the flag-of-convenience camp, a battle along the procedural lines followed, since the delegate of Liberia, claiming that a new legal situation had arisen as a result of the voting, submitted that the proposal he had made at the previous meeting, that an advisory opinion of the International Court of Justice be sought on the interpretation of art. 28, should take precedence over the voting on the United Kingdom draft resolution, and over the elections to the Maritime Safety Committee.[32] He also proposed that until the Assembly should receive the advisory opinion of the Court, an Interim Committee on Safety at Sea be established for the purpose of discharging the functions of the Maritime Safety Committee. The Liberian motion being found out of order, the president of the Assembly (Mr. Audette of Canada) ruled that the voting on the United Kingdom draft resolution should proceed forthwith. The resolution was adopted by eighteen votes to nine,

(1959), p. 10. Therefore the criticism of the action of the American delegation, which supported the United Kingdom motion to bar India from voting and thereby deprived itself of allies in voting, seems to be not unfounded, although the chairman of the American delegation rebutted these charges. See *The New York Times*, February 15, 1959, p. 88. Mexico and Burma were not in attendance.

30. IMCO/A.I/Working Papers 6 & 11 (1959). This text amended the amendment that was tabled earlier by Liberia; IMCO/A.I/Working Paper 10 (1959).

31. Paragraphs I, II, and III were rejected by 17 votes to 11. Favoring the amendment were: Pakistan, Panama, the United States, China, Dominican Republic, Ecuador, Haiti, Honduras, Iran, Israel, Liberia. For the details of the alignment of the votes, see IMCO/A.I/SR. 8 (1959), pp. 5–6.

32. See IMCO/A.I/SR. 7 (1959), p. 13; IMCO/A.I/Working Paper 6 (1959).

with one abstention.[33] Subsequently, the Assembly voted separately on the eight countries to be elected to the Maritime Safety Committee as the largest shipowning nations under art. 28, in the order given in *Lloyd's* 1958 Tables. The United States and the United Kingdom were each elected by 27 votes, with one abstention.[34] Liberia's candidature was rejected, only eleven votes being in favor, fourteen against, with three countries abstaining.[35] Norway, Japan, Italy, and the Netherlands were elected without any opposing vote, but with Liberia, Panama, and Argentina abstaining.[36] The vote in the case of Panama, the eighth nation on *Lloyd's* list, was negative, with nine votes in favor, fourteen against, and five abstentions.[37] Since so far only six nations had obtained the majority of votes necessary for election to the Maritime Safety Committee, the voting continued, with France and the Federal Republic of Germany, the next nations on Lloyd's list being elected by equal votes of 23 in favor, 2 against, and 3 abstentions.[38] To

33. IMCO/A.I/SR. 8 (1959), pp. 8–11. See also the statements of the delegates of the United Kingdom and the Netherlands; *id.*, pp. 8–9. The Liberian motion was supported only by the delegate of the Dominican Republic. Panama, the United States, Argentina, the Dominican Republic, Ecuador, Haiti, Honduras, Israel, and Liberia voted against the United Kingdom resolution; China abstained.

34. Argentina abstained from voting altogether because, in the opinion of her delegate, "the only possible legal solution was to refer the matter to the ICJ. IMCO/A.I/SR. 9 (1959), p. 3.

35. Honduras, Iran, Israel, Liberia, Pakistan, Panama, the United States, China, the Dominican Republic, Ecuador, and Haiti supported Liberia. Ireland, Italy, Japan, the Netherlands, Norway, Turkey, the United Arab Republic, the United Kingdom, Australia, Belgium, Canada, Federal Republic of Germany, France, and Greece voted against Liberia's election. Switzerland, the U.S.S.R., and Argentina abstained. IMCO/A.I/SR. 8 (1959), p. 13.

36. *Id.*, pp. 14–17.

37. Honduras, Iran, Israel, Pakistan, the United States, China, the Dominican Republic, Ecuador, and Haiti voted for Panama. Ireland, Italy, Japan, the Netherlands, Norway, Turkey, the United Arab Republic, the United Kingdom, Australia, Belgium, Canada, the Federal Republic of Germany, France, and Greece were opposed to the election of Panama. Among those abstaining were Liberia, Panama, Switzerland, the U.S.S.R., and Argentina; *id.*, p. 18. The delegates of the two flag-of-convenience countries explained that they had abstained from voting on all the nations after the failure of Liberia because the remainder of the election proceedings was, in their opinion, null and void in the light of art. 28 of the convention. See the statements of the delegates of Liberia (*id.*, p. 21) and Panama (IMCO/A.I/SR. 9 (1959), p. 2).

38. Honduras and the United States voted against, and Liberia, Panama, and Argentina abstained; IMCO/S.I/SR 8 (1959), p. 20. The delegate of the United States was opposing France and the Federal Republic of Germany "only as two of the first eight members, to be consistent with the legal principle it had maintained throughout, but certainly was not opposing them for election to other seats on the Committee" (*id.*, p. 21). The delegate of Honduras explained that he had voted against

the six seats left were elected Argentina, Canada, Greece, Pakistan, the U.S.S.R., and the United Arab Republic. The Panamanian delegate refused the nomination proposed by the Dominican delegate, regarding the election as null and void.[39]

After the legality of the election had been challenged by Liberia, Panama, Honduras, and the United States, the next objective of the Panlibhon nations was to secure the referral of the legal points in dispute to the ICJ for an advisory opinion. For this purpose the Liberian delegate introduced a draft resolution under which the Assembly should, acting under art. 56 of the convention, refer the legal issues arising from the interpretation of art. 28 to the Court. Also the formulation of the questions to be put to the Court should be referred to the legal committee and then to the Assembly "for approval."[40] The Assembly's consensus, the Netherlands excepted,[41] was for referring the case to the ICJ. After a discussion in the legal committee, a resolution to this effect, firmly supported also by the United Kingdom,[42] was adopted by the Assembly with one abstention.

With respect to the interpretation of art. 28 regulating the election of the eight "largest" shipowning nations to the Maritime Safety Committee of IMCO, the convention lays down two criteria. The first of these — the governments of the shipowning nations must have "an important interest in maritime safety" — was to be satisfied by all 14 members of the committee. The second was that, of these 14, "not less than eight shall be the largest shipowning

those two countries because, in his opinion, Liberia and Panama were entitled to membership on the committee, and two of the eight seats should therefore have remained unfilled pending an advisory opinion of the ICJ; IMCO/A.I/SR. 9 (1959), p. 2.

39. *Id.*, p. 5. Honduras, the third flag-of-convenience country, succeeded in gaining one vote. The criteria laid down in art. 28(a) for the six members are that they "shall be elected so as to ensure adequate representation of Members, governments of other nations [of nations other than the eight largest ones] with an important interest in maritime safety, such as nations interested in the supply of large numbers of crews or in the carriage of large numbers of berthed and unberthed passengers, and of major geographical areas."

40. IMCO/A.I/Working Paper 12 (1959). The words "for approval" were changed to "for further action." IMCO/A.I/SR. 9 (1959), p. 6.

41. IMCO/A.I/SR. 10 (1959), p. 3. The Netherlands delegate was referring to art. 55 of the convention providing for the settlement of disputes by the Assembly, and art. 16(j), under which the Assembly might refer to the Council for consideration or decision any matters within the scope of IMCO.

42. IMCO/A.I/SR. 9 (1959), p. 7; IMCO/A.I/SR. 10 (1959), p. 4.

nations." The anti-flag-of-convenience group of nations assumed a priori the existence of certain facts prejudicial to Liberia and Panama, from which a conclusion was drawn that those two nations should not be elected to the Maritime Safety Committee. Although "there was clearly no question of dealing with the problem of flags of convenience, which lay outside the limits of (the) discussion," [43] in reality the battle fought was largely one of prestige, in which the recognition of the flags of convenience was at stake. The delegate of the Netherlands, reminding the Assembly that his government deplored "the institution of the so-called flags of convenience," openly stated that he would vote against the Liberian and American amendments, because to support them would be "tantamount to accepting the institution of flags of convenience." At another juncture he said that "an important matter of shipping policy lay behind the question and involved more important factors than merely legal considerations." [44] Therefore, the interpretation of art. 28 was approached by the traditional maritime countries with the "special position of Liberia and Panama" as "totally different from that of the other nations at the top of the world tonnage list" taken as an established fact.[45] This element of political bias appeared also at the later stage of the case, namely in the statements submitted to the International Court of Justice which — as the Court said — "have shown that, linked with the question put to it, there are others of a political nature." [46]

The wide divergence of views on the relevant requirements of art. 28(a) can be clearly seen from the following comparison of the arguments of both groups.

The nations opposed to the flags of convenience maintained that Liberia and Panama did not meet any of the criteria laid down in art. 28. Their argument was as follows:

As to the first criterion set forth in art. 28, that is, "governments of those nations having an important interest in maritime safety,"

43. The statement of the delegate of the United Kingdom; IMCO/A.I/SR. 7 (1959), p. 2.

44. IMCO/A.I/Working Paper 11 (1959); IMCO/A.I/SR. 8 (1959), p. 3; IMCO/A.I/SR. 10 (1959), p. 3.

45. IMCO/A.I/SR. 7 (1959), pp. 2, 6. Therefore the interpretation of the delegate of the United Kingdom was found "tendentious" by the delegate of the Dominican Republic who sided with the flag-of-convenience nations; *id.*, p. 10.

46. [1960] ICJ Rep. 153.

one had to consider how far *governments* were interested in maritime questions and to what extent they were able, through their knowledge and experience, to make contributions in various fields connected with maritime safety. Liberia and Panama did not satisfy that criterion because their governments did not have the necessary technical knowledge and were not at present in a position to make any important contribution to maritime safety. If Liberia and Panama made progress in the field, there would exist the possibility of their entry to the committee at a later date.

With regard to those countries' interest in questions of maritime safety, it was undeniable that the vessels registered there were among the most modern in the world. However, this was so not because those governments were interested in maritime safety, but because those fleets belonged to foreign shipowners and because Liberia and Panama left questions of maritime safety and administration to the very experienced classification societies. The matter was not to elect United States shipowners or the classification societies to the Maritime Safety Committee, but the governments, and the governments of Liberia and Panama were not sufficiently equipped for membership in a highly technical body like the Maritime Safety Committee. The delegations of those governments were equal only to the task of the Assembly, and, besides, the committee acting under art. 32 might invite any member of the IMCO to participate, without vote, in its deliberations on any matter of particular concern to that member.[47]

As to the second criterion, namely, that of "the largest shipowning nations" the delegations of the traditional maritime nations based their interpretation on the notion of the genuine link accepted at the United Nations Conference on the Law of the Sea held in 1958. They agreed that art. 28 in fact embodied an imperative criterion that "not less than eight [members of the Maritime Safety Committee] shall be the largest shipowning nations," but, at the same time, claimed that the article did not provide any guidance for the interpretation of that criterion, and accordingly the Assembly was in duty bound to interpret it. The words "eight shall be the largest shipowning nations" provided no basis

47. The statement of the delegate of the United Kingdom; IMCO/A.I/Sr. 7 (1959), pp. 2–4. See also the statement of the delegate of Norway; *id.*, p. 6.

for any individual member to enter a claim to sit on the committee. There was no reserved seat on the committee for any particular country.[48]

Interpreting the phrase "the largest shipowning nations" in the light of the genuine-link concept, the majority of the Assembly, as represented by the opinions of the delegates of the United Kingdom, Norway, and the Netherlands, contended that the concept of the largest shipowning nations was not necessarily identical with that of the nations having the largest registered tonnage. A country's registered tonnage might in no way reflect its actual importance as a shipowning nation.[49] For the United Kingdom delegate the expression "largest shipowning nations" was used for the first time, but it was perfectly clear. "Vessels had really to belong to the countries in question, which was obviously not the case with Panama and Liberia." It would be in accordance with both the letter and the spirit of art. 28, and large fleets flying flags of convenience would be adequately represented on the Maritime Safety Committee if those countries whose nationals had the owning and controlling interests in those ships were elected to the committee.[50]

In the interpretation of the anti-Panlibhon camp, non-admission of Panama and Liberia to the Maritime Safety Committee resulted from the negation of both criteria with regard to those two countries. If Panama and Liberia, as was assumed by their opponents, did not have an "important interest in maritime safety," they could not be among the 14 members of the committee, and *ipso facto* were not among the selected inner 8. And, again, Liberia and Panama were not considered by their opponents as "largest shipowning nations," and therefore they could not have important interest in maritime safety, having, in the eyes of their opponents, virtually no fleets.[51]

48. This was expressly stated by the delegate of the Netherlands; IMCO/A.I/SR. 10 (1959), p. 3. Similarly, the delegate of the U.S.S.R., explaining his votes, stated that he had abstained from voting on Panama and Liberia because discussion in the Assembly had shown that the existence of a genuine link between the states of Liberia and Panama and the ships flying their flags was disputed by a number of delegations and that the principle of genuine link clearly applied to the interpretation of art. 28; IMCO/A.I/SR. 9 (1959), pp. 2, 3.

49. IMCO/A.I/SR. 7 (1959), p. 12; IMCO/A.I/SR. 8 (1959), pp. 2–3.

50. IMCO/A.I/SR. 7 (1959), p. 3.

51. The argument of the anti-Panlibhon group of nations was further exposed in

The interpretation of art. 28(a) as understood by the delegates of Liberia and Panama, as well as the United States and other countries supporting the flags of convenience, was as follows:

The two criteria of eligibility set forth in art. 28 were not independent of each other, and therefore the largest shipowning nations were *ipso facto* those having an important interest in maritime safety.[52] The requirement of governments "having an important interest in maritime safety" could be understood to refer only to the governments which had given proof of the widest expert knowledge in maritime safety matters. It was practically impossible to grade 14, or even 8, nations from that point of view, and such a criterion must, therefore, be rejected as too vague. On the other hand, important interest in maritime safety was clearly established by active participation in international regulation of the problem of maritime safety or by adoption of codes based on internationally approved safety regulations.[53] Even if the criteria of important interest in maritime safety be taken independently, Liberia and Panama were capable of contributing to maritime safety, possessed the necessary expertise, and had many highly qualified persons in their service who were able to make a valuable contribution to the Maritime Safety Committee's work.[54] The largest shipowning nations being *ipso facto* those

---

the written and oral statements in the proceedings before the ICJ. See ICJ *Pleadings*, Constitution (1960), as follows: France, pp. 124–132 (written statement); Italy, pp. 219–226, 331–350 (written and oral statements); Netherlands, pp. 247–252, 351–359, 430, 439–440 (written and oral statements); Norway, pp. 242–246, 360–369 (written and oral statements); Switzerland, pp. 216–218 (written statement); United Kingdom, pp. 228–241, 370–394, 431–433 (written and oral statements). In addition, Belgium, which did not submit any argument of its own, informed the Court that its point of view followed that of the great maritime countries [i.e., European countries] (*id.*, p. 23). Denmark declared concurrence in the point of view set out in the statement of the United Kingdom (*id.*, p. 227). For a summary of the argument of the anti-Panlibhon group see [1960] ICJ Rep. 156–157.

52. The statement of the Liberian delegate; IMCO/A.I/SR. 8 (1959), p. 4, and the statement by the United States delegate; *id.*, p. 2.

53. The statement of the United States delegate; IMCO/A.I/SR. 7 (1959), p. 9. The impossibility of ascertaining accurately the degree of interest in maritime safety was one of the reasons why the United States submitted the proposal for the establishment of a provisional Maritime Safety Committee; IMCO/A.I/Working Paper 7 (1959), p. 3.

54. The statements by the delegates of Liberia and Panama; IMCO/A.I/SR. 8 (1959), p. 4; IMCO/A.I/SR. 7 (1959), p. 6. The Panamanian delegate, Alfaro, referring to the remarks of the representative of the United Kingdom about the incapability of Liberia and Panama to contribute to maritime safety, drew attention

having an important interest in maritime safety, the next task was to determine the eight largest shipowning nations to be members of the Maritime Safety Committee.

As interpreted by the flag-of-convenience nations and the United States, the eight largest shipowning nations were the first eight nations shown on the *Lloyd's Register of Shipping*, because the criterion of registered tonnage was the sole criterion for judging the size of a fleet. The election of the eight largest shipowning nations under art. 28 of the IMCO convention was not an election in the usual sense of the word, for, once those eight nations had been determined in the list contained in the official document of the organization, the Assembly was bound to elect them and electing others would be a breach of the convention. Therefore, all the eight nations should be voted upon as a whole, not separately. The meaning of art. 28(a) could not be assumed to be ambiguous, and even if it were so for purposes of discussion, the criterion of the "largest shipowning nations" could not refer to the nationality of the owning corporation, since it was the country whose flag the vessel was flying that was directly interested in its safety, rather than the country in which the corporation was legally constituted. But even if the criterion of the nationality of the shipowners were acceptable, both Liberia and Panama would still have to be elected, because from the legal point of view practically all the Panamanian and the majority of Liberian vessels were owned by national corporations, which still placed Liberia as fifth on the list of *Lloyd's Register,* and Panama as eighth. As to the criterion of the nationality of the beneficial owners of the vessels, that also had to be discarded because of the difficulty of establishing stock ownership of corporations. Besides, quite apart from the case of Liberia, and Panama, there were many ships flying, for example, the British flag, which in fact were not controlled by the United Kingdom interests.

The phrase "largest shipowning nations" could not, of course, mean that the vessels must be owned by the state. Gross registered tonnage was, therefore, the only evidence by reference to which

---

to the fact that the modern world was changing quickly. He pointed out that, *e.g.*, prior to the nationalization of the Suez Canal, Egypt had been considered incapable of operating the canal and yet one year later, everyone was compelled to admit that Egypt was doing so quite successfully (*ibid*).

the size of a shipowning nation should be determined. Further corroboration of this interpretation of art. 28 was found by the flag-of-convenience camp in the fact that art. 28 stipulated that not less than eight of the members of the committee should be the *largest* shipowning nations, and not merely *large*. Therefore the eight states did not stand as candidates, but should be elected automatically. Article 28 was drawn up in mandatory terms, and was not merely the expression of a desirable result. The acceptance of the criterion of registered tonnage was further substantiated by the argument that nothing in the preliminary drafts indicated that the phrase had any meaning other than nations with the largest registered tonnage.[55]

As a result of the differences of opinion as to the interpretation of art. 28(a) of the IMCO convention discussed above, the case of the constitution of the Maritime Safety Committee of IMCO was referred to the International Court of Justice for an advisory opinion. This was done under art. 56, providing that "any legal question which cannot be settled as provided in art. 55 [56] shall be referred by the Organization to the International Court of Justice for an advisory opinion in accordance with art. 96 of the Charter of the United Nations."

The delegate of the Netherlands expressed some doubt as to whether submitting the matter to the Court was "justifiable from both the legal and the policy standpoint." [57] However, his doubts do not seem to have been well founded. Article 55 of the conven-

55. The argument of the Panlibhon group was fully set forth in the statements presented before the ICJ. See ICJ *Pleadings,* Constitution (1960), as follows: Panama, pp. 165–215, 302–319, 409–424, 437 (written and oral statements); Liberia, pp. 33–113, 269–301, 395–408, 434–436 (written and oral statements); United States, pp. 114–163, 320–330, 425–429, 438 (written and oral statements). In its written statement India favored the Panlibhon stand (*id.,* pp. 253–259). China, in its written statement, declared that the *Lloyd's Register* could be adopted as a basis for designating the eight "largest shipowning nations," and that all shipowning nations so designated were nations "having an important interest in maritime safety" within the meaning of art. 28(a). See *id.*, p. 164.

56. Article 55 (which with art. 56 constitutes part XV of the convention, entitled "Interpretation") reads: "Any question or dispute concerning the interpretation or application of the Convention shall be referred for settlement to the Assembly, or shall be settled in such other manner as the parties to the dispute agree. Nothing in this article shall preclude the Council or the Maritime Safety Committee from settling any such question or dispute that may arise during the exercise of their functions."

57. IMCO/A.I/SR. 9 (1959), p. 6.

tion entitles "the parties to the dispute" concerning the interpretation of the convention to refer the question on the dispute to the Assembly, or settle it in such other manner as they agree. In the case in question, the Assembly, confronted with the dispute, agreed to settle it by referring the matter to the Court. The Assembly was entitled to do so because the question was legal and could not be settled as provided in art. 55.

The formulation of the request passed through three stages. Initially, the Liberian delegate formulated it in three points as follows:

> I. Is gross registered tonnage the appropriate test for determining the size of a ship-owning nation for the purpose of electing the eight largest ship-owning nations under art. 28 of the Convention?
>
> II. Alternatively, is registration in the name of nationals the appropriate test for the purpose referred to in question I above?
>
> III. If the answer to either question is in the affirmative, and having regard to the fact that by the first test Liberia ranks third and Panama ranks eighth among States, and by the second test Liberia ranks fifth and Panama ranks eighth among States, is the Assembly under a duty to elect Liberia and Panama to the Maritime Safety Committee? [58]

The formulation of the United Kingdom delegate was similar, but emphasized the problem of whether tonnage is the sole criterion, and did not mention Liberia and Panama explicitly. It read:

> I. Must the "eight largest ship-owning nations" be determined solely according to the tonnage on the national register?
>
> II. If so, is the Assembly under a legal obligation to elect to the Maritime Safety Committee the governments of the nations having the largest registered tonnage? [59]

This formulation, however, reproduced only half of the legal issue to be solved in the interpretation of art. 28. It dealt only with the second criterion of the "largest shipowning nations," and did not refer to the Court the question of the criterion of "important interest in maritime safety" which was also in issue.

Therefore, the question as it was eventually phrased: "Is the Maritime Safety Committee of the Intergovernmental Maritime Consultative Organization, which was elected on January 15, 1959,

58. IMCO/A.I/SR. 8 (1959), p. 7.
59. IMCO/A.I/SR. 10 (1959), p. 4.

constituted in accordance with the Convention for the Establishment of the Organization?"[60] rendered in the briefest and most comprehensive way the essence of the dispute, leaving to the Court the detailed elaboration of the various possible modalities of the legal issue in question. The request also satisfied the requirement that it should contain "an exact statement of the question upon which an opinion is required."[61]

The opinion of the Court was given on June 8, 1960. Having discussed the circumstances in which the issue came to it, the Court, first of all, dealt with the question whether art. 28(a) granted the IMCO Assembly a discretionary power to determine which members of the IMCO had "an important interest in maritime safety," and consequently to exclude as unqualified for election those nations which in the Assembly's judgment did not have such an interest. The anti-Panlibhon group of nations in the IMCO Assembly asserted that the Assembly had that power, and that the expression "elected" implied a notion of choice and a free appraisal of the qualifications of each member to be elected both in the eight largest ship-owning nations group and in that of the remainder of six. This approach, according to the Court, "assumes a meaning to be accorded to the word 'elected' and then applies that meaning to Art. 28(a) and interprets its provisions accordingly. In so doing it places in a subordinate position the specific provision of the Article in relation to the eight 'largest ship-owning nations.' "[62]

In its argument the Court started from the proposition that the word "elected" in art. 28 must be interpreted in the light of the context in which it was used. As in arts. 16(d) and 17 (c)(d), so in art. 28 the margin of choice allowed to the Assembly in relation to the election of the members of IMCO to the respective organs was no greater than the terms of the relevant articles permitted. Applying the well established rule of interpretation that words must be read in their natural and ordinary meaning, in the

60. IMCO/A.I/Working Paper 20 (1959); [1960] ICJ Rep. 151.
61. The Statute of the ICJ, art. 65, para. 2. The Chinese delegate abstained from voting on the resolution submitting the request for an advisory opinion because he was not convinced "that the question put to the International Court of Justice was so drafted that the Court could render an advisory opinion," but he did not give any reasons for his view; IMCO/A.I/SR 11 (1959), pp. 2–3.
62. [1960] ICJ Rep. 158.

sense which they would normally have in their context, and that resort to other methods of construction must be had only if the words were in any way ambiguous,[63] the Court came to the conclusion that "the draftsmen deliberately contemplated that the preponderant control of the Committee was in all circumstances to be vested in "the largest ship-owning nations." [64]

The words "of which not less than eight shall be the largest ship-owning nations," read in their natural and ordinary meaning, involved an obligatory designation and expressed the underlying principle of art. 28(a) that the largest ship-owning nations should be in preponderance on the committee. "Whichever were the largest ship-owning nations they were necessarily to be appointed to the Committee." [65]

As to the criterion of "an important interest in maritime safety" which must be satisfied by all the fourteen members of the committee the Court stated that "in the context of the whole provision, possession of this interest is implied in relation to the eight largest ship-owning nations as a consequence of the language employed. The particular condition of being one of the eight such nations describes the nature of the required interest in maritime safety and constitutes that interest." [66]

The Court rightly found this interpretation to accord with the structure of the relevant article. Indeed the structure and the contents of art. 28 show that in the case of the second group of nations the interest has its source in the fact of supplying large numbers of crews or in the carriage of large numbers of passengers.[67] In the case of the first group this interest is manifested simply by the fact that the members of this group are "the [say, eight] largest ship-owning nations." Thus, in the second group there are crews and passengers as elements protected by maritime safety, and in the first group the emphasis is laid on ships. Consequently, the conclusion must be drawn that the first group, by

63. Competence of the General Assembly for the Admission of a State to the United Nations [1950], ICJ Rep. 8.

64. [1960] ICJ Rep. 160.

65. *Id.*, 161. *Contra:* Dissenting Opinion of President Klaestad (*id.*, 173); Dissenting Opinion of Judge Moreno Quintana (*id.*, 177).

66. *Id.*, 161.

67. The clause including nations interested in the supply of crews and carriage of passengers was added to the draft at the maritime conference in 1948 at the request of India and Pakistan. See UN Doc. E/CONF.4/SR. Rev. (1948), p. 78.

owning the largest shipping of all the members of IMCO, *eo ipso* has an important interest in maritime safety.[68] As the Court put it "that [the largest ship-owning nations] each possessed an important interest in maritime safety was accepted as axiomatic; it was inherent in their status of the eight largest ship-owning nations." [69]

One could add to the Court's argument that from the standpoint of logic there was no need for the delegates of the Netherlands, the United Kingdom and Norway to use the argument that Liberia and Panama were not sufficiently equipped to participate in the work of the Maritime Safety Committee.[70] If, as the opponents of Liberia and Panama contended, those two countries were not among the eight largest ship-owning nations, their fleets being owned by foreigners, then Panama and Liberia had virtually no mercantile marines at all. Consequently, they could not have any important interest in maritime safety.[71] What was, then, the use of having maritime safety experts or using their absence as argument? If the anti-flag-of-convenience camp had been consistent, it should have simply stated that Liberia and Panama had no fleets at all (since such is the situation from its point of view, the ultimate ownership of these fleets being vested outside Liberia and Panama) and had no reason to be interested in the matters of maritime safety.[72]

The Court supported its argument also by reference to the *travaux préparatoires* which had taken place in the United Maritime Consultative Council, and which were discussed above.[73]

68. See Boczek, "Flags of Convenience," an unpublished Ph.D. thesis submitted to the Department of Government of Harvard University in May 1960. The argument of the ICJ is almost identical and also refers to the "structure" of the article. *Cf.* [1960] ICJ Rep. 160.

69. [1960] ICJ Rep. 161.

70. This was quite apart from the fact that the objection was denied by Liberia and Panama.

71. Panama and Liberia do not supply large crews, nor are they interested in the carriage of large numbers of passengers.

72. To the argument of the United Kingdom delegate that the governments of Liberia and Panama were not interested in maritime safety because they left these problems to classification societies, one could again reply that under the Convention for the Safety of Life at Sea of 1948 inspection and survey of ships might be entrusted by the government of the state of registry to special organizations, the respective governments guaranteeing the completeness and efficiency of the inspection and survey; Regulation 6, Annex to the Convention; 3 U.S.T 3450; T.I.A.S. 2495; 164 U.N.T.S. 113.

73. [1960] ICJ Rep. 161–164.

The first part of the Court's argument referring to the words "of which not less than eight shall be the largest ship-owning nations" ended with the conclusion that the words in question "have a mandatory and imperative sense and precisely carry out the intention of the framers of the Convention." [74]

The next question to be solved by the Court was the meaning of the words "the largest ship-owning nations" which was crucial for the interpretation of art. 28(a). There was general agreement that art. 28(a) embodied an imperative criterion and, hence, that the first group of the members of the Maritime Safety Committee should consist of not less than eight *largest* ship-owning nations.[75] Incidentally, this does not necessarily mean the eight largest ship-owning nations of the world, but the eight largest members of IMCO. However, when the Assembly met in 1959 all the major maritime nations were members of the new agency.

In approaching the problem the Court could choose one of the following ways: either apply an objective test which could be accepted as the basis of the measurement of the ship-owning status of a nation, and which would make it possible to assess a comparative size *vis à vis* other nations, owners of tonnage, or else find that the IMCO Assembly was bound by no ascertainable criteria and had the authority to appraise by its discretion which were ship-owning nations and which were the largest among them, by looking "at the realities" on the basis of "true situation."

The latter solution was represented by the anti-Panlibhon group of the IMCO Assembly, in particular by the Netherlands and the United Kingdom. In the written statement of the United Kingdom it was suggested that

> The expression "the largest ship-owning nations" has no apparent clear-cut or technical meaning. . . . It is submitted that the intention of those words was to enable the Assembly in the process of election to look at the realities of the situation and to determine according to its own judgment, whether or not candidates for election to the Maritime Safety Committee could properly be regarded as the "largest ship-owning nations" in a real and substantial sense . . . these words, while intended to guide the Assembly, were at the same time deliberately framed so as

74. [1960] ICJ Rep. 165.

75. This, in fact, was admitted by the delegate of the Netherlands; IMCO/A.I/SR. 10 (1959), p. 2.

to enable the Assembly to deal with the matter on the basis of the true situation and the real interest in maritime safety of the State concerned.[76]

Similarly in the opinion of the Netherlands government set out in its written statement it was said that

the term "ship-owning nation" is . . . not suitable for legal analysis; it cannot be decomposed into elements which have any specific legal connotation . . . even the fact that the merchant fleet flying the flag of a particular State is owned by nationals of that State cannot in itself qualify that State as a ship-owning nation. . . .[77]

This solution to the problem, in its vagueness and contradictions so reminiscent of the notion of genuine link was with emphasis rejected by the Court which stated:

If Article 28(a) were intended to confer upon the Assembly such an authority, enabling it to choose the eight largest ship-owning nations, uncontrolled by any objective test of any kind, whether it be of tonnage registration or ownership by nationals or any other, the mandatory words "not less than eight shall be the largest ship-owning nations" would be left without significance. To give to the Article such a construction would mean that the structure built into the Article to ensure the predominance on the Committee of "the" largest ship-owning nations in the ratio of at least eight to six would be undermined and would collapse. The Court is unable to accept an interpretation which would have such a result.

In order to determine which nations are the largest ship-owning nations, it is apparent that some basis of measurement must be applied. . . .[78]

The Court decided that tonnage possessed by a nation was the only practical means of measuring the size of ship-owning nations. However, this was not yet the answer to the problem under consideration. The next question was in what sense art. 28(a) contemplated tonnage as owned by or belonging to the largest ship-owning nations.

To begin with, the Court rejected the possibility that the phrase "ship-owning nations" meant ownership by the state (government) itself. In this respect the Court, naturally enough, shared the

76. [1960] ICJ Rep. 166 (as quoted by the Court). See also ICJ *Pleadings*, Constitution (1960), p. 239.
77. ICJ *Pleadings*, Constitution (1960), pp. 249–250.
78. [1960] ICJ Rep. 161.

general opinion that the criterion of the ownership by the state would displace the maritime nations whose fleets were owned primarily not by government or its agencies.

For this reason only two meanings of the phrase in question could — according to the Court — be seriously considered. Either it referred to the tonnage beneficially owned by the nationals of a state or to the registered tonnage of a state regardless of its private or state ownership. One can note that the Court did not consider the test of ownership as such (the "formal" ownership), but the actual, ultimate, beneficial ownership.

In facing the problem the Court took a firm stand that the test of registered tonnage was the only one by which the size of a shipowning nation should be determined. The Court arrived at this conclusion by the examination of 1) certain articles of the IMCO convention and the actual practice which was followed in giving effect to them, and 2) international practice and maritime usage.

The Court relied first of all on art. 60 providing for the entry into force of the convention:

> The present Convention shall enter into force on the date when 21 states of which seven shall each have a total tonnage of not less than 1,000,000 gross tons of shipping, have become parties to the Convention in accordance with Article 57.

The Court found that the convention meant the tonnage *registered* in each of the seven states. After the required conditions had been fulfilled on March 17, 1958, the legal counsel of the United Nations stated in a letter to the United States Mission to the United Nations, of April 10, 1959:

> In so far as concerns the requirement of Article 60 that seven among the States becoming parties should "each have a total tonnage" of the stated amount, no question was raised, and no consideration was given, as to whether the total tonnage figure of any State then a party, as indicated by Lloyd's Register, should be altered for any reason bearing upon the ownership of such tonnage.[79]

79. Quoted by the Court; *id.*, 167. See also ICJ *Pleadings*, Constitution (1960), p. 163. The Court corroborated its argument by taking recourse to the equally authentic French and Spanish texts of the convention; these use equivalent words ("posséder" and "poseer" respectively) in art. 60 and art. 28(a), whereas the English text uses "have" in art. 60 and "own" in art. 28(a). This means that "own" in art. 28(a) is equivalent to "have" in art. 60.

The Court also referred to art. 17(c) providing that two members of the IMCO Council "shall be elected by the Assembly from among the governments of nations having a substantial interest in providing international shipping services." Although the tonnage criterion was not mentioned the countries elected (Japan and Italy) were recommended to these vacancies because they "clearly surpassed the others in size of their tonnage." [80] The tonnage mentioned is the tonnage registered in the respective countries, not that beneficially owned by their nationals. The data were taken from *Lloyd's Register of Shipping* for 1958, which was also before the Assembly in the election under art. 28(a).[81]

One could add that in 1948 the formulation of the draft art. 28(a) did not differ, in the parts relevant for the present discussion, from the text eventually adopted.[82] At the working party on maritime safety a proposal was made that the Maritime Safety Committee should be composed of equal numbers of nations interested in providing international shipping services and of nations interested in international seaborne trade. Since the working party rejected this proposal, it can be concluded that the phrase "the largest ship-owning nations" does not refer to nations "with the largest interest in providing international shipping services." [83] Six such nations are, under art. 17, members of the IMCO Council, at whose election in 1948 the criterion of the registered tonnage statistics was not strictly followed. The working party's rejection of this proposal implies its acceptance of the registered tonnage criterion for the composition of the Maritime Safety Committee. If, on the other hand, the words "ship-owning nations" had been intended to have a meaning different from that accepted in international practice, then the framers of the convention would have certainly indicated it. However, as the Court observed: "The absence of any discussion on their meaning as the draft article developed strongly suggests that there was no doubt as to their meaning; that they referred to registered ship tonnage." [84]

80. IMCO/A.I/SR 3 (1959), p. 3.
81. [1960] ICJ Rep. 168.
82. In the original draft prepared by the United Maritime Consultative Council it was art. VII, §1. See also paper submitted by the United States at the conference of 1948; UN Doc. E/CONF.4/13 (1948), p. 23; *DSB* 16:1096 (1946).
83. UN Doc. E/CONF.4/SR. Rev. 76 (1948).
84. [1960] ICJ Rep. 170.

Another argument of the Court referred to the way in which the apportionment of the expenses of the organization amongst its members was regulated under the provisions of art. 41 of the convention. Under resolution A. 20(I) adopted by the IMCO Assembly on January 19, 1959, the assessment of the contribution of each member state was determined principally by its respective gross registered tonnage as shown in the latest edition of *Lloyd's Register of Shipping*. The states whose registered tonnages were the largest paid the largest contributions.[85] In this respect Liberia and Panama were considered among the largest ship-owning nations as the delegates of Liberia and the United States had observed at the IMCO Assembly in 1959.[86]

Finally, at the very election of the Maritime Safety Committee the list of the ship-owning nations with their respective registered tonnages, formulated after *Lloyd's Register of Shipping*, served as the basis for the election of the members of the committee.

All these reasons persuaded the Court to the view that "it is unlikely that when [art. 28(a)] was drafted and incorporated into the Convention it was contemplated that any criterion other than registered tonnage should determine which were the largest ship-owning nations."[87] In particular the Court rejected the test of the nationality of the beneficial owners of the ships, as difficult to ascertain, and neither practical nor certain. Such a test "finds no basis in international practice, the language of international jurisprudence, in maritime terminology, in international conventions dealing with safety at sea or in the practice followed by the Organization itself in carrying out the Convention."[88]

One might add that not only the test of beneficial ownership

85. [1960] ICJ Rep. 168. For a list of IMCO documents relating to the apportionment of expenses among the member states see ICJ *Pleadings*, Constitution (1960), p. 21.

86. IMCO/A.I/SR. 7 (1959), pp. 4–5, 7–9, 12–13. See also the written statement of the government of Liberia (ICJ *Pleadings*, Constitution (1960), pp. 56–58), and the written statement of the United States of America (*id.*, pp. 146–147). One can add that also under art. 1 of the Agreement on the Financial Support of the North Atlantic Ice Patrol, 1956, the annual contributions of the parties are determined by the ratio which the total gross tonnage of the given party's vessels bears to the combined total gross tonnage of the vessels of all parties. Here also the registered tonnage is meant since the test of registry is expressly adopted in art. 2; T.I.A.S. 3597; 7 U.S.T. 1969.

87. [1960] ICJ Rep. 169.

88. *Ibid.*

but also the test of "formal" ownership by nationals (individuals and, in particular, corporations) must be rejected in the light of what has been proved in the preceding chapter. But even if the criterion of ownership by nationals were accepted, the answer to the question put to the International Court of Justice would have to have been negative since, on this criterion, Liberia would be fifth and Panama eighth on the list of the largest ship-owning nations in 1958.[89]

In the second part of its argument the Court pointed to certain aspects of international practice and maritime usage confirming the thesis that a ship is considered as belonging to a state if it is registered by that state. In particular, the Court referred to the conventions mentioned in the preceding chapter, namely to art. 3 of the Load Line Convention of July 5, 1930, which stated that "a ship is regarded as belonging to a country if it is registered by the Government of that country," and that "the expression 'Administration' means the Government of the country to which the ship belongs . . .";[90] and to the provisions of the Convention for the Safety of Life at Sea of 1929,[91] as well as to the London Convention on Safety of Life at Sea of 1948.[92] The Court also mentioned the Brussels Conventions of 1910 respecting Collisions, and Assistance and Salvage at Sea[93] and the Convention for Prevention of Pollution of the Sea by Oil, 1954.[94] As the Court added "numerous bilateral treaties also give expression to [the principle under consideration]." [95]

The consistency of the registry criterion with the general purposes of the IMCO convention and the special functions of the

89. See the argument of the Liberian delegate at the IMCO Assembly, 1959; IMCO/A.I/SR. 8 (1959), p. 7. See also the statement of Weeks, in ICJ *Pleadings*, Constitution (1960), p. 271. One can add that if the criterion of beneficial ownership were accepted, Greece would be qualified for election as one of the eight largest shipowning nations.

90. T.S. 858; 47 Stat. 2228; 135 L.N.T.S. 301.

91. T.S. 910; 50 Stat. 1121; 136 L.N.T.S. 81. In this convention a ship is regarded as belonging to a country if it is registered at a port of that country.

92. In this convention, which replaced that of 1929, art. II establishes the criterion of registry for the application of the provisions of the convention, and the annexed regulation 20 specifies the duties of each "Administration" towards "its" ships. Regulation 2(b) defines "Administration" as "the government of the country in which the ship is registered"; 3 U.S.T. 3450; T.I.A.S. 2495; 164 U.N.T.S. 113.

93. 37 Stat. 1658; T.S. 576.

94. This convention has not yet come into force.

95. [1960] ICJ Rep. 170. On these treaties see Ch. IV.

Maritime Safety Committee was found to be additional argument in favor of the Court's interpretation of art. 28(a).[96] One can add that one of the duties of IMCO, in particular of the Maritime Safety Committee, is to coordinate international activities in the field of safety at sea. Adopting one test for the conventions on safety at sea, and a different one for the IMCO convention, would result in much confusion and could lead to results which would render the convention ineffective.

Finally, the Court briefly disposed of the problem of the genuine link which — according to the adversaries of the flags of convenience — should exist between ships and the countries where they were registered, and which should allegedly be taken into consideration in assessing "the largest ship-owning nations." Having reached the conclusion that the determination of the largest ship-owning nations depends solely upon the tonnage registered in the countries in question, the Court said: "any further examination of the contention based on a genuine link is irrelevant for the purpose of answering the question which has been submitted to the Court for an advisory opinion." [97]

One cannot agree with the view of Judge Moreno Quintana, expressed in his dissenting opinion, that the genuine link provision of art. 5 of the Convention on the High Seas of 1958 should be interpreted as meaning that the genuine link should exist between the owner of a ship and the flag it flies, and that "this provision, by which international law establishes an obligation binding in national law, constitutes at the present time the *opinio juris gentium* on the matter." [98] To the contention of Judge Moreno Quintana one can reply, first, that art. 5 does not speak about the genuine link between the owner of a ship and the flag it flies, but between the state and the ship; secondly, that the element of ownership was discarded by the conference, and even before, by the International Law Commission; and thirdly, that the *opinio juris gentium* on the matter is that registration is the test of a ship's nationality.[99]

96. [1960] ICJ Rep. 171.
97. [1960] ICJ Rep. 171.
98. *Id.*, p. 178.
99. On the genuine link see Chapters VIII and IX. It is interesting to note that President Klaestad did not touch the problem of genuine link in his dissenting

The final conclusion of the International Court of Justice was that the IMCO Assembly, by not electing Liberia and Panama to the Maritime Safety Committee, failed to comply with art. 28(a) of the convention which "must be interpreted as requiring the determination of the largest shipowning nations to be made solely on the basis of registered tonnage," and that therefore the committee was not constituted in accordance with the Convention for the Establishment of the Organization.[100]

The decision of the Court must be accepted as consonant with the practice and doctrine of international law of the present day. It should also be noted that the Court, faithful to the requirements of its judicial character, limited itself to the judicial interpretation of the convention, eliminating — as it emphasized — in advance all political aspects of the case.[101] In spite of that, the opinion of June 8, 1960, will certainly be an argument for the case of Panlibhon not only in direct application to the constitution of the Maritime Safety Committee of the IMCO which in future elections will certainly follow the directives of the Court's opinion, but also in the international legal situation of the flag-of-convenience fleets in general. One must add, however, that for Panama the Court's decision has lost its practical significance since already in 1960 when the decision was given Panama was no longer among the eight nations possessing the largest registered tonnage of shipping. As statistics show, in 1960 Panama was eleventh on *Lloyd's Register of Shipping*, and the present trend in international shipping does not point to any increase of the Panamanian tonnage.[102]

---

opinion. One might add that he had opposed the principle expressed by the ICJ in the *Nottebohm* case. See [1955] ICJ Rep. 30.

100. [1960] ICJ Rep. 171. The decision of the Court was taken by nine votes to five. President Klaestad and Judge Moreno Quintana appended their dissenting opinions.

101. For this reason the Court's decision was criticized as based on the "formal" interpretation of art. 28 — *i.e.*, on the interpretation that fails to take into account the underlying "reality." See Monaco, "Sulla composizione del Comitato della sicurezza marittima dell'IMCO," *Rivista di Diritto Internazionale* 43:679 (1960). Monaco was the representative of the Italian government at the hearings before the ICJ.

102. *Cf.* Table 1. See also *The New York Times*, September 13, 1961, p. 74.

Chapter VI. The Problems of Labor Jurisdiction

The foregoing discussion shows that the criterion of registry is the only valid criterion for the recognition of the national character of a merchant ship. But beyond this one must distinguish the occasions on which a state may, under certain circumstances, assert its authority over a merchant vessel not registered under its flag. This problem impinges upon the international-labor aspect of flags of convenience. It is related to the attempt of the American maritime unions to raise wage levels and to improve working conditions for the crews aboard Panlibhon vessels by asserting that American labor laws are applicable in labor disputes involving seamen on these vessels. This is a subject touching the borderline between private and public international law, since the assertion raises important issues that relate in general to the jurisdiction exercised over merchant ships in international navigation, a problem which has been the subject of countless judicial decisions and volumes of doctrine in international law, both public and private.

In international shipping situations continuously arise, mostly controversies, which entail legal consequences and which require the application of law to a given set of facts. It is in the nature of shipping that very often events occurring aboard ships (or sometimes originating on land) affect and involve various interpenetrating legal systems.[1] These events may take place either upon

1. McDougal, Burke, & Vlasic divide the jurisdictional claims resulting from these controversies into two kinds: 1) "Claims relating to events occurring on board ship on the high seas" (claims relating to public order of ship and those relating to events not affecting public order of ship). 2) "Claims with respect to events primarily affecting value processes within territorial communities and not directly related to the enjoyment of the high seas." See McDougal, Burke & Vlasic, pp. 43–45, 46, 81–84, 94–97.

the high seas, which are not subject to the sovereignty and jurisdiction of any state, or within the ports or territorial waters of a coastal state. In the former case the institution of the nationality of a ship serves to subject it, in principle, to the jurisdiction of the nation whose flag it flies. In the latter case, the ocean areas are in varying degree subject to the jurisdiction of the littoral state. However, these two rules are only a simplified and prima facie view of the allocation of jurisdiction, since the competence to exercise jurisdiction may be concurrent, depending on various factors which may be relevant in the allocation of this competence.

Determining which of several simultaneously valid legal systems is applicable to a given set of facts comes within the scope of private international law, or conflict of laws, and is not, in principle, the main subject of this discussion.[2] However, the outer limits of private international law border on public international law. This introduces the problem of the relation between these two spheres of law. The question is whether public international law imposes upon various states an obligation in their relations with one another to make their rules on conflict of laws conform to certain principles. In other words, does international law demarcate the respective spheres of the legislative competence of these states?[3] Applying this to the flag-of-convenience situation, one can pose the question whether state *X* is obliged by public international law (hereinafter referred to merely as international law) to apply to labor relations on board the flag-of-convenience ship *Y*, finding itself transitorily in a port of state *X*, the law of the flag state *Y*, or that of the state of ownership, which may also be, and, in fact, very often is, the law of state *X*. Note, in addition, that states may be bound by a lawmaking treaty to apply the law of one or the other state, and that in this case, what is termed private international law, may become public international law.[4]

It is a well established principle of international law that a vessel

2. For the various definitions of private international law see Beale, *A Treatise on the Conflict of Laws* (1935), I, 2–4. See also in general: Wolff, *Private International Law* (1950), pp. 3–7; Ehrenzweig, *Conflict of Laws* (1959), which contains a very rich bibliography; Rabel, *The Conflict of Laws: A Comparative Study*, vols. I–IV (1945–1958).

3. Wolff, pp. 12–14. On the relation of private to international law see, *e.g.*, Stevenson, "The Relationship of Private International Law to Public International Law," *Columbia Law Review* 52:561 (1952).

4. Oppenheim, I, 6–7; Wolff, p. 12.

on the high seas is, with exceptions not relevant here, subject to the exclusive jurisdiction of the state whose flag it flies.[5] There is no need to explain this jurisdiction by regarding ships as floating portions of a state's territory,[6] a fiction which has now given way to a theory of jurisdiction based on practical necessity that "*some* law must prevail on ships, and there is no other law to compete with that of the flag state," [7] or that the jurisdiction of a state over its ships on the high seas "partakes more of the characteristics of personal than of territorial sovereignty." [8] For this reason it is often concurrent with the jurisdiction of another state with which the given event has a point of contact.

This concurrence is more clearly brought into focus when one considers the jurisdiction over a merchant vessel in a foreign port. It is in these circumstances that the problems arise relating to the jurisdiction over the flag-of-convenience shipping. According to the well established practice and prevalent doctrine of international law, a non-governmental merchant ship entering a foreign port becomes subject to the laws and jurisdiction of the foreign nation.[9] However, for the practical necessities of international commerce,

5. This has been confirmed by practically all writers. To mention only a few: Oppenheim, I, 330; Colombos, p. 257; Westlake, *International Law* (1910), I, 191; Schwarzenberger, *International Law* (3d ed. 1952), p. 56; Smith, p. 61. See also art. 6 of the Convention on the High Seas (UN Doc. A/CONF. 13/53).

6. This fiction was expressed, *e.g.*, in the case of *The Costa Rica Packet;* Moore, *Arbit.*, V, 4948; the S.S. *Lotus,* PCIJ, Ser. A, No. 10 (1927). For the literature on the fiction of the vessel as a floating portion of the state's territory, see Gidel, I, 239–245, and the accompanying notes.

7. Brierly, *The Law of Nations* (5th ed. 1955), p. 238. See also Scharrenberg v. Dollar Steamship Co., 245 U.S. 122, 127 (1917). In the latter the Court observed: "It is, of course, true that for purposes of jurisdiction a ship, even on the high seas, is often said to be a part of the territory of the nation whose flag it flies. But in the physical sense this expression is obviously figurative (Moore, *Digest,* I, §174), and to expand the doctrine to the extent of treating seamen employed on such a ship as working in the country of its registry is quite impossible." For criticism of the fiction of the territoriality of the ship and for literature on this subject see Gidel, I, 245–256, and the accompanying notes. See also Hall, *International Law* (7th ed. 1917) §§76–78; Colombos, p. 249; Jessup, *The Law of Territorial Waters and Maritime Jurisdiction,* pp. 191–192.

8. Cunard Steamship Co. v. Mellon, 262 U.S. 100, 123 (1923).

9. Wildenhus' case, 120 U.S. 1 (1887); The Ester, 190 Fed. 216 (E.D.S.C. 1911); Cunard Steamship Co. v. Mellon, 262 U.S. 100, 123–124 (1923); Benz v. Compañía Naviera Hidalgo, S.A., 353 U.S. 138, 142 (1957); Marine Cooks & Stewards, AFL v. Panama Steamship Co. Ltd., 362 U.S. 365, 372 (1960). For the American practice see Moore, *Digest,* II, 272–286. See also Hackworth, II, 230–248; Hyde, I, 735–739; Gidel, II, 81; Jessup, *The Law of Territorial Waters and Maritime Jurisdiction,* pp. 144–145, 191–194; Briggs, pp. 349–354. From the codifications on the subject one can mention "Regulations concerning the Regime of Ships and Their Crews in Foreign

states have long found it inexpedient to exercise their jurisdiction over foreign merchant vessels in the matters affecting only the internal discipline or economy of the foreign vessel, and have left the exercise of this jurisdiction to the authorities of the flag state, notably to consular officers. As was stated by the United States Supreme Court in the famous *Wildenhus'* case:

> From experience . . . it was found long ago that it would be beneficial to commerce if the local government would abstain from interfering with general regulation of the rights and duties of the officers and crew towards the vessel, or among themselves. And so by comity it came to be generally understood among civilized nations that all matters of discipline, and all things done on board, which affected only the vessel, the peace or dignity of the country, or the tranquility of the port, should be left by the local government to be dealt with by the authorities of the nation to which the vessel belonged as the laws of that nation, or the interests of its commerce should require.[10]

The *Wildenhus'* case dealt with the problem of criminal jurisdiction by the coastal sovereign,[11] but a similar principle obtains in cases of civil jurisdiction as well.[12] In both cases, however, the coastal state has the discretion and remains the sole judge of whether to refrain from the exercise of jurisdiction or enforcement of its laws against a foreign vessel. The exercise of jurisdiction being "not mandatory but discretionary," [13] the local sovereign "may out of considerations of public policy choose to forego the exertion of its jurisdiction or to exert the same in only a limited way, but this is a matter resting solely in its discretion." [14] If the state waives its right to exercise jurisdiction when the affair concerns the internal

---

Ports in Time of Peace," *Annuaire de l'Institut de Droit International* 34:736, 746 (1928). See also Harvard Research, "The Law of Territorial Waters," *AJIL* 23 Supp. (1929), pp. 307–328 (art. 18, with rich comments).

10. 120 U.S. 1, 12 (1887).

11. For the practice of states see: Moore, *Digest*, II, 272–318; Jessup, *The Law of Territorial Waters and Maritime Jurisdiction*, pp. 145–182; Hackworth, II, 208–230; Hyde, I, 735–741; Gidel, II, 200–252; Harvard Research, "The Law of Territorial Waters," pp. 307–328; Briggs, pp. 350–352; Rienow, pp. 189–213. As to criminal jurisdiction, Rienow concludes that the criminal statutes of the United States assuming jurisdiction over crimes committed aboard ships on high seas on the basis of ownership in whole or in part by the citizens of the United States are probably a violation of international law.

12. The American practice is summarized in *The Ester;* 190 Fed. 216, 221 (E.D.S.C. 1911).

13. Benz v. Compañía Naviera Hidalgo, S.A., 353 U.S. 138, 142 (1957).

14. Cunard Steamship Co. v. Mellon, 262 U.S. 100, 124 (1923); *accord,* The Belgenland, 114 U.S. 355 (1885); The Ester, 190 Fed. 216, 221 (E.D.S.C. 1911).

economy of the vessel, this is not to be considered evidence of the recognition of a principle of international law,[15] but is motivated by reasons of convenience or other policy considerations of the state.

The practice of mutually waiving jurisdiction over foreign vessels in ports in matters of the internal economy and order of the vessels has found its way into the conventional law of nations, and is included in many bilateral consular conventions. From the international-law point of view, such a treaty provision is the only restriction that may limit the authority of the coastal state to enforce its law, in a given matter, on the foreign merchant vessels in its port. Whether a state, for its own policy reasons, wants to extend the application of its laws even to matters of internal economy of the foreign ships can be seen from the language of the respective municipal enactment. The intention of the state may either be clearly expressed by the law, or it may be construed by the adjudicating court. As the Supreme Court of the United States observed:

> It follows that if Congress had so chosen, it could have made the Act applicable to wage disputes arising on foreign vessels between nationals of other countries when the vessel comes within our territorial waters. The question here therefore narrows to one of intent of the Congress as to the coverage of the Act.[16]

In the practice of maritime states, certain matters are generally recognized as subject to the exclusive jurisdiction of the littoral state. For example, immigration, customs, health, and safety laws apply both to national and foreign flag vessels.[17]

The extension of the legislation of the coastal state on matters coming within the internal economy of the foreign vessel is exceptional, and requires specific and express authorization of the legislative authority of the coastal state, which puts the foreign vessels on notice before entering a given port. This doctrine is accepted by the United States Supreme Court, which, though

15. The Belgenland, 114 U.S. 355, 363 (1885). See also Jessup, *The Law of Territorial Waters and Maritime Jurisdiction*, p. 189; Harvard Research, "The Law of Territorial Waters," p. 308; Hyde, I, 743.

16. Benz v. Compañía Naviera Hidalgo, S.A., 353 U.S. 138, 142 (1957).

17. Hyde, I, 676–702, 735–739; Briggs, p. 350; ACFN *Memorandum*, p. 56, nn. 44–50, and the accompanying text. See also "Flag-of-Convenience Fleet" *YLJ* 69:506 notes 56–60 and the accompanying text.

admitting "the power of Congress to condition access to [United States] ports by foreign-owned vessels [here foreign-registered ships are meant] upon submission to any liabilities it may consider good American policy to exact," [18] has been aware of the international importance of such decisions of the Congress "where the possibilities of international discord are so evident and retaliative action so certain." [19] For this reason the Court stated: "For us to run interference in such a delicate field of international relations there must be present the affirmative intention of the Congress clearly expressed." [20]

This affirmative intention of the Congress with regard to labor relations on foreign vessels has been expressed by the Congress in statutes dealing with wage payments to seamen on foreign vessels in American ports, the so-called "Seamen's Wages Acts.[21] These Acts of Congress were actuated by the American flag shipping's apparent interest in reducing the competitive advantage of the foreign-flag operators by indirectly forcing them to pay higher wages, and so equalizing the operating costs of American- and foreign-flag operations.[22] The applicability of these Acts was confirmed by the Supreme Court on several occasions,[23] but in three

18. Lauritzen v. Larsen, 345 U.S. 571, 592–593 (1953).

19. Benz v. Compañía Naviera Hidalgo, S.A., 353 U.S. 138, 147 (1957).

20. *Ibid.*

21. 23 Stat. 55 (1884), "The Dingley Act," 46 U.S.C., §599 (barring the payment of advances to seamen, with express reference to foreign vessels); Rev. Stat. §4529 (1875), 46 U.S.C. §596 (1952) (provision giving the seamen right to immediate payment after discharge of cargo or seaman); Rev. Stat. §4530 (1875), 46 U.S.C. §597 (1952) (granting seamen on both American and foreign vessels the right to receive one-half of their then earned wages while their vessels are in American waters). These three statutes were embodied in the La Follette Seamen's Act of 1915, 38 Stat. 1164 (1915); Rev. Stat. §4527 (1875), 46 U.S.C., §594 (1952) (granting a seaman discharged unlawfully the right of one month's wages even if these have not been earned).

22. In particular this is true of the La Follette Seamen's Act of 1915. See H.R. Rep. No. 645, 62d Cong., 2d Sess. (1912), p. 7; Bickel, *The Unpublished Opinions of Mr. Justice Brandeis* (1957), pp. 47–50 [dealing with his opinion in *Strathearn Steamship Co. v. Dillon*, 252 U.S. 348 (1920)]; ACFN *Memorandum*, pp. 49–52; Harolds, "Some Legal Problems Arising Out of Foreign Flag Operations," *Fordham L. Rev.* 28:295, 305–306 (1959).

23. See, *e.g.*, Patterson v. The Bark Eudora, 190 U.S. 169 (1903). (The statute prohibiting the payment of advance wages to seamen was found applicable to a British vessel which had shipped seamen in New York.) Strathearn Steamship Co. v. Dillon, 252 U.S. 348 (1920). (A British subject, shipped on a British ship in a British port under articles stipulating that wages were payable at the end of the voyage, was given the benefit of collecting one-half the wages due to him when his vessel put in at an American port.)

cases the La Follette Act was construed as not covering wage advances made in foreign ports sanctioned by the foreign law.[24] Here again the refusal to apply American law was motivated by the Court by the lack of specific intention of the Congress:

> Had Congress intended to make void such contracts and payments [*i.e.*, advance of money to foreign seamen in foreign port under foreign law] a few words would have stated that intention, not leaving such an important regulation to be gathered from implication. . . . Such sweeping and important requirement is not found specifically made in the statute.[25]

Thus, even within a statute expressly applicable to foreign vessels in American ports, the Supreme Court, weighing the interests of the coastal and foreign states gave priority to the contact of the transaction with the foreign state and declared the American law inapplicable.

The two sets of facts represented by the case of *Patterson v. The Bark Eudora* and *Sandberg v. McDonald* have two corresponding situations which placed the issue on the plane of international law. The first illustrates the fact that there is no principle of international law forbidding the application of a coastal state's labor legislation to foreign vessels transitorily staying at its ports. When the Dingley Act of 1884 was passed[26] prohibiting the payment of advances to seamen hired at American ports both on American and foreign flag vessels, this provoked the protest of the French minister, who claimed the violation of the Franco-American Consular Convention of February 23, 1853,[27] and contended that the application of the Act to the enlistment of French sailors in the ports of the United States was an infringement of "the legislative sovereignty of each nation with regard to its subjects." [28] In reply to this protest, the United States Secretary of State, emphasizing that the Act of 1884 dealt only with seamen hired in *American* ports — and those only — concluded his argument that the

24. Sandberg v. McDonald, 248 U.S. 185 (1918); Neilson v. Rhine Shipping Co., 248 U.S. 205 (1918); Jackson v. S.S. Archimedes, 275 U.S. 463 (1928).

25. Sandberg v. McDonald, 248 U.S. 185, 195 (1918). *Accord,* Jackson v. S.S. Archimedes, 275 U.S. 463, 470 (1928); Benz v. Compañía Naviera Hidalgo, S.A., 353 U.S. 138, 146, 147 (1957).

26. 23 Stat. 55–56 (1885).

27. 10 Stat. 992; T.S. 92; Malloy, I, 528.

28. Roustan, French Minister, to Bayard, Secretary of State, July 31, 1885; [1885] *Foreign Rel.* (1886), p. 384; Moore, *Digest,* II, 305–307.

Act of 1884 was not in conflict with the consular convention with France and did not infringe upon any principle of international law.[29] Dealing with similar facts in *Patterson v. The Bark Eudora,* the Supreme Court upheld the applicability of the American law to the situation examined.

The other situation shows that at a certain point the claim of jurisdiction may be forced too far with ensuing diplomatic protests indicating the violation of international comity and the danger of retaliation by the state whose law has not been respected. After the refusal of the Supreme Court, in *Jackson v. S.S. Archimedes,* to extend the advancement provisions of the seamen's wage laws to foreign vessels in foreign waters, several proposals were made by Senator La Follette to extend these provisions to such vessels. It was contemplated

> that foreign seamen who signed shipping articles at the lower wage scale prevailing at foreign ports would, since no longer prevented by legal process, take advantage of higher American wage level on reaching ports of the United States and find new jobs at the higher wages. The foreign ship must then fill up its crew at the current wages in the United States port. Thus, both vessels of the United States and foreign vessels running to and from ports of the United States would have the same labor operating costs.[30]

These proposals resulted in a storm of diplomatic protests from Great Britain, Italy, Sweden, Norway, Denmark, the Netherlands, Germany, and Canada,[31] denouncing vigorously the proposal as "contrary to fundamental principles of law commonly acknowledged among nations." and "contrary to conventional understanding of international law." [32] The British Embassy protested, pointing out that

> the bill by seeking to vary forcibly the provisions of a contract, perfectly valid under British law, made within British jurisdiction, and in many cases between British subjects, and purporting apparently to regulate

29. Bayard, Secretary of State, to Roustan, French Minister, August 26, 1885; [1885] *Foreign Rel.* (1886), p. 386; Moore, *Digest,* II, 307–310.

30. S. Rep. 833, 70th Cong., 1st Sess. (1928), p. 1; S. Rep. 1583, 71st Cong., 3d Sess. (1931), p. 1 (Memorandum of the Senate Committee proposing the bill).

31. Briggs, p. 353; ACFN *Memorandum,* pp. 138–141; Benz v. Compañía Naviera Hidalgo, S.A., 353 U.S. 138, 146 (1957).

32. The Swedish Legation to the Department of State, April 30, 1928; [1928] *Foreign Rel.* (1942), I, 834, 835.

The Netherlands Legation to the Department of State, May 3, 1928; *ibid.*

the manner in which a master of a British ship may engage a British crew in a British port, appeared to be contrary to the generally accepted principles of international law.[33]

Under this diplomatic pressure and the dissuasion of the Department of State, the bill failed to be enacted by the Congress.[34]

The question now arises as to what policies and principles ought to guide the authorities of a state deciding whether to assert its laws upon the foreign ship in port, or to apply the law of the flag of the vessel in question, or perhaps the law of another country which also has some national interest in the given situation. In this respect, two elements should be distinguished. First, there are certain general principles applicable in all conflicts of interests in the international community and common both to public and private international law, both of which are "ultimately concerned with the possibility of maintaining a unified economic and social order for the conduct of international trade and intercourse among independent political units of diverse cultures and stages of civilization, different legal and economic systems and varying degrees of physical power and position." [35] Secondly, the considerations resulting from this first element will be important directives for the decision makers in the *method* adopted in the concreate case in which a coastal state's authority is facing the problem of applying one of the several competing laws to the given "shipping" situation.

These two elements have been extensively discussed by commentators upon private international law and admiralty[36] and by judicial decisions dealing with maritime labor cases — in particular by the United States Supreme Court as well as lower courts. In recent years the courts have faced increasing numbers of conflict-of-law cases connected with the rise of the fleets flying flags of convenience, where the interaction of various national elements is particularly marked.

The doctrine, as developed by these decisions, is that in absence of express congressional intent, the following considerations should

33. Memorandum of March 19, 1930; [1931] *Foreign Rel.* (1946), I, 808.

34. Briggs, p. 353; Benz v. Compañía Naviera Hidalgo, S.A., 353 U.S. 138, 146 (1957).

35. Dunn, *The Protection of Nationals* (1932), p. 1; also quoted in Stevenson, p. 567.

36. See, *e.g.*, Rabel, II, 346–351; Yntema, "The Objectives of Private International Law," *Canadian Business Review* 35:721 (1957).

be taken into account in the interpretation of the law by the adjudicating court: The principle of balancing divergent interests should be the "controlling consideration." [37] This principle stresses the main function of law in general. Applying it to the problem of jurisdiction of the coastal state over foreign ships transitorily staying in its port, it can be said that the coastal state must consider both its own interests and the interests of the various states which may have interest in the vessel.[38] As it was put in *Lauritzen v. Larsen,* the American courts have long been accustomed to "dealing with admiralty problems in reconciling our own with foreign interests and in accommodating the reach of our own laws to those of other maritime nations." [39] In another, more recent case, the Court referred to the controlling considerations of "the interacting interests of United States and of foreign countries." [40]

Closely connected with the principle of balance is that of mutual tolerance and restraint and circumspection in the exercise of sovereign authority. "[I]n assessing [the interacting interests of the United States and of foreign countries] we must move with the circumspection appropriate when this Court is adjudicating issues inevitably entangled in the conduct of our international relations" stated Justice Frankfurter, emphasizing the delicate nature of the problem of jurisdiction over foreign vessels.[41] The recognition of reciprocal interests, and restraint in the assertion of jurisdiction is a "self-regarding respect for the relevant interests of foreign nations." [42] It is, therefore, in the self-interest of all the states, because of the dangers of retaliation which may be applied by the state whose interests have — in its view — been impinged upon

37. Romero v. International Terminal Operating Co., 358 U.S 354, 383 (1959).

38. McDougal and Burke speak of the concurrence of the "inclusive" interest (by which they mean the self-interest of the coastal state shared with other nations in free commercial navigation in addition to the local interests) with various exclusive interests of foreign nations. See in general McDougal & Burke, "Crisis in the Law of the Sea: Community Perspectives versus National Egoism," *YLJ* 67:539 (1958). See also McDougal, Burke, & Vlasic, pp. 26, 51, and "Flag-of-Convenience Fleet," *YLJ* 69:505–506.

For the criticism of the concept of McDougal and Burke of the conflict between community interests and national egoism, see Mender, pp. 289–292; see also Sørensen, p. 199.

39. Lauritzen v. Larsen, 345 U.S. 571, 577 (1953).

40. Romero v. International Terminal Operating Co., 358 U.S. 354, 383 (1959).

41. *Ibid.*

42. *Ibid.*

and because of the interests of international commerce. Mr. Justice Jackson expressed the first reason in his opinion in *Lauritzen v. Larsen:*

> In dealing with international commerce we cannot be unmindful of the necessity for mutual forbearance if retaliations are to be avoided; nor should we forget that any contact which we hold sufficient to warrant application of our law to a foreign transaction will logically be as strong a warrant for a foreign country to apply its law to an American transaction.[43]

In another case, Mr. Justice Clark, refusing to apply the Labor-Management Relations Act of 1947 [44] to a controversy involving damages resulting from the picketing of a Liberian vessel, owned by a Liberian corporation (but whose stockholders were not Americans), operated entirely by foreign seamen under foreign articles, while the vessel was temporarily in an American port, substantiated his opinion by the absence of an affirmative intention of the Congress which — as he said — "alone has the facilities necessary to make fairly such an important policy decision where the possibilities of international discord are so evident and retaliative action so certain." [45]

The Supreme Court's awareness of international complications obviously influenced the Court's decision in *Romero v. International Terminal Operating Co.*, where Mr. Justice Frankfurter, following *Lauritzen v. Larsen,* referred to "the accommodations that become relevant in fair and prudent regard for the interests of foreign nations in the regulation of their own ships and their own nations, and the effect upon our interests of our treatment of the legitimate interests of foreign nations." [46]

The danger of retaliation was a major consideration in the refusal of the Department of State to endorse the amendment to the La Follette Bill in 1929.[47] The Secretary of State, opposing the Bill, stated that "the enactment into law of the amendment in question may render the American Merchant Marine subject to retaliatory measures by foreign Governments which in their effect

43. 345 U.S. 571, 582 (1953).
44. 61 Stat. 136 (1947), 29 U.S.C., §141 (1958).
45. Benz v. Compañía Naviera Hidalgo, S.A., U.S. 138, 147 (1957).
46. 358 U.S. 354, 384 (1959).
47. See notes 30–34 above, and the accompanying text.

may far outweigh any advantages which might be secured by this legislation."[48] Mutual restraint is also imperative because of the dangers to international commerce, involved in the indiscriminate application of local law. In *Lauritzen v. Larsen*, Mr. Justice Jackson, stating that "the virtue and utility of sea-borne commerce lies in its frequent and important contacts with more than one country," warned that "if, to serve some immediate interest, the courts of each [country] were to exploit every such contact to the limit of its power, it is not difficult to see that a multiplicity of conflicting and overlapping burdens would blight international carriage by sea."[49]

The principle of stability is a close corollary of the preceding principle. Stability is an overriding objective of international law, indispensable, in particular, for the efficient fulfillment of international transactions, which does not, of course, exclude the promotion of beneficial changes.[50] This was meant by Mr. Justice Jackson when he said, in *Lauritzen v. Larsen*, that "international or maritime law in such matters as this does not seek uniformity and does not purport to restrict any nation from making and altering its laws to govern its own shipping and territory. However, it aims at stability and order through usages which considerations of comity, reciprocity and long-range interest have developed to define the domain which each nation will claim as its own."[51]

It was also for the sake of stability that the Court, determining the law applicable to *Lauritzen v. Larsen*, gave the preference to the law of the flag, rejecting both "the territorial standard so unfitted to an enterprise conducted under many territorial rules and none," and the criterion of the place of contract, which "would subject a ship to a multitude of systems of law." The law of the forum was also rejected because "the purpose of a conflict-of-laws doctrine is to assume that a case will be treated in the same way under the appropriate law regardless of the fortuitous circumstances."[52] Similarly, in *Romero v. International Terminal Operating Co.*, Mr. Justice Frankfurter stated that "to impose on ships

48. Secretary of State Stimson to Senator Wesley L. Jones, June 10, 1929; [1929] *Foreign Rel.* (1946), I, 1006.
49. 345 U.S. 571, 581 (1953).
50. See McDougal, Burke, & Vlasic, p. 51.
51. 345 U.S. 571, 582 (1953).
52. *Id.*, 584, 588, 591.

the duty of shifting from one standard of compensation to another as the vessel passes the boundaries of territorial waters would be not only an onerous burden but also an unduly speculative burden, disruptive of international commerce and without basis in the expressed policies of this country." [53]

Finally, last but not least, the overriding consideration in determining whether to apply a local law to a foreign merchant vessel should be the principle that domestic law ought never to be construed to violate the law of nations. Reaffirming expressly this old doctrine of construction,[54] Mr. Justice Jackson observed, in *Lauritzen v. Larsen,* that "by usage as old as the Nation, such statutes [i.e., the shipping statutes of the United States] have been construed to apply only to areas and transactions in which American law would be considered operative under prevalent doctrines of international law." [55]

Besides mentioning the treaties, the Court referred to one further source of the law of nations as accepted by the present practice and theory. These are the words of Mr. Justice Jackson:

> Courts of this and other commercial nations have generally deferred to a non-national or international maritime law of impressive maturity and universality. It has the force of law, not from extra-territorial reach of national laws, nor from abdication of its sovereign powers by any nation, but from acceptance by common consent of civilized communities of rules designed to foster amicable and workable commercial relations.[56]

These words presumably refer to general principles of law recognized by civilized nations,[57] in particular those dealing with international maritime transactions.

The general principles outlined above are implemented by the courts in concrete cases which pose the question of the applicability of local law with respect to persons or things aboard a foreign

53. 358 U.S. 354, 358 (1959).

54. See The Charming Betsy, 6 U.S. (2 Cranch) 64, 118 (1804) (the opinion of Chief Justice Marshall). See also McLeod v. United States, 229 U.S. 416, 434 (1913) (the opinion of Justice Day).

55. 345 U.S. 571, 577 (1953). See also Hyde, I, 727: "The scope of the operation of a domestic statute, in a geographical sense, or with respect to the nationality of the individuals or the character of ships to which it is applicable, is determined by the will of the legislator. In the endeavor to ascertain its design, there may be reason to impute to the legislative body knowledge of the law of nations and the absence of a deliberate attempt to defy its injunctions."

56. Lauritzen v. Larsen, 345 U.S. 571, 581–582 (1953).

57. Statute of the ICJ, art. 38(1)c.

merchant vessel staying transitorily in the port of the coastal state. This concrete implementation requires analysis of the weight and significance of the various factors which, alone or in combination, influence the choice of the law to govern the claim in the concrete maritime case.

The United States Supreme Court gave, in *Lauritzen v. Larsen,* a classic exposition of the method to be followed in this situation. The decision in *Lauritzen v. Larsen* dealt with a tort action for injury under the Jones Act[58] but the principle enunciated by the Court can also be useful in the cases dealing with the assertion of jurisdiction over employer-employee relations aboard foreign-flag ships in general. In the words of Mr. Justice Jackson:

> Maritime law, like our municipal law, has attempted to avoid or resolve conflicts between competing laws by ascertaining and valuing points of contact between the transaction and the states or governments whose competing laws are involved. The criteria, in general, appear to be arrived at from weighing of the significance of one or more connecting factors between the shipping transaction regulated and the national interest served by the assertion of authority.[59]

The Court listed the following factors which can be taken into consideration in determining the law applicable to a claim of actionable wrong:

1. The place of the wrongful act.
2. The law of the flag.
3. The allegiance or domicile of the claimant.
4. The allegiance of the shipowner.
5. The place of contract between the parties.
6. The inaccessibility of the foreign forum.
7. The law of the forum.[60]

Among these points of contact the law of the flag and the allegiance of the shipowner are of particular interest for the flag-of-convenience ships. However, there is one factor more, relevant for flag-of-convenience ships, namely the nationality of the ultimate owner.[61] Discussing the factor of the allegiance of the defendant shipowner, the Court observed: "until recent times this factor was

58. 41 Stat. 1007 (1920), 46 U.S.C., §688 (1952).
59. 345 U.S. 571, 582 (1953).
60. *Id.,* 583–592.
61. This was not taken into account by the Court in *Lauritzen v. Larsen,* since the owner was an individual Danish citizen.

not a frequent occasion of conflict, for the nationality of the ship was that of its owners. But it is common knowledge that in recent years a practice has grown, particularly among American shipowners, to avoid stringent shipping laws by seeking foreign registration eagerly offered by some countries." [62] Here, no doubt, the phenomenon of the flags of convenience is alluded to by the Court which, however, in *Lauritzen v. Larsen* was not interested in the issue directly.

The rules relating to the jurisdiction by the coastal state over foreign vessels calling at this state's ports have already been discussed in the first part of this chapter. Now the question must be answered as to what the scope of this jurisdiction is in application to flag-of-convenience ships where the competing links of the ownership of the vessel (very often both corporate and ultimate ownership, e.g. in the frequent case of a Liberian flag vessel owned by a Panamanian corporation whose stock is owned by Americans) and the "nominal" nationality thereof are at work in the events occurring aboard these ships. Besides these two (or three) major links, some others, such as the nationality or domicile of the seaman may also affect the decision as to the applicability of the given law to the particular event.

First of all, one must state that flag-of-convenience ships entering a foreign port become, like other foreign ships, subject to local jurisdiction, and the fact that they are ultimately owned or controlled by nationals of a state other than the flag state is largely irrelevant for the general application of the principle of the jurisdiction of the littoral state which may be the state of ultimate ownership of the vessel.

The principle that in matters of internal economy, the coastal state exercises restraint in asserting its jurisdiction over foreign ships in its ports also obtains with regard to flag-of-convenience ships. The fear of retaliatory measures by the flag-of-convenience state does not seem to be of decisive importance considering that the number of foreign ships putting in at the ports of flag-of-convenience states is negligible compared with the number of flag-of-convenience ships which call at the ports of other states. However, as discussed below, the assertion of jurisdiction by the United

62. *Id.*, 587.

States National Labor Relations Board over certain Panamanian and Liberian-flag vessels has already created international conflicts and danger of retaliatory measures of various kinds. There are also other factors, such as the need for certainty and stability of law, which speak against the application of local laws in matters of the internal economy of the flag-of-convenience ships. Even if due notice were given that the law of the coastal state would be applied to such ships, this situation would negatively affect international commerce; the operators of these vessels — a considerable percentage of the world merchant fleet — might be deterred from entering ports where a law unfavorable for their interests might be applied. Another important argument is that the non-application of the law of the flag state to flag-of-convenience ships would amount to discrimination against this shipping, since the practice of all states is that they either decline to assert their jurisdiction as a matter of international comity and usage (the Anglo-American courts) or "prefer to rest their judgments upon the ground that it is the invariable rule to leave the ship herself, and the authorities of her flag-state, all questions solely affecting her internal discipline and legal relations."[63]

The American practice is of particular interest here because a large number of Panlibhon ships stay transitorily in United States ports, and it has become inevitable that many disputes between employers and employees aboard these vessels eventually end up in the United States courts and even create international disputes.

The principle that express congressional authorization is necessary for American labor acts to regulate the internal economy of foreign vessels also obtains in the case of flag-of-convenience ships ultimately controlled by American interests. The American labor laws, with the exception of the Seamen's Wages Acts, do not have express extraterritorial application, and the examination of the legislative history of the American labor legislation does not indicate any congressional intention to apply this legislation to alien seamen on foreign-flag vessels, whether foreign- or American-owned.[64] The leading case in this respect is *Benz v. Compañía Naviera Hidalgo, S.A.*, in which the Supreme Court held that the

63. Colombos, p. 286.
64. For a detailed analysis of this legislation, see ACFN *Memorandum,* pp. 9–56.

Labor Management Relations (Taft-Hartley) Act of 1947[65] did not apply to a controversy involving damages resulting from the picketing of a foreign (Liberian) ship owned by a foreign (Panamanian) corporation, operated entirely by foreign seamen under foreign articles while the vessel was temporarily in an American port, though American unions, to which the foreign seamen did not belong, participated in the picketing. The Court found that an intent on the part of Congress to change the contractual agreement made by the foreign shipowner and the foreign seamen in that case could not be read into the Taft-Hartley Act.[66]

In *Benz* the ultimate owners of the ship were apparently not American,[67] but the nationality of the ultimate owners seems to have been irrelevant for the rationale of the case, since neither the lower courts nor the Supreme Court were interested in this problem. The important point was that — as the Court concluded, considering the legislative history of the Act —

> our study of the Act leaves us convinced that Congress did not fashion it to resolve labor disputes between nationals of other countries operating ships under foreign laws. The whole background of the Act is concerned with industrial strife between American employers and employees. In fact, no discussion in either House of Congress has been called to our attention from the thousands of pages of legislative history that indicates in the least that Congress intended the coverage of the Act to extend to circumstances such as those posed here. It appears not to have even occurred to those sponsoring the bill. . . . What was said [in the report made by Hartley] inescapably describes the boundaries of the Act as including only the workingmen of our own country and its possessions.[68]

The settled American practice and doctrine that the law of the flag, regardless of ownership, governs the internal economy of the

65. 61 Stat. 136, 29 U.S.C., §141.

66. 353 U.S. 138, 138–147 (1957).

67. The Court said: "The *only* [emphasis added] American connection was that the controversy erupted while the ship was transiently in a United States port and American labor unions participated in its picketing," *id.*, p. 142.

68. *Id.*, 143–144. *Accord,* Marine Cooks & Stewards, AFL v. Panama Steamship Co., 265 F. 2d 780 (9th Cir. 1959), where in view of *Benz* the Norris-La Guardia Act of 1932 was held inapplicable to picketing a flag-of-convenience vessel. But see Afran Transport Co. v. N.M.U., 169 F. Supp. 416 (S.D.N.Y. 1958); *motions to dismiss denied,* 175 F. Supp. 285 (S.D.N.Y. 1959), where the Court declined to halt picketing by unions and, refusing to follow *Benz,* held that the unions could show whether the facts constituted a bona fide dispute within the Norris-La Guardia Act, or whether the NLRB had jurisdiction.

foreign vessel, in particular wages of the crew, has been confirmed in several cases involving flag-of-convenience ships. In these cases the courts, referring to the dictum in *Lauritzen v. Larsen* that "perhaps the most venerable and universal rule of maritime law [relevant in the problem of conflict of laws] is that which gives cardinal importance to the law of the flag," and that "the weight given to the ensign overbears most other connecting events in determining applicable law,"[69] have decided that seamen's contracts are treated as matters of internal order or economy of the vessel and that in these matters the law of the flag is the controlling factor. In *McQuade v. Compañía de Vapores San Antonio, S.A.*, an alien seaman who had signed articles in a United States port to serve on a vessel registered in Honduras but owned by a Panamanian corporation sued under the law of Panama, the domicile of the shipowner, but the court held that the law of Honduras, the state of registry, was applicable.[70] An additional argument was the fact that both Panama and Honduras were parties to the Bustamante Code, which expressly provides that the internal order of the vessel is subject to the law of the flag.[71] The court, basing itself on *Lauritzen v. Larsen,* also found the signing of articles in an American port insufficient to bring American law into the case.[72]

Two other cases, *Grivas v. Alianza Compañía Armadora, S.A.*, and *Evangelinos v. Andreavapor Compañía Naviera, S.A.* deal with analogous situations. In both of them, the ship was registered in Liberia, but owned by a Panamanian corporation. In both cases, plaintiffs sought to have the Panamanian Labor Code applied, but the court applied the principle of the law of the flag. In *Grivas* the court observed that:

> The Panama Labor Code does not by its terms apply to ships registered in another country and flying the flag of another country, merely because they are owned by a Panamanian corporation. Panama might, of course, impose requirements on Panamanian corporations requiring them to comply with the provisions of the Panama Labor Code, but there has been no evidence offered to the Court that would establish that Panama has imposed such requirements or that the Labor Code applied

69. 345 U.S. 571, 584, 585 (1953).
70. 131 F. Supp. 365 (S.D.N.Y. 1955).
71. Article 281; 86 L.N.T.S. 246, 326 (1929).
72. 131 F. Supp. 365 (S.D.N.Y. 1955).

to a ship of foreign registry merely because it is owned by a Panamanian corporation.[73]

Rejecting explicitly jurisdiction by ownership, the court concluded that the fact that the vessel was owned by a Panamanian corporation did not in itself entitle the crew to the benefits of the Panamanian Labor Code.[74]

In *Evangelinos,* the Court, replying to the libellant's brief urging that the courts were frequently using the term "law of the flag" loosely and in contexts in which "law of the owner's domicile" could have been used with equal, or perhaps better, effect, stated positively: "We have not, however, been cited to any case in which the distinction between those terms, when material, was overlooked. The cases which apply the principle that the law of the flag is to govern matters such as the one before us are a legion." [75]

In none of the cases discussed above did the court inquire into the ultimate ownership of the vessel, and therefore the National Labor Relations Board cases in which the Board applied American labor statutes on Panlibhon-flag vessels ultimately owned and controlled by American corporations do not follow the line of *Benz.* The NLRB has considered several cases involving disputes between owners of flag-of-convenience vessels and American maritime unions. In *Compañía Marítima Sansoc Ltda* the Board in an administrative opinion refused a petition of the unions to represent seamen aboard a Panamanian vessel operated by aliens, but indicated that it would place considerable weight upon the fact of beneficial ownership.[76] In *Peninsular & Occidental Steamship Company and Green Trading Company* the Board accepted juris-

73. 150 F. Supp. 708, 711–712 (S.D.N.Y. 1957).

74. *Id.,* p. 712.

75. 162 F. Supp. 520, 521 (S.D.N.Y. 1958). Among other cases the court cited the following: *In re* Ross, 140 U.S. 453 (1891) (the decision where it was ruled that a sailor's nationality is deemed that of the vessel on which he serves): The Hanna Nielsen, 273 Fed. 171 (2d Cir. 1921); Taylor v. Atlantic Maritime Co., 179 F. 2d 597 (2d Cir. 1950); Radovcic v. The Princ Pavle, 45 F. Supp. 15 (S.D.N.Y. 1942); Cunard Steamship Co. v. Mellon, 262 U.S. 100 (1922); The Belgenland, 114 U.S. 355 (1884); Grivas v. Alianza Compañía Armadora, 150 F. Supp. 708 (S.D.N.Y. 1957); McQuade v. Compañía de Vapores San Antonio, S.A., 131 F. Supp. 365 (S.D.N.Y. 1955).

76. CCH N.L.R.B. Decisions 1950–1951, para. 10081 (1950). See also the discussion in "Panlibhon Registration of American-owned Merchant Ships: Government Policy and the Problem of the Courts" [Note] *Colum. L. Rev.* 60:711, 735–737 (1960).

diction over representation election on board two Liberian-flag vessels nominally owned by Liberian subsidiaries but ultimately controlled by an American corporation. The vessels in question sailed regularly from American ports and most of the crew signed articles in an American port.[77]

The leading case in the issue of labor jurisdiction over flag-of-convenience ships is that of *West India Fruit and Steamship Company, Inc.*, decided by the Board on February 16, 1961. Here the Board held that the Labor Management Relations Act applied to American-owned ships flying foreign flags, manned by non-resident aliens and operating from United States harbors. In particular the case involved an unfair labor practice charge brought against the company by the SIU, Atlantic and Gulf District, AFL-CIO, which attempted to organize the crew of the SS *Level*, owned and operated by the United States incorporated and controlled company. The ship was for the most part repaired and serviced in the United States. The NLRB found the *Lauritzen v. Larsen* guidelines applicable in the case and asserted that the fact that an American employer was involved and that the vessel was continually engaged in American commerce constituted substantial contacts warranting the application of American labor law notwithstanding foreign registry, alien crew and the fact that the unfair labor practices had been committed outside the United States waters. The argument (advanced by the two dissenting members of the board) that the national defense policies of the United States compelled the NLRB to decline to assert its jurisdiction was dismissed by the board. The majority of the NLRB concluded that the encouragement of transfers to Panlibhon does not rest upon any stated congressional policy, that the present national policy as established by the Congress is directed towards building up an American flag fleet manned by citizen personnel, that any conclusion that the application of the Act in question to flag-of-convenience vessels would have adverse effects on Department of Defense and Maritime Administration policies was necessarily speculative in nature, that, even assuming a conflict of national

77. 120 N.L.R.B. 1097 (1958). The case was again considered before the NLRB on unfair labor practices charge (case no. 12-CA-255) and in consolidated proceedings with Eastern Shipping Corp., McCormick Shipping Corp. (case no. 12-RC-415) and United Fruit Co. (case no. 2-RC-10379).

defense and labor relations law policies, the matter was one to be resolved by the Congress not by the NLRB, and that the board was without discretion under sec. 14 (c) (1) of the Act to decline to assert its jurisdiction.[78]

The case of the West India Fruit and Steamship Corp., the American owners of the SS *Level,* inaugurated a significant development with respect to the jurisdiction of American laws over the Panlibhon vessels involved in labor disputes. It was followed by other cases in which the NLRB examining the facts in each particular case, determined that substantial contacts existed between the given maritime operations and important United States interests, which warranted the application of the domestic law. Thus, in July 1961, an NLRB panel decided two to one that the Peninsular and Occidental Steamship Co., a Connecticut corporation, was the real owner of the steamship *Florida,* cruising out of Miami to Nassau, chartered to a subsidiary company in Liberia and flying the Liberian flag but leased back to the American concern for operation.[79] The next case was another step forward in the assertion of jurisdiction by the NLRB over Panlibhon shipping, since it involved a Panamanian concern — operating out of Miami in the Caribbean, manned mostly by a non-resident alien crew, owned by a Panamanian concern — the McCormick Shipping Corp. — in turn owned 95 per cent by foreign nationals. The NLRB, by a two to one vote, ordered that an election be held aboard the ship to determine whether its unlicensed seamen wanted to be represented by the SIU. It was held by the majority of the board that it was not necessary that "all significant contacts be American to warrant the application of a domestic law to a maritime operation having foreign attributes." It said that since the McCormick Shipping Corp. was engaged in "an essentially domestic enterprise, having a continuing and substantial impact on the domestic and foreign commerce of this nation," the NLRB could perceive "no reason why the foreign incorporation and ownership of McCormick should be held to bar jurisdiction over the company." [80]

In the case of the American-owned fleet of the Hamilton Bros.

78. West India Fruit and Steamship Corp., Inc., case no. 15-CA-1454, 130 N.L.R.B. No. 46 (1961).

79. *The New York Times,* July 12, 1961, p. 50. 130 N.L.R.B. No. 1 (1961).

80. *Id.,* August 12, 1961, p. 30.

Inc., trading with Central America, the NLRB ruled in favor of a Honduran seamen's union petitioning for a representation election on the company's Honduran-flag vessels. Applying the "contacts" method, the NLRB found that the company's operations "clearly possess those substantial United States contacts which bring them within the jurisdictional coverage of the [American] act." This was ruled notwithstanding the fact that the petitioning union was organized under the laws of Honduras and although the employer's vessels were engaged in trading with Honduras, the flag state of the ships in question.[81] A major victory for the seamen's unions in their efforts to organize foreign-flag ships controlled by United States interests was the NLRB ruling in favor of the NMU for a representation election on a fleet of 17 ships operated under the Honduran flag by Empresa Hondureña de Vapores, S.A., the wholly-owned Honduran subsidiary of the United Fruit Co., a New Jersey corporation with headquarters in Boston. Rejecting the company's contention that the 500 seamen involved were employees of a foreign corporation, serving on foreign-flag vessels and subject to Honduran labor laws, the NLRB ruled that Empresa Hondureña de Vapores and United Fruit Co. were "joint employers" of the seamen, that the United Fruit Co., virtually owned by United States citizens, chartering the vessels from the Honduran subsidiary, directed the operations of the fleet, and that those operations were "wholly integrated" in the company's shipping operations with its American vessels.[82]

In the foregoing cases the NLRB followed in its decisions the method used by the lower courts which deciding claims under the Jones Act had in some cases pierced the corporate veil of the

81. *Id.*, October 13, 1961, p. 56; 133 N.L.R.B. No. 85 (1961).

82. *Id.*, November 17, 1961, p. 57; 134 N.L.R.B. No. 25 (1961). However, the election aboard the *Empresa Hondureña* vessels was stayed by a temporary restraining order of the District Court of the District of Columbia, and subsequently the U.S. Court of Appeal for the Second Circuit reversed the lower court's order denying the temporary injunction against holding the election. The decision of the Court of Appeal may well be the first of a series of decisions pronouncing against the application of American labor laws aboard the Panlibhon vessels. See Empresa Hondureña de Vapores, S.A. v. McLeod, F.2d (2d Cir. 1962), decided January 12, 1962 (Docket No. 27314). See also *The New York Times*, November 17, 1961, p. 57; December 18, 1961, p. 58; December 19, 1961, p. 58; December 21, 1961, p. 48; December 22, 1961, p. 40; January 2, 1962, p. 32; January 12, 1962, p. 61.

nominal shipowning corporation. The nature of the application of the Jones Act[83] against the owners of foreign-flag vessels in American ports differs from that of the application of the Wagner and Taft-Hartley Acts. The essential difference is that the American courts, granting to foreign-flag seamen the remedy of the Jones Act, have acted on the assumption that this assertion of jurisdiction does not violate any principles of comity because "matters of 'internal management' are not involved in an action by a seaman to recover damages for injuries suffered through the negligence of the shipowner." [84]

The scope of the application of the Jones Act is in each particular case a problem of the court's interpretation of the Act, which, using general language, refers to "any seaman" and makes no explicit requirement of any connection with the United States. The method of finding the answer to each particular case before the court was analyzed by the Supreme Court in *Lauritzen v. Larsen*, but neither the outcome of this case, in which the Jones Act was held inapplicable, nor the language of the Court precludes the possibility of applying the Jones Act to flag-of-convenience vessels substantially controlled by American interests. In *Lauritzen v. Larsen* the factor on which the injured seaman chiefly relied to invoke American law was that of place of contract in the United States, which has no substantial influence in the choice between competing laws to govern a maritime tort. In addition, the Court in *Lauritzen v. Larsen* explicitly stated that the Jones Act was not applicable just "in this case." The law of the flag was found to be of cardinal importance, but the Court pointed out that the law of the place of allegiance of the defendant shipowner could also be determinative. Mentioning the practice of the flags of convenience, the Court observed:

Confronted with such operations, our courts on occasion have pressed beyond the formalities of more or less nominal foreign registration to

83. 41 Stat. 1007 (1920), 46 U.S.C. §688 (1952): "Any seaman who shall suffer personal injury in the course of his employment may, at his election, maintain an action for damages at law, with the right of trial by jury, and in such action all statutes of the United States modifying or extending the common-law right or remedy in cases of personal injury to railway employees shall apply. . . ." The act referred to by §688 is the Employers' Liability Act, 35 Stat. 65 (1908), 45 U.S.C. §§51–60 (1952).

84. Gerradin v. United Fruit Co., 60 F. 2d 927, 929 (2d Cir. 1932).

enforce against American shipowners the obligations which our law places upon them. But *here again* [emphasis added] the utmost liberality in disregard of formality does not support the application of American law in this case, for it appears beyond doubt that this owner is a Dane by nationality and domicile.[85]

Similarly, the recent case of *Romero v. International Terminal Operating Co.*,[86] ruling that the Jones Act is inapplicable to foreign seamen injured on a foreign-owned vessel flying a foreign flag, even if the injury occurred in a United States port, does not affect the cases of American-owned vessels sailing under flags of convenience.

Therefore, the foregoing two cases decided by the Supreme Court do not seem to provide a sound basis for the view that the Jones Act is not applicable to flag-of-convenience ships controlled by American interests;[87] they only substantiate the view that not every contact, no matter how ephemeral or fortuitous it might be, can be the basis for applying American law.[88] A restatement of the method of approach in Jones Act cases, in particular those in which American-owned flag-of-convenience ships are involved, was undertaken by the United States Court of Appeal (Second Circuit) in *Bartholomew v. Universe Tankships, Inc.*, where the Court comes to the conclusion that for the Jones Act to be applied in a particular case, a "substantial" contact is necessary, which is "something between minimal and preponderant contacts." [89] In the words of the Court:

the decisional process of arriving at a conclusion on the subject of the application of the Jones Act involves the ascertainment of the facts or groups of facts which constitute contacts between the transaction involved in the case and the United States, and then deciding whether or not they are substantial. Thus each factor is to be 'weighed' and 'evaluated' only to the end that, after each factor has been given consideration, a rational and satisfactory conclusion may be arrived at on the question of whether all the factors present add up to the necessary substantiality.

85. 345 U.S 587, 588–589 (1953).
86. 358 U.S. 354 (1959).
87. These two cases provide such basis for the argument in the ACFN *Memorandum*, pp. 54–55.
88. The view opposite to that expressed in the ACFN *Memorandum* is represented in Harolds, pp, 299, 305–313. Studying the legislative history of the Jones Act Harolds comes to the conclusion that "Congress *purposely* phrased section 688 [of the Jones Act] in broad terms so as to make it applicable to foreign seamen injured aboard foreign vessels in our ports."
89. 263 F. 2d 437, 440 (2d Cir. 1959).

Moreover, each factor, or contact, or group of facts must be treated in the light of the underlying objective, which is to effectuate the liberal purposes of the Jones Act.[90]

A study of the Jones Act cases involving American-owned flag-of-convenience vessels (Table 10) shows that ultimate ownership

TABLE 10. Jones Act cases involving American-owned flag-of-convenience ships.

No.[a]	Flag	Nominal ownership	Control	Nationality or domicile of seaman	Situs of injury	Seaman signed on in—
			Jones Act remedy held applicable			
1	Hond.	Hond.	U.S.	U.S.	High seas	U.S.
2	Pan.	Pan.	U.S.	Alien	High seas	
3	Hond.	Pan.	U.S.	U.S.[b]	Foreign	
4	Lib.	Lib.	U.S.	Alien	High seas	
5	Pan.	Pan.	U.S.	Alien	Foreign	U.S.
6	Lib.	Lib.	U.S.	Alien	Foreign	U.S.
7	Lib.	Lib.[c]	U.S.	U.S.[b]	Foreign	
			Jones Act remedy refused			
8	Pan.	Pan.	Alien	Alien	High seas	
9	Lib.	Pan.	Alien	Alien	Foreign	U.S.

[a] Numbers refer to cases as follows:

1. Gerradin v. United Fruit Company, 60 F. 2d 927 (2d Cir.) *cert. denied*, 287 U.S. 642 (1932).
2. Carroll v. United States, 133 F. 2d 690 (2d Cir. 1943).
3. Zielinski v. Empresa Hondureña de Vapores, 113 F. Supp. 93 (S.D.N.Y. 1953).
4. Rodr'guez v. Solar Shipping Ltd., 169 F. Supp. 79 (S.D.N.Y. 1958).
5. Bobolakis v. Compañía Panameña Marítima San Gerassimo, S.A., 168 F. Supp. 236 (S.D.N.Y. 1958).
6. Forde v. Urania Transportation Inc., 168 F. Supp. 240 (S.D.N.Y. 1958).
7. Bartholomew v. Universe Tankships, Inc., 263 F. 2d 437 (2d Cir. 1959).
8. Argyros v. Polar Compañía de Navegación Ltda., 146 F. Supp. 624 (S.D.N.Y. 1956).
9. Mproumeriotis v. Seacrest Shipping Company, 149 F. Supp. 265 (S.D.N.Y. 1957).

[b] Domicile.

[c] Owned by Panama.

of these vessels combined with actual control thereof are contacts sufficient for the application of the Jones Act. This means that in

90. *Id.*, p. 441. *Accord,* Firipis v. S/S Margaritis, 181 F. Supp. 48 (E.D. Va. 1960).

order for the purposes of the Jones Act not to be frustrated by American shipowners by registration under the flags of convenience, American courts have looked "through the façade of foreign registration and incorporation to the American ownership behind it." [91] Giving effect to the nationality of the actual control of the ship, the courts do not disregard the corporate entity of the subsidiary base company, and do not impose liability directly on the American stockholders, but use the fiction that the foreign subsidiaries are American, not foreign (Honduran or Panamanian, respectively) corporations.[92]

The two cases of *Argyros v. Polar Compañía de Navegación, Ltda.*[93] and *Mproumeriotis v. Seacrest Shipping Co.*,[94] in which the stock ownership alone was found insufficient warrant to apply the Jones Act, seem to be exceptions to the rule that American-owned flag-of-convenience vessels are covered by Jones Act jurisdiction. In the later case of *Rodríguez v. Solar Shipping, Ltd.*[95] the Court explained the outcome of those two cases by the fact that in them the plaintiffs had not alleged both ownership and control of the vessels, whereas the *Rodríguez* case, alleging operation and control by citizens of the United States, went beyond the allegations in the *Argyros* and *Mproumeriotis* cases and fell within the "control" test in the *Zielinski* case.[96]

91. 263 F. 2d 441 (2d Cir. 1959). In *Bartholomew v. Universe Tankships, Inc.*, the American owners took the trouble to insert an additional nominal foreign corporation between the flag and the true beneficial ownership. The vessel was flying the flag of Liberia and was owned by a Liberian corporation whose stock was held by a Panamanian; all stock of the latter was owned by U.S. citizens. However, the court brushed all this aside, believing that "complicating the mechanics of evasive schemes cannot serve to make them more effective." *Accord*, Bobolakis v. Compañía Marítima San Gerassimo, 168 F. Supp. 236, 238 (S.D.N.Y. 1959). Here the court stated: "Under the view pressed by [the defendant] Compañía, an American owner might escape his statutory liability merely by interposing a foreign corporation between himself and the vessel, both of which, for all practical purposes, he owns. I do not believe that the law can be so easily baffled. . . . For the purposes with which we are concerned such corporate intervention is but a weak fortress."

92. Zielinski v. Empresa Hondureña de Vapores, 113 F. Supp. 93, 95 (S.D.N.Y. 1953); *Accord*, Bartholomew v. Universe Tankships, Inc., 263 F. 2d 437 (2d Cir. 1959).

93. 146 F. Supp. 624 (S.D.N.Y. 1956).

94. 149 F. Supp. 265 (S.D.N.Y. 1957).

95. 169 F. Supp. 79 (S.D.N.Y. 1958).

96. Zielinski v. Empresa Hondureña de Vapores, 113 F. Supp. 93, 95 (S.D.N.Y. 1953). (Not the stock ownership but the fact that "actual control" of the vessel is by U.S. citizens, permits the application of the Jones Act.) In *Bartholomew v. Universe Tankships, Inc.*, the cases of *Mproumeriotis* and *Argyros* are considered

The American nationality or domicile of the injured seaman and the occurrence of the tort in the waters of the United States give, of course, additional weight to the application of the Jones Act to American-controlled flag-of-convenience ships, but American ownership and control of the vessel seem to be the key contact in such cases.[97] The cases of *Uravic v. F. Jarka Co.*[98] and *Gambera v. Bergoty,*[99] in which the Jones Act was held applicable, the only contacts being American domicile of the seaman and American situs of injury, support the thesis that the Jones Act might be applicable under these circumstances to foreign-owned flag-of-convenience ships in American ports.[100]

Now the question remains to be solved whether the commercial and consular treaties of the United States with the flag-of-convenience countries limit the United States in the assertion of its jurisdiction on board American-owned flag-of-convenience vessels. The United States has the following treaties of this kind with the flag-of-convenience countries: Treaty of Friendship, Commerce and Navigation with Liberia, August 8, 1938;[101] Consular Convention with Liberia, October 7, 1938;[102] Treaty of Friendship, Commerce, and Consular Rights with Honduras, December 7, 1927;[103] Treaty of Friendship, Commerce, and Navigation with Costa Rica, July 10, 1851;[104] and Consular Convention with Costa Rica, January 12, 1948.[105] There are no such treaties with Panama.

The flag recognition provisions binding the United States in the

"of doubtful validity"; 263 F. 2d 437, 443 (2d Cir. 1959). On the other hand the counsel for the ACFN used the same expression for the cases of *Rodríguez* and *Bobolakis;* see ACFN *Memorandum,* p. 55: "Such a construction, even for welfare purposes, is of doubtful validity."

97. The cases of Gerradin v. United Fruit Co., 60 F. 2d 927 (2d Cir.), *cert. denied,* 287 U.S. 642 (1932), and Zielinski v. Empresa Hondureña de Vapores, 113 F. Supp. 93 (S.D.N.Y. 1953).

98. 282 U.S. 234 (1931).

99. 132 F. 2d 414 (2d Cir. 1942), *cert. denied,* 319 U.S. 742 (1943).

100. But if the seaman were an alien, the courts would refuse the Jones Act remedy, following *Romero v. International Terminal Operating Co.,* 358 U.S. 354 (1959). Thus, *e.g.* in *Penedo Compañía Naviera v. Maniatis,* 262 F. 2d 284 (2d Cir. 1959) in a personal injury action by a Greek seaman against a foreign owner of a Liberian vessel, the court applied the general law of Liberia and not the Jones Act. Cf. Markakis v. Mparmpa Christos, 161 F. Supp. 487 (S.D.N.Y. 1958).

101. 54 Stat. 1739; T.S. 956; 201 L.N.T.S. 163.

102. 54 Stat. 1751; T.S. 957; 201 L.N.T.S. 183.

103. 45 Stat. 2618; T.S. 764; 87 L.N.T.S. 421.

104. 10 Stat. 916; T.S. 62; Malloy, I, 341.

105. 1 U.S.T. 247; T.I.A.S. 2045; 70 U.N.T.S. 27.

treaties with Liberia and Honduras were discussed in Chapter IV. The conditions relating to the exercise of jurisdiction over events and persons aboard ships in ports are laid down in the Consular Convention with Liberia and the above mentioned treaty with Honduras. The Consular Convention with Liberia provides:

> A consular officer shall have exclusive jurisdiction over controversies arising out of the internal order of private vessels of his country, and shall alone exercise jurisdiction in cases, whenever arising, between officers and crews, pertaining to the enforcement of discipline on board, provided the vessel and the persons charged with wrongdoing shall have entered a port within his consular district. Such an officer shall also have jurisdiction over issues concerning the adjustment of wages and the execution of contracts relating thereto provided, however, that such jurisdiction shall not exclude the jurisdiction conferred on local authorities under existing or future laws.[106]

The provision in the treaty with Honduras is almost identical,[107] and the formulation in the Consular Treaty with Costa Rica is essentially the same.[108] The above-mentioned provisions are representative of the practice of maritime states, the United States included, and can be found in many other treaties of this kind.[109]

The consular treaties with Liberia and Honduras grant to the consular officers exclusive jurisdiction over "controversies arising out of the internal order" of private vessels of their respective countries, and specifically refer to sole jurisdiction of the consuls the cases pertaining to "the enforcement of discipline," and "wrongdoing" between officers and crews. In the treaty with Costa Rica, both kinds of matters are included within the exclusive jurisdiction of the consular officers. The question arises of the interpretation of the phrase "controversies arising out of the internal order" of the vessel. This sentence is usually interpreted to refer to disciplinary matters between captain and crew, minor offenses on board and suits for certain wage claims, but does not seem to imply that applying American labor legislation aboard the vessels flying

106. Consular Convention with Liberia, October 7, 1938, art. X, para. 1; 54 Stat. 1751; T.S. 957; 201 L.N.T.S. 183.

107. Treaty of Friendship, Commerce, and Consular Rights with Honduras December 7, 1927, art. XXII, para. 1; 45 Stat. 2618; T.S. 764; 87 L.N.T.S. 421.

108. Consular Convention with Costa Rica, January 12, 1948, art. X; 1 U.S.T. 247; T.I.A.S. 2045; 70 U.N.T.S. 27.

109. For the earlier treaties of the United States see Harvard Research, "The Law of Territorial Waters," pp. 312–314.

Liberian, Honduran or Costa Rican flag would be in conflict with it.[110]

Thus, for example, the relevant article of the treaty with Honduras has been interpreted as not affecting the right of seamen to recover under the Jones Act for negligence against the American ultimate owner of the Honduran ship.[111] Moreover, the consuls have only concurrent jurisdiction over "issues concerning the adjustment of wages and the execution of contracts relating thereto," because the treaties explicitly lay down that the jurisdiction conferred in these matters on local authorities under existing or future laws is not excluded.[112] It is interesting to note that in the earlier treaties of the United States, the matters relating to the adjustment of wages and the execution of contracts were also within the exclusive jurisdiction of the consular officers; and only in treaties which have been concluded since the First World War has this kind of jurisdiction been conditioned upon the requirement that the local laws of the contracting parties so permit.[113] Such are the treaties with the flag-of-convenience countries, Liberia, Honduras, and Costa Rica.

The application of American labor laws aboard American-owned flag-of-convenience ships would not conflict with the consular treaties with Liberia, Honduras, and Costa Rica,[114] but if these labor statutes were to be applied only to flag-of-convenience vessels, this would amount to the violation of the non-discrimination clauses in the commercial treaties with Liberia and Honduras,

110. See "Flag-of-Convenience Fleet," *YLJ* 69:512 (1950) notes 102–104 (citing cases) and the accompanying text. And see also the opinion of the counsel for the ACFN who, analyzing the treaties in question, concluded that "our courts, the National Labor Relations Board and other agencies of our government are without jurisdiction to act in labor disputes arising on vessels registered under the laws of Liberia and Honduras." ACFN *Memorandum*, p. 118. This view is criticized in "Flag-of-Convenience Fleet," *YLJ* 69:511–513 (1960).

111. Gerradin v. United Fruit Co., 60 F. 2d 927 (2d Cir.), *cert. denied*, 287 U.S. 642 (1932).

112. This provision is narrowly interpreted by the counsel for the ACFN as referring only to "the remedial functions exercised by courts in interpreting and enforcing seamen's wage contracts and wage claims and to provide an alternative method for seamen to sign and execute articles of agreement in foreign ports." ACFN *Memorandum*, p. 117.

113. For the examples of such treaties, see Hyde, I, 742, n. 1.

114. The case of Costa Rica is of negligible importance, since there are virtually no American-owned vessels under the flag of Costa Rica.

and would bring about protests by these countries.[115] Therefore, the statutes would have to be consistently applied also on other American-owned ships flying the flags of various European states, in particular the United Kingdom. Since labor relations aboard these vessels are governed by well-developed bodies of the flag states' labor laws, serious international conflicts and protests would result, similar to those which followed the attempt to extend the La Follette Act to foreign vessels in 1928. If, despite the diplomatic protests, the American jurisdiction were asserted, the American merchant ships calling at foreign ports would be subject to retaliatory measures applied by the foreign government, affected by the American measures. Thus the violation of the principle of restraint and forbearance in the exercise of jurisdiction would negatively affect international commerce and the common use of the oceans. As events have shown, the decisions of the NLRB to assume jurisdiction in labor disputes over Panlibhon vessels have already produced international disputes. After the Board's decision in *West India Fruit and Steamship Co., Inc.* the Panamanian Foreign Minister making in March 1961 a special visit to Washington met with Secretary of State Rusk, and expressing his concern about the decision, warned that his government might find it necessary to take retaliatory measures. Claiming that the NLRB practically assumed control over vessels flying foreign flags and over acts performed on the high seas, the Panamanian Minister stated:

> This decision is very far-reaching and violates century-old rules of international law to the effect that vessels are governed as to their internal regime and order by the laws of the flag they fly. In line with this decision, United States authorities can make rules for the entire shipping world without regard to the sovereign independence of foreign nations . . . [The decision] may open the door to reprisals by other nations, including Panama, who could subject American-flag vessels entering their ports to their domestic rules as to the internal matters of vessels such as the type of labor relations contracts they should have.[116]

115. Treaty of Friendship, Commerce and Navigation with Liberia, August 8, 1938, art. VII; 54 Stat. 1739; T.S. 956; 201 L.N.T.S. 163. Similar provisions are found in the treaties with Honduras and Costa Rica. See Treaty of Friendship, Commerce, and Consular Rights with Honduras, December 7, 1927, art. VII; 45 Stat. 2618; T.S. 764; 87 L.N.T.S. 421; Treaty of Friendship, Commerce, and Navigation with Costa Rica, July 10, 1851, art. II; 10 Stat. 916; T.S. 62; Malloy, I, 341.

116. *The New York Times,* March 27, 1961, p. 44.

The Panamanian Minister did not conceal the reasons for Panama's preoccupation: drop in the registration of ships in Panama constituting a decrease in revenue for his nation. Another Panamanian protest followed the NLRB decision in the *Yarmouth* case. The Panamanian note to the United States Department of State threatened that Panama might assert, as a reprisal method, her 12-mile jurisdiction over her national waters including the waters near the Panama Canal.[117] The Liberian government also protested with the government of the United States against the pressure being imposed on Liberian-flag vessels by American maritime unions.[118]

From the foregoing considerations the following conclusions can be reached concerning jurisdiction over the flag-of-convenience ships, in particular jurisdiction in labor cases: The jurisdiction of the flag-of-convenience states over their vessels does not, in principle, differ from the jurisdiction exercised by other states over their own shipping. The Panlibhon states are entitled to establish the law and exercise authority over their ships in national waters and on the high seas. In foreign waters, these ships, according to the general rule of international law, become subject to the jurisdiction of the local state whose courts may have jurisdiction even in matters which originated on the high seas.

Reasons of interest in the unhampered flow of international commerce as well as danger of retaliation, point to the conclusion that the coastal state should waive the exercise of its sovereign rights in matters of civil jurisdiction, in particular those pertaining to "internal economy," including labor relations, aboard flag-of-convenience vessels. In case of the United States, although the application of the Jones Act could not seriously affect the future of the flags of convenience, the assertion of labor jurisdiction, in general, over the American-controlled Panlibhon vessels might force the owners of these vessels to transfer them to other flags, which would conflict with important considerations of the United States

117. *Id.*, September 1, 1961, p. 45.

118. *Id.*, September 13, 1961, p. 75 (According to the Liberian delegate to the 20th International Navigation Congress meeting in Baltimore in September 1961.) Honduras also protested against the NLRB decision ordering elections aboard the Honduran-flag vessels of Empresa Hondureña de Vapores, S.A. See *The New York Times*, December 21, 1961, p. 48; January 12, 1962, p. 61. Honduras charged that the decision violated treaty provisions between the United States and Honduras.

shipping policy. Therefore the problem, from the American point of view, must be viewed "in a broader context than a labor bargaining issue"[119] and the Administration's policy on the matter should take into account not only the private rights of the parties but also considerations of public policy, in particular the availability of the shipping in question to the United States in case of national emergency. This is closely related with the concept of the so called "effective U.S. control" whose international-law implications are discussed in Chapter VII.

119. Statement of R. L. Gilpatrick, Deputy Secretary of Defense; *The New York Times*, August 1, 1961, p. 44. The matter was discussed jointly by the Departments of Labor, Defense, and State, in connection with the maritime strike in the summer of 1961. *Cf.* a leading article by Krock, "A Reminder to Congress of a Dangerous Deadline," *id.*, August 29, 1961, p. 30.

Chapter VII. The Doctrine of "Effective United States Control"

The state that has attributed its national character to a merchant vessel has an unquestionable competence to control its movements and activities. This prerogative is of particular importance for the flag state in time of national emergency or war, when it has also the right to requisition private merchant ships possessing its nationality[1] — ships that may be within or without its territorial waters.[2] Since the foregoing prerogatives of the states are based on the criteria of registry, and not ownership, they would seem to obtain also in the case of Liberia, Panama, and other flag-of-convenience countries.

In view of the peculiar situation of the fleets of these countries, which are beneficially owned by nationals of other states, various international law problems arise in connection with the right to control and requisition their ships in case of war or other serious emergency.

It is true that Liberia, Panama, and other flag-of-convenience states have, under general international law, the right to requisition in wartime the vessels flying their ensigns, but, on the other hand, the question may be raised whether the state of which the beneficial, ultimate owners of the vessels are citizens has the right

1. See Texas Co. v. Hogarth Shipping Co., 256 U.S. 619, 628 (1920).

2. See The Adriatic, 258 Fed. 902, 903 (C.C.A. 3d 1919); Linea Sud-Americana, Inc. v. 7,295.40 Tons of Linseed, 29 F. Supp. 210 (S.D.N.Y. 1939); The Luigi, 230 Fed. 493 (E.D. Pa. 1916); Lorentzen v. Lydden [1942] 2. K.B. 202.

to expect that the property of its nationals, in this case, the ships, will be available to it for defense purposes in case of war or other serious national emergency. This is particularly true of the American-owned flag-of-convenience vessels which — as is well known — are of vital interest for the defense of the United States.

From the practical point of view, the simple fact that neither Liberia, Panama, or Honduras would be able, in the case of an emergency, to enforce their control or to requisition the vessels registered under their flag has, of course, decisive impact upon the whole problem, but from the strictly legal point of view, the situation of the flag-of-convenience vessels in case of war presents a multitude of problems, some of which may be of only academic value, but others of quite practical significance.

The first question this situation poses is whether a state is entitled in time of national emergency to control the movements of, and to requisition, the vessels ultimately owned by its nationals but registered under a foreign flag. In concrete terms, what is the international law aspect of the so-called "effective United States control" over the American-owned Panlibhon vessels?

This aspect of the problem came to the attention of the congressional committee at the hearings on vessel transfer. A discussion between the then Maritime Administrator Morse and the chief counsel of the Committee on Merchant Marine and Fisheries, Mr. Drewry, is revealing. It shows that the international-law aspect of the whole problem of "effective control" is rather obscure to the competent authorities:

Mr. Drewry: Mr. Morse, I believe you said that you could requisition American-owned foreign-flag ships. Under what authority can you do that?

Mr. Morse: Section 902 of the 1936 act.

Mr. Drewry: That is without the consent of the country under whose flag it flies?

Mr. Morse: I think that has never been treated in the courts or in international law but I am sure that the statute says we have authority to do so.

Mr. Drewry: The statute says, "any vessel or other watercraft owned by citizens of the United States," is that correct? I was interested in what might occur with some nationalities at least if we were to decide we wanted to requisition a ship flying their flag.

Mr. Morse: My speculation would not be any more valuable than yours,

Mr. Drewry.
Mr. Drewry: Thank you.[3]

It will be recalled here that defense considerations are the major reason for the commitment of the United States government to the practice of operating vessels under the flags of convenience. The American-owned vessels flying flags of convenience are believed by the Maritime Administration, the Department of Defense, and the Department of the Navy to be under "effective United States control" or "effective United States management control." As a spokesman for the Navy presented the problem:

> Effective U.S. control applies to selected American-owned ships which have been registered by their owners under the so-called "flags of convenience" (Panama, Honduras and Liberia) in order to reduce operating costs . . . It is important that U.S. "effective control" of this shipping be retained . . . Over the past few years, the American-owned merchant fleet registered under the so-called "flags of convenience" has become significant in national defense planning.[4]

The meaning of this "planning concept" is that the vessels in question will be available on request to the United States in case of a national emergency and that, although the whole arrangement

3. *Hearings* (House) 1957, p. 168.

4. Statement of Vice Admiral John Silvester, U.S. Navy, Deputy Chief of Naval Operations (Logistics) on March 10, 1961, *The New York Times,* June 21, 1961 p. 10. Similar statements were made by others, including: Vice Admiral Emory S. Land, U.S. Navy (Ret.), former chairman of the United States Maritime Commission, in his report to the Business Advisory Council, May 13, 1961; former Secretary of Defense Thomas S. Gates in his letter to the Attorney General, October 26, 1960; *ibid.* [also statement of Secretary Gates in *Hearings* (House) 1957, pp. 630–633]; Deputy Secretary of Defense Roswell L. Gilpatrick, *The New York Times,* August 31, 1961, p. 44. See also the testimony of then Maritime Administrator Morse, *Hearings* (House) 1957, pp. 129–135; *id.,* pp. 552–554, 601–606; statement of Rear Admiral Collins, Assistant Chief of Naval Operations for Logistics, *Hearings* (Senate) 1957, pp. 223–224. See also report prepared by the MARAD-Navy Planning Group, April 12, 1957: "Ocean Shipping to Support the Defense of the United States," *Hearings* (House) 1957, pp. 556–561; letter of then Secretary of the Navy Thomas, *id.,* pp. 566–567; statements by Vice Admiral Wilson, then Deputy Chief of Naval Operations, *The New York Times,* October 17, 1959, p. 46; April 5, 1960, p. 62; Schade, pp. 40–43.

The "U.S. effective control" concept was referred to also by representatives of various shipowning companies in *Hearings* (Senate) 1957, pp. 15, 74. See also the full-page advertisement of the ACFN in *The New York Times,* June 21, 1961, p. 10. The concept was discussed in pleadings before the NLRB. See, *e.g.,* the brief of the Department of Justice in *West India Fruit and Steamship Co., Inc.,* Case No. 15 CA-1454; 130 N.L.R.B. No. 46 (1961). The concept was also presented to the ICJ in the oral statement of Hager, who was representing the government of the United States at the proceedings; see ICJ *Pleadings,* Constitution, (1960), pp. 427–429.

"has its faults," there is "reasonable prospect of gaining control" of these ships.[5] Therefore, the American-owned flag-of-convenience vessels are included in the plans of mobilization capability and the assumptions used in determining the size of the operating national defense fleet.[6] "If we lost them [flag-of-convenience ships] — stated a United States Navy specialist — "our defense mobilization plans are so much waste paper . . . In my opinion the ships that are fighting the battle [here the battle between the shipowners and the unions is meant] will be flying flags, not of convenience, nor even necessity, but of survival." [7]

Whereas the United States government's and the American shipowners' position is that the American-owned Panlibhon ships would be available for the United States in an emergency, the American maritime unions reject as fallacious and as "nonsense" the doctrine of "effective U.S. control." The unions, which for well-known reasons fight the flags of convenience, contend that a ship sailing in foreign waters under a foreign flag with a foreign crew cannot be effectively controlled by the United States government in time of international crisis.[8] One must add that doubts as to whether there is real assurance that the Panlibhon vessels would, in time of war, come indisputably under "effective U.S. control," are harbored also among members of various congressional committees.[9] The importance of the United States-owned Panlibhon shipping to the defense of the United States is also objected to by certain European shipping circles for which the emphasis on the importance of this fleet is an attempt to belittle

5. Testimony of Rear Admiral Collins, *Hearings* (House) 1957, p. 602.

6. *Hearings* (House) 1957, pp. 552–553; *cf.* Report of the MARAD-Navy Planning Group, *id.*, p. 557. From the operational point of view, the flag-of-convenience ships are more valuable for mobilization requirements than the reserve fleet because, unlike the reserve ("mothball") fleet, they are modern and are available without going through the time-consuming process of reconditioning and activating; *id.*, pp. 554, 570, 602, 604, 632.

7. Quoted by the ACFN in the full-page advertisement in *The New York Times*, June 21, 1961, p. 10.

8. *The New York Times*, August 6, 1961, p. 11. See also the statement of Haddock, executive secretary of the AFL-CIO Maritime Committee, *Hearings* (Senate) 1957, p. 176.

9. Statements of Senator Magnuson, chairman of the Committee on Interstate and Foreign Commerce, *Hearings* (Senate) 1957, pp. 3, 26, and statements by members of the House Committee on Merchant Marine and Fisheries, *Hearings* (House) 1957, pp. 601, 631. *Cf.* also National Academy of Sciences–National Research Council, *The Role of the U.S. Merchant Marine in National Security* (1959), pp. 31–32.

the importance of West European merchant fleets to the North Atlantic Treaty Organization defense plans.[10]

The factors which United States government agencies believe ensure the effective control of the American-owned flag-of-convenience vessels have both a legal and a factual basis. The legal arguments are based on domestic legislation. The first legal factor within the scope of domestic law which is designed to establish the "effective control" is the statutory authority of the Secretary of Commerce to requisition, during any national emergency proclaimed by the President, "any vessel or other watercraft owned by citizens of the United States." [11] Then, there are contractual agreements between the Maritime Administration and the owners of vessels transferred to foreign registry, which guarantee, under penalties, ultimate American ownership of the vessels and American majority in the directorship of the corporations, and form "a genuine link in the control concept." [12] The owners also contract, under severe penalties, to make their ships available to the government in case of emergency.[13] There are even written agreements between the Department of the Navy and American operators of certain categories of flag-of-convenience ships about the taking over of these ships. These agreements provide that a United States fleet commander may take over control of a flag-of-convenience ship immediately, without consent of the owner, the formalities to be arranged later. In case of resistance of the crew, the taking over of the control is effected by seizure.[14] Recently, the Maritime Administration announced that it would provide United States government war risk insurance or re-insurance for

10. See the statement of Jorgen Jahre, president of the Norwegian Shipowners Association, challenging statements made before the House Ways and Means Committee by E. D. Naess, *The New York Times,* June 30, 1961, p. 54. See also Mender, pp. 343–347.

11. Merchant Marine Act, 1936, §902: 49 Stat. 2015 (1936), as amended, 53 Stat. 1255 (1939), 46 U.S.C., §1242 (1952).

12. Statement of then Secretary of the Navy Gates, *Hearings* (House) 1957, p. 632.

13. See the Statement of Policy on Foreign Transfers of the Maritime Administration, November 5, 1956, 21 Fed. Reg. 8588 (1956), as amended, 21 Fed. Reg. 8920 (1956), 22 Fed. Reg. 4289 (1957), 22 Fed. Reg. 4448 (1957), 22 Fed. Reg. 7397 (1957), 23 Fed. Reg. 5956 (1958). See also the statement of then Maritime Administrator Morse, *Hearings* (House) 1957, p. 135.

14. Testimony of Rear Admiral Collins, *id.,* pp. 579–580, 583, 584, 605–606.

vessels flying the flags of Panlibhon but majority-owned by United States citizens.[15]

The foregoing legal factors are all based on the municipal law of the country of ownership of the vessels, and do not take into account the international law aspect of the problem, which presents the following picture: Flag-of-convenience countries have, under customary international law, the unquestionable right to control the movements and activities of the vessels registered under their flags.[16] Such was also the conclusion reached by the congressional committee inquiring into the subject of the transfer of ships to the flags of convenience. The problem of control over American-owned flag-of-convenience shipping was discussed, in particular, on the basis of the experience of the Second World War, the Korean conflict, and the Suez crisis in 1956.

It is difficult to give the exact data as to the actual availability of these ships in the Second World War.[17] Senator Magnuson, presiding at the Hearings of the Senate Subcommittee on Merchant Marine and Fisheries, correctly understood the essential legal point at issue when he, first of all, wanted to ascertain who, during the Second World War, directed the movements and use of the American-owned vessels under the Panamanian flag, "whether there was a directive from the Panamanian Government as to their use or whether . . . [the United States] Government made that decision."[18] From the various contradictory testimonies, it results that although in most cases the American-owned Panamanian flag ships became available to the United States, a number of them, especially those which happened to be in harbors where the United States had no physical control, were not avail-

15. *The New York Times*, December 3, 1959, p. 65.

16. About this prerogative of the states in general see McDougal, Burke, & Vlasic, p. 63, where the relevant case of *Furness, Withy & Co. v. Rederiaktiebolaget Banco* [1917] 2 K.B. 873 is discussed.

17. As to the First World War, the Maritime Administrator testified that "[Panama and Liberia] have made their ships available to us in past wars." *Hearings* (Senate) 1957, p. 129. This statement is hard to understand since there was no Liberian fleet in the First or Second World War and hardly any Panamanian fleet in the First. On the other hand, the executive secretary of the AFL-CIO Maritime Committee stated that "World War I proved very conclusively that American-owned foreign-flag ships were not available to the United States," *id.*, p. 176.

18. *Hearings* (House) 1957, pp. 17, 74.

able.[19] In the cases where the United States directed the movements of the Panamanian flag vessels beneficially owned by American citizens, this was done with the friendly acquiescence of Panama. However, Panama, being the country of registry, was, from the international law point of view, entitled to direct the movement of its ships. In this respect, Senator Magnuson stated:

> I think that the record would probably show — I am not sure about this — that during the war, although a ship flying the Panamanian flag was technically and legally under the Panamanian Government's regulations, they cooperated with us in any directions through them and sort of acted as our agent. But technically they could pass regulations or could direct a ship under the Panamanian flag in case of emergency, to do what they suggested it do, rather than us.[20]

In recent years, the Suez crisis of 1956 brought to the fore the question of controlling the movements of merchant vessels in the war zones. Congressional hearings revealed that the state of actual ownership, that is, the United States, did not direct American-owned flag-of-convenience ships as to what their movement should be in the Suez combat area.[21] Similarly, only American-flag vessels were mentioned in the statement prepared by the Department of State with regard to the American position on the transit of the

19. The use of the two Socony Mobil Oil Co. tankers flying the Panamanian flag was directed by the United States War Shipping Administration; *id.*, p. 57. The Panamanian flag vessels of the Esso Shipping Company were promptly offered to the War Shipping Administration on the same terms as applied to United States flag tankers which that Administration had requisitioned; *id.*, pp. 73–74. These ships are also probably those meant by Vice-Admiral Land in his report "The Merchant Marine of Panama as an American Asset," *Hearings* (House) 1957, pp. 100–102. On the other hand, many American-owned ships flying the Panamanian flag either could not or did not want to come to American-controlled waters; statement of Senator Magnuson, *id.*, p. 53. Therefore the statement of Vice Admiral Land in his report to the Business Advisory Council, May 13, 1961, that the ships in question were immediately available to the U.S. in the Second World War does not seem to be entirely correct; statement quoted in advertisement of the ACFN, *The New York Times*, June 21, 1961, p. 10.

20. *Hearings* (House) 1957, p. 53.

21. Testimony of Maritime Administrator, *id.*, p. 133–134; testimony of Rear Admiral Collins, *id.*, p. 580. One American-owned tanker, "The Statue of Liberty," flying one of the flags of convenience was caught in the closure of the Suez Canal. Its master had asked the United States Maritime Administration for advice as to whether to transit the Canal. The Administration recommended that the ship should not do so, but this was not a binding direction. The tanker ran the risk of transiting the Canal and was caught; *id.*, pp. 133, 149–150. However, during that period even American-flag vessels were not given any directions by the United States government as to their movements; testimony of the Maritime Administrator, *id.*, p. 134.

Suez Canal.[22] Also in connection with the passage through the Gulf of Aqaba, Secretary of State Dulles, mentioning the possibility of using force to protect the control over American vessels, expressly referred to American flag vessels, and said: "I do not think that the United States, in the absence at least of a treaty or congressional action, has authority to use force to defend the rights of ships of another registry." [23] An agreement with the flag-of-convenience countries was also found to be necessary in case the United States Navy should undertake to convoy through the Suez Canal the ships registered in those countries.[24]

So far as requisition itself is concerned, the rules of international law are much similar. The state of the vessel's national character, that is, the state of its registry, has the right, in case of national emergency, to appropriate for its own purposes, by requisitioning, those ships registered under its flag.[25] Rienow comes to the conclusion that the documentation of a ship is the exclusive basis upon which the rights of requisition are founded,[26] and categorically states that "no case has come to the attention of the author in which a State has succeeded in requisitioning a vessel on the grounds of ownership by its nationals over the protests of another State having other more highly regarded connections with the vessels." [27]

The main incident leading to this conclusion was the requisitioning by Great Britain during the First World War of Dutch-registered vessels controlled by companies incorporated in the Netherlands, whose shareholders were, however, British subjects.[28] From

22. *Id.*, pp. 167–168. The Maritime Administrator could not say, however, whether the terms "United States shipping industry" or "United States shipowners" meant American-controlled companies or American-flag companies; *id.*, p. 150.

23. *The New York Times*, February 20, 1957, p. 8. See also *Hearings* (House) 1957, pp. 129–130; *Hearings* (Senate) 1957, p. 76.

24. Opinions of Rear Admiral Collins and Drewry, Chief Counsel of the House Committee on Merchant Marine and Fisheries, *Hearings* (House) 1957, p. 580.

25. Rienow, p. 7 ("There are apparently no limits on this power, and the State in applying it is answerable to no other.") and pp. 100–104, 185–186; McDougal, Burke & Vlasic, p. 65.

26. Rienow, p. 186.

27. *Id.*, p. 104.

28. *Id.*, pp. 100–104, 185–186. See also Harvard Research, "Draft Convention on the Rights and Duties of Neutral States in Naval and Aerial War," *AJIL* 33 Supp. 375–378 (1939) (comment on art. 21), Harley, "The Law of Angary," *AJIL* 13:267, 290–293 (1919); Bullock, "Angary," *British Yearbook of International Law*, 3:99, 117 (1922); Hackworth, VI, 641–642; Wilson, "Taking Over and Return of Dutch

the point of view of ownership relations, this situation was, then, analogous to the present flag-of-convenience relation between the United States and, for example, Panama.

The decision to requisition the Dutch vessels gave rise to a prolonged and interesting diplomatic correspondence between Great Britain and the Netherlands, in which the right to requisition neutral-flag vessels by belligerents was discussed.[29] From this correspondence the opinions concerning the test employed by states in determining over which ships they may exercise the power of requisition are of interest for the present inquiry. The British government initially based their decision to requisition the Dutch-flag ships on the necessity to protect British interests vested in the vessels, which were "really British-owned or chiefly British-owned," but sailing under a neutral flag and defenseless against German naval forces.[30] The Dutch government, protesting against the British decision, pointed out that even though the shareholders of the shipowning Dutch corporation were British subjects, it was not Great Britain as the state of ultimate ownership but only the state of registry, that is, the Netherlands, that had, under international law, the right to requisition the vessels:

> C'est le Gouvernement néerlandais seul, à l'exclusion de tout autre, qui est libre de réquisitionner des navires battant pavillon néerlandais. L'unique cas où la réquisition par un belligérant serait admissible est celui d'absolue nécessité militaire . . . C'est le pavillon seul et non le propriétaire qui entre en jeu pour déterminer la place que le navire occupe comme sujet du droit international. . . . Il ne s'agit même point de navires étant en entier ou en majeure partie propriété britannique, mais de bâtiments appartenant en totalité à des sociétés néerlandaises, quelle que soit la nationalité de leurs actionnaires . . .
>
> Il est parfaitement possible que la plupart des actions de ces sociétés se trouvent actuellement entre les mains de personnes de nationalité

Vessels, 1918–1919," *AJIL* 24:694 (1930) — discussing primarily the requisition by the United States; Oppenheim, II, 763; Colombos, p. 507. The United States and other allies also requisitioned Dutch vessels lying in their ports, but the British case is of particular interest in this context.

29. For the British-Dutch correspondence in 1917–1918 see *British Parliamentary Papers*, Miscellaneous No. 5 (1918) and No. 11 (1918), Cd. 8986 & 9025. See also *B. & F. St. Pap.* 1917–1918, 111:465–473 (1921). For the reference to the Dutch sources see Harvard Research, "Draft Convention on the Rights and Duties of Neutral States in Naval and Aerial Warfare," pp. 375–378 (comment on art. 21).

30. Sir. W. Townley to M. Loudon, May 22, 1917, *B. & F. St. Pap. 1917–1918* 111:465–466 (1921)

britannique. Si, toutefois, le Gouvernement britannique veut bien se rendre compte des conséquences qu'aurait pour la navigation internationale l'adoption d'une règle d'après laquelle la nationalité de la majorité des actionnaires — d'ailleurs souvent inconnus — d'une société à laquelle appartient un bâtiment de haute mer constituerait le critérium de la nationalité du navire même, il ne pourra manquer de s'apercevoir à quel point sa décision récente est contraire au principe très rationnel qui régit la matière . . .[31]

The Dutch protest caused a shift in the argument of Great Britain which, taking advantage of the phrase in the Dutch note referring to absolute military necessity, subsequently based its measure on the right of angary, and the further exchange of correspondence turned on the question of whether the circumstances of the case justified the exercise of that right:

2. The right of a belligerent to requistion neutral property, and especially neutral ships, in certain circumstances is admitted by M. Loudon, and is of course so well established that it cannot be contested. M. Loudon appears to doubt, however, whether the circumstances of the present case are such as to justify the exercise of this right . . . His Majesty's Government do not base their right to requisition these ships upon the fact of their being actually British-owned or controlled; and therefore I think it necessary to discuss M. Loudon's contention that a belligerent is not entitled to look beyond the flag in order to ascertain the actual ownership of a nominally neutral vessel.[32]

That a state has the right to requisition ships registered under its flag in spite of the fact that they are ultimately owned by foreign nationals was recognized by the United States in connection with the wholesale transfer of ships from foreign to American registry after the passing of the Act of August 18, 1914, which enabled American-owned vessels under foreign flags, formerly ineligible for American registry because of foreign build, to be registered under the American flag.[33] Most of these ships had been under the British flag, and "had Great Britain issued a requisition order immediately on the outbreak of the War, as she did subsequently, the transfer of these vessels would have been impossible" reported Senator Jones in the Senate Committee of

31. M. Loudon to Sir W. Townley, 11 juin 1917; *id.*, pp. 467, 468.
32. Mr. Balfour to Sir W. Townley, July 18, 1917; *id.*, pp. 468, 469. A copy of this dispatch was communicated to M. Loudon; *id.*, p. 471.
33. 38 Stat. 698.

Commerce.[34] Actually, some of the American-owned ships which remained under the British registry were requisitioned by Great Britain. This fact was later used as argument by the United States in an attempt to secure the release of some American-flag vessels which were seized by Great Britain because of alleged German beneficial interest in them. It was argued by the American side that:

> This Government has also observed that the British authorities have in several instances requisitioned vessels flying the British flag, although the entire beneficial interest in them was owned by American citizens, and in connection with requests on the part of such beneficial owners for the release of such vessels, the British Government apparently has taken the position that the vessels, flying the British flag and being owned by British corporations, must, of course, be regarded as British and not as American vessels.[35]

The American argument was irrelevant, because, although registry is the test of the right to requisition vessels, in the case of capture the enemy character is a consequence, not only of registry but also of enemy ownership or enemy service.[36] One can also recall here the fact that fearing the imminent outbreak of the war in 1939, a number of European shipowners transferred their vessels to the Panamanian flag. This change of registry made it possible for them to avoid requisition by their governments.

The range of the requisitioning power of the state of registry includes not only ships in the territorial waters, but also those on the high seas and in foreign waters. The question of the extra-territorial operation of requisitioning decrees, particularly in foreign

34. Report of Mr. Jones of the Committee of Commerce, December 9, 1922; 1 Sen. Rep. No. 935, 67th Cong., 4th Sess. (1922–1923), p. 6; quoted in Rienow, p. 102 n. 83. *Accord, Annual Report* of the Commissioner of Navigation (1915), pp. 12–14: "Under the ship registry Act of August 18, 1914, during the year ended June 30, 1915, American registers were issued to 148 vessels of 523.361 gross tons . . . Nearly all of these vessels had been owned by American capital for a considerable period of time . . . British authorities would have been quite within the law to have declined to assent to the transfer to the American flag under the act of 1914 of any or all of the 96 ships of 332.258 gross tons which were under the British flag and British law, and to have requisitioned them for Government purposes." Quoted in Rienow, p. 103 n. 84.

35. The Secretary of State to the British Ambassador, Spring Rice, Washington, May 10, 1916 [1916] *Foreign Rel.*, Supp. (1929), pp. 388, 389.

36. Rienow, p. 117–139; Hyde, III, 2074–2078.

waters, has been the subject of numerous judicial decisions, and presents complex problems beyond the scope of this inquiry.[37]

If it is the state of registry that has the right to control and requisition the vessels flying its flag, then what is the course to be followed by the state of the vessel's beneficial ownership in order to exercise its effective control over the vessels in case of national emergency without the risk of falling into conflict with the principles of international law?

A state has the power to command its own citizens, wherever they may be, and has the prerogative to issue orders to them requisitioning their property for national purposes in time of emergency, wherever this property may be.[38] This is expressly stated by the United States law which provides for the requisition by the Executive, in case of emergency, of any vessel owned by a citizen of the United States.[39] This provision, however, because of the special nature of ships which are endowed with nationality, can be effective only so far as it does not conflict with the right of requisition which the state of registry is, under international law, entitled to exercise. The state of registry may acquiesce in the taking over and requisition by the state of ultimate ownership of vessels flying its flag, as was the case with Panama during the Second World War, but, as the incident with the Dutch ships in the First World War shows, the action of the state of ultimate ownership may provoke protest by the flag state which has a more

37. For a review of the judicial decisions on this subject, with particular reference to the British practice, see McNair, "Problems Connected with the Position of the Merchant Vessel in Private International Law, with Particular Reference to the Power of Requisition," *The Grotius Society* [1945] *Transactions* 31:30–46 (1946). See also the discussion on McNair's paper, *id.*, pp. 46–58. This paper is also reprinted in McNair, *Legal Effects of War* (3d ed. 1948), appendix IV; "The Requisitioning of Merchant Ships," pp. 433–447, reprinted from *The Journal of Comparative Legislation*, (1945). On the requisitioning of ships, see also McNair, *Legal Effects of War*, pp. 377–382. For an exhaustive review of the position of the British and American courts with respect to the cases which arose out of the Spanish Civil War requisitions see: Preuss, "State Immunity and the Requisition of Ships during the Spanish Civil War, I: Before the British Courts," *AJIL* 35:263 (1941); Preuss, "State Immunity and the Requisition of Ships during the Spanish Civil War, II: Before the Courts of the United States," *AJIL* 36:37 (1942). However, neither McNair nor Preuss touches the question of whether the state of beneficial ownership may requisition ships if these ships are registered under a foreign flag.

38. McNair, *Legal Effects of War*, p. 447.

39. Merchant Marine Act, 1936, §902; 49 Stat. 2015 (1936), as amended, 53 Stat. 1255 (1939), 46 U.S.C., §1242 (1952).

perfect right to control the ships flying its flag. The conflict may be more complex if, for example, the ship is registered in state *L*, but is owned by a corporation which is a national of state *P*, and the corporation is controlled by nationals of state *A*. In this case, even if state *L* waives its right, a conflict may arise between the state of nominal ownership, *P*, and the state of actual control, *A*.

From the point of view of the state of ultimate ownership, there exists the possibility of an agreement with the state of registry providing for the taking over, upon the outbreak of the emergency, of the control of the vessels by the state of ultimate ownership. The agreement could also stipulate the consent of the state of registry (the flag-of-convenience state) to the transfer of registry of the vessels to the state of ultimate ownership.[40]

In this respect, the facts in the concrete case of the United States-beneficially owned but foreign-registered fleet are as follows: There is a kind of agreement between the United States and the two major flag-of-convenience countries, Panama and Liberia, that the latter countries would make their ships available to the United States in case of emergency. It is not a treaty arrangement; "at most it would be an informal letter of concurrence."[41] Most probably the taking over of the control would be accompanied by the transfer of the vessels to the American registry. This can be assumed from the existence of an understanding to this effect between Panama and the United States, about which it was testified before a Senate committee in 1950 that

> There is an understanding with at least one of the Latin American governments which provides for *the return to United States registry* [emphasis added] in the event of an emergency of American-owned vessels doc-

40. The laws of Liberia, Panama, and Honduras provide for the possibility of transferring vessels to another registry: UNLS, p. 97 (Liberia); *id.*, p. 133 (Panama); *id.*, p. 77 (Honduras). In the Honduran law transfer to another flag requires prior consent of the Executive if Honduras is at war. In Liberia the government's approval is required for any agreement under which a Liberian-flag vessel is made available to another country; Rep. of Liberia, Treasury Department Regulations Promulgated by the Commissioner of Maritime Affairs, §1.41 (1960).

41. Testimony of the Maritime Administrator, *Hearings* (House) 1957, p. 129. See also *The New York Times*, August 31, 1961, p. 44. However, Hager, representing the government of the United States before the ICJ in the case of the Constitution of the Maritime Safety Committee of the IMCO, categorically stated that the "effective United States control" concept was not founded on any treaties, conventions, or intergovernmental agreements of any kind but depended purely on private arrangements of the U.S. government with the shipowners; ICJ *Pleadings*, Constitution (1960), pp. 427, 428.

umented in that country. The Navy Department therefore considers that American-owned ships under the flags [sic] of such a country are potentially available on request of the United States Government in time of war.[42]

In response to a senator's question, the testifying admiral said further that such a country is Panama. It is not clear whether there is any agreement with Honduras. Neither is it quite clear which countries' ships are believed to be under "effective United States control." The Maritime Administration specifically limits the transfers of American ships to Liberia, Panama, and Honduras as the countries which will not impose any restrictions on the use by the United States of their ships in the event of war or other emergency[43] whereas the Department of the Navy, in one statement, includes among these states also Venezuela,[44] and in another, besides these four countries, also the Philippines.[45] It seems appropriate that in order to clarify the legal status of the American-owned ships under Panlibhon flag for purposes of the right of control and requisition in case of national emergency, the United States should have this right explicitly guaranteed by treaties with the countries concerned.

Other American-owned vessels, registered not in Panlibhon but in other foreign countries, for example, in the United Kingdom, will not, in case of emergency, be available to the United States, since there are no agreements to this effect, and the states of registry will have full right to control and requisition them for their own needs.[46]

42. Testimony of Admiral Callaghan, *Hearings* (House) 1957, p. 76. In the Report of the Board of Inquiry into the maritime strike in summer, 1961, submitted to President Kennedy, it is stated that "a measure of national control is preserved by agreements with the friendly governments to the effect that these ships will be returned to the American flag in the event of a national need." *The New York Times*, July 4, 1961, p. 8.

43. Maritime Administration Policy Statement of November 5, 1956, 21 Fed. Reg. 8588 (1956), as amended, 21 Fed. Reg. 8920 (1956), 22 Fed. Reg. 4289 (1957), 22 Fed. Reg. 4448 (1957), 22 Fed. Reg. 7397 (1957), 23 Fed. Reg. 5956 (1958).

44. Statement of Rear Admiral Gano, Deputy Commander of the Military Sea Transportation Service, *Hearings* (House) 1957, p. 627. As the Maritime Administrator explained, Venezuela was not included in the Maritime Administration's list "primarily because of either inadvertence or the fact that there are so few vessels under the Venezuela flag"; *id.*, p. 132.

45. Letter of Secretary of the Navy Thomas, *id.*, p. 567.

46. Testimony of president of Esso Shipping Co., stating that in case of a worldwide emergency such vessels owned by the wholly-owned subsidiaries of Esso Ship-

One could also consider the international law status of the flag-of-convenience fleet in various hypothetical situations involving war, in which some of the states concerned would be belligerents. Supposing that Panama were at war with state *X*, what would happen to vessels registered under her flag, nominally owned by her corporations but ultimately controlled by foreign nationals? Panama would undoubtedly have, under international law, the right to requisition these ships. But how would she exercise and enforce the power of requisition if the ships under her flag, except for coastal shuttles, usually ply the high seas and very rarely put into the Panamanian ports, and Panama has practically no capability to intercept ships on the high seas? On the other hand, the Panamanian ships would be subject to capture by the enemy state,[47] which in turn would raise the problem of their transfer, in many cases, back to the state of ownership, for example, to the United States.[48] In fact, such possibility was even taken into consideration at a congressional hearing. The counsel of the hearing subcommittee, arguing with the shipowners' representatives on the legal status of flag-of-convenience ships in case of emergency, envisioning the situation, said: "[I]f some Panamanian vessels were tied up or seized by some foreign country, where we were not at war, I don't think that the Panamanian vessels would be able to switch back to American registry while under their control." [49]

A difficult question is what the legal grounds are on which a state can requisition, in time of war to which it is a party, vessels beneficially owned by its nationals but registered under the flag

ping Co. "will be governed by the countries under which . . . [they] were registered"; *Hearings* (Senate) 1957, p. 98. Neither have these ships been offered war risk insurance by the Maritime Administration. See *The New York Times*, December 3, 1959, p. 65. The fact that a number of American-owned Panlibhon vessels have been transferred to some European flags under the impact of the unions' anti-Panlibhon campaign has caused understandable concern of the United States administration since those ships cannot any more be considered under "effective U.S. control." See *The New York Times*, September 12, 1961, p. 54; September 13, 1961, p. 75.

47. Lord Stowell in *The Vrow Elizabeth* (1803) 5 C. Rob. 2; The Declaration of London, art. 57, Charles' *Treaties*, p. 278.

48. On the transfer of enemy ships to neutrals see The Declaration of London, arts. 55 and 56, Charles' *Treaties*, p. 278. See also in general Hyde, III, 2078–2083; Harvard Research, "Draft Convention on the Rights and Duties of Neutral States in Naval and Aerial War," pp. 681–689.

49. *Hearings* (Senate) 1957, p. 77. See also p. 54.

of a foreign state if there is no agreement on the matter between the two states and the state of registry protests the requisitions, or even itself issues the requisition decree. This question is not even mentioned by McNair in his discussion on requisition of merchant vessels, and on the whole such a conflict between the state of ultimate ownership and the flag state is not discussed by the literature of international law. Neither are there any judicial decisions on this issue. The only author who touches this problem is Rienow, who, reporting the incident of the requisition of Dutch ships by Great Britain, in the First World War, comes to the conclusion that only the state of registry has, under international law, the right to requisition the merchant vessels flying its flag.[50] In the case of the Dutch ships, Great Britain, the state of beneficial ownership, pleaded the right of angary, that is, "the right of a state in time of war or public danger to requisition for its own use ships, aircraft, rolling-stock and other means of transport belonging to the nationals of other Powers but lying within its jurisdiction at the time of requisition." [51]

However, the right of angary may be exercised only within the territorial waters of the requisitioning state,[52] and must be justified by imperative necessity. If the vessel is on the high seas, it may in principle be seized only by the navy of its state of registry. In practice, the success of the control would depend to a high degree on the behavior of the master, the crew, and the actual owners of the ship, who would probably give an order to set course for the country of actual control of the vessel. That is why the crews of the flag-of-convenience ships are considered by the defense agencies of the United States an important element in the implementation of effective control. The plans of this implementation provide for replacing the large numbers of aliens aboard these ships with properly screened personnel. The possibility of the refusal by the alien crew to conform to routing instructions is also

50. Rienow, pp. 104, 186.

51. Bullock, p. 129. To Bullock's definition one should add that in time of war the ships should belong to the nationals of neutral states. On angary, see also Harley; Hackworth, IV, 638–655; Hyde, III, 1760–1764; Colombos, pp. 505–513; Oppenheim, II, 759–766; Harvard Research, "Draft Convention on the Rights and Duties of Neutral States in Naval and Aerial War," pp. 359–385.

52. But see Oppenheim, II, 761, where the author extends the exercise of angary to the high seas.

taken into account, although it is believed that, in general, the actions of the crews would be influenced by the desire to draw their wages.[53]

Should the vessel arrive at a port of a third state, the question arises whether the authorities of that state would recognize the requisition order of the state of ultimate ownership or trust of the state of registry, in case the latter state issued a requisition order.[54]

In time of war, as the practice has shown, the prize courts look beyond the registry and the nominal corporate owner to the real ownership and control of the neutral flag vessel, and have the right to declare it as a lawful prize if it proves to be beneficially owned by enemy nationals.[55] The rule of international law as to the enemy character was succinctly stated in the American Court of Claims in these words: "If a ship flies an enemy flag, it will not be permitted to show, in a prize Court, that its true ownership was neutral, but . . . the fact that it flies a neutral flag, does not prevent the seizing nation from proving that its true ownership was in the enemy."[56] From this rule it can be seen that in case of war in which the state of ultimate control is a belligerent, flag-of-convenience ships, even if they should remain under neutral flags of convenience, would be treated by the opposing side as enemy vessels and captured.

As is well known, Panama, Liberia, and Honduras would be virtually unable to provide protection at sea for the many vessels registered under their respective flags. Their own needs for transportation are and would, in case of war, be negligible compared with those of the states of actual control, such as the United States. Ships registered under Panlibhon flags are not in their bulk used to convey supplies to these countries, and so the requisi-

53. Statement of then Secretary of the Navy Gates, *Hearings* (House) 1957, p. 632. See also *Hearings* (Senate) 1957, pp. 52, 54, 75. *Cf.* National Academy of Sciences–National Research Council Publication no. 748, p. 32.

54. Of course, the enforcement of foreign decrees of requisition in general is a separate problem and does not touch directly the subject under inquiry. Concerning it, see McNair's paper in *Grotius Society Transactions* and the discussion on the paper; *id.*, pp. 47–58.

55. The St. Tudno (1916) P. 271; The Unitas [1950] A.C. 536; American Transatlantic Co. v. United States, 83 F. Supp. 832 (Ct. Cl. 1949); Rienow, pp. 117–139; Hyde, III, 2074–2078.

56. American Transatlantic Co. v. United States, 83 F. Supp. 832 (Ct. Cl. 1949).

tion by the state of ownership would not grievously distress the economic life of the neutral flag-of-convenience countries. Neither would, in reality, requisition be detrimental to the property rights of the flag-of-convenience countries' nationals because the compensation for the requisitioned ships would, in reality, be due to the citizens of the state of actual ownership. It is therefore possible that the neutral state in whose port a flag-of-convenience ship happened to be on the outbreak of war would give priority to the requisition claims of the state of beneficial ownership. These reasons of equity, outweighing those which a flag-of-convenience country might put forward, could also be advanced as arguments by the state of ultimate ownership to support its claim to requisition on the high seas, and against the protests of the state of registry of convenience vessels beneficially owned by its citizens.

Speculations could also be made on the international law aspect of the situation in which the government of a flag-of-convenience country would expropriate or confiscate the property of foreign corporations established in its territory. This would, of course, touch, first of all, the property of owners of seagoing vessels, since the majority of them are nominally owned by such corporations. Still larger in scope would be the nationalization of all the ships flying the particular flag of convenience. The possibility of such development has been taken into account by the United States. Thus, for example at a congressional hearing, the Chairman of the Subcommittee on Merchant Marine of the House Committee on Merchant Marine and Fisheries, doubting the validity of the "effective United States control" over flag-of-convenience shipping, cited examples of other nations, such as Mexico, having seized American-owned corporations and properties. He also raised the question as to how the United States control concept might be affected by a revolution in one of the flag-of-convenience countries to which American shipowners have transferred their vessels.[57] Similarly, in a dialogue between the Chairman of the Merchant Marine and Fisheries Subcommittee of the Senate Committee on Interstate and Foreign Commerce and the representative of a shipowning company, the question was put as follows:

57. *Hearings* (House) 1957, pp. 601–602.

The Chairman: What if Panama passed some legislation or issued decrees to the contrary? Would you have any control over them? [i.e., the ships]

Mr. Teitsworth: I wouldn't want to speculate about that. They haven't done it.[58]

It has also been stated by the Liberian representative before the ICJ that the vessels registered under a foreign flag are subject to the sovereign acts of the flag state, such as modification of the relevant substantive law, changes in the tax rate, "and even possibly requisition or expropriation." "Owners who seek foreign registration accept these risks" added the Liberian counsel.[59] The question posed above touches the very large subject of expropriation and its validity under international law, and has a substantial body of international practice embodied in diplomatic and judicial cases, as well as rich literature. Applying the principles governing in international law the expropriation of foreign property to the case of the expropriation of foreign-owned shipping by a flag-of-convenience state, one can reach the following general conclusions:

A flag-of-convenience state is entitled, under international law, to expropriate foreign-owned shipping,[60] provided that effective, prompt, and adequate compensation is paid to the owners. If this condition is not observed, the expropriation would amount to confiscation, unlawful under international law.[61] In this case, the general rule denying extraterritorial effect to a decree of confiscation would have to be applied by the coastal state in respect of a ship which would be claimed by the confiscating government for delivery. Precedents of this category are known in international practice. In *The Jupiter*, the British court, holding that decrees

58. *Hearings* (Senate) 1957, p. 15. *Cf.* similar concern of the chairman about the American position in the Panama Canal; *id.*, p. 16. *Cf.* also the Panamanian threats of reprisals against the United States; *The New York Times,* March 27, 1961, p. 44; September 1, 1961, p. 45.

59. ICJ *Pleadings,* Constitution (1960), p. 276.

60. Here "foreign-owned" would, in a majority of cases, mean beneficially owned. Besides, if a majority of shareholders of, for instance, a Liberian corporation are American nationals, this is a sufficient basis to treat the case as interference with foreign property. See, *e.g.*, Herz, "Expropriation of Foreign Property," *AJIL* 35:243, 244 (1940).

61. This is a truism, and the rule is generally adopted by international courts and is prevailing in doctrine. See, *e.g.*, Briggs, pp. 568–570; Oppenheim, I, 351–354; Friedman, *Expropriation in International Law* (1953); Herz, p. 254. The items cited here contain extensive bibliography.

of the Soviet government were ineffectual to confiscate ships which were outside the territorial waters of Russia, stated: "It was not suggested that ships were to be governed by any principles other than those applicable to other chattels. If the *Jupiter* was not within the territory of the R.S.F.S.R., I do not see how the mere passing of a decree could transfer the property. This seems to me to be recognized in all the cases . . ." [62]

Of course, in case of an expropriation legislation in one of the Panlibhon countries, the fact that vessels registered under the flags of convenience have rare occasion to put into ports of their registries would have decisive importance for the enforcement of the expropriation. The countries in question, besides, possess practically no capability to seize ships on the high seas.[63] They also lack the potential and facilities requisite to proper maintenance of a sizeable merchant fleet. For these reasons, the possibility of expropriation does not present a real menace for the states whose citizens beneficially own the flag of convenience vessels.

In conclusion, the following general propositions are submitted on the right to control the movements of the flag-of-convenience ships and to requisition them in case of war:

Under the general principles of international law, the right to control and requisition the flag-of-convenience ships rests with their countries of registry. With their consent or acquiescence, the country of ultimate ownership is fully entitled to control and requisition the vessels in question in time of emergency. Without the consent of the state of registry, the state of ultimate ownership may requisition citizen-owned vessels finding themselves within its territorial domain. The requisition of the vessels on the high seas and in ports of third states could be justified by the motive of providing the ships with necessary protection, which the flags of convenience are unable to afford.

62. (No. 3) [1927] P. 122, 144; *Accord,* The El Contado (No. 2) LL.L. Rep., 63, 83 (1939). *Cf.* also The Elise, where the Supreme Court of Canada held that it would be contrary to public policy to enforce a foreign confiscatory decree purporting to have extraterritorial effect by seeking to reach in a Canadian port a ship that was never in the possession of the foreign government in question. [1949] S.C.R. 530. The rule relating to confiscation does not obtain in case of requisition. See Lorentzen v. Lydden, [1942] 2 K.B. 202.

63. In 1957 Liberia's navy consisted of two coast guard cutters; *Hearings* (House) 1957, p. 129.

Of decisive practical importance in the whole issue is the fact that the flag-of-convenience vessels in their bulk never put in at the ports of registry, and that the flag-of-convenience countries would be unable in case of emergency to enforce their control over the ships flying their flags on the high seas.

Chapter VIII. The Attack on the Traditional Principle before the 1958 Geneva Conference

The legal argument of the anti-Panlibhon group of nations is based on the doctrine that mere registration is not sufficient to establish such a relation between the ship and its flag state that the nationality of the ship is recognized by other states. It is claimed by the representatives of this doctrine that a "genuine link" must exist between an individual country and the ships registered there. As the analysis of the IMCO case before the International Court of Justice shows, the representatives of the traditional maritime states of Europe have repeatedly referred to this concept in their endeavor to support their contention that the Maritime Safety Committee of the IMCO was elected without any violation of art. 28 of the IMCO convention.

The attempts to limit the traditional principle of the exclusive competence of each state to determine the conditions for the grant of nationality to merchant vessels are not entirely new, but have been stimulated recently by the emergence in the last decade of the large Panlibhon fleets. As far back as the end of the nineteenth century a doctrine proclaimed the limitation by international law of the legislative authority of the state in the matter of attributing nationality to merchant vessels. Based upon two premises, namely, various requirements found in the domestic laws of the states and analogy with the nationality of individuals, this doctrine tried to find some minimum allegedly imposed by international law, which should be adopted by all the maritime states in legislation dealing with the nationality of ships.

Two methods of delimiting the scope of the states' competence have been proposed: 1) to lay down specific provisions to be incorporated by the states in their domestic laws, and 2) to limit the states' rights by some general principle, without imposing any detailed requirements.

The first method was used in 1896 by the Institute of International Law at its Venice session and in 1950–1955 by the International Law Commission of the United Nations in the early stages of its work on the nationality of ships. The Institute of International Law aspired to achieve, if not entirely uniform regulations, which might be difficult to bring about, at least more similarity among the laws of various states.[1] Since the formulation of this principle, carried out by the Institute's rapporteurs, Asser and Reay, became the basis of the codifying work done by the Institute in 1896 and more recently of the initial work of the ILC,[2] it is worthwhile to cite it in its entirety:

> In principle every sovereign state is free to fix the rules after which the nationality of the merchant vessels is acquired or lost. But in order that the legislation of a state in this matter should be effective in any circumstances that may arise, it should not depart too much from the principles which have been adopted by the greater number of states and which may therefore be considered to constitute the basis of international law in that respect.[3]

The 1896 report accepted the current doctrine of the states' freedom as a general rule, but admitted the possibility that if nationality were granted without taking into account some international law directives, there might be cases where the legislation of a state in the matter of the nationality of ships in general, and the nationality of the particular vessel, would be ineffective and presumably not recognized by other states. As an instance of such a situation, the 1896 report mentions the possibility of non-recognition in naval warfare of the nationality of a merchant vessel by

1. *Annuaire* 15:51, 52 (1896).

2. ILC *Yearbook 1950*, II, 38 (Doc. A/CN.4/17, First report on the regime of the high seas by François); ILC *Yearbook 1951*, II, 75–77 (Doc. A/CN.4/42, Second report on the regime of the high seas by François).

3. *Annuaire* 15:51, 52: "Règles relatives à l'usage du pavillon national pour les navires de commerce," Report by Asser and Reay [translated by the present author].

a prize court, if the nationality were based on a "much more liberal law than that of the majority of states."[4] Another example would be a conflict of laws whose solution depended on which municipal law should be applied to determine the nationality of a vessel.[5]

Having stated general principles, the Institute had to solve the problem of a method by which the general principles adopted by the majority of states could be discovered and made precise. It adopted one of fixing the precise material conditions which must be fulfilled before a ship is entitled to a grant of nationality. Further, the Institute tried to find the relevant conditions by a comparative study of the provisions in the municipal laws of various countries, and for this purpose collected the provisions of fifteen states on the grant and loss of the nationality of the merchant vessels.[6] Then, after receiving the members' opinions on the principles to be recommended, the Institute prepared a "Draft Resolution on the Acquisition of the Right to Fly the Flag, on Its Loss, and the Provisional Right to Fly the Flag." This draft resolution, after a short discussion and some modifications, was adopted as "Règles relatives à l'usage du pavillon national pour les navires de commerce."[7] Section I, dealing with the right to fly the flag, provided that the ships must be listed in a register, which could be effected only if more than half of a ship was owned by nationals or a partnership or a simple commandite company in which more than half of the partners with personal liability were nationals, or a national joint-stock company in which not less than two-thirds of the members of the board of directors were nationals. The enterprise must have its head office in the state whose flag the ship would fly, or in which it was to be registered. The nationality of the captain and the other members of the crew were not — ac-

4. *Id.*, p. 52. It was rightly pointed out by Neumeyer that in this example the report had confused the nationality of a ship with its enemy character in naval warfare; Neumeyer, III, 91 n. 20. See also Rienow, pp. 117–139 and Ch. VII above.

5. *Annuaire* 15:52. Here the Institute appears to have confused the irrelevancy of the vessel's nationality in the given case with its non-recognition in general.

6. *Id.*, pp. 54–67. The fifteen states were Germany, Austria-Hungary, Belgium, Denmark, Spain, France, Great Britain, Greece, Italy, Norway, the Netherlands, Portugal, Russia, Sweden, and the United States. The Institute did not take into account the legislations of the Latin American countries which in some cases differed from the legislations of European countries and which already, at that time, did not require the owners of the ships to be nationals. See Ch. I above.

7. *Annuaire* 15:72–74.

cording to the Institute's proposal — a condition for acquiring or forfeiting the right to fly the flag.[8]

The Institute found ownership relations to be the main factor governing the right of the vessels to fly the flag of a particular country. These conditions were proposed by the Institute as basis for unification. But the Institute necessarily encountered difficulties connected with the definition of national owner, in particular so far as corporate ownership was concerned. In this respect, the Institute adopted the criterion of the preponderance of the national element in the administrative board, and of the national seat of the head office. As the discussion of 1896 further shows the members of the Institute were aware of the difficulty of conciliating various national legislations, but came to the conclusion that "one cannot conciliate everything," and agreed to the rules without serious controversies.[9]

This consensus among the members of the Institute of International Law in 1896 is not surprising. It represented the practice of the traditional maritime countries, all of which had more or less stringent ownership requirements for granting nationality to ships. There were at that time already cases of vessels beneficially owned by nationals of one country but registered under a different country's flag. However, this phenomenon had not assumed sufficient proportion to cause international friction.[10] Nonetheless, even under those circumstances, more favorable than today, no unification of the laws on the nationality of ships could be reached. The principle of the states' freedom to determine individually the prerequisites of granting nationality to ships was too well established in the sovereign power of the states to be modified by the Institute's proposals, which remained only "guidance and advice,"[11] not followed by the states as they enacted new laws on nationality of ships. Their contents were dictated, even though some may have

8. *Id.*, pp. 201–203.

9. As Desjardins, a member of the Institute, said, "On ne peut tout concilier." The rules were adopted by 18 votes against 1 (den Beer Portugael, the Netherlands), with one abstention (Beirão, Brazil). The prerequisite of the captain's nationality, proposed by den Beer Portugael, prompted some controversy and was rejected. See *Annuaire* 15:196–198.

10. The *Muscat Dhows* case was a specific problem, although of the same nature. See Ch. IV.

11. Hudson called the rules of the Asser-Reay Report a "typical example of a platonic problem"; ILC *Yearbook 1951,* I, 330.

conformed to the rules of 1896, not by the obligation to observe principles of international law, but by national interest. The principle of the states' freedom was affirmed also by the decision of the Permanent Court of Arbitration in the *Muscat Dhows* case.

The theory of the limitations imposed upon the states' right to grant the right to fly the flag was for a long time a subject not comprehensively worked out by the doctrine.[12] It is pertinent here to mention the criticism of the *Muscat Dhows* decision by some international publicists. Discussing this case, Fleischmann questioned the Court's opinion that each state has the right to determine the rules governing the grant of nationality to ships. According to Fleischmann, this right might be restricted not only by treaty provisions but also by certain general principles conditioned by the order of international intercourse. These international-law requirements also should be taken into account. However, Fleischmann did not develop his thought any further, stating only that the problem of granting the right to fly the flag to foreign-owned vessels had not been explored by the literature of international law. Fleischmann's view was closely followed by Kaufmann, whereas Gidel endorsed virtually the same idea as had been formulated by the Institute of International Law in 1896.[13]

Analogy with the nationality of individuals was at the basis of the views of Neumeyer, who, in principle, recognized the absence of any limitations imposed by international law upon the states in the matter of granting the right to fly the flag, but admitted of the possibility that a "transgression of the competence of granting the flag might entail the loss of the protection of international law." [14] Similarly, Verdross speaks of a "factual domestic link between the ship and the state of registration," which must exist

12. Speaking in the ILC, François rightly stated that the principle of limiting the states' rights in question had been formulated by only a few writers. He is wrong, however, in mentioning only Neumeyer and Verdross as the legal authorities in this respect (ILC *Yearbook 1951*, I, 328). These two authors mention the principle only in one or two sentences in their more general works. François omits the fact that Gidel also endorsed the opinion of the Institute (see Gidel, I, 81), as did Fleischmann and Kaufmann. He ignores Quadri, who elaborated a whole theory on the subject in question.

13. Fleischmann, "Der Maskat Fall," *Das Werk von Haag* (Schücking ed. 1917, pt. I, 2d ser.), pp. 345, 414, 418; Kaufmann, p. 376; Gidel, I, 81.

14. Neumeyer, III, 90. He refers to Triepel, *Virtuelle Staatsangehörigkeit* (1921), p. 30.

in the case of the nationality of ships, as in that of individuals.[15]

These writers on international law did not work out any theory on the subject under discussion, but only stated the principle itself without trying to prove it or develop it in a comprehensive way. Attempts to do this were undertaken by representatives of the Italian school of international law. Among them, Quadri elaborated a uniform dogmatic construction of the legal situation of merchant vessels in time of peace. According to Quadri, it is international law "in coincidence with municipal law" that lays down the principles regulating the nationality of ships. Quadri stated with emphasis that the power of granting nationality to private vessels that international law accords to the states is not without limitations, and that this power is restricted not only by the existence of possible conventional provisions, as it was established in the *Muscat Dhows* case, but also by common international law. Since in Quadri's dogmatic construction the foundation of the flag state's jurisdiction over its ships is laid in the governing power (*potestà di governo*) of the state over the ship's community, the right of the state to grant nationality to ships is limited by the state's ability to control effectively all the elements of the said community. This criterion of effectivity, being a link between the ships and state, was for Quadri the characteristic feature of all the municipal systems. For this reason Quadri held that a pirate ship automatically lost its nationality, and that the inland states could not, under international law, have the right to grant the flag, having no way of rendering effective the governing power over the ship's community. Quadri pushed his conclusions so far that for him a ship, as an individual, might from the point of view of municipal law have the nationality of a state, and at the same time not have this nationality from the point of view of international law.[16]

The construction of Quadri omits the reality of the present state of international practice and international law, as evidenced by treaties and judicial decisions, which show that the international

15. Verdross, p. 247: "doch muss auch hier eine tatsächliche inländische Anknüpfung zwischen dem Fahrzeug und dem Registerstaat vorliegen."

16. Quadri, *Le navi private nel diritto internazionale* (1939), pp. 39, 40–41. ("Ed è nella effettiva capacità di governo della comunità viggiante che trova i suoi limiti la potestà degli Stati di cui è parola.")

order refers to municipal law so far as the granting of nationality to ships is concerned, and that international law does not lay any minimum requisites guaranteeing the exercise of the "governing power" of the state over its ships.

A pertinent criticism of Quadri's views has recently been given by another representative of the Italian school of international law, Florio,[17] who, besides, criticized all the theories claiming that the grant of the right to fly the flag beyond some alleged limits prescribed by the international order would conflict with international law. Florio's solution is that international law does not lay any limits to the municipal rules on the nationality of ships, but accepts them only so far as they are effective. Beyond the limits of effectivity the municipal requisites are simply ineffective, without being, *per se*, illicit. Giuliano, another Italian writer, comes to the conclusion that in spite of the new tendencies of international law, expressed, for example, by the ILC, the old principle of states' rights is still valid.[18]

In recent years, the demanding task of finding some theoretical basis for the limitation of the competence of states to grant their nationality to merchant vessels has become particularly urgent for the opponents of the flags of convenience. The matter was discussed, first of all, by the ILC, where Mr. François, a Dutch jurist and rapporteur of the ILC on the regime of the high seas, became the chief exponent of the doctrine of the anti-Panlibhon group.[19]

The work of the International Law Commission was the first stage in the codification work accomplished by the United Nations Geneva Conference on the Law of the Sea in 1958, which was mainly based on the drafts prepared by the ILC, and also dealt with the problem under inquiry.

17. Florio, *Nazionalità della nave*, pp. 140–143.

18. Giuliano, I, 371.

19. François reiterated his views, expressed in the ILC, in his publications. See, *e.g.*, François, "La Cour Permanente d'Arbitrage, son origine, sa jurisprudence, son avenir," *RCADI* 87:461, 490–491 (1955, pt. I), where he criticizes the decision in The *Muscat Dhows* case. See also François, "Le tendenze moderne nel diritto internazionale pubblico marittimo," *La Comunità Internazionale* 13:30, 41–42 (1958). For the most comprehensive theoretical exposition of the anti-Panlibhon camp see Mender, "Nationality of Ships — Politics and Law," *Arkiv for Sjørett* 5:265–369 (1961).

The ILC was meeting in the period when the flags of Panlibhon were growing rapidly and were beginning to cause serious concern in the old European maritime nations. This development found greater and greater reflection in the discussions of the ILC devoted to the issue of the nationality of ships and did not fail to provoke controversial debates and to align the members of the ILC according to the national interest of their respective countries.

The ILC, a body of fifteen persons "of recognized competence in international law," elected by the General Assembly from a list of candidates nominated by the governments of members of the United Nations,[20] was established by Resolution 174 (II) adopted by the General Assembly at its 123d plenary meeting on November 21, 1947.[21] This was done in recognition of the need to give effect to a provision of the Charter of the United Nations stipulating that "the General Assembly shall initiate studies and make recommendations for the purpose of . . . encouraging the progressive development of international law and its codification."[22]

According to its Statute, the ILC's work was to have two aspects, on the one hand the "progressive development of international law" or, in the words of the Statute, "the preparation of draft conventions on subjects which have not yet been regulated by international law or in regard to which the law has not yet been sufficiently developed in the practice of states," and, on the other hand, the "codification of international law" or "the more precise formulation and systematization of rules of international law in fields where there already has been extensive State practice, precedent and doctrine."[23] Although different procedures were prescribed for the two approaches, the truth that the distinction between these two kinds of activity could, in practical codifying work, hardly be established and that no "clear-cut distinction between the formulation of the law as it is and law as it ought to be could be rigidly maintained in practice"[24] came also to be under-

20. The ILC Statute, arts. 2 and 3. [UN Doc. A/CN.4/4, reprinted, *e.g.*, in 1947–1948 UN *Yearbook*, p. 211 or in *AJIL* Supp. 44:1, 6–7 (1950).]

21. UN.GA. ILC A/CN.4/4 (1949), p. 1.

22. UN Charter, art. 13, para. 1(a).

23. The ILC Statute, art. 15.

24. The final report of Brierly, the rapporteur of the committee on the progressive development of international law; A/A.C. 10/50 (1947), p. 7.

stood by the ILC.[25] The problem of the nationality of ships is an example of the fact that the terms "codification" and "progressive development" as used for the sake of convenience by the Statute of the ILC are not mutually exclusive. The solution given to this issue must, therefore, be viewed in the light of the above remarks.

The problem of the flags of convenience was the principal issue at the discussion by the ILC of the question of the nationality of ships — one of various subjects under the topic of the regime of the high seas. The topic was among fourteen provisionally selected for codification by the ILC at its first session in 1949, and was subsequently given priority, along with the topics of the law of treaties and the arbitral procedure.[26]

The very question whether nationality of ships should be discussed by the ILC at once revealed the divergence of views between the traditional school proclaiming the states' unlimited right to determine the conditions of granting nationality to merchant vessels and the proponents of limitations allegedly imposed on the states in this matter, by international law.

In his first report on the high seas (1950), François devoted the fourth section to the question of the nationality of ships, basing his views entirely upon quotations from Gidel such as "The attribution of an identity and a nationality to seagoing ships is the corollary of the principle of the free use of the high seas"[27] and from the Asser-Reay Report at the Venice Session of the Institute of International Law in 1896.[28]

The first problem, as the rapporteur put it before the ILC, was whether to retain the subject of the nationality of ships for consideration or drop it altogether. It is characteristic that the latter possibility was suggested by François himself,[29] who, apparently discouraged by the fact that it was impossible to establish uniform regulations on the subject in question because of divergence be-

25. ILC *Yearbook 1956*, II, 255–256. [ILC Report covering the work of the 8th session, April 23–July 4, 1956; UN.GA.*OR*, 11th sess., Supp. No. 9 (A/3159) (1956); *AJIL* 51:154, 159 (1957).]

26. ILC *Yearbook 1949*, pp. 280–281. [ILC Report covering the work of the 1st session, April 12–June 9, 1949; UN.GA.*OR*, 4th sess., Supp. N. 10 (A/923) (1949); *AJIL* 44 Supp.: 1, 6–7 (1950).]

27. ILC *Yearbook 1950*, II, 38.

28. *Annuaire* 15:52.

29. This interesting detail is not mentioned in McDougal, Burke, & Vlasic, p. 104.

tween municipal legislations, believed the problem not to be worthwhile considering. He stated, at the same time, that there were certain common principles to be found in many countries.[30] Since, however, the members of the ILC voted for retaining the subject on the agenda, the next question facing that body was whether to confine themselves to the expression of the principle that each state is free to grant the right to fly its flag, or to consider the possibility of determining some general principles and unifying the various national laws on that point.[31] Alfaro, from Panama, the major flag-of-convenience country at that time, expressed the view that the ILC should only restate the principle as it existed at the moment (that is, the principle of the freedom of states to fix the conditions of granting nationality to ships), and proceed only *de lege lata,* since only treaties could change the practice followed in this respect by the states.[32] To support this view, Alfaro quoted a passage from the report of the rapporteur concerning the states' right to establish the regulations governing the grant of nationality to ships. However, he did not quote it *in extenso,* omitting the very essential modification that "in order that the legislation of a state . . . should be effective in any circumstances that may arise, it should not depart too much from the principles which have been adopted by the greater number of states and which may therefore be considered to constitute the basis of international law in that respect." [33] In this connection we must mention the liberal formulation found among the principles relating to the high seas, proposed by Amado which — as the framer thereof wished — were to serve as a basis for discussion for the ILC. Paragraph 2(a) of these principles states that "every sovereign State shall be entitled to decide to whom it will give the right to fly its flag and to establish the regulations governing

30. ILC *Yearbook 1950,* II, 38. See also ILC *Yearbook 1950,* I, 190 (Summary Records of the Second Session).

31. The following members of the ILC were present at the meeting: Chairman Scelle (France), Rapporteur Alfaro (Panama), Amado (Brazil), Brierly (the United Kingdom), Córdova (Mexico), François (the Netherlands), Hsu (China), Hudson (United States), el-Khouri (Syria), Sandström (Sweden), Spiropoulos (Greece), Yepes (Colombia). Secretariat: Kerno and Liang.

32. ILC *Yearbook 1950,* I, 190.

33. ILC *Yearbook 1950,* II, 38. The report copied the formulation from the Asser-Reay report at the Venice session of the Institute of International Law of 1896 (*Annuaire* 15:51–52).

the granting of that right."[34] However, the ILC did not want to follow the traditional doctrine.

The first skirmish between the old school of thought (which happened to serve as a weapon for Panlibhon) and the new doctrine of the limitation of the states' rights (which served the old European nations, *i.e.*, the anti-Panlibhon camp) initiated a series of defeats of Panlibhon in the ILC, since that body decided by nine votes to two that "it was desirable to endeavor to determine the general principles which might permit the achievement of a certain degree of uniformity in the matter."[35] The special rapporteur was invited to submit a further report on the subject at the next, third session of the ILC.[36]

Having agreed on the necessity to determine the general principles governing the grant of nationality to ships, the ILC subsequently faced the problem of choosing an appropriate method to reveal the principles in question. This was exactly the same task as had been posed before the Institute of International Law in Venice in 1896. The method followed by the ILC in the first stage of its debates on the subject in question, that is, at its second and seventh sessions, was also analogous to that used by the Institute in 1896, from whose Venice session the rapporteur of the ILC largely drew his inspiration.[37] Moreover, the rules accepted at the seventh session of the ILC did not differ greatly from the rules of the Institute.

Before considering what these rules were, the question to be decided by the ILC was whether the grant of nationality to ships was limited by certain principles of international law or not. Here

34. ILC *Yearbook 1950,* I, 188 n. 1. Scelle, the chairman of the meeting, quite wrongly pointed out that para. 4 of François' report and Amado's proposal were in agreement, whereas it was obvious that they represented opposing views on this issue (*Id.,* p. 190).

35. *Id.,* p. 191.

36. ILC *Yearbook 1950,* II, 387. [ILC Report to the General Assembly covering the work of the 2d. sess., June 5–July 29, 1950; (A/1316) (1950); *AJIL* Supp. 44:105 (1950).]

37. See ILC *Yearbook 1950,* II, 38; ILC *Yearbook 1951,* II, 75–77. *Cf.* the discussion at the third session of the ILC (ILC *Yearbook 1951,* I, 328, 337); at the seventh session (ILC *Yearbook 1955,* I, 62); see also ILC *Yearbook 1955,* II, 19, 22–23 [ILC Report covering the work of the 7th session; UN.GA.*OR,* 10th sess., Supp. No. 9 (A/2934) (1955); *AJIL:* 50:190 (1956), (Provisional articles concerning the regime of the high seas, art. 5, comment).] The affiliations of François' reports are not discussed in McDougal, Burke & Vlasic.

again, in this issue, Mr. Alfaro was the only member of the ILC to vote against the motion to recognize the above-mentioned principle of limitation, although he nonetheless admitted that the rules governing the nationality of ships should respect the interests of other states.[38]

Thus, on this essential question of principle, two views clashed in the ILC, one view continuing the traditional doctrine of the states' freedom to fix the conditions of granting nationality to ships, and the other view proclaiming the limitation of this freedom by international law. The former doctrine was represented only by the Panamanian, Alfaro, and the new trend found followers in the majority of the ILC, François being its chief exponent.

The reasoning of the majority proceeded along the lines followed by François in his report. He had studied the manner in which the legislation of various countries regulated the matter, and tried to discover what the rules were with which a ship must comply in order to be considered as possessing the right to fly the flag of a particular state. This study led the rapporteur to the conclusion that in a great majority of states the nationality of merchant vessels was governed by the requirements of national ownership or national crew. The argument of François was that since those requirements were included in almost all legislations they must be regarded as part of the existing international law by which the states — though possessing the right to fix the conditions to grant the flag — were limited in the exercise of the said right. Theoretically, the principle of limitation was deduced — after Gidel[39] — from the institution of the nationality of ships, a corollary of the principle of the freedom of the high seas.

The ILC found an analogy between the nationality of individuals and the nationality of ships. It referred to the statement in the basis of discussion no. 1 of the preparatory committee of the Hague Conference for the Codification of International Law of 1930 that: "Questions as to . . . nationality are within the sovereign authority of each state. Any question as to the acquisition or loss by an individual of a particular nationality is to be decided in accordance with the laws of the state whose nationality is claimed

38. ILC *Yearbook 1951*, I, 330.
39. Gidel, I, 73.

or disputed. The legislation of each state must nevertheless take account of the principles generally recognized by states." [40] In this respect the views of the rapporteur continued the ideas of some writers who had referred to the analogy between the nationality of individuals and ships, without, however, entering into the question at length.[41]

The conclusions of the ILC are best presented by this comment: ". . . with regard to the national element required for permission to fly the flag, a great many systems are possible; but there must be a minimum national element, since control and jurisdiction by a State over ships flying its flag can only be effectively exercised where there is in fact a relationship between the State and the ship other than that based on mere registration." [42]

This principle of the effectivity which must be satisfied by the flag state in the exercise of its control and jurisdiction found its expression at the early stage of the ILC's debates, but it was not further developed, and the ILC subsequently got entangled into the intricate question of the definition of national-ownership requirement and even nationality of crew as the minimum national elements required for the recognition of the right to fly the flag.

The view of the traditional school of international law was represented by Alfaro from Panama. It had a solid background of states' practice, precedents, and doctrine. The Panamanian member of the ILC stated that the matter of granting nationality to ships was entirely one of national law, the only limitation, based on the *comitas gentium*, being that no country might accept registration of a ship if the country whose flag that ship had formerly flown was opposed to such registration. Alfaro emphasized that the situation *de lege lata* confirmed absolute freedom of states. On the other hand, he proposed, in view of the decline of the principle of absolute sovereignty, which was generally being supplanted by the concept of the interdependence of states, that the ILC should *de lege ferenda* restrict the states' freedom on that subject by a general principle couched in negative terms, namely that the

40. Quoted by François; ILC *Yearbook 1951*, II, 76.
41. Neumeyer, III, 90; Verdross, p. 247.
42. ILC *Yearbook 1955*, II, 22–23. (ILC Report 1955; Provisional articles concerning the regime of the high seas, art. 5, comment.)

national legislations should not prejudice the interests of other states, particularly in regard to dues, taxes, and to industrial legislation.[43] This proposal was interesting from the methodological point of view, since it implied the formulation of the limitation of the states' right not by casuistic rules but by general principles.[44]

The voting which followed this discussion showed that the eight members of the ILC represented the view that the grant of nationality to ships was limited by certain principles of international law. One member (Alfaro) was against this view, and two abstained.[45]

The following three rules sum up the question of principle as decided by the ILC at its first stage of approach to the question of the nationality of ships: 1) Each state lays down the conditions for the registration of ships under its flag. 2) The right to register ships is restricted by certain principles of international law resulting from the practice of a great majority of states, which principles impose some minimum requirements on the states. 3) If these minimum requirements are not met in a given case, the other states are not bound to recognize the national character of the ship.[46]

The next objective of the ILC was to find and formulate the minimum requirements governing the permission to fly the flag. It was a very demanding task in view of the large variety in municipal legislations and the consequent divergence in the determination of national element.

The substance of the rules adopted at the seventh session of the ILC in 1955 did not differ much from the rules of 1896. The

43. ILC *Yearbook 1951,* I, 330.

44. In this connection one can mention the proposal of Yepes as to the conditions of the recognition of foreign ships' nationality in the state's own territorial waters. At the 1950 session of the ILC Yepes had submitted some principles, taken in modified form from Bluntschli's *Code of International Law,* as a basis of discussion for the ILC. Point 4, dealing with the nationality of ships, laid down that the conditions under which the states recognize the nationality of foreign ships in their own territorial waters should not be such as to render navigation and seaborne trade impossible or too difficult for a foreign nation; ILC *Yearbook 1950,* I, 190 n. 4. *Cf.* Bluntschli, *Das Moderne Völkerrecht der Civilisirten Staten* (3d. ed. 1878) §327, p. 195.

45. ILC *Yearbook 1951,* I, 330. Sandström, who at first abstained, subsequently declared his support for the majority view; *ibid.*

46. This last clause was proposed to be added to the future text of the draft by Hudson; *ibid.*

principles on the nationality of ships were embodied in art. 5 of the provisional articles, having previously undergone a few drafting changes and one modification referring to the requirement of the nationality of the captain.

For purposes of clarity, the sequence of the proceedings of the ILC and the metamorphosis of the relevant provisions until the adoption of the provisional articles of 1955 are given in the following summary.

In his second report the special rapporteur, François, proposed the following rules on the matter of the nationality of ships:

1. More than one-half of the vessel should be owned by
   a) nationals or persons established in the territory of the state to whom the flag belongs;
   b) A partnership or commandite company in which more than half the partners with personal liability are nationals or persons established in the territory of the flag state;
   c) A national joint-stock company which has its head office in the territory of the flag state.
2. The captain should possess the nationality of the flag state.[47]

These rules were given first reading at the third session of the ILC.[48] On the basis of this discussion the special rapporteur prepared a new draft, which he included in his sixth report as art. 10, reading:

> Each state may fix the conditions on which it will permit a ship to be registered in its territory and to fly its flag. Nevertheless, for the purposes of the recognition of its national character by other states, not less than 50 per cent of the ship must be owned by
> a) nationals of or persons permanently resident in the territory of the state concerned; or
> b) a partnership or commandite company in which half the partners with personal liability are nationals or persons permanently resident in the territory of that state; or
> c) a joint-stock company organized under the laws and having its registered office in the territory of that state.[49]

After having discussed this revised proposal of the special rapporteur at its seventh session in 1955,[50] the ILC adopted the pro-

47. ILC *Yearbook 1951,* II, 77.
48. *Id.,* I, 327–334.
49. A/CN.4/79 (1954), pp. 12–13 [mimeographed].
50. ILC *Yearbook 1955,* I, 61–66.

visional articles with comments, in which the subject in question was included in article 5. The provisional articles were subsequently submitted to governments for observations. The relevant article reads as follows:

Right to a flag
Art. 5

Each state may fix the conditions for the registration of ships in its territory and the right to fly its flag. Nevertheless, for purposes of recognition of its national character by other states, a ship must either:

1. Be the property of the state concerned; or
2. Be more than half owned by:
   a) Nationals of or persons legally domiciled in the territory of the state concerned and actually resident there; or
   b) A partnership in which the majority of the partners with personal liability are nationals of or persons legally domiciled in the territory of the state concerned and actually resident there; or
   c) A joint-stock company formed under the laws of the state concerned and having its registered office in the territory of that state.[51]

The method of fixing the precise criteria of national ownership as a condition for the international recognition of a vessel's nationality has its advantages, but only if all the maritime states adopt uniform regulations on the definition of the "national owner." However, the study of the national legislations shows a large number of various definitions of "national owner," the main obstacle in the acceptance of uniform rules. The ILC at the first stage of its discussion of the nationality of ships was apparently not quite aware of the intricacy of the problem. The classification of various laws given by the special rapporteur in his second report was too general and did not point to the possibility of conflicts between the municipal legislations on the matter of the concept of the national ownership of merchant vessels.[52] This defect in the preparatory work of the ILC was later, at the eighth session, rightly pointed out by Zourek, who claimed that the ILC had insufficient materials from which to draft a satisfactory formulation.[53]

The less complicated forms of ownership, namely, ownership by

51. *Id.*, II, 22.
52. For some of the possible conflicts, see Rienow, pp. 79–83.
53. ILC *Yearbook 1956*, I, 37.

individuals and ownership by partnerships, were promptly dealt with by the ILC, which deemed the rules of 1896 acceptable in a slightly amended form, subscribing to the rule of more than 50 per cent ownership of the vessel. The complications of corporate ownership provoked more discussion in the ILC. It was in this sphere that some members of the ILC felt that it was impossible to formulate such criteria of corporate ownership as would be both acceptable to all states and fulfill the aim set by the ILC, that is, the "elimination of friction and the prevention of abuse," by which the growing practice of registering ships under the Panlibhon flags was certainly meant. The question of what criterion or criteria are to be applied for the purposes of considering a "national" a given juristic person, such as a private or public corporation in Anglo-American law or, *société anonyme, sociedad anónima, Aktiengesellschaft,* and other forms of business organization, is known to be complex and disputable. Since a large number of ships are owned by such associations, the question of which of them is to be regarded as "national" for purposes of owning a vessel is also differently settled by municipal laws (see Chapter II). The ILC departed from the combined test of control by the administrative organs and *siège social,* adopted in 1896 by the Institute of International Law, and preferred to combine the test of *siège social,* with that of the law of the state under which the joint stock company[54] was created.

There is no doubt that the action of the majority of the ILC, led by the special rapporteur, was directed against the registration of ships under the flags of Panama (the primary target at that time) as well as those of Liberia, Honduras, and Costa Rica. Objections were raised against Panama that it was registering ships with a "very frail link between them and Panamanian law," and in general against "states whose merchant fleets had grown to abnormal proportions for very special reasons.[55]

The possibility of easily evading the spirit of art. 5, para. 2c of the provisional articles of 1955 was envisioned not only by the Panamanian member of the ILC who, already at the beginning of the discussion, readily stated that the rules laid down by art. 5

54. This was the only kind of juristic person mentioned in art. 5.
55. ILC *Yearbook 1951,* 333, 334 (François).

were in conformity with Panamanian law and that he would vote for their adoption,[56] but also by other members representing national interests opposed to those of Panama, who expressed their objections against the formulation of art. 5, both at the third and seventh sessions of the ILC.[57]

On the whole, the attitude of the members of the ILC varied, ranging from the most moderate and cautious approach, emphasizing that the time was not yet ripe for achieving an ideal in the form of a generally accepted and universally applicable law on the nationality of ships,[58] to the most radical, demanding a far-reaching unification of the national laws to contribute towards the "integration of the international community" and to prevent the "anarchy created by the exercise of sovereign rights."[59]

The criticism of para. 2c of art. 5 emphasized the formalistic and liberal attitude of the provision, under which shipping companies would be given every facility of choosing for their ships whatever nationality they wished.[60] The critics pointed out that that provision made the apparent stringency of the subparagraphs (a) and (b) illusory, since it would be easy to transfer the ownership of vessels to a joint stock company formed for that sole purpose with a purely fictitious office in the country of refuge.[61] The famous case of the *I'm Alone*[62] was adduced as an instance of the procedure in which nationals of one state (the United States) could utilize the nationality of a vessel to institute proceedings against their own country. On the other hand, Alfaro, defending the proposed provision (which favored the Panamanian interests), pointed out that in the case of the *I'm Alone* no attempt had been made to define the right of a state to permit a company to be

56. *Id.*, p. 328.

57. The problem of the nationality of ships was not on the agenda of the ILC at the intervening sessions.

58. ILC *Yearbook 1955*, I, 3 (Spiropoulos).

59. *Id.*, pp. 12–13 (Scelle).

60. ILC *Yearbook 1951*, I, 332 (Sandström).

61. ILC *Yearbook 1955*, I, 63. (Sandström, Zourek). *Cf.* in this respect the comment by the government of the Union of South Africa, which considered it necessary for a shipping company to have its principal place of business in the flag country; ILC *Yearbook 1956*, II, 78. See also the comment by the government of the United Kingdom; *id.*, pp. 80–81. The solution of accepting the principal place of business as the criterion of the nationality of a joint stock company is open to many uncertainties in localizing this place in cases of large international corporations.

62. UN Reports of International Arbitral Awards 3:1609 (1949); Briggs, p. 385.

formed in its territory under its law, and that the right of Canada to decide on the conditions of setting up a company was within Canada's domestic law.

In this connection it is worthwhile to discuss briefly the case of the *I'm Alone,* since it has caused some confusion, in particular in discussions of the basis for the protection of a merchant vessel. In the ILC the case was cited by the rapporteur as a warning that absolute freedom in granting the right to fly the flag would increase the tendency of other states to "look behind the flag" not only in war time but also in peace.[63]

The *I'm Alone,* a vessel registered in Canada and owned by a Canadian company whose shareholders were Canadians was in reality beneficially owned and controlled by United States citizens. The vessel was sunk in 1929 on the high seas by an American revenue cutter because it had allegedly been engaged in smuggling liquor in violation of the United States law. The Claims Commission "looked behind the flag" and refused to grant compensation to Canada for the loss of the vessel and the cargo, but, notwithstanding the fact that the vessel had been actually owned and controlled by American citizens, the Commission held the act of sinking the vessel unlawful and ordered the United States to apologize and pay the Canadian government compensation for the wrong done.[64]

The case of the *I'm Alone* seems to be a paradox for those who, inspired by the *Nottebohm* decision, divorce protection from nationality and adopt actual ownership as a basis for protection of ships, rejecting registry. Watts, forgetting the fact that the Claims Commission found the sinking of the *I'm Alone* unlawful and ordered compensation to be paid to the state of registry, gives the explanation that the Commissioners considered the *I'm Alone* "a British vessel for jurisdictional purposes, but held . . . [her] not to be a British vessel for purposes of protection."[65] He also explains that the damages were awarded because of the indignity

63. ILC *Yearbook 1951,* II, 76. This reference is based entirely on a quotation from Schwarzenberger, *International Law* (2d ed. 1949), p. 183, as was pointed out by Hudson (ILC *Yearbook 1951,* I, 332).

64. UN Reports of International Arbitral Awards 3:1618 (1949).

65. Watts, "The Protection of Merchant Ships," *British Yearbook of International Law* 33:67 (1957).

directed at the Canadian flag, lawfully flown, and thus, in reality, at British sovereignty, and introduces a distinction between the protection of the flag and the protection of the vessel flying the flag.[66] The practice of states, however, is different from Watts' suggestions. The state of the vessel's nationality has the right to extend its protection to the vessel. This is the rule. On the other hand, the protection of the property of nationals is a privilege of the states, and therefore they may have concurrent competence to protect a ship in virtue of the fact that it is owned by nationals. Yet, as Rienow observes, the right of protection based on ownership "is an imperfect one, due to the special nature and qualities of the ships. It can be made effective so long as it does not conflict with the control which the state to which the vessel legally belongs is, under international law, permitted to effect and does, in fact, effect." [67]

As to the criterion of the national character of the ship-owning company, the views of the members of the ILC were, to a certain degree, affected by the legislative approach of their respective countries. Thus, the French criterion of the control of the juristic person by means of securing national representation in the administrative organs thereof[68] was put forward by Scelle as "the only valid criterion for the nationality both of a company and of any ship it owned." [69] On the other hand, the Swedish member of the ILC rightly pointed out that even the requirement of the directors' nationality might prove illusory, since it was possible to appoint nominees with no effective powers, who would administer the company on the instructions given by the real owners. For the Swedish delegate, the solution of securing the ownership of the shares to the nationals seemed the best.[70] Such a solution, however, in order to be effective, would require the provision on

66. *Id.*, p. 71.

67. Rienow, pp. 104–105. On the right to protect ships to which national character has been attributed, see in general McDougal, Burke, and Vlasic, pp. 60–62, where a pertinent criticism of Watts' view can also be found.

68. *Cf.* Code des Douanes du 8 Décembre 1948, art. 211; *Journal Officiel,* No. 1 (1949); UNLS, p. 54. On this type of legislation see Ch. II.

69. ILC *Yearbook 1955,* I, 63.

70. ILC *Yearbook 1951,* I, 331. According to art. 1 of the Swedish Maritime Law of June 12, 1891, the shareholders of the joint stock company must be Swedish subjects, if the ship owned by the company is to be considered Swedish; UNLS, p. 162.

registered (nominative) shares as it was suggested by Córdova.[71] This, in turn, touching Panama's sensitive spot, provoked a strong protest by Alfaro against the involvement of the ILC in the questions of domestic law which might allow companies to issue bearer shares.[72]

All this discussion and the contradictory proposals advanced indicated the complexity of the problem and the difficult situation of the ILC, whose majority found themselves undecided between a desire for legal strictness and easy application of the law, and the motivation to curtail the practice of the flags of convenience. At this deadlock there was even a proposal not to go into the details of partnership or corporate ownership, but simply to state the principle of recognizing the flag, if the ship was registered by a natural person or legal entity of the same nationality as the flag state.[73] This solution would have the obvious advantage of simplicity, since it would be very easy to ascertain where a given juristic person is established.

The hesitancy of the ILC is best illustrated by the problem of the captain's (master's) nationality as a requirement for the recognition of the vessel's national character, concurrent with the requisite of national ownership. This possibility had been considered and rejected by the Institute of International Law in 1896, but the rapporteur of the ILC, regarding the captain's nationality as a very important link between the ship and the flag state, proposed that "the captain should possess the nationality of the flag state." [74] At the third session of the ILC, this rule was rejected by eight votes to three, but at the seventh session, which was the direct continuation of the discussion of the nationality of ships, it was

71. ILC *Yearbook 1951*, I, 331.

72. *Ibid. Cf.* in this respect the comment of the Union of South Africa on art. 5 of the provisional articles to the effect that "it would be more in accord with the intention which appears to underlie paragraphs 2(*a*) and 2(*b*) if paragraph 2(*c*) were expanded by the addition of the following words: '. . . provided that more than half the issued share capital of such company is registered in the names of nationals or of persons legally domiciled in the territory of the State concerned and actually resident there.'" ILC *Yearbook 1956*, II, 78. This kind of provision would hit the practice of registering ships in Panlibhon.

73. ILC *Yearbook 1955*, I, 62 (Zourek). The Czechoslovak member of the ILC also insisted on adopting the criterion of operation as an important element in recognizing the nationality of the ship. This criterion, along with ownership, is recognized by art. 6 of the Czechoslovak Shipping Act of October 29, 1952; UNLS, p. 36.

74. ILC *Yearbook 1951*, II, 77.

reinstated on the agenda, to be rejected again by four votes to four, and four abstentions.[75]

It was the issue of the captain's nationality that prompted much discussion touching Panlibhon, in particular Panama. The ILC's opinion was divided. One group[76] considered that in view of the "widespread" practice of requiring by domestic legislation that the captain must possess the nationality of the state under whose flag the ship sailed[77] and because of the important position of the captain in the exercise of the state's jurisdiction and control over the vessel, it would be advisable to introduce the captain's nationality as one of the requirements in the rules under discussion. It was argued by this group that one could not expect a foreign master to apply properly the law to which his ship was subject. The Panamanian vessels were cited as an example. Their captains, as François claimed, being foreigners, could not enforce the laws of which they were ignorant. Besides, those ships, he added, never entered Panamanian waters.[78] The source of this information must have been the report of the International Labor Organization according to which none of the masters of the thirty Panamanian ships selected for inspection were of Panamanian nationality.[79] The sample of thirty ships selected at random was likely to be representative of the situation in the Panamanian fleet as a whole[80]

It was hoped by the adversaries of the flags of convenience in the ILC that the introduction of the requirement of national captain "would serve as a protection against the growing use of 'fictitious flags.'"[81] This requirement is undoubtedly desirable and its value for the control of the ship's community is not to be denied. However, it must be regarded as too radical and going absolutely too far because of several reasons. First of all, it cannot be regarded as *lex lata* adopted by a majority of states. On the

75. ILC *Yearbook 1951,* I, 334; ILC *Yearbook 1955,* I, 63.

76. François, Yepes, Sandström (at the third session) and also Scelle and Krylov and two other members (at the seventh session).

77. François' second report mentions 19 countries imposing this requirement (ILC *Yearbook 1951,* II, 77). This is a minority but represents a large percentage of the merchant tonnage in relation to the global world tonnage.

78. ILC *Yearbook 1951,* I, 333. This is certainly true. *Cf.* statement of then Secretary of the Navy Gates, *Hearings* (House) 1957, p. 632.

79. ILOffice, *Panama Conditions,* appendix V, pp. 74–75.

80. ILC *Yearbook 1951,* I, 333.

81. ILC *Yearbook 1955,* I, 63 (Scelle).

contrary, some important maritime countries, such as Norway and Germany, do not know this rule and employ foreigners as captains of their ships. The introduction of this rule would therefore upset international shipping and lead to confusion. Therefore, even starting from the premises of the ILC of the existence of general rules limiting the right of the states of granting nationality to ships, one must come to the conclusion that, no universal rule on the national captain being in existence, the question is entirely a matter of domestic jurisdiction. The same obtains in the case of crew in general whose nationality has never been considered under international law as evidence of the nationality of the vessel. There are also practical reasons against the feasibility of the prerequisite of captain's nationality being accepted by all the states, namely, that certain countries have not yet sufficient trained personnel to enable them to comply with such a requirement.[82] In view of the above reasons, the common sense solution prevailed, and the ILC dropped the demand for the nationality of captain, although at the seventh session in 1955 this demand found more followers than in the previous discussion of this topic in 1951. This can be attributed to the fact that in the meantime, that is, in the period 1951–1955, the amount of tonnage registered under Panlibhon (especially Liberia) flags had continued to grow rapidly. This development found its reflection in the attitude of the ILC, the majority of whose members made attempts to find legal checks on this tendency by laying down various safeguards limiting the right of the states to register ships under their flags.[83]

The whole text of the article dealing with the nationality of ships was approved by the ILC at the seventh session by seven votes to four, with two abstentions,[84] and became art. 5 of the provisional

82. Such were the opinions of Alfaro, el-Khouri, Hsu, Spiropoulos, Amado (ILC *Yearbook 1951*, I, 333–334) and Sandström (ILC *Yearbook 1955*, I, 63). See also *id.*, II, 23 (ILC Report 1955, Provisional articles, art. 5, comment).

83. An example of inconsistency in the views on the subject of captain's nationality is provided by the attitude of Amado. At the third session (1951) this member of the ILC considered it to be going too far if at that stage the ILC laid down the requirement of the captain's nationality; Amado was in favor of deleting this requirement from the rapporteur's proposal; ILC *Yearbook 1951*, I, 334. However, at the seventh session (1955) the same member came to the conclusion that in view of the inadequacy of the ownership criteria, "the only possible way to ensure that the flag really represented the nationality of the ship was to insist that the captain be a national of the flag State." ILC *Yearbook 1955*, I, 63.

84. *Ibid.*

articles concerning the regime of the high seas. However, lack of enthusiasm and an undertone of discouragement could be seen in the debates of the ILC on the subject of nationality of ships. In its comment, the ILC admitted that it was aware of the fact that "if the practical ends in view are to be achieved, States must work out more detailed provisions when they incorporate the . . . rules in their legislation.[85]

The provisions concerning the right to fly the flag, as agreed upon by the ILC at its seventh session, did not have much chance of survival. From the point of view of strictness, the approach of the ILC was correct; it laid down specific conditions for the grant of nationality which were intended to be binding on all the states. But, besides the difficulties of practical implementation of the rules, draft art. 5 caused a considerable degree of dissatisfaction among the majority of the members of the ILC, bent on curtailing the flags of convenience, because they felt that it did not remove a practice the elimination of which was the apparent objective of the ILC. So far as this aim was concerned, art. 5, as it was put by Sandström, "amounted to little more than a stop-gap."[86]

The ILC had set itself the goal of curbing the expansion of the flags of convenience, and bringing about a regulation of the grant of nationality to merchant vessels under which the relation between state and vessel would be based on something more than mere registration. If this was the aim of the ILC, the following objections might be, and were, raised against its first solution:

Article 5, para. 2(c) could be easily evaded, being wide enough to permit the establishment of flags of convenience by the device of subsidiary companies incorporated in other countries. Besides this, with regard to ownership by individuals and partnerships, the draft admitted the possibility of a ship entirely owned by aliens and, nevertheless, entitled to being recognized as national, since the criteria required by art. 5 would be satisfied if the ship were owned, say, 51 per cent by aliens domiciled and actually

85. ILC *Yearbook 1955,* II, 23 (ILC Report 1955, Provisional articles, art. 5, comment).

86. ILC *Yearbook 1956,* I, 37.

resident in the state concerned, and 49 per cent by aliens living outside the flag state.[87] Under the provisional articles of 1955, ships owned by fictitious companies would have to be internationally recognized, satisfying the formal requirement of national ownership, whereas a number of ships registered bona fide in some other countries could not be recognized. To this category would belong, for example, ships of the countries which knew only the requirement of national crew (Argentina, Uruguay, Guatemala, Ecuador) or the countries whose ownership requirements were not within the scope of art. 5 for example, Chile, Colombia, Lebanon, Vatican, Mexico, Ethiopia or the countries in which the nationality of the operator (charterer) provides sufficient link for granting the right to fly the flag, even though the ship be entirely owned by aliens (Czechoslovakia, Austria, Yugoslavia, German Federal Republic).

There might also arise difficulties as to the recognition of the ships sailing, as a matter of custom or historical right, under the flag of, and being registered in, one of the British Commonwealth countries, although it was wholly owned and controlled by another Commonwealth country.[88] The objections against the draft of the ILC were particularly strong in the comment by the government of the Netherlands, for whom the proposed solution did not seem to prevent possible abuse, and seemed rather to be likely to cause complications and leave a number of problems unsolved.[89]

There is no doubt that the ILC, in its first approach to the unification of the rules concerning nationality of ships, was too ambitious, undertaking the task of reducing to a few rules the divergent criteria governing this subject in various domestic legislations. In the present state of unequal economic development and conflicting legislations, the task of devising a formula which would embrace all possible combinations of links between the ship and the state seems unfeasible. The ILC also overlooked the fact that, due to particular local conditions, criteria different from those laid down by the ILC might, in some states, better fulfill the objective of establishing control and jurisdiction, which is the rationale of

87. See the critical remarks of Zourek and Sandström (ILC *Yearbook 1955*, I, 63).
88. Comment by the government of the United Kingdom (ILC *Yearbook 1956*, II, 81).
89. *Id.*, 63.

the institution of nationality and which was also sought by the ILC, although it was not included in the text of art. 5, but only referred to in the comment. Finally, there was nothing in the draft about the ship's documents, which under international law are the evidence of the ship's right to fly its flag. There were also some drafting omissions, adding to the other uncertainties of the draft.[90]

It was a foregone conclusion that, in view of these reasons, which were also voiced by some governments in their comments, the ILC would reexamine the problem of the connection between the state and the ship at its next, eighth session in 1956. It was at the eighth session that the concept of the genuine link made its first appearance in the discussion of the nationality of ships. The inspiration came, this time, from the comments of the government of the Netherlands, and to a lesser degree from the government of the United Kingdom. The governments of these two countries criticized severely the draft of 1955 in their comments, unlike the government of the United States which expressed agreement with the draft, stating that "the articles in this chapter [*i.e.*, Chapter I, Navigation, of the provisional articles, where art. 5 was included] constitute as a whole a sound exposition of the principles applicable to problems of navigation."[91]

Both the Netherlands and the United Kingdom submitted proposals concerning the problem of the nationality of ships. Since these two proposals originated a new approach to this problem which culminated at the Geneva Conference, they are quoted here *in extenso:*

The Proposal of the Netherlands

Replace art. 5 by two other articles:

> 5a. "Each State may fix the conditions for the registration of ships in its territory and the right to fly its flag. Nevertheless, for purposes of recognition of the national character of the ship by other States, there must exist a genuine connection between the State and the ship."

90. Thus, *e.g.*, para. 2c of the relevant article mentioned only the joint stock companies as juristic persons; the article did not provide for ships owned more than half by a state (comment by Italy, *id.*, p. 60) or for ships operated by national charterers but owned by aliens.

91. *Id.*, p. 91.

5b. "States shall issue for their ships regulations in order to ensure the safety at sea *inter alia* with regard to:

1. The adequacy of the crew and reasonable labour conditions;
2. The construction, equipment and seaworthiness of the ship;
3. The use of signals, the maintenance of communications and the prevention of collisions.

In issuing such regulations the States shall observe the standards internationally accepted for the vessels forming the greater part of the tonnage of seagoing ships.

States shall take the necessary measures in order to guarantee the observance of the said regulations. To that effect they shall provide *inter alia* for the registration of the ship in the territory of the State and for the documents showing that the pertinent regulations of national legislation have been observed." [92]

The Proposal of the United Kingdom

Art. 5: "A ship has the nationality of the State whose flag it is entitled to fly. A State may not, however, allow a ship to fly its flag, nor need other States recognize the ship as entitled to do so, unless, both under its own domestic law and under international law, the flag State is in a position to exercise, and does exercise, effective jurisdiction and control over ships flying its flag, and the right to fly its flag is limited and regulated accordingly by its domestic law. A State may permit a ship that would be entitled to fly its own national flag under domestic law, to fly the flag of another State, provided the requirement of the exercise of effective jurisdiction and control on the part of that other State is fulfilled." [93]

As can be seen from their contents, the two proposals used a new approach to the problem, discarding the detailed criteria and substituting for them a general principle. The main difference between them is that, whereas the Netherlands' proposal found the criterion of the recognition of the ship's nationality in the existence or non-existence of the "genuine connection" between the state and the ship, the United Kingdom's proposal saw this criterion in the exercise of effective jurisdiction and control over the ship by the flag state. The Dutch proposal showed the tendency to the extreme of generality, while the English one "was an attempt, while eliminating controversial detail, to give some content to the idea of a substantial connection between the state and the ship flying its flag.[94] To express it in another way, the

92. ILC *Yearbook 1956*, II, 15 (also p. 63).
93. *Id.*, p. 15 (also p. 81).
94. *Id.*, I, 38 (Sir Gerald Fitzmaurice).

Dutch proposal found the center of gravity in the relation between the state and the ship, whereas the British one was more concerned with the result of that relation which must, as its consequence, bring about effective jurisdiction and control of the ship on the high seas, since — as the United Kingdom member of the ILC claimed — "some States tended to grant the right to fly their flag without being able to exercise control over the ships in question or assume international responsibility for them." [95] This problem, so far as control by the flag state over the safety regulations (conceived broadly to include labor conditions) is concerned, is dealt with in the Netherlands' proposal in art. 5b, combined with 5a. The provisional articles had mentioned safety at sea in art. 9.[96]

The United Kingdom's proposal contained an important innovation, since it limited not only the right to grant the flag, but also restricted states in granting permission to the transfer of their ships to another flag. Under the United Kingdom proposal, this transfer would be permissible only if the requirement of the exercise of effective jurisdiction and control on the part of the other state had reasonable chance of being fulfilled. This provision was obviously directed against the transfer policy of some states, in particular the United States, which, without greater difficulties, allowed ships owned by their nationals to be registered under one of the flags of convenience.

The Dutch and the English proposals were found so attractive that the ILC unanimously decided that the article dealing with the nationality of ships "should be redrafted on the basis of formulation of a general principle," [97] instead of enumeration of detailed ownership criteria. The subcommittee set up for the purpose of preparing the text of the article in question gave preference to the proposal of the Netherlands which stressed the necessity for a genuine link between the state and the ship as a condition for recognizing the grant of its nationality.[98]

95. *Id.*, p. 72.

96. Signals and rules for the prevention of collisions, art. 9: "States shall issue for their ships regulations concerning the use of signals and the prevention of collisions on the high seas. Such regulations must not be inconsistent with those concerning the safety of life at sea internationally accepted for the vessels forming the greater part of the tonnage of sea-going ships." ILC *Yearbook 1955,* II, 23.

97. ILC *Yearbook 1956,* I, 38.

98. *Id.*, p. 67.

The concept of the genuine link, which, in connection with the flags of convenience, was to provoke so much discussion at the Geneva Conference on the Law of the Sea (see Chapter IX) at the ILC also revealed conflicts of interests and opinions on this issue, as well as much confusion and vagueness. The real, economic nature and background of the whole flag-of-convenience controversy was exposed in the ILC by Salamanca (Bolivia), who pointed out that "behind the stress on the necessity for 'genuine connection between the State and the ship' was probably the fear of competition from States with very liberal registration laws." [99] This was certainly true, but this aspect of the problem had its reflection in the ILC as a conflict of two theoretical views of which one attempted to introduce into international law the principle of limiting the states' right of granting nationality to ships.[100]

The opposition against adopting the genuine-link clause was motivated by practical and legal arguments. From the practical point of view, the advisability of the genuine link was questioned because of its vagueness and lack of precision. It was pointed out that it would be extremely difficult to define that term.[101] The ILC itself agreed with this objection, but the majority of its members "preferred a vague criterion to no criterion at all." [102] and the term was not defined even in the commentary, the task which was expected to be fulfilled.[103] Some suggestions as to the tests which might be applied in order to decide whether there was a genuine connection were given by the government of the Netherlands, the author of the principle adopted by the ILC. The ownership or the administration of the ship, or the nationality of the captain or the crew, were among these criteria.[104] However, the ILC, obviously discouraged by its previous efforts, did not attempt to make the genuine link more precise. It left the states a wide latitude in this respect and only "wished to make it clear that the grant of [the] flag to a ship cannot be a mere administrative

99. *Id.*, p. 37.
100. Scelle emphasized that "the Commission's primary concern was the public interest and not the interests of shipowners, though the latter, of course, must not be overlooked." (*Id.*, p. 71.)
101. *Id.*, pp. 67, 69, 72 (Salamanca).
102. ILC *Yearbook 1956*, II, 279 (The Law of the Sea, art. 29, commentary).
103. ILC *Yearbook 1956*, I, 67 (Zourek, chairman of the drafting subcommittee).
104. *Id.*, II, 63.

formality, with no accompanying guarantee that the ship possess a real link with its new State." [105] The addition of the adjective "new" was not precise, since it implied that the ILC meant only a transfer to a new flag, although — as it is well known — a number of newly launched vessels are granted registration in Liberia or Panama directly, without any transfer from another flag.

The legal arguments against the genuine-link clause reflected the views of the traditional school of international law, and were also strengthened by the international practice of the states in the matter of the nationality of ships. In connection with the unclarified problem of who should bear the burden of proving the existence of the genuine link, it was argued, in accordance with the traditional doctrine, that the link between the state of registration and the ship was created precisely by the granting of nationality. Only the states themselves could decide whether a genuine link existed between them and the ship whose owner was seeking registration, and only they could lay down the conditions for the registration of ships. States should not be suspected of fraudulent practice in that regard. The necessity of deleting the genuine-link clause was motivated, also, by its being in conflict with international practice, particularly with the treaties which laid down that the nationality of a ship was determined by the law of the state to which it belonged, and in which treaties the parties reciprocally recognized the nationality of each other's vessels as granted under the municipal law of the flag state, and not because of the existence of a genuine connection of the ship with the flag state. In such treaties, the link of nationality effected by registration was the only one recognized by the states.[106] The adversaries of the flags of convenience, against all international practice, advanced the view that in case of a transfer or registry, it was for third states to decide whether a genuine link existed between the ship and the state of new registration, and consequently whether the ship was entitled to its new flag.[107] The analogy with the nationality of individuals was incidentally mentioned, but

105. *Id.*, p. 279 (The Law of the Sea, art. 29, commentary).

106. ILC *Yearbook 1956*, I, 69, 70, 72 (statements by Padilla Nervo from Mexico, and el-Khouri from Syria). The members of the ILC meant the bilateral treaties of friendship, commerce, and navigation, discussed in Ch. IV.

107. *Id.*, p. 71 (Scelle).

there were no attempts at the ILC to develop this point or to defend this position by some legal argumentation. Neither was the *Nottebohm* case expressly invoked at the sessions of the ILC as an analogy in the matter of the nationality of ships.[108]

In discussing the debates of the ILC, we must note the separate position taken by Sir Gerald Fitzmaurice, who repeatedly affirmed the view that the correct criterion for the recognition of a ship's nationality was the exercise of effective jurisdiction and control over it by the flag state, as had been suggested in the proposal of the United Kingdom.[109] It was not until the Geneva Conference that this element was taken into account, serving to define, at least partially, the essence of the genuine link. For the time being, the point was mentioned only in the commentary to art. 29 of the 1956 draft, stating that the "jurisdiction of the State over ships, and the control it should exercise in conformity with article 34 of these articles, can only be effective where there exists in fact a relationship between the State and the ship other than mere registration or the mere grant of a certificate of registry." [110]

As to the text of the relevant article, it was adopted by the ILC, after a few drafting amendments, in the following provisional formulation:

> Art. 5. 1. Each State shall fix the conditions for the grant of its nationality to ships, for the registration of ships in its territory and for the right to fly its flag. Ships have the nationality of the State whose flag they are entitled to fly. Nevertheless, for the national character of the ship to be recognized by other States, there must exist a genuine link between the State and the ship.
>
> 2. The nationality of merchant ships, and hence their right to a flag, shall be established by documents issued by the authorities of the State of the flag.[111]

108. Nottebohm case (Liechtenstein v. Guatemala) (Second Phase), Judgment of April 6, 1955; [1955] ICJ Rep. 4. On the correlation between the *Nottebohm* case and the genuine link between ship and state, see Ch. IV.

109. ILC *Yearbook 1956*, I, 68, 72, 262.

110. *Id.*, II, 279. Article 34 deals with the safety of navigation. Unlike the text in the provisional articles (1955) it was extended (following the Netherlands' proposal) to cover not only the rules concerning signals and the prevention of collisions but also to cover those concerning the construction, equipment, and seaworthiness of the ships and the labor conditions of the crews. About the reason for this extension, see Ch. IX.

111. ILC *Yearbook 1956*, I, 70, 72.

The ILC subsequently agreed to reverse the order of arts. 4 and 5, and after additional drafting changes[112] art. 4 (the former art. 5) assumed the following definitive formulation:

> 1. Each State shall fix the conditions for the grant of its nationality to ships, for the registration of ships in its territory, and for the right to fly its flag. Ships have the nationality of the State whose flag they are entitled to fly. Nevertheless, for purposes of recognition of the national character of the ship by other States, there must exist a genuine link between the State and the ship.
> 2. A merchant ship's right to fly the flag of a State is evidenced by documents issued by the authorities of the State of the flag.[113]

As a result of voting sentence by sentence, the first two sentences, expressing the traditional rule of international law, were adopted by the ILC, without any dissenting vote (there was one abstention on the second sentence), while the disputed geninue-link clause was adopted by nine votes to three, with three abstentions. From their enunciations in the discussion, one can assume that Padilla Nervo, el-Khouri, and Salamanca voted against it. Paragraph 2, dealing with the documents evidencing a merchant ship's right to fly the flag was adopted unanimously since it reflected the undisputed rule of customary international law. It was added this time by the ILC, which had omitted to do so in the provisional articles in 1955. The article as a whole was adopted by eleven votes to none, with four abstentions.[114]

After this analysis of the flag-of-convenience problem, in the light of the codification work of the ILC, the following can be said by way of summary and conclusion:

The growing practice of the flags of convenience seized the attention of the ILC from the very beginning of the discussion of

112. *Id.*, pp. 262–263.

113. This article became art. 29 of the Law of the Sea, in Subsection A, Navigation, of Section I, General Regime, of Pt. II dealing with the high seas, ILC Report 1956 (ILC *Yearbook 1956*, II, 278). It provided the basis of discussion of the flags of convenience at the Geneva Conference on the Law of the Sea in 1958.

114. ILC *Yearbook 1956*, I, 72. The following 14 members were present: Chairman García-Amador (Cuba), Rapporteur François (the Netherlands), Amado (Brazil), Edmonds (United States), Fitzmaurice (United Kingdom), Hsu (China), el-Khouri (Syria), Krylov (U.S.S.R.), Padilla Nervo (Mexico), Pal (India), Salamanca (Bolivia), Sandström (Sweden), Scelle (France), Spiropoulos (Greece), Zourek (Czechoslovakia). Liang represented UN Secretariat.

the nationality of ships, to which discussion it chiefly contributed. The divergence of interests underlying the issue found its reflection within the ILC, the attitude of whose members was certainly influenced by the position taken in the dispute by their respective countries. The purely legal aspect of the problem revealed once again that although in any field of international law "there is, as a rule, a consensus of opinion on broad principle . . . there is no semblance of agreement in relation to specific rules and problems." [115]

In the subject discussed here, the general traditional principle of the states' right to establish by their own legislation the conditions of flying their flag, was not questioned by anyone, but the limits of this right and the recognition of its effect by other states provided essential disagreement. Due to the rise of the flags of convenience, the problem of the nationality of ships became an example of a case which could not fit neatly either into the concept of codification or of progressive development of international law as provided by art. 15 of the statute of the ILC. For there was agreement evidenced by long practice, precedent, and doctrine as to the freedom of fixing the conditions of registration of ships, and this was *lex lata* and codification of international law in the strict sense of the word. On the other hand, the ILC provided an opportunity for those who, in view of the growing practice of the flags of convenience, found the traditional rule no longer convenient, to weaken that rule by the *de lege ferenda* provision on the genuine link as a condition of recognizing the nationality of a given ship. Thus, art. 5, as adopted by the ILC, became one of those provisions which, "based on a 'recognized principle of international law,' have been framed in such a way as to place them in the 'progressive development' category." [116]

The formulation of a principle of international law is always difficult in a period when the states' practice begins to outgrow the hitherto obtaining rules, causing conflict and the need for revaluation of these rules. This was the case in the question of the nationality of ships. The successive alternative proposals and hesitant

115. Lauterpacht, "Codification and Development of International Law," *AJIL* 49:16, 17 (1955).
116. ILC *Yearbook 1956*, II, 256 (ILC Report 1956, para. 26).

attitude of the ILC revealed the intricacy of the problem, which was also made more difficult by the fact that the ILC had not adequate materials prepared on the subject of the nationality of ships. The documentation here was very weak, compared with that in other fields of the law of the sea. The concept of the genuine link adopted by the ILC was not developed, and the essential question of its elements was left obscure. As to the sanction in case of the absence of the genuine link, it was formulated in a very general way, without making the legal consequences of this rule more precise. Hence, the adopted attitude presaged the dangers of an interpretation which, in disregard of all international practice, would introduce the possibility of unilateral non-recognition of a ship's nationality. All these doubts and obscurities, and potential dangers, were left by the ILC to the Geneva Conference, for which the ILC draft of 1956 was to provide a basis of discussion.

Chapter IX. The 1958 Geneva Conference on the Law of the Sea

Attempts to limit the competence of the states to confer their nationality upon merchant vessels culminated at the first United Nations Conference on the Law of the Sea, which met at Geneva, Switzerland, from February 24 to April 27, 1958.[1] The initiative in summoning the conference was taken by the International Law Commission which, pursuant to the provisions of its statute,[2] submitted the articles concerning the law of the sea to the General Assembly. In so doing, the ILC could choose one of the recommendations provided for by its statute:

1. The Commission may recommend to the General Assembly:
   a. To take no action, the report having already been published;
   b. To take note of or adopt the report by resolution;
   c. To recommend the draft to Members with a view to the conclusion of a convention;
   d. To convoke a conference to conclude a convention.
2. Whenever it deems desirable, the General Assembly may refer drafts back to the Commission for reconsideration or redrafting.[3]

The ILC chose to recommend in its 1956 report to the General Assembly, in conformity with art. 23, para. 1d of the statute,

that the General Assembly should summon an international conference of plenipotentiaries to examine the law of the sea, taking account not only of the legal but also of the technical, biological, economic and politi-

1. UN.CLS.*OR* 2:146–147, Final Act of the Conference. The last meeting rose on April 28, 1958, at 2:20 a.m.; *id.*, p. 79; and the Final Act itself was signed on April 29; *id.*, p. 147.
2. ILC Statute, art. 22.
3. *Id.*, art. 23.

cal aspects of the problem, and to embody the results of its work in one or more international conventions or such other instruments as it may deem appropriate.[4]

The reason for this recourse to conventional means is to be found in the fact that in the course of its work the ILC became convinced that the distinction established by the statute between the two kinds of ILC activity, that is, the codification of the law as it was, and the "progressive development," or creation of, new law,[5] could hardly be maintained, since the two elements were in several cases intermingled and the elaboration of some existing rule of law amounted to the formulation of a new law, which belonged to the category of "progressive development."[6] This was the proper course to be taken in order to give effect to the project of the ILC as a whole, and therefore the recommendation of the ILC was approved by the General Assembly of the United Nations on February 21, 1957, which decided to convene a conference, in a resolution faithfully following the wording of the above-mentioned recommendation of the ILC.[7]

The Geneva conference was attended by more than 700 delegates from 86 countries, and by observers from seven specialized agencies and nine intergovernmental bodies.[8] The fact that the conference had both a legal and a practical character was emphasized by the participation in its sessions of not only diplomats and legal experts but also experts in maritime matters, such as navigation, shipping, fisheries, oceanography, etc. Among the advisers and unofficial advisers of some delegations there were also representatives of shipowners' associations and seamen's unions.[9] The diversity of members within the delegations allowed

4. ILC *Yearbook 1956*, II, 256 (Report of the ILC, para. 28).
5. ILC Statute, art. 15.
6. ILC *Yearbook 1956*, II, 255–256 (Report of the ILC, para. 26).
7. UN.CLS.*OR*. 2:xi [Resolution 1105 (xi); UN.GA.XI.*OR*., Supp. 17, (A/3572) (1957)].
8. Only the German Democratic Republic, the Korean People's Democratic Republic, Outer Mongolia, and the Democratic Republic of Viet-Nam did not participate, China being represented by the nationalist government. The original number of 87 states was reduced by the merger of Egypt and Syria into the United Arab Republic. For the list of the delegations, see UN.CLS.*OR* 2:xiii–xxvii.
9. For example, in the delegation of Norway, UN.CLS.*OR* 2:xxi; the United Kingdom, *id.*, xxv. In connection with the issue of the flags of convenience one might mention that the ITWF suggested (in *Panlibhonco*) that the delegations should also include seafarers' representatives, which was the case with some delegations.

one to hope that the technical, biological, economic, and political aspects of the problem of the law of the sea would be taken into account in accordance with resolution 1105 (xi) of the General Assembly. Hence one could also hope that the participation of so many experts in maritime matters and maritime law would contribute to the formulation of the provisions relating to nationality of ships which would best correspond to the interest of community of states.

The task of the Geneva conference was facilitated by the work of the ILC, whose final report, setting forth the Draft Articles on the Law of the Sea with commentaries, was referred by the General Assembly to the conference "as the basis for its consideration of the various problems involved in the development and codification of the law of the sea." [10] The report of the ILC was debated upon during the eleventh (1957) session of the General Assembly in the Sixth Committee.[11]

In fact, the conclusions of the ILC found in the Law of the Sea of 1956 were, with few changes, embodied by the Geneva conference in four conventions, namely, Convention on the Territorial Sea and the Contiguous Zone, Convention on the High Seas, Convention on Fishing and Conservation of the Living Resources of the High Seas, and Convention on the Continental Shelf.[12] The conference also adopted the Optional Protocol of Signature concerning the compulsory settlement of disputes,[13] and nine resolutions.

A wide variety of conflicts among states, based on their national economic, political, and military interests, was brought to light in the debates of the conference. The Geneva Conference on the Law of the Sea is mainly associated with the still unresolved issue of the breadth of the territorial sea, with which the literature of the conference is primarily concerned, but in addition the issue of flags of convenience was along with nuclear tests on the high seas the main disputed issue in the discussion on the regime of the high seas, and revealed the material interests of the states and national groups involved in the dispute. This had manifested

10. Resolution 1105 (xi), para. 9 (UN.CLS.*OR*. 2:xi).
11. Doc. A/CONF. 13/19 (1957) [mimeographed].
12. UN.CLS.*OR* 2:132–143 (Documents A/CONF. 13/L. 52–55).
13. *Id.*, pp. 145–146 (Doc. A/CONF. 13/L. 57).

itself to a certain extent in the sessions of the ILC, but at the conference, which was a meeting of plenipotentiaries of practically all governments, the division became more complete and the official views of the interested governments found an appropriate forum.

The documentation of the conference was, in general, extensive, but so far as the subject in question is concerned, the ILC did not leave to the conference sufficient auxiliary materials, in particular those related to the economic, technical, and social aspects of the problem of the flags of convenience.[14] The provisions relating to the flags of convenience are included in the Convention on the High Seas, elaborated by the second committee dealing with the general regime of the high seas.[15]

The working basis for the second committee, in which practically all the discussion took place, was provided by arts. 26 to 48 and 61 to 65 of the Law of the Sea, adopted by the ILC at its eighth session.[16] Article 29 dealt with the nationality of ships. The articles dealing with the status of ships (art. 30), and especially with the safety of navigation (art. 34) also have relevance to the subject in question. The traditional rule of customary international law, that each state is free to lay down the conditions under which it will register ships and thereby grant them the right to fly the flag, and that ships have the nationality of the state whose flag they are entitled to fly, was not questioned at Geneva, and this found its confirmation in the first two sentences of art. 5 of the Convention on the High Seas, which literally reiterated the corresponding sentences of art. 29 of the ILC's 1956 draft: "Each state shall fix the conditions for the grant of its nationality to ships, for the registration of ships in its territory, and for the right to fly

14. The lack of sufficient documentation in this field was pointed out by the delegate of Israel; UN.CLS.*OR* 4:28.

15. UN.CLS.*OR* 2:135–139 [Doc. A/CONF. 13/L. 53 (1958)]. For the text of the convention in question see also, *e.g.*, *DSB* 38:1115 (1958) or *AJIL* 52:842 (1958). The chairman of the second committee was O. C. Gundersen (Norway), the vice-chairman was E. Glaser (Roumania), and the rapporteur was J. Madeira (Portugal). Prince Wan Waithayakon (Thailand) was president of the conference; UN.CLS.*OR* 2:xxvii.

16. The General Assembly placed, besides, on the agenda of the conference the question of free access to the sea of land-locked countries; Resolution 1105 (xi), para. 3.

its flag. Ships have the nationality of the state whose flag they are entitled to fly."

The third sentence of art. 29, reading: "Nevertheless, for purposes of recognition of the national character of the ship by other states, there must exist a genuine link between the state and the ship," became the pivotal point for the discussion of the flags of convenience at the 1958 conference. Neither the legal content of the requirement of the genuine link (in French "*lien réel*" in the ILC's draft) nor the exact legal consequences had been defined by the ILC, which was quite aware that the term "genuine link" was imprecise and vague, but "[did] not consider it possible to state in any greater detail what form this link should take." [17]

Now, the conference had to decide which course to follow. There were several possibilities: to retain the genuine-link clause as it had been drafted by the ILC, to define in general terms the essentials of the genuine link, to define them in detail, or, finally, to reject the concept altogether. It would also have been possible to refer the whole issue to a specialized body, such as IMCO.

More difficult was the problem of the sanction of nonrecognition of the nationality of the vessel flying a flag of convenience without a genuine link existing between it and the state of its registration. The conference could either retain the general expression "for purposes of recognition of the national character of the ship by other states," or specify precisely the legal consequences of the absence of the genuine link, or reject the nonrecognition clause. The task was difficult, and, as François, expert to the conference,[18] remarked, there was little likelihood that the conference, already overburdened with work, would be able to deal with the matter in detail and would specify both the nature of the genuine link and its legal consequences.[19]

The positions taken by the states' delegates on these legal issues reflected, on the whole, the national interests of the states directly or indirectly interested in the problem. The traditional maritime countries of Europe, desiring to check the practice of flags of

17. ILC *Yearbook 1956*, II, 279 (commentary on art. 29 of the Law of the Sea prepared by the ILC).
18. UN.CLS.*OR* 2:xviii.
19. UN.CLS.*OR* 4:34.

convenience, were in favor of the introduction of the genuine-link clause, and of providing it with the nonrecognition sanction. The hopes of these countries, in particular the shipping circles of these countries, were best expressed by the government of Denmark, stating in its comment on art. 29 that

> In this connexion, the Danish authorities emphasize that the implementation of the proposed rules, which assumes the existence of certain guarantees or evidence of the actual relationship of the ship with the State concerned, may serve to support the various endeavours of international shipping circles (including the Danish shipping trade) to prevent the nationality and registration of a ship from being established on the basis of such mere formalities as to come within the concept of 'flag of convenience.' [20]

The flag-of-convenience states, in particular Liberia and Panama (the delegates of Honduras and Costa Rica did not take active part in the discussions), vehemently opposed the principle of genuine link as it had been formulated by the ILC. They were backed by the United States, particularly interested in the continuance of the flag-of-convenience practice, by some Latin American countries (for example, San Salvador, Mexico, Uruguay), by Greece, and by some of the new, ex-colonial states (Lebanon, India, Ghana), whose interest is served by having complete freedom to take such measures as they deem necessary to promote the development of their small merchant marines. Already in the committee stage, the nonrecognition clause found a fairly large number of adversaries, and later at the plenary session, surprisingly enough, these adversaries increased so much that they succeeded in eliminating the dangerous phrase.

The real, economic background of the whole controversy surrounding the flags of convenience, namely, the competition between European and American shipowners, had already emerged in the preparatory stage of the Geneva conference. Besides statements at the sessions of the ILC, it is interesting to quote the official comment of the government of the Netherlands on art. 29 of the ILC's draft. It was stated with concern by this government

20. UN.CLS.*OR* (Preparatory documents) 1:83. About pressure exercised by these circles, see Ch. III. See also Jessup, "The Geneva Conference on the Law of the Sea; A Study in International Law-Making," *AJIL* 52:730, 731 (1958), noting that national interests affected voting on certain matters such as flags of convenience,

that "it is feared that if ships avail themselves of those facilities [*i.e.*, flags of convenience] to an ever increasing extent, the competitive position of other countries will be undermined." [21] This fear of what some called "unfair competition" [22] was pointed out at the Geneva conference by the delegate of Liberia, as the true reason for the introduction by the ILC of the genuine-link clause into the working of art. 29.[23] The Panamanian delegate also made allusions to the concern of "certain maritime states, but by no means all of them." [24]

The attitude of the states toward the genuine-link clause as proposed by the ILC revealed a variety of views, from full acceptance of this principle without any changes to vehement rejection thereof as a "dangerous" and even "provocative" concept which, if adopted, would create confusion and misunderstanding. It was no wonder that the foremost exponents of the two opposing views were the states most directly involved in the issues, whose national interests were most at stake, namely, Norway on the one hand, and Liberia on the other. The Norwegian shipowners showed concern and anxiety over losing to Liberia the position of the third greatest shipping power. "Norway attached the greatest importance to the essential need for a genuine link between a ship and a state whose flag it flew," stated the Norwegian delegate at the meeting of the second committee of the conference.[25] On the other side was Liberia, for which the practice of registering foreign-owned ships was an important source of income, contributing much to her economic development.

There was general agreement among the states endorsing the requirement of the genuine link that this conception, although useful and, for some delegates, even "almost self-evident" [26] was very difficult to grasp in strict, legal terms, and although a more

21. UN.CLS.*OR* 1:108.

22. Doc. A/CONF. 13/19 (1957), p. 275 [mimeographed] (statement by Pinto, delegate of France, in the 6th Committee of the G.A., 11th session).

23. UN.CLS.*OR* 4:22. The Liberian delegate quoted in this respect the words of Salamanca, member of the ILC, without, however, mentioning the latter's name.

24. *Id.*, p. 29. *Cf.* the statements of Weeks (Liberia) and Fábrega (Panama); ICJ *Pleadings*, Constitution (1960), pp. 276–277, 417.

25. UN.CLS.*OR* 4:62. See also the statement by the delegate of the Netherlands: "The Netherlands attached great importance to the principle of a genuine link . . ." p. 64.

26. As it was put by the delegate of Sweden, *ibid.*

detailed definition of the principle of genuine link would be welcome, the difficulties involved were great because of a considerable variety of registration requirements in the domestic laws of various countries.[27] Other opinions pointed out the fact that the genuine link was a fair expression of the internationally accepted standard which all the traditional maritime states observed, but that the laying down of detailed requirements for this genuine link was extremely difficult.[28] It was difficult to find an infallible and comprehensive definition of genuine link,[29] or agree on any exact criteria for it.[30] And the formulation of more definite rules explaining the meaning of that principle did not appear feasible to several other delegations, since such might fail to take account of differing national practices.[31]

On the whole, the conclusion can be drawn from the lengthy discussion in the second committee of the Geneva conference that the conference, like the ILC, did not consider it possible to state in precise terms the elements of the genuine link. However, a number of delegations believed, as it was put by the delegate of the Netherlands, that the "difficulty of definition in no way invalidated the force of a principle,[32] and therefore insisted on retaining the genuine-link clause merely as a statement of a general guiding principle.[33] The same position was taken by François.[34] The need for laying down a guiding principle was additionally substantiated by the argument that a general principle did not necessarily increase the chances of conflicts between states; on the contrary, "International Law must rely upon the application of guiding principles to give direction and consistency to the findings of international tribunals and to the practice of states." [35]

At the same time, the majority of states calling for the inclusion of a genuine-link clause in the instrument to be adopted, suggested

27. Statement by the delegate of Denmark, *id.*, p. 5.
28. Statement by the delegate of Norway, *id.*, p. 8.
29. Italy, *id.*, p. 10. The United Kingdom, *id.*, p. 62.
30. Czechoslovakia, *id.*, p. 24.
31. Switzerland, *id.*, p. 3. New Zealand, *id.*, p. 64.
32. *Ibid.*
33. Norway, UN.CLS.*OR* 4:8, 62; the United Kingdom, pp. 4, 62; Portugal, p. 20; Italy, p. 10; Ireland and Australia, p. 13; China, p. 25; Pakistan, p. 64; New Zealand, p. 65.
34. For his statement to this effect, see UN.CLS.*OR* 4:32, 34, 35.
35. The statement by the delegate of New Zealand; *id.*, p. 65.

that the conference, though endorsing the principle, should make it clear that it was not the last word on the matter, that it was not enough merely to enunciate the principle and leave to each state the decision of what the genuine link was, and that the criteria of the genuine link should be elaborated by some other, more appropriate body (a conference or a specialized agency) possessing the necessary technical and expert knowledge of the problem and sufficient time to discuss it in detail. As the delegate of the United Kingdom put it:

> Such study must initially be the task of States working together in international organizations and conferences which had the time and expert knowledge to deal fully with the subject. The magnitude of other tasks before the Conference and the limited time available to it would preclude it from giving full consideration to the particular problem of the genuine link.[36]

In this connection, it was rightly pointed out that there was not a sufficient documentation of the economic and social factors involved in the problems of the flags of convenience.[37]

The lack of precision and vagueness of the term "genuine link" — admitted even by its supporters[38] who recommended its further consideration — was one of the arguments used against it by the flag-of-convenience countries.[39] There was also a small group of states which, recommending further study of the issue, were, for various reasons, against the retention of the genuine-link clause.[40]

On the other hand, the staunchest sponsors of the genuine-link principle, Norway and the Netherlands, contended that the term was not too vague or too general. They argued that if equally

36. *Id.*, p. 4. *Cf.* also Ireland and Australia, p. 13; Portugal, p. 20; Pakistan, p. 26; Israel, p. 28; Switzerland, p. 63; and even François, p. 35.

37. Statement by the delegate of Israel; *id.*, p. 28. This delegate also proposed entrusting the task of preparing this documentation to the convention on IMCO — when that convention came into force. The delegate of Israel could not yet know that the convention on IMCO had just entered into force on the preceding day. See Ch. V, n. 14.

38. See, *e.g.*, ILC *Yearbook 1956*, II, 278–279. See also UN.CLS.*OR* 4:4 (Statement by delegate of the United Kingdom). The term "genuine link" is found rather vague by Colombos, p. 256 n. 2.

39. Liberia, U.N.CLS.*OR* 4:22.

40. Greece, *id.*, p. 14; the United States of America, p. 15; India, p. 12. The Indian delegate believed that art. 29 should not be included in a convention for the time being because the principle of a genuine link — which India supported only as such — was not stated precisely enough.

vague phrases, such as "with reasonable regard to" had been found acceptable, then the genuine-link clause should be treated in the same way.[41] The objections against general terms were not found justified by François either, in whose opinion "a codification of international law can no more do without these expressions than can national law." In specific cases the disputes as to the interpretation of these vague expressions should be submitted to some impartial bodies.[42] Even fundamental constitutional principles of different countries required interpretation by the court.[43] Besides — it was added — an analogous imprecise term, "genuine connection," had been used by the International Court of Justice as the basis for its judgment in the *Nottebohm* case.[44]

Yet the majority of the second committee felt that some specification must be given to the requirement of the genuine link and the vagueness of this expression prompted some delegations to call for continued attempts at formulating a more precise draft of art. 29, and at finding a satisfactory solution at the conference itself, without referring the problem to other bodies for detailed examination.[45] The exponents of the genuine-link principle had made several attempts at the conference to indicate some possible elements of this concept, until eventually the final draft providing for the effective exercise of control and jurisdiction over the ship by the flag state found general acceptance.

After the ILC it is possible to say that the genuine link is "a relation between the state and the ship other than mere registration or the mere grant of a certificate of registry." [46] In order to know what the ILC, the author of the draft, meant by this "relation," it is useful to quote the relevant passage from the statement made by François at the session of the second committee of the conference:

> The essential corollary to the freedom of the seas must be that states exercise the same jurisdiction over ships sailing the high seas under their

41. Norway, *id.*, pp. 63, 67. The phrase "with reasonable regard to" was used in the United Kingdom amendment to art. 27 of the ILC Law of the Sea. See *id.*, p. 134.
42. *Id.*, pp. 33–34.
43. The Netherlands, *id.*, p. 64.
44. Norway, *id.*, p. 62.
45. Denmark, *id.*, p. 5; China, p. 25; Uruguay, p. 30; Mexico, p. 29.
46. ILC *Yearbook 1956*, II, 279. (Commentary on art. 29 of the Law of the Sea prepared by the ILC.)

flag as they exercise in their own territory. It is in this sense that ships are regarded as floating extensions of the flag state's territory. This regime is based on the notions that the ship must in the main belong to nationals of the flag state; that the owners must be domiciled in that state; that the officers and at least the major part of the crew must be nationals of that state; that in foreign ports the consular officers of the flag state shall exercise the necessary control over such ships putting in at those ports, and, where appropriate, grant them such protection as they may need, and, finally, that the ships shall return to their home ports at regular intervals. That is, what the I.L.C. understands by the link between the ship and the flag state. . . .[47]

However, this was only a description in general terms of various possible elements of the genuine link without a strict legal definition acceptable to the conference. The majority of the delegates agreed that the formulation of the criteria for determining the existence of the genuine link between the state and the ship involved great technical difficulties, in view of a great diversity of domestic laws. This was the old obstacle, which the ILC had not been able to overcome. Besides the elements referred to by François, the following features of the genuine link were mentioned by way of example: 1) the operation of the ship by the flag state of its nationals,[48] 2) the possession by the flag state of a body of laws regulating maritime questions, 3) adequate provisions for effective administration and enforcement of the law wherever the ships operate,[49] 4) the extent to which parties suing the shipowners can effectively have recourse to the courts of the flag state.[50] The last two criteria had been suggested earlier by the Maritime Transport Committee of the OEEC which particularly emphasized the criterion of suing in the courts of the flag state as probably reflecting "to a greater degree than most aspects of shipping the true relationship between the ship and her flag."[51] It was also pointed out by the OEEC that:

47. UN.CLS.*OR* 4:34.
48 Czechoslovakia; *id.*, p. 24. *Cf.* also A/CONF. 13/19 (1957), p. 463 [mimeographed] (the statement of the Czechoslovak delegate at the sixth committee of the General Assembly, 11th session). The element of the operation of the ship was repeatedly stressed by Czechoslovakia and Yugoslavia as a link entitling the state to grant its flag to the ship.
49. The Netherlands, UN.CLS.*OR* 4:3. The United Kingdom, p. 4. Portugal, p. 20.
50. Norway; *id.*, p. 62.
51. OEEC.MTC, "Study" (1958), p. 11.

> Where a shipping company has no assets in the flag state, and the owners, directors and managers are not nationals, it is useless to have recourse to the Courts in those countries, as they cannot enforce their decisions. It is significant that even the owners of vessels under flags of convenience prefer to have their disputes settled in the courts of the maritime countries.[52]

The OEEC study, however, does not give any statistical data; neither does it refer to any source for this information.

Among the various approaches to the genuine-link problem, the proposal of Switzerland should also be mentioned. Since the formulation of more definite rules explaining the meaning of this expression did not seem feasible, the delegate of Switzerland proposed to embody "purely permissively" all the suggested conditions in an annex to a convention and enunciate only the general principle.[53] This proposal, however, did not find any response, and, like the other suggestions, did not have much chance of being adopted by the conference. Almost all the delegations were aware of the fact that it was futile to enunciate the detailed conditions of the genuine link because the diverse practices of the states did not allow of any common denominator acceptable to the entire community of nations.

The genuine-link clause is presented in some accounts of the Geneva Conference as having been readily accepted except by the countries directly concerned, Liberia and Panama.[54] Such a presentation is not accurate, since not only the delegates of Panama and Liberia opposed the genuine-link concept as it was worked out by the ILC, but some other delegations as well, first of all the United States, demanded its cancellation.

The vagueness of the term had already been severely criticized by the governments of Ethiopia and Finland at the preparatory stage of the conference. According to the note of the Foreign Ministry of Ethiopia, the phrase "genuine link" was a "standard so vague and imprecise as to be virtually meaningless" and would result "in a plethora of conflicting definitions with different tests

52. *Ibid.*
53. UN.CLS.*OR* 4:63.
54. See, *e.g.*, Verzijl, "The United Nations Conference on the Law of the Sea, Geneva, 1958 (II)," *Nederlands Tijdschrift voor Internationaal Recht* 6:115, 117 n. 46 (1959).

being adopted to different purposes." [55] Quite exceptional was the attitude of Finland, which was the only state to revive the provisional draft prepared by the ILC in 1955, whose rules — as the delegate of Finland stated at the 6th committee of the General Assembly, 11th session — unlike the vague term "genuine link," "established clear and sound rules on the relationship which should exist between the State and the ship for purposes of recognition of the national character of the ship by other states." [56]

The return to the criterion of ownership was also supported by the German Federal Republic. Its delegate, in his criticism, correctly pointed out that the draft of the ILC did not make nationality of ships obligatory; neither was there obligation for states to register all ships when a genuine link existed. There might be situations in which ships could, on the one hand, not be registered, because of the lack of a genuine link, in states offering convenient conditions, and on the other hand, could not qualify for registration in the state with which they were connected by a genuine link because that state imposed too stringent conditions of registration. To avoid the possibility of stateless ships, the German delegate suggested three principles to be considered by the conference, namely, 1) all ships would be obliged to have nationality, 2) every state should be obliged to register ships entirely owned by its nationals or by companies domiciled in its territory, and also ships which regularly received orders in its territory, provided, of course, that they were not registered in another state, and 3) the state should not grant its registration if the ship was already registered elsewhere.[57] The German proposal would be difficult to introduce in practice because it would require a revision of domestic laws in many countries. On the other hand, it would not necessarily bring about the cessation of the practice of registering ships under the flags of convenience because of the possibilities inherent in corpo-

55. UN.CLS.*OR* 1:12.

56. A/CONF. 13/19 (1957), p. 78–80 [mimeographed]. See also the statement by the delegate of Mexico: "I believe that the correct approach is this: either the state is given the right to fix, at its discretion, the conditions governing the grant of its nationality, in which case this right is valid *erga omnes* or else international law lays down specific conditions on which the state can validly grant its nationality to ships with binding effect, *vis à vis* other states, and, in this case it is necessary to state exactly what these conditions are as the Commission did last year [1955] in art. 5 of the earlier Report." *Id.*, p. 172.

57. UN.CLS.*OR* 4:11–12.

rate ownership. At a later stage of the debates in the second committee, the German delegate proposed an amendment to art. 29 under which the genuine link would have to exist not only between the state and the ship but also between both of these and the shipowner. He also emphasized that the criterion of ownership should be defined in precise language as a prerequisite for registration, since it was registration that established the link between the state and the ship.[58]

Reluctance to include the provision on the genuine link was manifested by the delegations of India and Greece. The delegate of Greece deemed it preferable not to include in the future instrument any version of the principle regarding the genuine link, since it would lead to controversy and misinterpretation.[59] The delegate of India thought that the article should not be included in a convention "for the time being," and that further study by an expert body was desirable.[60] The attitude of these two delegations was significant. Greece was a state much interested in the whole issue because a sizeable amount of Greek-owned shipping was registered under flags of convenience, and India was just preparing a new maritime codification providing for more liberal rules than the old British Merchant Shipping Act of 1894.[61] Similarly, the delegate of Lebanon, paying lip service to the principle of genuine link, sceptically stated that it would not solve anything unless some states modified their domestic legislation.[62] It is significant, however, as was mentioned in Chapter II, that Lebanon itself had, four years before, enacted legislation following the path of the flag-of-convenience countries.

The main argument against the principle of genuine link came from the two major flag-of-convenience countries, Liberia and Panama, with the support of the United States. In discussing the attitude assumed by these states (and others as well) one should

58. *Id.*, pp. 67, 126.
59. *Id.*, p. 14.
60. *Id.*, p. 12. *Cf.* the written statement of the government of India before the ICJ favoring the stand of Liberia and Panama; ICJ *Pleadings*, Constitution (1960), pp. 253–259.
61. The new Indian Merchant Shipping Act, 1958, was eventually passed on October 30, 1958. For its text, see ILOffice, *Legislative Series* (July–August, 1958) (1959).
62. UN.CLS.*OR* 4:5.

bear in mind a certain distinction concerning the genuine-link clause as proposed by the ILC, namely the genuine-link phrase alone, and the sanction of nonrecognition added thereto. We cannot forget that a fairly large number of states, though supporting in principle the genuine link, were against the non-recognition provision. This was the case already in the committee stage (where practically all the discussion took place), and later this was the position taken by the majority in the plenary session. Liberia and Panama showed much diplomatic elasticity in defending their position. One can distinguish three stages in the attitude of these flag-of-convenience countries at the Geneva conference. At first, they rejected not only the non-recognition provision but the genuine-link clause itself, and proposed to lay down in the future instrument only the traditional liberal principle of the states' right to fix the conditions for granting nationality to ships. Subsequently they agreed to add the provision on the effective jurisdiction and control which states should exercise over their ships, and finally at the plenary session of the conference, Liberia and Panama endorsed the genuine-link principle, but only after having succeeded in depriving it of the sanction of non-recognition, which was their main target of attack.

It is interesting to note that the theoretical international law basis of the Panlibhon argument rested — paradoxically enough — in the same principle which was invoked by its adversaries, namely, in the principle of the freedom of the seas. Thus both sides dubbed themselves as champions of this venerable principle of international law, each using it for their own respective exclusive interests. The anti-Panlibhon group of states argued that the vessels sailing under the flags of convenience, having no genuine link with the states of registration, contained nuclei of disorder and anarchy, and were a potential menace to the freedom of the seas. On the other hand, for the Panlibhon states, freedom of the seas implied, among other things, absolute freedom of the states to register vessels under their flags. "It was surprising," stated the Panamanian delegate, "that maritime powers which declared themselves in favor of the freedom of the high seas wanted that freedom to be limited by making it impossible for the shipping companies to register their ships where they wished."[63] The Liberian delegate, concluding his long argument in the second committee, urged "that the Conference should accept freedom as the guiding principle of its deliberations — the freedom of the high seas."[64]

Consequently, Liberia and Panama agreed only with the first two sentences of paragraph 1 of art. 29 of the ILC Law of the Sea of 1956, which provisions codified the traditional freedom of each state to determine under what conditions it would register ships under its flag. On the other hand, these two countries recommended "in the interests of the progressive development of International Law and the promotion of better international relations" complete deletion of the third sentence providing for the existence of a genuine link between the state and the ship for purposes of recognition of the national character of the ship. This sentence — they claimed — rendered the rest of the article contradictory and ambiguous.[65] The deletion of all reference to the relation between the vessel and the state was preferable even to the provision that the genuine link should be determined by the domestic law of the state of registration; the genuine-link concept was not a concept of international law and represented an attempt to inject into international law a novel principle which could create confusion and misunderstanding. It was a provision of "so provocative a nature that some of the principal maritime nations would not subscribe to it."[66] The delegate of Liberia vehemently attacked the states sponsoring the genuine-link concept, and referring to the functions of the ILC embodied in art. 15 of its statute, sarcastically pointed out that there was no genuine link between the insistence upon the desire to inject this novel principle of genuine link and the need for the more precise formulation and systematization of rules of international law in fields where there had already been extensive state practice, precedents, and doctrine.[67]

Following the well established doctrine, supported by inter-

63. *Id.*, p. 29.
64. *Id.*, p. 23.
65. *Id.*, p. 22.
66. *Id.*, p. 29; *id.*, p. 22. The Liberian delegate must have meant the United States and presumably Liberia and Panama.
67. *Id.*, p. 21.

national practice, the Liberian delegate correctly argued that the only true criteria for the determination and recognition of the nationality of a ship were the ship's documents. The other criteria suggested for the determination of the genuine link, such as the nationality of the owners or the nationality of the crew, or the country of construction, were based on the states' national, economic, or social policies. The fact that they were adopted even by a large number of states did not invest them with an imperative character, or make them a rule of international law, argued the Liberian delegate, following views expressed by the doctrine of international law.

Taking all these arguments into account, it must be said that the second committee of the conference did not make much progress, and after a few days of discussion found itself at the same deadlock as the ILC after its seventh session, when it found that the provisional articles specifying the ownership criteria could not fulfill the aim set by the ILC, that is, the limitation of the flags of convenience.

This being so, it is no wonder that the proposals suggesting a search for the genuine link in the effective control and jurisdiction of the flag state over its ships in administrative, technical, and social matters found general approval, since everybody, Panama and Liberia included, agreed with this requirement.

The rationale of the institution of the nationality of ships is that ships on the high seas, which are not within the exclusive territorial jurisdiction of any particular state, must be under some control in order that order and safety of navigation be secured. This control is exercised by the flag state, to which exclusive jurisdiction of the ship is, as a general rule, accorded on the high seas.[68] For reasons of safety and order of navigation, there must be certainty that control over the vessel is exercised effectively. As it was stated at the Geneva conference by the delegate of the United States: "The right of a state to sail vessels on the high seas carried with it the corresponding duty to exercise control and effective jurisdiction over those vessels in the interests of order on the high seas."[69] Similarly, the spokesman of the opposite camp,

68. Convention on the High Seas, art. 6.
69. UN.CLS.*OR* 4:64.

the delegate of the Netherlands, stated that the "counterpart of the freedom of navigation must be the obligation of the flag state to maintain order on the high seas." [70] That the flag state is under international law obliged to exercise effective jurisdiction and control over its vessels on the high seas was agreed upon generally both in the ILC and at the Geneva Conference on the Law of the Sea.

This point of view had already been insisted upon by the United Kingdom in its comment on the provisional articles adopted by the ILC in 1955, as well as in its proposal, and by Sir Gerald Fitzmaurice at the eighth session of the ILC, who repeatedly supported the view of the United Kingdom government that the ability of the state to exercise, and the actual exercise of, the control and jurisdiction over its vessels should be the criterion of the recognition of the ship's nationality.[71] The ILC did not include this principle in the relevant text of its 1956 Law of the Sea, but pointed out in the comment that "the jurisdiction of the State over ships, and the control it should exercise in conformity with art. 34 . . . can only be effective when there exists in fact a relationship between the State and the ship other than mere registration or the mere grant of a certificate of registry." [72]

At the Geneva conference, the delegates, taking part in the discussion, agreed that effective jurisdiction and control, "the twin components of the exercise of sovereignty," [73] were "an indispensable feature of the genuine link," "the real point" in proving its existence, "the test of the genuine link," "the only truly decisive factor," "one of the most important factors in the determination of nationality," and in any case "an indispensable element." [74] So far as Liberia is concerned, her first proposal contained only the traditional principle of the freedom to fix the conditions of granting nationality to ships, but then the same

70. *Ibid. Accord,* the delegate of Israel and Jenks, delegate of the ILO; UN.CLS.*OR* 4:26.

71. ILC *Yearbook 1956,* I, 67, 72, 262. *Cf.* comment by the government of the United Kingdom; *id.,* II, 80–81.

72. *Id.,* II, 279.

73. Italy; UN.CLS.*OR* 4:61.

74. Norway, *id.,* p. 62; the Netherlands, p. 3; Uruguay, p. 30; the Holy See, p. 59; Italy, p. 61; Sweden, p. 64. See also the statements by the delegates of: Denmark, p. 5; Portugal, pp. 20, 64; the United Kingdom, p. 62; Spain, p. 63; Switzerland, *ibid.;* China, p. 66.

country added an amendment to the proposal, laying down that "the State shall exercise effective jurisdiction and control over the ship." [75] The Liberian delegate stated that the purpose of his proposal was to eliminate the expression "genuine link" along with the non-recognition clause, and to ensure that the flag state exercised effective and constant control over its ships. Panama also expressed her approval of the requirement of effective jurisdiction and control.[76]

Thus there was general agreement in the second committee that effective exercise of jurisdiction and control should be the responsibility of the state of the ship's nationality. The difference of opinion was that the opponents of the flags of convenience tied this exercise to the concept of genuine link, whereas the flag-of-convenience group of states, though recognizing this principle, did not want to connect it with the vague concept of genuine link.

A number of delegations sponsoring the genuine link did not fully realize that "effective jurisdiction and control" did not constitute a criterion of the genuine link which a state might lay down as a condition of granting its nationality to a ship. Effective jurisdiction and control is only an objective, a result which the still undefined criteria of the genuine link must guarantee.[77] The determination of the criterion or criteria, that is, the definition of the genuine link, falls within the internal competence and domestic jurisdiction of each state. This is the general principle laid down in the first sentence of art. 29 of the ILC Law of the Sea of 1956, but the effective exercise of jurisdiction and control over the ship by the flag state must be the final result of this genuine link. Therefore, the wording of the proposal by France, stating that the criteria applied by the state of registration for the grant of its nationality must in any event *provide for* effective and constant control,[78] or by Brazil, laying down that "no state shall grant its nationality to a ship unless there is a genuine link between the state and the ship *that guarantees* effective jurisdiction and control over the ship," [79] were, from the logical point of view, stricter than

75. *Id.*, p. 119.
76. *Id.*, p. 63.
77. *Cf.* the remarks by the French delegate, Gidel; *id.*, p. 61 and the remarks by the United States delegate; *id.*, pp. 64–65.
78. *Id.*, p. 116.
79. *Id.*, p. 118.

the eventually adopted Italian proposal supplemented by a French subamendment.

Eventually, the second committee adopted the Italian proposal by 34 votes to 4, with 17 abstentions, after having approved by 24 votes to 16 with 14 abstentions a subamendment thereto, proposed by France. The French delegate proposed to add to the Italian requirement of effective jurisdiction and control the words "in administrative, technical and social matters," since he felt that some further specification was needed in the matter.[80] After the Italian delegate had agreed to the French addition, France withdrew its own proposal on art. 29.[81]

The genuine link has not been defined by the drafters of the convention. The question must now be answered of what is meant by the effective exercise of jurisdiction and control over the ship in administrative, technical, and social matters.

The terms "effective," and "effectively" were many times repeated at the debates of the second committee of the Geneva conference, but no attempt was made to specify the meaning of these terms, which are rather vague and not easy to define, since the notion of "effectivity," although so important in international law, evades any comprehensive, general definition.[82]

One can only suggest that in this context it means such an exercise of jurisdiction and control in the specified matters as satisfies the provisions of international conventions on navigation, and certain minimum standards of safety and maintenance of order at sea. True, the term "effectively" used in art. 5 is vague, and so may be the interpretation given to it here, but, on the other hand, such general, vague terms are also found in other articles of the convention, for example, the expression "with reasonable regard," used in art. 2. In this respect, François seems to have been right when he said that "any attempt to codify international law without using such expressions will prove vain." [83]

The term "jurisdiction" is used both in art. 5 and art. 6 of the

80. *Id.*, p. 61. For the results of the voting see: UN.CLS.*OR* 4:75, and 2:95 (Report of the second committee).

81. UN.CLS.*OR* 4:61.

82. On the subject of effectivity in international law, see Charles de Visscher, "Observations sur l'effectivité en droit international public," *Revue Générale du Droit International Public* (3rd. ser., vol. 29) 62:601 (1958).

83. UN.CLS.*OR* 4:33–34.

convention. Article 6 lays down the "law of the flag" rule of subjecting ships on the high seas to the exclusive jurisdiction of the flag state. Here the term jurisdiction is used in the broadest sense. This is indicated by the ILC which in the comment to the corresponding article in the provisional articles of 1955 explained that the term "jurisdiction" was used in the same meaning as in art. 2 of the provisional articles, that is, "including not merely the judicial function but any kind of sovereignty or authority" [84] over the vessels and acts occurring on board the vessels. This general term embraces civil, criminal, administrative, and "protective" jurisdiction.[85] On the other hand, the term "jurisdiction and control" is used in art. 5 in its more narrow meaning, including that type of the states' authority which refers to the administrative, social, and technical matters, dealing in particular with safety of navigation. This interpretation is confirmed by the ILC which in its comment on art. 29 of the Law of the Sea (art. 5 of the convention) observed that control over vessels should be exercised in conformity with art. 34 (art. 10 of the convention), and art. 34 lays down only rules concerning safety at sea (though it gives a wide scope to these rules).

The discussions at the conference did not provide much guidance as to the terms "control" and "jurisdiction." The delegate of Sweden observed on this subject that

> any attempt to define control and jurisdiction in more detail was unlikely to result in greater precision at the present juncture, since though there was a general consensus about what was the responsibility of ships [it should be rather "states in respect of ships"] which had been reflected in Art. 34, it was difficult to go further without a risk of confusing two different things, namely, the enforcement of the observance by ships of national regulations and international conventions and the means whereby that could be done, which was a matter for national action, and unsuitable for regulation in an international convention.[86]

According to art. 10 of the Convention on the High Seas (art. 34 of the ILC Law of the Sea, with some changes) the control which a state should effectively exercise over the ships flying its flag is made up of two elements. *First,* the state must:

84. ILC *Yearbook 1955,* II, 21.
85. Colombos, p. 257.
86. UN.CLS.*OR* 4:64.

take such measures for ships under its flag as are necessary to ensure safety at sea with regard *inter alia* to

a) the use of signals, the maintenance of communications and the prevention of collisions;
b) the manning of ships and labour conditions for crews, taking into account the applicable international instruments;
c) the construction, equipment, and seaworthiness of ships.

and *second,* the state must "take any steps which may be necessary" to ensure the observance of the above-mentioned measures.[87]

As a result of the tenor of art. 10 of the convention, the regulations to ensure safety at sea cover not only the rules concerning signals and the prevention of collisions, as was done in art. 9 of the first, provisional draft of 1955, but, following art. 34 of the ILC 1956 draft, have been extended to regulations concerning the construction, equipment, and seaworthiness of ships and the labor conditions of crews, which also contribute to the safety of navigation. The insertion by the ILC of these provisions in an article dealing with the safety of navigation was due to the allegedly substandard safety and labor conditions aboard the vessels flying the flags of convenience. As the ILC stated: "Objections to the transfer of ships to another flag have often been accentuated by the fact that such regulations, and an effective control over their application, were lacking in the State of the new flag." [88]

At the Geneva conference, too, the adversaries of Panlibhon laid emphasis on the administrative, social, and technical safety aspects of the control that the flag state must effectively exercise over its vessels. It was claimed that "the main danger involved in the flags of convenience was the undermining of public order on

87. The questions of safety at sea and labor conditions of seamen are regulated in detail by a large number of multilateral conventions, and the conference faced the problem of the relation of the Convention on the High Seas to these detailed regulations. Following the recommendation of the ILC, the conference took the course of including in the new instrument the principles underlying the detailed conventions and not conflicting with them. See in particular the statement by François, *id.*, pp. 32–33. *Contra,* the delegation of the United Kingdom; *id.*, pp. 49–50.

The states would either ratify the conventions or insure the application of the relevant principles in some other way, *e.g.*, by the insertion of detailed regulations in their domestic laws. For the list of the conventions regulating labor conditions of seamen see A/CONF. 13/C.2/L. 8 and Add. 1 & 2, and A/CONF. 13/C.2/L. 9 [mimeographed].

88. ILC *Yearbook 1956*, II, 280 (commentary on art. 34 of the Law of the Sea prepared by the ILC).

the high seas,"[89] and that the lack of supervision by the flag-of-convenience countries was detrimental to the safety of navigation.[90]

It was argued by the ILC, that if a ship flying the flag of a state, with a crew consisting of aliens, does not sail to or from the ports of that country, the national authorities have no opportunity of inspecting it or of satisfying themselves at regular intervals that the working conditions on board comply with the law of the land.[91]

Objections were also raised that the flag-of-convenience countries were unable "to ascertain whether navigational regulations were being complied with or to enforce such regulations by imposing penalties or taking other measures against persons responsible for the operation of the ship."[92] The work of the International Labor Organization, which was just preparing its maritime session, was referred to by some state delegates,[93] and, first of all, by the delegate of the International Labor Organization, who, in his statement, stressed the endeavors of his organization "to defend, in matters falling within its competence, the responsibilities of States in relation to vessels flying their flags, with a view of ensuring safety on the high seas and the welfare of crews, irrespective of changes in world distribution of shipping arising from various factors."[94]

Now, in view of all objections against Panlibhon, the question imposes itself whether these countries effectively exercise control over ships flying their flags, as is enjoined by art. 10 of the Convention on the High Seas. The definitive answer to this question would require extensive study of concrete data on all aspects of the states' control over their ships but the fact that since the 1949 ILO inquiry the safety and labor conditions aboard the flag-of-convenience ships have improved and are not inferior to the con-

89. Italy; UN.CLS.*OR* 4:10.

90. Comment of the Netherlands government on art. 29 of the ILC's draft; UN.CLS.*OR* 1:108.

91. ILC *Yearbook 1951*, II, 75–76 (Second report by François).

92. The Netherlands; UN.CLS.*OR* 4:3. See also the statements by the delegates of: Denmark, *id.*, p. 5; Italy, p. 10; Israel, p. 28; New Zealand, p. 65.

93. Italy, *id.*, p. 10; Israel, p. 28; New Zealand, p. 65. See also comment by the government of Denmark on the ILC draft of 1956, UN.CLS.*OR*. 1:83.

94. UN.CLS.*OR* 4:26.

ditions aboard the vessels of the European countries is recognized even by the adversaries of the flags of convenience.

At the Geneva conference, Liberia and Panama themselves advocated the principle of effective jurisdiction and control of the flag state over its vessels. As to art. 34 of the ILC draft, dealing with safety at sea, Panama expressed her support for it,[95] whereas the Liberian delegate, though stressing Liberia's observance of the rules envisaged by art. 34, opposed the inclusion of art. 34 (as well as other articles of related contents, namely art. 35 on collisions at sea, art. 36 on assistance at sea, art. 48 on oil pollution, and art. 61 on laying submarine cables and pipelines) in the instrument to be adopted, contending that all those matters were already covered by the existing conventions and that including them in a new one might give rise to confusion and even involve a country in adherence to a convention to which it did not subscribe.[96]

The way in which Liberia discharges her duty to exercise effective jurisdiction and control over vessels registered under her flag in 1960 was described by the Liberian representatives before the ICJ in the proceedings concerning the constitution of the Maritime Safety Committee of the IMCO. In particular the government of Liberia attached to its written statement before the Court a special appendix (Appendix III) entitled "The Liberian Maritime Programme" where Liberian registration requirements, compliance with international conventions, other standards and controls as well as participation in international maritime affairs are presented as proof of the effective Liberian control and jurisdiction. Similar statement was presented by the government of Panama.[97]

As to the measures necessary to ensure safety at sea, both Liberia and Panama have ratified the International Load Line Convention, signed at London, July 5, 1930,[98] the Convention on Safety of Life at Sea, signed at London, June 10, 1948,[99] and Regulations for preventing collisions at sea, approved by the International Conference on Safety of Life at Sea, London, April 23–June 10,

95. *Id.*, p. 29.
96. *Id.*, p. 22. Incidentally, a similar position was taken by the United Kingdom; *id.*, p. 49.
97. ICJ *Pleadings*, Constitution (1960) pp. 104–113, 190–193.
98. 47 Stat. 2228; T.S. 858; 135 L.N.T.S. 301.
99. 3 U.S.T. 3450; T.I.A.S. 2495; 164 U.N.T.S. 113.

1948.[100] Liberia also, on April 23, 1958, ratified the Agreement regarding financial support of the North Atlantic Ice Patrol, opened for signature at Washington, January 4, 1956.[101] The same was done by Panama on August 31, 1959.[102] Honduras, however, is a party only to the International Load Line Convention.[103] All three Panlibhon countries have enacted laws providing for various aspects of safety at sea, Liberia having a comprehensive codification of maritime law, which, as the Liberian delegate at the conference pointed out, was constantly being changed to meet the requirements of standards of the times. Revised laws on the subject, which, as he claimed, might well be copied by other states, came into force on March 1, 1958.[104] In addition the Liberian maritime law adopts the non-statutory maritime law of the United States of America in so far as it does not conflict with the specific provisions of the Liberian law. As the Liberian representative before the ICJ stated: "This provides a 'common law' background which would not otherwise have been available because of the more recent appearance of Liberia as a maritime power." [105]

Panama has the provisions relating to maritime matters embodied in several acts and decrees. Honduras enacted a National Merchant Marine Act, March 2, 1943.[106] All these regulations impose requirements concerning construction, seaworthiness, and equipment of the ships to be registered under the flags of Panlibhon. These ships, like ships of other countries, carry safety certificates issued by the classification societies.[107]

100. 47 U.S.T. 2956; T.I.A.S. 2899.

101. 7 U.S.T. 1969; T.I.A.S. 3597. For the information about the ratification, see *Liberia Today*, September 1958, p. 15. See also ICJ *Pleadings*, Constitution (1960), pp. 112–113.

102. American Bar Association, Section of International and Comparative Law, *Proceedings* (1960), p. 96; ICJ *Pleadings*, Constitution (1960), p. 191.

103. For the state of ratification of the maritime conventions see A/CONF. 13/C.2/L. 8, Add. 2 (1958), p. 19 [mimeographed].

104. UN.CLS.*OR* 4:22.

105. ICJ *Pleadings*, Constitution (1960), p. 68, quoting §30 of the Maritime Law.

106. A new Labor Code of June 1, 1959 was enacted in Honduras, dealing, among other things, with labor conditions of seamen. See ACFN *Memorandum*, p. 133 n. 28.

107. Liberian vessels are classified in the American Bureau of Shipping, Lloyd's *Register*, Bureau Veritas, Dat Norske Veritas, and, since February 1958, in Germanischer Lloyd. See the statement of Liberian government delegate; ILConf.*RP*. 41 Sess. (Geneva, 1958), p. 73. See also ICJ *Pleadings*, Constitution (1960), p. 111. Panamanian and Honduran vessels are classified in American Bureau of Shipping, Bureau Veritas and Lloyd's *Register*; ACFN *Memorandum*, pp. 130, 132. See also ICJ *Pleadings*, Constitution (1960), p. 191.

The Liberian maritime law requires that no vessel be navigated unless there is on board the complement of officers and crew necessary for safe navigation.[108] All officers are required to have Liberian licenses of competence, which are issued not by consular officers, but by the Commissioner of Maritime Affairs or his deputy, and only upon the presentation of a valid license issued by a recognized maritime country or the successful completion of a Liberian examination. It is characteristic that the Liberian Deputy Commissioner of Maritime Affairs has his seat in New York, and some 17 examination centers located at strategic ports throughout the world have been set up. Recently, Liberia decided to supplement the licensing system for its merchant marine officers by providing for the issuance of radar observer certificates.[109] Certificates of competence are also required by Honduran law.[110] Provisions on manning the vessels, signing articles of agreement, and labor conditions are also provided for by the laws of Panlibhon.[111]

There is no doubt, then, that Panlibhon countries possess some body of laws dealing with questions provided for by art. 10 of the Convention on the High Seas.[112] The enactment of regulations is not a difficult problem in itself. The questions arise, however, first, whether these regulations "conform to generally accepted standards," and, second, whether these states take the steps necessary to ensure the observance of these regulations. As to the first question, the precise specification of the legislative measures which a state is bound to take in order to comply with art. 10 of the convention is practically impossible, and many states have not issued regulations which could cover every single aspect of the matters included in art. 10. Therefore, it would be extremely difficult to state with precision whether the legislative measures

108. *Liberian Code of Laws of 1956,* vol. II, title 22 ("Maritime Law"), ch. 10, §10.

109. See statement by the Liberian delegate, ILConf.*RP*. 41 Sess. (Geneva, 1958), pp. 73–74. *Cf.* ICJ *Pleadings,* Constitution (1960), pp. 108–111.

110. Act of March 2, 1943, art. 20.

111. See *e.g.,* Liberian Maritime Law, ch. 8, §311; Panama: Decree No. 199 of August 5, 1947, arts. 1 and 2; Honduras: Labor Code, arts. 220–265.

112. This legislation is believed by some to be very limited in scope. See *YLJ* 69:499 n. 3 (1960), referring to Goldberg, *The Maritime Story: A Study in Labor-Management Relations* (1958), p. 220. Reference is also made to ILOffice *Panama Conditions* and to Berguido, "The Rights of Seamen on a Ship Under Panamanian Registry," *Temp. L.Q.* 19:458, 460–461 (1946).

taken by Panlibhon satisfy the "generally accepted international standards," which are not specified in art. 10. So far as safety at sea, in the strict meaning, is concerned, these standards would perhaps be less difficult to elaborate because the conventions dealing with this problem have been ratified and complied with by a great majority of maritime states. Particular difficulties would, however, arise if one were to make concrete what standards concerning labor conditions aboard the ships are binding upon the states. Though a large number of conventions and recommendations have been made under the auspices of the ILO,[113] many of them have not been ratified by a number of states, although some of these conventions and recommendations have influenced domestic legislation and collective agreements. This lack of international standards in matters of labor relations and the need for their elaboration was one of the main topics at the Maritime Session of the International Labor Conference held in Geneva in 1958.[114]

It should be pointed out finally that none of the above-mentioned labor relations conventions has as yet been ratified by Panlibhon countries,[115] which, however, does not prove that wages and working conditions and safety standards aboard Panlibhon vessels do not meet the standards generally accepted by the traditional maritime countries of Europe. It is even claimed that they are often superior.

The next question is how, by what machinery, the flag-of-convenience states effectively enforce the observance by their vessels, wherever they are, of the measures dealing with safety at sea, if those vessels practically never call at their ports and do not even go there for registration. No concrete answer to this question was given at the Geneva conference by the delegates of Liberia and Panama. The Liberian delegate only stated that "Liberia was genuinely anxious by efficient administration of its maritime law and regulations to maintain the high standards it had set." [116] On the other hand, no concrete evidence was

113. For the maritime conventions adopted by the International Labor Conference see A/CONF. 13/C.2/L.9 (1958) [mimeographed].

114. ILConf.*RP*. 41 Sess. (Geneva, 1958), *passim*.

115. The status of the ratification of these conventions is indicated in ILOffice, *Report* I (1957), pp. 54–55.

116. UN.CLS.*OR* 4:22.

advanced at the conference to show that there were any cases where the flag state did not exercise effective jurisdiction over its vessels.[117] But here again the anti-Panlibhon group contends that the credit for efficiency must go not to the Panlibhon governments but to the foreign shipowners who are obliged to apply measures internationally adopted, because otherwise the port authorities in various countries would not allow the Panlibhon ships to proceed on their voyages.[118]

In view of the fact that practically no Panlibhon vessels trade to and from the ports of these countries, the main responsibility of seeing that the laws are effectively applied in respect of these ships seems to lie with the consular services of Panlibhon. These services must be built up proportionately to the size and the composition of the respective fleet. As the above-mentioned inquiry into the conditions on ships flying the Panamanian flag showed, it must be a staff of career, not honorary, consuls, thoroughly acquainted with all the relevant laws and collective agreements, not only of the flag country, but also of other legislations, if, for example, they are to approve the articles as being in accordance with the standards of their countries.

Liberia has consuls and vice-consuls stationed at almost all major ports throughout the world. Every master of a Liberian vessel is required to report to the consul upon his arrival at a foreign port.[119] Similar functions are fulfilled by the Panamanian and Honduran consuls.

So far as the seaworthiness of the vessels is concerned, the Panlibhon countries should have a widely organized network of nautical inspectors and surveyors who would carry out inspections of the vessels at regular intervals. The Committee of Enquiry advised Panama in 1949 to make arrangements with one of the classification societies to undertake these inspections, which was subsequently effected by Panama. As the Liberian sources indi-

117. *Cf.* the statement by the delegate of the United States; *id.*, p. 64.

118. *The Shipping World & World Shipbuilding,* December 31, 1958, p. 560. *Cf.* the statement by the United Kingdom delegate at the IMCO session in London, 1959; IMCO/A.I/SR. 7 (1959), pp. 2–3.

119. ACFN *Memorandum,* pp. 129–130. The memorandum does not indicate the per cent of career and honorary consuls. *Cf.* ICJ *Pleadings,* Constitution (1960), p. 271.

cate, Liberian vessels are subject to such periodic inspections, carried out in accordance with international conventions.[120]

The inspections are carried out by the classification societies with which Liberia "maintains close contacts . . . to be sure of the continuing classification of the vessels." [121] Here one should add that under the provisions of the International Convention for the Safety of Life at Sea, 1948, the inspection and survey of ships need not be carried out by officers of the country in which the ship is registered, and these functions may be entrusted to recognized organizations, the governments concerned fully guaranteeing the completeness and efficiency of the inspection and survey.[122] There is also an agreement signed in 1957 between the United States and Panama, allowing Panamanian nautical inspectors to board Panamanian-flag vessels in the Panama Canal Zone in order to inspect safety and working conditions aboard these ships.[123]

These are only some brief facts pointing to the way in which the Panlibhon countries exercise jurisdiction over vessels registered under their flags. The picture is not complete, but the fact that no concrete instances of the absence of effective exercise of jurisdiction have been adduced by the opponents of Panlibhon certainly strengthens the position of the flag-of-convenience countries. Such an instance, for example, could be afforded by the operation of ships under the Costa Rican flag. Mention has already been made of the memorandum submitted to the Costa Rican Legislative Assembly on the new draft law on registration of ships. Among other interesting details this memorandum reveals such facts as repeated violations of Costa Rican labor legislation by the ship operators flying the Costa Rican flag, lack of inspection and survey and safety regulations, and inefficiency in the consular service.[124]

120. Statement by the Deputy Commissioner of Maritime Affairs of the Republic of Liberia; *Liberia Today*, May 1959, p. 7. See also ICJ *Pleadings*, Constitution (1960), pp. 104–112.

121. Statement by the government delegate of Liberia; ILConf.*RP*. 41 Sess. (Geneva, 1958), p. 73.

122. 3 U.S.T. 3450; T.I.A.S. 2495; 164 U.N.T.S. 113 (ch. I, regulation 6). For this reason the argument against Panlibhon of the United Kingdom delegate at the IMCO conference, 1959, was irrelevant.

123. T.I.A.S. 3893; 8 U.S.T. 1413.

124. [Costa Rica] *La Gaceta, Diario Oficial* 80:3771–3772 (No. 252, 1958) (Fernando Fournier, "Proyecto").

The situation as to the facts would be much clearer if an inquiry similar to that of 1949 were carried out, possibly by the IMCO, in order to ascertain whether or not the Panlibhon countries effectively exercise jurisdiction and control in administrative, technical, and social matters over their ships, because, so far, both the ILC and the Geneva conference have discussed the problem without a solid basis of facts.

From the legal standpoint, however, there are no differences of opinion among the states, since both the Panlibhon camp and their adversaries expressly recognize the duty imposed by international law upon the flag state to exercise effective jurisdiction and control over its ships. This duty is also laid down in art. 5 of the Convention on the High Seas.

Recapitulating the state at which the second committee of the Geneva conference found itself after its frustrations in the attempt to define the genuine link, one finds that:

1) The attempt to give a direct definition of the genuine link was abandoned, the conference pursuing thus the course taken previously by the ILC.

2) All delegations agreed that the exercise of effective jurisdiction and control over vessels in administrative, technical, and social matters was the duty of the flag state.

3) The adversaries of the flags of convenience proposed that the exercise should serve to define the genuine link and, even more important, insisted that the genuine link must exist "for purposes of recognition of the national character of the ship by other states."

4) The flag-of-convenience camp proposed complete elimination of the expression "genuine link" along with the non-recognition clause, but was for the insertion of a provision stipulating the duty of effective exercise of jurisdiction and control.

For purposes of clarity, the outcome of voting on the respective proposals in the second committee, and the final result of voting in the plenary session, will be reported first, and subsequently the results of the Geneva conference in relation to the flag-of-convenience issue will be interpreted and evaluated.

The results of voting in the second committee were as follows:

The Liberian proposal (omitting the genuine link but requiring effective jurisdiction and control)[125] was rejected by 36 votes to 16, with 6 abstentions.[126] It is significant that the flag-of-convenience point of view could muster as many as 16 votes. The genuine-link provision, with the non-recognition clause, as framed by Italy and supplemented by France,[127] was adopted by 34 votes to 4, with 17 abstentions.[128] Following this, the Liberian delegate resorted to the device of putting the non-recognition clause to the vote separately. The vote showed that although 39 states endorsed the non-recognition clause, as many as 13 states were against it, and 6 states abstained. The results of the voting show that some delegations were hesitant and inconsistent in their votes. Thus, for example, three more delegations voted for the adoption of the Liberian proposal than against the non-recognition clause. Which states supported Panlibhon can be only presumed from the discussion, and also from the vote on the Panamanian amendment[129] to the Liberian proposal.[130] This vote, being at the request of Panama taken at roll call, gives some indication as to the position taken by the states. Honduras, Liberia, Panama, Colombia, Cuba, Ecuador, and Ghana were in favor of the Panamanian amendment. Israel, Venezuela, Republic of Korea, Mexico, Philippines, United States of America, Argentina, Brazil, China, Costa Rica, Dominican Republic, Greece, and Guatemala abstained. The other states whose delegates were present at the session of the second committee were against. Upon this basis, one can make a fairly substantiated conjecture that in the committee stage the flag-of-convenience states were supported, or at any rate not opposed, by the United States, the Latin American countries, Greece, and by Ghana.[131]

The whole of the text of art. 29 submitted by the ILC, as

125. UN.CLS.*OR* 4:119.

126. *Id.*, p. 75.

127. The Italian proposal (*id.*, p. 123), with the French amendment adding the words "in administrative, technical and social matters" (*id.*, p. 141). In the French text the phrase *lien réel* was replaced by *lien substantiel*.

128. *Id.*, p. 75. The French amendment was adopted by 24 votes to 16, with 14 abstentions.

129. *Id.*, p. 144.

130. *Id.*, p. 119.

131. Ghana had just started to build up a merchant fleet, establishing the Black Star Line, originally a common Ghana-Israeli venture, *The New York Times*, December 31, 1959, p. 31.

amended, was adopted by 40 votes to 7, with 11 abstentions.[132] Thus the committee stage ended with the defeat of the flag-of-convenience camp. But that was only the first round of the encounter. The final battle, which was a matter of a few minutes (extremely short, compared with the prolonged discussions at the committee) took place at the plenary session of the conference.

During the consideration of the report of the second committee, the delegate of El Salvador stated that

> although the Conference was entitled to lay down certain general conditions governing the grant of nationality to ships, the provisions of the instrument finally adopted should maintain complete respect for national sovereignty. In his delegation's view, the words 'Nevertheless, for purposes of recognition of the national character of the ship by other states' appearing in paragraph 1, seemed to offend against the principle of sovereignty and he would therefore ask for a separate vote on that phrase.[133]

The motion of El Salvador was supported by the United Arab Republic and Iran. This time, surprisingly enough, the nonrecognition clause was rejected by 30 votes to 15, with 17 abstentions, and art. 29 of the ILC draft of 1956, as amended by the conference, was adopted unanimously by 65 votes without even any abstentions.[134] This article became art. 5 of the Convention on the High Seas, which, as the conference decided, was to embody the work of the second committee.[135]

The sentence of art. 5 which is relevant for the present inquiry reads: "There must exist a genuine link between the State and the ship; in particular, the State must effectively exercise its jurisdiction and control in administrative, technical and social matters over ships flying its flag." The question is how to interpret this requirement in which several points are left obscure.

What could be understood by effective jurisdiction and control in the matters mentioned by the article has already been suggested. The next question which must be answered is the following: Is the requirement as to control and jurisdiction, introduced by the words "in particular," an additional test which

132. UN.CLS.*OR* 4:75.
133. UN.CLS.*OR* 2:20.
134. *Ibid.*
135. UN.CLS.*OR* 2:61. The convention as a whole was adopted by 65 votes to none, with 1 abstention.

must be satisfied besides the requirement of the undefined genuine link, or should it be interpreted as something that is included in the concept of genuine link itself?

The statement of Sørensen that "this sentence . . . in effect relates the 'genuine link' not only to the qualities of the ship and its owner, but also to the legal possibilities of the state to control the ship"[136] shows that the fears of the possible interpreting of art. 5 as embracing not one but two tests are not without foundation.[137] Sørensen, however, forgets that the problem of the qualities of the owner was discarded, already by the ILC at its eighth session. That ownership need not be element of the genuine link, even according to the authors of this concept, was also overlooked by Judge Moreno Quintana in his dissenting opinion to the advisory opinion of the ICJ of June 8, 1960 concerning the constitution of the Maritime Safety Committee of the IMCO.[138]

The failure of the second committee of the conference to define the genuine link points to the fact that the center of gravity has been shifted by the framers of the article from the various criteria, such as ownership, which the states are free to choose (as it is stipulated by the first sentence of art. 5) and which are indifferent provided that the objective of effective control over the ships plying the high seas is secured, to the exercise of jurisdiction and control. This interpretation is consonant with the institution of nationality, and is also corroborated by the French text of art. 5, where the English words "in particular" are rendered by the adverb "notamment," which in English corresponds more to the words "that is" than "in particular." Therefore the view expressed in a recent edition of a textbook of international law that "there must exist a genuine link between the state and the ship, *i.e.*, the state must exercise its jurisdiction and control effectively in administrative, technical and other related matters," correctly solves the problem under inquiry.[139]

136. Sørensen, p. 205.

137. The danger of such an interpretation is signalled by McDougal, Burke, & Vlasic, *YLJ* 54:29–30 (1960).

138. [1960] I.C.J. Rep. 179.

139. Brittin & Watson, *International Law for Seagoing Officers* (2d ed. 1960) p. 107. *Cf.* also this answer given by the Department of State, March 2, 1960, to a question of Senate Foreign Relations Committee, concerning the difficulties of defining the genuine link by the Geneva conference: ". . . While the conference did not

In other words the concept of the genuine link, finally accepted by the conference, does not refer to conditions which should exist prior to registration, but, as it was rightly pointed out by the Liberian representative before the ICJ,

> The particulars given of the concept, namely, the effective exercise by the flag State of jurisdiction and control in administrative, technical and social matters, indicate that the concept was in its final form intended to relate not to events before registration, but to events after registration. It became, in effect, an exhortation to States to do something vis-à-vis ships under their flag.[140]

Potential dangers are inherent in the possible interpretation of the question, also left unspecified by the convention, what sanctions are to be attached to the absence of genuine link (*whatever* it may mean) in a given case. The most dangerous for the traditional system of the conclusive competence of states to attribute nationality to ships is the interpretation which allows other states to determine unilaterally that genuine link does not exist in a given case and that they will deny the national character of the ship as evidenced by its registry. Although the non-recognition clause was rejected by the plenary session of the conference, and the final text does not specify any sanction, Verzijl expresses the view that "under these conditions international tribunals, municipal legislatures, and municipal courts would seem to have been given a free hand to attach to the general requirement of 'genuine link' the legal consequences they deem fit and proper." [141]

Discussing the result of the conference, it should be emphasized

---

agree on the definition of the term 'genuine link' it was able to agree on the requirement of 'effective jurisdiction and control' as a particularization of the concept of the 'genuine link.' The addition of this particularization to the article gives to the concept of the 'genuine link' a degree of specificity which it did not have in the original draft of this article submitted by the International Law Commission." *Hearings on Conventions on the Law of the Sea before the Committee on Foreign Relations,* United States Senate 86th Cong., 2d Sess., January 20, 1960 (1960), p. 86.

140. ICJ *Pleadings,* Constitution (1960), p. 297.

141. Verzijl, p. 118. McDougal, Burke & Vlasic attribute to Sørensen the opinion that in view of art. 5 of the convention states are free not to recognize the nationality of a ship if no genuine link exists. However, the sentence of Sørensen, quoted by them, refers to his interpretation not of art. 5 of the convention, but of art. 29 of the ILC Law of the Sea which *was* provided with an explicit non-recognition clause. In view of the rejection of the non-recognition clause Sørensen further only states that, if a state has no legal possibilities to control the ship, it is "not entitled to enter or to maintain the ship on its register." *Cf.* McDougal, Burke & Vlasic pp. 28–29 with Sørensen, p. 205.

that the main disputed point was not the genuine-link concept itself, however inconvenient it might have been to Panlibhon. The main target of the Panlibhon argument was the non-recognition clause "for purposes of recognition of the national character of the ship by other states," giving other states explicit right to refuse the recognition of the registration in case of the absence of the genuine link between the ship and the state of the questioned registration.

Since its first debates on the problem of the nationality of merchant vessels, the ILC had always made it quite clear that the absence of a minimum national element in a ship, defined first by precise ownership requirements and then by the requirement of a genuine link, would carry the sanction of the non-recognition of its national character by other states. This sanction was expressly stated and endorsed by the majority of the members of the ILC, whereas some members were opposed to it as being in conflict with international practice.[142]

The ILC did not define strictly the legal consequences of the absence of the genuine link and left this question open to various conjectures,[143] but the general effect of the phrase was clearly understood by the delegations of both camps at the Geneva conference: a state holding that no genuine link existed between the ship and its flag state would presumably have the right, and perhaps even the duty, to refuse unilaterally to recognize the ship's nationality. This would entail quite an avalanche of dangerous consequences in many spheres of international legal relations.

If, for example, state *A* were to decide unilaterally that a ship registered in state *X* had no genuine link with state *X*, state *A* would be free to disregard the nationality of the ship obtained in state *X*. But what nationality would that ship then have in the view of state *A*? Would it have the nationality of some other

142. In Sørensen, p. 203, the recommendation of the non-recognition clause is mistakenly attributed to the "International Labor Conference," and this misleading error is repeated by the counsel of the ACFN in his memorandum to the chairman of the Senate Foreign Relations Committee. See *Hearings on Conventions on the Law of the Sea* (1960), p. 122.

143. There was no time for a thorough analysis of the non-recognition sanction, states Verzijl, who was a member of the Netherlands delegation to the Geneva conference (Verzijl, p. 117.)

state, say state *Y*, with which — according to state *A* — it was connected by a genuine link? Or would it, perhaps, have no nationality at all, and would it be treated as stateless, a status very awkward indeed for a vessel and so far extremely rare? Or, third (a case even more paradoxical), there might conceivably be a situation in which state *A* would claim the ship to be connected by a genuine link with itself, and regard it as its own ship. All these possibilities would be in conflict with the generally accepted rule of international law that "the regularity and validity of a registration can be questioned only by the registering state."[144] In disregard of all these dangers, the Netherlands delegate at the conference made it plain that the ship's documents only certified the ship's rights to fly its flag under the municipal law of the flag state, but were not conclusive evidence of a genuine link with that state.[145]

The possibility of stateless ships plying the high seas was envisaged at the conference, and some of the untoward consequences inherent in such a situation were pointed out by the delegates of Liberia, Panama, Mexico, and the United States.

Pursuing the effects of non-recognition of the nationality of a ship to its furthest logical conclusions, one could presume that a ship registered without a genuine link would practically be prevented from sailing the seas. The Netherlands delegate even declared that it would be difficult to recognize the right of such a ship to use the high seas and enjoy immunity from foreign interference.[146] This interference would take the form of an unexpected and undesirable extension of the right to visit in time of peace.[147] If the nationality of a ship were questioned, it might not be allowed port clearance, as a stateless ship, on the ground that it had not declared its "true" nationality.[148] This, again, would raise the question of responsibility for the financial loss incurred by the

144. Lauritzen v. Larsen, 345 U.S. 571, 585 (1953).
145. UN.CLS.*OR* 4:64.
146. *Id.*, p. 3.
147. Liberia; *id.*, p. 22. The right of visit is provided for by art. 46 of the ILC Law of the Sea of 1956, corresponding to art. 22 of the Convention on the High Seas.
148. Rienow, pp. 14–15. *Cf.* OEEC.MTC, "Study" (1958), p. 12. See also "The Link between Ship and Flag," *The Shipping World & World Shipbuilding*, February 26, 1958, p. 195.

shipowner whose ship had to remain in the port until the settlement of the dispute.[149]

The hope that the Geneva Conference on the Law of the Sea would devise a legal provision enabling the old maritime countries to refuse entry to ships which could not produce proof of a genuine link with their flag state was cherished, and openly confessed, by shipping circles in some countries. There were also suggestions of a radical approach to the problem of the flags of convenience. Thus, some English shipping circles demanded that the government take direct legislative action by forbidding the Panlibhon ships entry to the ports of the United Kingdom.[150] It was hoped that if the ships of, say, Liberia were excluded from the ports of the United Kingdom and other European maritime nations, the United Kingdom and those nations would be able to endure losing the Liberia trade to Honduras, and *vice versa*. Even an agreement between "the dozen or so of nations who are significant in the world shipping position (as opposed to the shipping registry position)" was suggested in order to "make the few and small countries who [*sic*] are thus threatening the interest of the world into a group of pariahs until they decided to find some other way of balancing their budgets."[151] The OEEC, however, deemed it useless to consider such a course, and rightly so, in the absence of international agreements and — what is more difficult to determine — international standards of effectiveness, which would establish the validity and correctness of the consequences of the non-recognition of the flags of convenience.[152]

Another possible source of conflicts would result within the sphere of jurisdiction. Thus, for example, state *A* might claim the right to exercise criminal jurisdiction over ships registered in state *X*, if there existed a genuine link between those ships and the claimant state *A*.

As it was pointed out at the conference, the non-recognition

149. Panama, UN.CLS.*OR* 4:63.
150. *The Shipping World & World Shipbuilding*, February 26, 1958, p. 240.
151. Nevin, "Notes on Current Events," *Business Law Review* 5:112, 113 (1958).
152. OEEC.MTC, "Study" (1958) p. 12. *Cf.* also the statement of Lord Mancroft in the House of Lords; House of Lords, *Parliamentary Debates* 208:369 (March 20, 1958).

of the vessel's national character would also result in conflicts in the sphere of private international law; it would affect relations between individuals, property rights, validity of contracts executed under the law of the flag, maritime insurance, and other legal relationships, making them dependent upon a fortuitous place of jurisdiction. In addition, it was not clear from the wording of the non-recognition clause whether a ship without a genuine link with the flag state would lose the diplomatic protection of that state.[153]

All these dangers were clearly seen by the government of India which rejecting the test of ownership expressed the following view in its written statement before the ICJ:

> In conclusion, the Government of India considers that the economic success of ship-owning and ship operating business depends upon a reasonably reliable forecast of the laws and regulations which will apply to the ship. The law as to the nationality of the ship must be definitely known in advance. It cannot be left to the general decision of a judge or a tax officer or a crew welfare administrator while the voyage is going on or after the voyage is concluded. The proposition that authorities may look behind the law of the flag to try to discover facts about national control of sums of money invested in the ships leads to the splitting of the nationality of the ship, which is destructive of the economic, social and legal conduct of the shipping business. It will result in international legal anarchy and in the disruption of the legal order which has already been established and followed.[154]

An argument against the non-recognition clause was also advanced from the position of logic. It was found to be a contradiction to allow a state — as did the first part of art. 29 — to fix the conditions under which it granted nationality to ships, but at the same time to lay down that other states had the right — if they held, notwithstanding the authenticity of the ship's papers, that no genuine link existed between the ship and the flag state — not to recognize the nationality granted under those conditions.[155] This situation would certainly lead to disputes and confusion.

153. Liberia, UN.CLS.*OR* 4:22; the United Kingdom, p. 64. Watts, following the doctrine of genuine link and applying the *Nottebohm* case to the protection of ships, comes to the wrong conclusion that only the state of ownership of the vessel may protect it. See Watts, "The Protection of Merchant Ships," p. 55.

154. ICJ *Pleadings*, Constitution (1960), p. 259.

155. Liberia, UN.CLS.*OR* 4:22; Panama, p. 62. *Cf.* also the statement of the Liberian delegate at the 6th committee of the G.A., 11th session; A/CONF. 13/19 (1957), p. 506 [mimeographed].

This opinion was expressed even by the delegate of Brazil, whose laws on the grant of the right to fly the flag are among the most stringent. He expressly stated that the existence of the genuine link should not be a condition for the recognition of the vessel's nationality.[156] The Mexican delegate at the Sixth committee of the General Assembly had put it this way: "Nothing would be more likely to create insoluble problems than to grant to a state the right to do something and at the same time to grant to other states the right not to recognize it. This is virtually the effect of Article 29 of the [International Law] Commission's draft." [157]

There was yet another contradiction inherent in art. 29, pointed out by the United States delegate: the ILC had admitted the vagueness of the term "genuine link" and the impossibility of its being defined, but at the same time it laid down that states were free not to recognize the national character of the ship concerned if they found that the genuine link did not exist.[158] One could also mention the possibility of the conflicts which would result between the non-recognition clause and treaties of commerce and navigation in which the signatory states recognized the nationality of each other's vessels as granted under the municipal law of these states.[159] Even in art. 42 of the ILC Law of the Sea, dealing with piracy, there was a provision that "the retention or loss of national character is determined by the law of the state from which the national character was originally derived.[160]

Bearing in mind all the potential harm that could be done by the introduction of the non-recognition clause into art. 5, it is not surprising that this clause was rejected by the plenary session of the conference. Sørensen suggests that the change in the minds of a number of delegations was a result of "extensive lobbying." [161]

156. UN.CLS.*OR* 4:66.

157. A/CONF.13/19 (1957), pp. 171–172 [mimeographed]. The same argument was reiterated by another Mexican delegate at the Geneva conference. He stated that "by conceding to other states the right to decide for themselves whether there was a genuine link between the ship and the flag state, the [International Law] Commission had opened the door to the creation of insoluble problems. UN.CLS.*OR* 4:29.

158. *Id.*, p. 65.

159. *Cf.* the statement by Padilla Nervo in the ILC, 8th sess. (ILC *Yearbook 1956*, I, 70, 72) and the statement of the Liberian delegate at the Geneva conference. (UN.CLS.*OR* 4:22.) See also Ch. IV.

160. *Cf.* substantially the same formulation in art. 18 of the Convention on the High Seas.

161. Sørensen, p. 205. Mender, p. 355.

There is one interesting fact, not mentioned by Sørensen, which throws a good deal of light upon the question. In the period of time between April 8, 1958 (the date on which the non-recognition provision was adopted) and April 23, 1958 (the date on which the plenary session rejected it), the International Chamber of Shipping had its annual meeting in London. Understandably enough, the problem of the flags of convenience was on the agenda. The proposed text of the second committee of the Geneva conference was also discussed, and the Chamber, recognizing the dangers of the non-recognition clause for international commercial intercourse and shipping, expressed disquiet over the wording of the clause. Consequently, many shipowners advised the delegates of their countries at the Geneva conference to oppose the clause at the plenary meeting.[162] Such is the explanation of the "lobbying," as a result of which the plenary session discarded the dangerous provision. The outcome of the voting at the plenary session must have been influenced not only by the fear of serious economic and political repercussions, but also by the weight of the policy arguments against the unilateral competence of one state to question the grant of nationality to ships by another.

The specific rejection of the phrase which was so amply discussed, and whose potential perils were understood both at the *travaux préparatoires* in the ILC and at the conference itself, cannot mean anything else but the intention of the framers of the convention to convey the idea that the absence of genuine link cannot give other states the right not to recognize the national character of the vessel which fails to meet this requirement. The striking of the clause showed that the majority of the delegations agreed with the argument of El Salvador that the non-recognition clause would "offend against the principle of sovereignty," and would allow a state to interfere with matters coming within the scope of the domestic jurisdiction of another state.[163]

162. *The Times,* April 17, 1958, p. 8; *The New York Times,* April 19, 1958, p. 37.

163. Reiff explains that the clause in question was struck out "to reduce the opportunities for discrimination" against the flag-of-convenience vessels; Reiff, *The United States and the Treaty Law of the Sea,* p. 331 (1959). The interpretation, given in ACFN *Memorandum,* pp. 81–84, is in its substance the same as of the present author, but the facts relating to the non-recognition clause and the adoption of the final text of art. 5 are misrepresented and confused. McDougal, Burke & Vlasic believe the deletion of the clause to be an expression of "some degree of recognition [by the Conference] of the perils inherent in the 'genuine link' doctrine"; McDougal,

Because of all the adduced reasons art. 5 of the convention cannot be interpreted to mean that if there is no link between the ship and the state the other states may refuse to recognize the ship's nationality, since this sanction is not laid down by the framers of the convention, and, on the contrary, was explicitly rejected.

In order not to fall into conflict with the long established practice and theory of international law of the sea the genuine link clause of art. 5 must be interpreted as a general rule laying down, in the interests of safety and order of navigation, the duty of the flag state to control effectively on the high seas the ships flying its flag.[164] Interpreted in this sense, the requirement of effective jurisdiction and control must be regarded as *lex lata*, a provision generally declaratory of an established principle of international law,[165] since there is universal agreement that the state of the vessel's nationality, besides issuing to the vessel its registration documents, has the duty to control effectively its vessels on the high seas, in the interest of all the users, as well as the corollary right of protecting its shipping. Even the Liberian delegate at the conference shared this view when he said that "in order to prevent abuse and friction, it should be laid down that the granting of a state's flag should not be a mere administrative formality with no accompanying guarantees," and added that "no state had acted as irresponsibly as that."[166]

In the declaration of the established principle of effective juris-

---

Burke & Vlasic, p. 116, n. 281. But see "Flag-of-Convenience Fleet," *YLJ* 69:510 n. 86 (1960), where the importance of the deletion of the clause is given more emphasis.

164. There are other rules of general importance for the regime of the high seas, belonging to this category, *e.g.*, the rule that the freedoms resulting from freedom of the seas should be exercised with reasonable regard to the interests of other states (Convention on the High Seas, art. 2.) Pinto explicitly states that effective jurisdiction and control provide genuine link (Pinto, p. 364).

165. *Cf.* the Preamble to the Convention on the High Seas. It is in this sense that international law has concern with nationality of ships. The change effected by Colombos in the latest edition of his textbook, from which he eliminated the sentence that international law has no concern with conditions of granting nationality to merchant vessels (which sentence was included in the previous editions, *e.g.*, in the edition of 1954), is the expression of Colombos' approval of genuine link as meaning that international law fixes the conditions of the grant of nationality to ships. *Cf.* Colombos, pp. 270, 250 with Higgins, *The International Law of the Sea* pp. 234, 216 (4th ed., Colombos ed. 1954).

166. UN.CLS.*OR* 4:22.

diction and control of the flag state over its shipping, the mention of the undefined and undefinable concept of genuine link is an intrusion which causes confusion and obscures the meaning of the article as it was finally agreed to by the conference.[167] Therefore, it should be discarded from the text of art. 5, para. 1, which, it is submitted, should read as follows:

> Each state shall fix the conditions for the grant of its nationality to ships, for the registration of ships in its territory, and for the right to fly its flag. Ships have the nationality of the state whose flag they are entitled to fly. Each state must effectively exercise its jurisdiction and control in administrative, technical, and social matters over ships flying its flag.

So far as the sanctions resulting from the non-fulfillment of this requirement are concerned, they would result from the facts attributable to the flag state, whenever the lack of effective control by that state over its ship should have proved detrimental to the interests of other states. Thus the matter would be placed on the plane of the general principles of responsibility of the states to be applied in each particular case. This is connected with one important defect of the convention, namely, that it does not provide for the duty of states to have recourse to arbitration or judicial settlement of disputes.[168] Proposals to this effect were rejected by the majority of states,[169] and only an optional protocol of signature concerning the compulsory settlement of disputes was adopted by the conference.[170] This protocol provides in art. 1 for the compulsory jurisdiction of the International Court of Justice in respect of "disputes arising out of the interpretation or application of any Convention on the Law of the Sea." However, since the protocol is optional, there is little chance that a large number of states would in advance agree to subject themselves to a judicial settlement of disputes that might arise in the future. But this is connected with the more general problem of lack of conditions in present international relations which would compel states to sub-

167. However, only American commentators see the dangers of this concept. See McDougal, Burke & Vlasic. See also "Flag-of-Convenience Fleet," YLJ, 69 (1960), and Kunz.

168. Only the Convention on Fishing and Conservation of the Living Resources of the High Seas provides for the settlement of disputes by arbitration (art. 9).

169. See, *e.g.*, the proposal by Colombia; UN.CLS.*OR* 4:135.

170. UN.CLS.*OR* 2:145–146.

mit their disputes to judicial settlement and would enforce their execution.

It is generally agreed that the Geneva conference has not solved the problem of the flags of convenience and, even if the Convention on the High Seas were eventually ratified by the prescribed number of states,[171] it is not likely to reduce the tonnage of ships sailing under the Panlibhon flags.[172] Article 5 does not take into account the criterion of ownership,[173] confirming thus the established principle of international law that foreign-owned vessels may be registered under the flag of any state. This means that the flags of convenience continue to be allowed under international law. Therefore the United States Department of State, asked by the Senate Foreign Relations Committee about the effect of the requirement of the genuine link upon the practice of registering American ships under the Panlibhon flags, answered: "The 'genuine link' requirement of Article 5 of the Convention on the High Seas need not have any effect upon the practice of registering American-built or owned vessels in such countries as Panama or Liberia . . . We are not aware of any reasons why such countries as Panama or Liberia could not maintain the existence of a 'genuine link' with vessels registered under their laws." [174]

The advisory opinion of the International Court of Justice of June 8, 1960, favorable for the flags of convenience, only confirms this conclusion. There the Court found the contention based on a genuine link irrelevant for the purposes of answering the question which had been submitted to it.

171. Article 34 provides that the convention shall come into force on the 30th day following the date of the deposit of the 22d instrument of ratification or accession with the Secretary-General of the United Nations. So far only a very negligible number of states have ratified the convention. The United States has ratified it.

172. *Cf.* the opinion of Sørensen, p. 205; Johnson, p. 87; Honig, "Die Vereinten Nationen und die Kodifikation des Völkerrechts," *Archiv des Völkerrechts* 8(No. 1); 1, 12 (1959). Reiff (p. 331) speaks about a "modest approach to a solution of a vexing problem." In *Hansa* 95:1164–1165 (1958) it is stated that, so far as the "danger" of the flags of convenience is concerned, the conference has made things worse instead of better. Pinto (p. 368) comes to the conclusion that the flags of convenience cannot be challenged in international law. See also "Flags of Convenience or Necessity," *Petroleum Press Service,* January 1959, pp. 13–15.

173. Some commentators still insist that, although it is not expressed in the convention, the domicile or nationality of the shipowners, or even the nationality of the crew, should be considered as element of genuine link. See, *e.g.*, Berber, *Lehrbuch des Völkerrechts,* I, 324 (1960).

174. *Hearings on Conventions on the Law of the Sea* (1960), p. 86.

On the other hand the 1958 Convention on the High Seas, although not ratified, may exert some influence upon the states' practice. It may, particularly, spur the ship-owning nations, including Panlibhon, to make the organization and control of their vessels in administrative, technical, and social matters more effective.

Chapter X. Summary and Conclusions

In concluding the present study, it is necessary for the clearer understanding of the whole issue of the flags of convenience to recapitulate briefly the various specific conclusions already reached and also to project some more general conclusions resulting from the international legal developments, in particular from art. 5 of the Convention on the High Seas and the advisory opinion of the ICJ of June 8, 1960.

The popular term "flags of convenience" refers to the registration and operation under the flags of Liberia, Panama, Honduras, (Panlibhon), and until recently, Costa Rica (hence also the name Panlibhonco) of merchant vessels which are beneficially owned and controlled by nationals of other countries, primarily Americans and Greeks, are manned by foreign crews, and hardly ever put into their ports of registry. Although the term "flags of convenience" itself was coined only a few years ago, the device of operating vessels under a foreign flag has long been known in maritime history. Panlibhon originated in the years after the First World War, but a spectacular growth of these flags started after the Second World War, especially when Liberia joined the group. After 1959 a slight decrease in the Panlibhon tonnage can be noticed; on the other hand a flag-of-convenience tendency has been clearly manifested by Lebanon.

The growth of the flags of convenience, in particular Panama, and still more Liberia, has been due to the specific competitive situation on the international shipping market in the period after the Second World War. Many unsubsidized American shipowners being unable — because of prohibitive high operating costs — to operate their ships (tankers and ore carriers) under the American flag transferred them wholesale to the flags of convenience, removing the handicap of operating costs and gaining, into the bargain, competitive advantage over their European rivals, because of tax immunities afforded by the flag-of-convenience countries. For Greek shipowners the reason of registration under the Panlibhon flags has been primarily the desire to avoid heavy taxation and inconvenient government regulations. For these reasons the problem of the flags of convenience, in which at first the labor aspect was in the foreground and justifiably aroused grievances on the part of seamen's unions, has now become first of all a problem of economic competition between American shipowners operating with lower costs under the tax-free flags of convenience new, big bulk carriers, and the shipowners of the European traditional maritime countries operating under heavy tax handicaps. Hence, the problem has also political repercussions, and is a cause of serious controversy within the Western bloc, between the United States administration, which approves transfers to and registration under the flags of convenience, and the governments of the European members of NATO, which consider the shipping policy of the United States an unfair competition. This shipping policy is also actively opposed by the American seamen's unions for which registration under Panlibhon flags means loss of labor opportunity for American seamen.

Another conclusion on the reasons for the rise of the Panlibhon flags is connected with the international law aspect of the problem, in particular with the question of nationality of ships. It has been proved that under international law each state is free to determine conditions under which it will register and thereby grant nationality to merchant vessels, and that this nationality as evidenced by registry and documents should be recognized by other states. Since international law does not impose upon the states the duty to register only such ships as are operated and owned, and manned by its citizens, the flag-of-convenience countries had the right to enact legislation allowing for registration of ships owned by nationals of other countries. As the analysis of the laws of the Panlibhon countries shows, it is not only the shipping registration laws, ignoring the requirement of national ownership, which make the flags of these countries so attractive for foreign shipowners — a view commonly held by commentators — but first of all, the very liberal taxation. However, these matters are also within the domestic jurisdiction of each state and the flag-of-convenience countries have the right to carry on such fiscal policy as serves their interests.

From the principle that nationality granted by a state to merchant vessels should be recognized for all purposes of international law, the conclusion results that the national character of the vessels, as shown by their registry, is also conclusive for situations where this national character is relevant for purposes of determining the right of the state to be a member of the organs of international organizations. This is the case of the constitution of the Maritime Safety Committee of IMCO, which, as the advisory opinion of the ICJ of 1960 proved, was not elected in accordance with the IMCO convention.

Neither is nationality of Panlibhon ships denied in cases where the authorities of a state, in cases justified by public and private international law, assert their jurisdiction aboard the Panlibhon vessels, as they do so also in respect to any other foreign vessels. In cases of conflict between the law of the flag and the law of the ultimate ownership of the vessel, the settled practice and doctrine, also as applied by the United States courts, is that, in absence of express language of the municipal law, the law of the flag governs the internal economy of the vessel, in particular the wages of the crew. This is done not in virtue of some rules of international law in this respect — since any merchant vessel entering the territorial waters of a foreign state subjects itself to its jurisdiction — but because of rules of international comity, which demand, in the interests of stability and certainty of international intercourse, mutual restraint in the assertion of jurisdiction by the coastal state. The analysis of the judicial decisions in injury cases as well as certain decisions of the NLRB shows, however, the tendency of the American courts and the NLRB to pierce the corporate veil of the Panlibhon companies and apply the American law to foreign seamen if the ship is ultimately owned and controlled by Americans. But the application of the American labor laws in general to the Panlibhon ships in order to equalize the costs of operation of American ships with those of foreign ships would be in open conflict with the whole shipping policy of the United States, which allows the registration under Panlibhon flags in order to lower these costs, and, on the other hand, the selective application of the American labor statutes only to non-Panlibhon foreign vessels would be a discriminatory measure and would result in retaliation.

The Panlibhon states also have the right to exercise protection over the ships registered under their flags, although here the concurrent protection by the state of ultimate ownership is under international law admissible as long as it does not conflict with the interests of the flag state.

The conclusions as to the right of control of movement and requisition of the Panlibhon vessels in time of war are:

Under customary international law only the Panlibhon states, as states of registry, have the right to control the movement of the vessels in question and to requisition them. The state of ultimate ownership could exercise these rights in virtue of an agreement with the Panlibhon states (no explicit agreement exists between the United States and the Panlibhon countries) or, if these states acquiesce in the exercise of these rights by the state of ultimate ownership. In the whole issue the inability of the Panlibhon states to control and requisition ships in case of war is a decisive factor. Since in case of war actual ownership is one of the tests of enemy character, the Panlibhon ships, in case of war, in which the state of actual ownership should be a belligerent, would be treated as enemy ships by the opposite party. In this case, the state of actual ownership could take control of and requisition its citizens' property in order to afford them necessary protection, even without the consent of the Panlibhon governments.

With the foregoing conclusions in mind, how should one evaluate the position of the flags of convenience in view of the attempts to restrict this practice by the introduction of the concept of genuine link into the article of the Geneva convention, dealing with nationality of ships? The general conclusions on this subject are as follows:

The genuine link concept in its application to ships has been devised by its framers as an international law medium to curb the practice of the flags of convenience which, for those who stimulated this concept, are dangerous competition, or are inconvenient because of other economic reasons. As originally designed and formulated by the ILC, the genuine link requirement was to be a *de lege ferenda* provision, aiming at terminating the traditional practice and rule of international law allowing the states exclusive competence in conferring their nationality upon merchant vessels. This concept of genuine link, inherited from the ILC by the Geneva conference, continued to be vague and undefinable and, at the same time, through the retention of the explicit non-recognition clause by the second committee of the conference, contained elements contrary to logic and international practice, and potentially harmful for international commercial intercourse and international relations in general. The dangers inherent in this unequivocal provision made the plenary session of the Geneva conference cancel the non-recognition clause, but the requirement of the genuine link has been retained, although with the edge taken off. No elements of the genuine link could be defined, but it has been generally agreed that effective jurisdiction and control in administrative, technical, and social matters by the flag state over its ships should be the result of this genuine link. The conclusion is submitted that the requirement of genuine link should be interpreted as implying a general rule enjoining the states to improve and make more effective their control over shipping registered under their flags, in the interests of order and safety at sea.

This interpretation of the provision in question is also consonant with the institution of the nationality of ships, whose rationale is to preserve order on the high seas. As art. 5 is now formulated, the mention of genuine link is an out-of-place survival from the text which once included the non-recognition clause, and therefore it should have been rejected along with that clause. Since it has been retained, it continues to cause confusion because it evokes association with the inapposite *Nottebohm* case and, by many commentators, and even in one of the dissenting opinions in the advisory opinion of the ICJ of 1960, is still interpreted contrary to the established practice of international law. As to the impact of the Geneva conference on the flags of convenience themselves, the conclusion must be drawn that this issue was not solved by the Geneva conference, and could not be solved because the roots of the problem lie not in the legal sphere but in the complex economic structure of the international shipping industry.

As things stand now, flags of convenience continue to be allowed under international law, since art. 5 of the 1958 convention affirms the prerogative of each state to determine the conditions under which it will grant nationality to merchant vessels, and since there is no mention at all of ownership, operation, or crew of the vessels registered. The advisory opinion of the ICJ on the constitution of the Maritime Safety Committee of the IMCO, following the traditional practice and doctrine of international law, recognized registry as test of the nationality of a merchant vessel, and has only strengthened the international law position of the Panlibhon fleets. On the other hand, art. 5 of the Convention on the High Seas stresses the duty of effective exercise of jurisdiction and control over the ships by the state of their nationality. A detailed elaboration of the elements of this requirement, without, however, unilateral questioning of one state's practice by another state, is necessary in order to ascertain whether the maritime nations, and in particular the flag-of-convenience states, satisfy the minimum standards of control and jurisdiction over their ships. But, as it has been emphasized above, this postulate is applicable with regard to international shipping in general; flags of convenience, though an important issue today, may eventually, under different economic and political conditions, prove to be only a transient phenomenon on the high seas.

Bibliography · Table of Cases Cited · Index

Bibliography

In addition to the titles listed below the following maritime periodicals are of special interest:

American Bureau of Shipping, *The Bulletin* [New York]
Arkiv for Sjørett [Oslo]
The Baltic and International Maritime Conference Monthly Circular [Copenhagen]
Diritto Marittimo [Genoa]
Le Droit Maritime Français [Paris]
Fairplay, Weekly Shipping Journal [London]
Hansa Zeitschrift fur Schiffahrt, Schiffbau, Hafen [Hamburg]
Journal de la Marine Marchande et de la Navigation Aérienne [Paris]
Marineblad [Netherlands]
Morskoi Flot [Moscow]
Norwegian Shipping News [Oslo]
Scandinavian Shipping Gazette [Copenhagen]
The Shipping World and World Shipbuilding [London]

Albion, R. G., "Flags of Convenience," in the *Grolier Encyclopedia* (1959).
Albion, R. G. and Pope, J. B., *Sealanes in Wartime* (1952).
American Bar Association, Section of International and Comparative Law, *Proceedings* (1960).
American Committee for Flags of Necessity (Donovan, Leisure, Newton, Irvine, Counsel), *Memorandum to the Department of State and to the General Counsel of the N.L.R.B.* (October 30, 1959). [Privately published.]
——— *Some Important Facts about Flags of Necessity Ships: A Fleet Vital to America's Defense and Economy, Summary.* (2d ed. Selvage & Lee, Inc., n.d.).

American University of Beirut, Economic Research Institute, "Business Legislation in Lebanon" (1955) [mimeographed].

Annuaire de l'Institut de Droit International, Session de Venise, vol. XV (1896).

Annuaire de l'Institut de Droit International, Session de Stockholm, vol. XXXIV (1928).

Annual Digest and Reports of Public International Law Cases 1948, ed. Sir Hersch Lauterpacht (1953).

Baker, R. Palmer, Jr., "Flags of Refuge for Shipping Industry — Federal Income Tax Considerations," *Tax Law Review* 13:137 (1957–1958).

Barlow, E. R. and Wender, I. T., *Foreign Investment and Taxation* (1955).

Bartos, M. F., "Kodifikacija i novi razvoj medunarodnog prava u Zenevskoj Konvenciji o Otvorenom Moru od 1958" ["Codification and New Development of International Law in the Geneva Convention on the High Seas of 1958"], *Jugoslovenska Revija za Medunarodno Pravo* 6:178 (1959).

Beale, J. H., *A Treatise on the Conflict of Laws,* vol. I (1935).

Becu, Omer, "Fighting the Pirate Flags," *Free Labour World,* No. 104, 59 (February 1959) [*Free Labour World* is the official organ of the International Confederation of the Free Trade Unions].

Benedict, E. C., *Admiralty,* vol. VI, ed. A. W. Knauth (7th ed., 1958).

Berber, F. J., *Lehrbuch des Völkerrechts,* vol. I (1960).

Berguido, Carlos, "The Rights of Seamen on a Ship under Panamanian Registry," *Temple Law Quarterly* 19:458 (1946).

Bickel, A. M., *The Unpublished Opinions of Mr. Justice Brandeis* (1957).

Bierzanek, Remigiusz, "Zagadnienie morza pełnego na konferencji Narodów Zjednoczonych w Genewie 24.II. — 27.IV. 1958" ["The Question of the High Seas at the United Nations Conference at Geneva, February 24–April 27, 1958,"] *Panstwo i Prawo* 13:811 (1958) [Warsaw, Poland].

Bluntschli, J. K., *Das moderne Völkerrecht der civilisirten Staten* (3d ed. 1878).

Bogaert, E. van., "Le droit que possède l'Etat pour déterminer les conditions d'après lesquelles les navires ont le droit d'arborer son pavillon," *Revue de Droit International et de Droit Comparé* 35:485 (1958).

Brajkovic, Vladislav and Pallua, Emilio, "Les conditions dans lesquelles les Etats accordent aux navires le droit d'arborer le pavillon national" (Académie Internationale de Droit Comparé—Le Congrès International de Droit Comparé 1958) [mimeographed].

——— "Lien substantiel et nationalité des navires," *Jugoslovenska Revija za Medunarodno Pravo* 7:258 (1960).

Brierly, J. L., *The Law of Nations* (5th ed. 1955).

Briggs, H. W., *The Law of Nations: Cases, Documents, and Notes* (2d ed. 1952).
British and Foreign State Papers 1917–1918, vol. CXI (1921).
Brittin, B. H. and Watson, L. G., *International Law for Seagoing Officers* (2d ed. 1960).
Bullock, C. Ll., "Angary," *British Yearbook of International Law* (1922), p. 99.
Bulushev, Iu., "Bluzhdaiushchie flagi," *Morskoi Flot* (Moscow, 1956, no. 12), pp. 25–26.
Burmistrov, M., "V tiskakh rastushchikh protivorechii," *Morskoi Flot* (Moscow, 1959, no. 11), pp. 23–26.

Calvo, Carlos, *Le droit international théorique et pratique*, vol. II (3d ed. 1880; 5th ed. 1896).
Cantillon de Tramont, Paul, *De la nationalité des navires* (1907).
Charles, Garfield, *Treaties, Conventions, International Acts, Protocols and Agreements between the United States of America and Other Powers: Supplement, 1913, to Senate Document N. 357, 61st Congress, 2d Session; Senate Document No. 1063, 62d Congress, 3d Session* (*1913*) [known as Charles' *Treaties*].
Colombos, C. J., *The International Law of the Sea* (4th rev. ed. 1959).
Conforti, Benedetto, "Le Convenzioni di Ginevra sul diritto del mare," Istituto di Diritto Internazionale e Straniero della Università di Milano, *Comunicazioni e Studi* 9:201 (1959).
[Costa Rica,] *Colección de leyes, decretos, acuerdos y resoluciones* (1941; 1958).
[Costa Rica,] *La Gaceta: Diario Oficial* (1958).

Dahm, Georg, *Völkerrecht*, vol. I (1959).
Das Werk von Haag, 2d series, pt. I, ed. W. M. A. Schücking (1917).
Demaurex, Claude, *La nationalité des navires de mer: Etude de droit suisse* (1958).
Diena, Giulio, "Principes du droit international privé maritime," *Recueil des Cours*, Académie de Droit International de la Haye 51:409 (pt. I, 1935).
"Le droit de la mer à la Conférence de Genève 1958," *Chronique de Politique Étrangère* 12:7 (1959, No. 1).
Dunn, F. S., *The Protection of Nationals: A Study in the Application of International Law* (1932).

"The Effect of United States Labor Legislation on the Flag-of-Convenience Fleet. Regulation of Shipboard Labor Relations and Remedies against Shoreside Picketing," [note] *Yale Law Journal* 69:498 (1960).
Ehrenzweig, A. A., *Conflict of Laws* (1959).

Fauchille, Paul, *Traité de droit international public,* vol. I, pt. 2 (1925).

Fedozzi, Prospero, "La condition juridique des navires de commerce," *Recueil des Cours,* Académie de Droit International de la Haye 10:5 (1929, pt. II).

Fenwick, C. G., *International Law* (2d ed. 1934).

Ferron, O. R. de, *Le droit international de la mer,* vol. I (1959).

Fleischmann, Max, "Der Maskat Fall," *Das Werk von Haag,* 2d series, pt. I, p. 345, ed. W. M. A. Schücking (1917).

Florio, Franco, "La conferenza di Ginevra sul diritto internazionale marittimo," *Jus: Rivista di Scienze Giuridiche* 9:557 (1958).

——— *Nazionalità della nave e legge della bandiera* (1957).

François, J. P. A. "La Cour Permanente d'Arbitrage, son origine, sa jurisprudence, son avenir," *Recueil des Cours,* Académie de Droit International de la Haye 87:460 (1955, pt. I).

——— "Le tendenze moderne nel diritto internazionale pubblico marittimo," *La Comunità Internazionale* 13:30 (1958).

Friedman, Samy, *Expropriation in International Law* (1953).

Friedmann, W. G., "Legal Problems in Foreign Investments," *Business Lawyer* 14:746 (1959).

Fulton, T. W., *The Sovereignty of the Sea* (1911).

Gibbons, W. J. *Tax Factors in Basing International Business Abroad* (1957).

Gidel, Gilbert, *Le droit international public de la mer,* 3 vols. (1932).

Giuliano, Mario, *I diritti e gli obblighi degli Stati,* vol. I (1956).

Goldberg, J. P., *The Maritime Story: A Study in Labor-Management Relations* (1958).

Gorter, Wytze, *United States Shipping Policy* (1956).

Green, L. C., "The Geneva Conventions and the Freedom of the Seas," *Current Legal Problems* 12:224 (1959).

Hague Court Reports, ed. J. B. Scott (1916).

Hackworth, G. H., *Digest of International Law,* vol. I (1941), vols. VI and VII (1943).

Hall, W. E., *International Law,* ed. A. P. Higgins (7th ed. 1917).

Harley, J. E., "The Law of Angary," *American Journal of International Law* 13:267 (1943).

Harolds, L. R., "Some Legal Problems Arising Out of Foreign Flag Operations," *Fordham Law Review* 28:295 (1959).

Harvard Law School, "Convention on the International Responsibility of States for Injuries to Aliens, Preliminary Draft with Explanatory Notes" (May 1, 1959) [published by Harvard Law School].

Harvard Research, *Draft Convention on the Law of Treaties* (1935).

——— "The Law of Territorial Waters," *American Journal of International Law,* 23 Supp. 307 (1929).

——— "Draft Convention on the Rights and Duties of Neutral States in Naval and Aerial War," *American Journal of International Law* 33 Supp. (1939).
Hawkins, H. C., *Commercial Treaties and Agreements* (1951).
Herz, J. H., "Expropriation of Foreign Property," *American Journal of International Law* 35:243 (1940).
Heyck, Heinrich, *Die Staatszugehörigkeit der Schiffe und Luftfahrzeuge* (1935).
Higgins, A. P., *The International Law of the Sea,* ed. C. J. Colombos (4th ed. 1954).
——— "Le régime juridique des navires de commerce," *Recueil des Cours,* Académie de Droit International de la Haye 30:19 (1929, pt. V).
——— and Colombos, C. J., *The Freedom of the Seas* (1943).
Honig, Frederick, "Die Vereinten Nationen und die Kodifikation des Völkerrechts," *Archiv des Völkerrechts* 8:1 (1959, No. 1).
House of Lords, *Parliamentary Debates,* vol. CCVIII (1958).
Hudson, M.O., ed., *International Legislation,* vols. I-IX (1931–1950).
Hyde, C. C., *International Law Chiefly as Interpreted and Applied by the United States,* 3 vols. (2d rev. ed. 1947).

Inter-Governmental Maritime Consultative Organization (IMCO), *United Nations Maritime Conference, Geneva 1948, Documents* (U.N. EcoSoc Council, Doc. E/CONF. 4/1–63) (1947–1948) [mimeographed].
——— *United Nations Maritime Conference, Geneva 1948, Summary Records* (U.N. EcoSoc Council, Doc. E/CONF. 4/SR. 1–6 (1948) [mimeographed].
——— First Session of the Assembly, London 1959, *Documents* (IMCO/A.I/Working Papers 1–20 (1959) [mimeographed].
——— First Session of the Assembly, London 1959, *Summary Records* (IMCO/A.I/SR. 1–12 (1959) [mimeographed].
International Labour Office, *Conditions in Ships Flying the Panama Flag: Report of the Committee of Enquiry of the International Labour Organization, May–November 1949* (1950).
——— *The International Labour Code 1951,* vol. I (1952).
——— International Labour Conference, Twenty-first and Twenty-second Sessions, Geneva 1936, *Record of Proceedings* (1936).
——— International Labour Conference, Forty-first Session, Geneva 1958, *Record of Proceedings* (1959).
——— *Report IV: Flag Transfer in Relation to Social Conditions and Safety* (1957).
——— *Report I: Report of the Director General* (1957).
[Note: These two reports were prepared for the 41st (Maritime) Session of the International Labor Conference, Geneva 1958.]

——— *Legislative Series* (July–August 1958), *India, Merchant Shipping Act 1958* (1959).

International Transport Workers' Federation, *Panlibhonco: The Modern Shipping Problem* (1958).

Jenks, C. W., "Nationality, the Flag and Registration as Criteria for Demarcating the Scope of Maritime Conventions," *Journal of Comparative Legislation and International Law* 19:245 (3d series, 1937).

Jessup, P. C., "The Geneva Conference on the Law of the Sea; A Study in International Law-Making," [Editorial Comment] *American Journal of International Law* 52:730 (1958).

——— *The Law of Territorial Waters and Maritime Jurisdiction* (1927).

——— "The United Nations Conference on the Law of the Sea," *Columbia Law Review* 59:234 (1959).

Johnson, D. H. N., "The Geneva Conference on the Law of the Sea," *Yearbook of World Affairs* 13:68 (1959).

Kaufmann, Erich, "Règles générales du droit de la paix," *Recueil des Cours,* Académie de Droit International de la Haye 54:313 (1935, pt. IV).

Keilin, A. D., *Sovetskoe morskoe pravo* (Moscow, 1954).

Kolodkin, A. L., "Predostavlenie sudam natsional'nosti po morskomu pravu kapitalisticheskikh stran," *Morskoe Pravo i Praktika* (Moscow, 1960, no. 8), pp. 10–27.

Korotaev, A., "Nekotorye problemy sudokhodstwa," *Morskoi Flot* (Moscow, 1956, no. 12), pp. 29–30.

Kunz, J. L., "The Nottebohm Judgment," *American Journal of International Law* 54:536 (1960).

Langavant, E. "Les conventions de Genève sur le droit de la mer," *Le Droit Maritime Français* 11:3, 67 (1959).

Lapradelle, A. G. de, and Niboyet, J. P., *Répertoire de droit international,* vol. X (1931).

Lauterpacht, Sir Hersch, "Codification and Development of International Law," *American Journal of International Law* 49:16 (1955).

League of Nations, "The Comparative Study of National Laws Governing the Grant of the Right to Fly the Merchant Flag," League of Nations *Official Journal,* 12:1631 (1931).

Legal Aspects of Foreign Investment, ed. W. G. Friedmann and R. C. Pugh (1959).

Legal Problems of International Trade, ed. P. O. Proehl (1959).

Liberian Code of Laws of 1956, vols. 1–3 (1957).

Liszt, Franz von, *Das Völkerrecht* (11th ed. 1918).

Magrassi da Sa, "A Organização Intergovernamental Consultiva de Navegação Marítima," *Revista Brasileira de Política Internacional* 1:76 (1958).

Malloy, W. M., *Treaties, Conventions, International Acts, Protocols and Agreements between the United States of America and Other Powers 1776–1909*, vols. I and II (1910).

Mance, H. O., *International Sea Transport* (1945).

Martens, G. F. von, *Recueil des Traités*, vol. II (1817).

——— *Nouveau Recueil des Traités*, vol. VI (1828).

McDonald, Eula and Cates, J. M. Jr., *Toward a World Maritime Organization* (1948).

McDougal, M. S. and Burke, W. T., "Crisis in the Law of the Sea: Community Perspectives versus National Egoism," *Yale Law Journal* 67:539 (1958).

——— *The Public Order of the Oceans: A Contemporary International Law of the Sea* (in press).

——— and Vlasic, I. A., "The Maintenance of Public Order at Sea and Nationality of Ships," *American Journal of International Law* 54:25 (1960).

McFee, William, *The Law of the Sea* (1950).

McNair, A. D., *Legal Effects of War* (3d ed. 1948).

——— "Problems Connected with the Position of the Merchant Vessel in Private International Law, with Particular Reference to the Power of Requisition," *Grotius Society [1945] Transactions* 31:30 (1946).

——— "The Requisitioning of Merchant Vessels," *Journal of Comparative Legislation and International Law* 27:68, 3d series, pts. 3 and 4 (1945).

Mender, Per Georg, "Nationality of Ships: Politics and Law," *Arkiv for Sjørett* 5:265 (1961).

Molodtsov, S. V., *Mezhdunarodno-pravovoi rezhim otkrytogo moria i kontinental'nogo shelfa* (Moscow, 1960).

Monaco, Riccardo, "Sulla composizione del Comitato della sicurezza marittima dell' IMCO," *Rivista di Diritto Internazionale* 43:679 (1960).

Moore, J. B., *A Digest of International Law*, vol. II (1906).

——— *History and Digest of the Arbitrations to Which the United States Has Been a Party*, vols. II and V (1898).

Morison, Samuel, *The Maritime History of Massachuetts 1785–1860* (1921).

[Morocco (Empire chérifien)], *Bulletin Officiel*, vol. XLVI (1957).

Mouton, M. W., "De Conferentie betreffende het Recht van de Zee, gehouden te Genève van 24 februari tot 29 april 1958," *Marineblad* 65:7 (No. 1, 1959).

Müller, Rudolf, "Das Flaggenrecht von Schiffen und Luftfahrzeugen," *Zeitschrift für Völkerrecht* 13:233, 353 (1926).

National Academy of Sciences — National Research Council, *The Role of the U.S. Merchant Marine in National Security* (NAS-NRC Publication No. 748, 1959).

Neumeyer, Karl, *Internationales Verwaltungsrecht,* vol. III (1926).

Oppenheim, L. F. L., *International Law,* ed. Sir Hersch Lauterpacht, vol. I (8th ed. 1955) and vol. II (7th ed. 1952).

Organization for European Economic Cooperation (OEEC): Maritime Transport Committee, *Maritime Transport* (Paris, December 1954) Trends in Economic Sectors.

——— *Maritime Transport* (Paris, July 1957) Trends in Economic Sectors.

——— *Maritime Transport* (Paris, June 1958) Trends in Economic Sectors.

——— *Maritime Transport* (Paris, May 1961) Trends in Economic Sectors.

——— "Study on the Expansion of the Flags of Convenience Fleets and on Various Aspects Thereof" [Doc. C (57) 246, 28 Jan. 1958, mimeographed].

Ortolan, T. J. F., *Règles internationales et diplomatie de la mer,* vols. I and II (4th ed. 1864).

Padwa, D. J., "The Curriculum of IMCO," *International Organization* 14:524 (1960).

Pallua, Emilio, "La nationalité des navires," *Jugoslovenska Revija za Medunarodno Pravo* 3:71 (1956).

——— "La nationalité des navires de commerce en droit international public et privé," *Jugoslovenska Revija za Medunarodno Pravo* 5:81 (1958).

"Panlibhon Registration of American-owned Merchant Ships; Government Policy and the Problem of the Courts" [Note] *Columbia Law Review* 60:711 (1960).

Patey, Jacques, "La conférence des Nations Unies sur le droit de la mer," *Revue Générale de droit international public* 62:446 (1958).

Pinto, Roger, "Flags of Convenience," *Journal du Droit International* 87:344 (1960).

Potamianos, Phocion, "L'hypothèque de préférence (mortgage) sur les navires," *Le Droit Maritime Français* 13:566, 633 (1961).

Pradier-Fodéré, P. L. E., *Traité de droit international public européen et américain,* vol. VIII (1906).

Preuss, Lawrence, "State Immunity and the Requisition of Ships during the Spanish Civil War, I: Before the British Courts," *American Journal of International Law* 35:263 (1941).

——— "State Immunity and the Requisition of Ships during the Spanish Civil War, II: Before the Courts of the United States," *American Journal of International Law* 36:37 (1942).

Quadri, Rolando, *Le navi private nel diritto internazionale* (1939).

Rabel, Ernst, *The Conflict of Laws, A Comparative Study*, 4 vols. (1945–1958).

Reiff, Henry, *The United States and the Treaty Law of the Sea* (1959).

Rienow, Robert, *The Test of the Nationality of a Merchant Vessel* (1937).

Ripert, Georges, *Droit maritime*, vol. I (4th ed. 1950).

Rousseau, Charles, *Le droit international public* (1953).

Scerni, Mario, *Il diritto internazionale privato marittimo ed aeronautico* (1936).

Schade, A. F., "The Strategic Importance of Control of the Seas" [mimeographed paper in the library of Center for International Affairs, Harvard University] (1960).

Schwarzenberger, Georg, *International Law*, vol. I (2d ed. 1949; 3d ed. 1952).

"Seven Maritime Sessions of the International Labour Conference," *International Labour Review* 78:429 (1958).

Singh, Nagendra, "The Indian Shipping Act, 1958, and International Law," *The Indian Journal of International Law* 1:10 (1960).

Smith, H. A., *The Law and Custom of the Sea* (3d ed. 1959).

Sørensen, Max, "Law of the Sea," *International Conciliation*, No. 520 (November 1958).

Stevenson, J. R., "The Relation of Private International Law to Public International Law," *Columbia Law Review* 52:561 (1952).

"Tableau des conditions imposées par les principales puissances maritimes pour le droit au pavillon national," *Recueil Général Périodique et Critique des Décisions, Conventions et Lois Relatives au Droit International Public et Privé* (1936, pt. VI), p. 1.

Triepel, Heinrich, *Virtuelle Staatsangehörigkeit* (1921).

[Tunisia] *Journal Officiel de la République Tunisienne*, vol. CI (1958).

United Nations Conference on the Law of the Sea, Geneva 1958, *Official Records*, vol. I: *Preparatory Documents* (1958); vol. II: *Plenary Meetings, Summary Records of Meetings and Annexes* (1958); vol. IV: *Second Committee* (High Seas: General Regime), *Summary Records of Meetings, and Annexes* (1958). [Note: These documents are numbered A/CONF.13. . .]

United Nations International Law Commission (ILC), *Yearbook of the International Law Commission 1949: Summary Records and Documents of the First Session including the report of the Commission to the General Assembly* (1956).

——— *Yearbook of the International Law Commission 1950*, vol. I: *Sum-*

mary Records of the second session 5 June–29 July 1950 (1958); vol. II: *Documents of the second session including the report of the Commission to the General Assembly* (1957).

——— *Yearbook of the International Law Commission 1951,* vol. I: *Summary Records of the third session 16 May–27 July 1951* (1957); vol. II: *Documents of the third session including the report of the Commission to the General Assembly* (1957).

——— *Yearbook of the International Law Commission 1955,* vol. I: *Summary Records of the seventh session 2 May–July 1955* (1960); vol. II: *Documents of the seventh session including the report of the Commission to the General Assembly* (1960).

——— *Yearbook of the International Law Commission 1956,* vol. I: *Summary Records of the eighth session 23 April–4 July 1956* (1956); vol. II: *Documents of the eighth session including the report of the Commission to the General Assembly* (1957). [Note: These documents are numbered A/CN.4/. . .]

United Nations *Reports of International Arbitral Awards,* vol. III (1949).

United Nations Secretariat, *Laws concerning the Nationality of Ships,* United Nations Legislative Series (1955).

——— *Supplement to Laws and Regulations on the Regime of the High Seas and Laws concerning the Nationality of Ships,* United Nations Legislative Series (1959).

United States Congress, *Hearings on S. 3823 before a Subcommittee of the Senate Committee on Interstate and Foreign Commerce,* 81st Congress, 2d Session (1950).

——— *Hearings on H.R. 6601, 7601 before the Subcommittee on Merchant Marine and Fisheries,* House of Representatives, 86th Congress, 1st Session (1959).

——— Senate Report No. 833, 70th Congress, 1st Session (1928).

——— Senate Report No. 1583, 71st Congress, 3d Session (1931).

——— Senate Report No. 2494, 81st Congress, 2d Session (1950).

——— *Ship Transfers to Foreign Flag, Hearings before the Merchant Marine and Fisheries Subcommittee of the Committee on Interstate and Foreign Commerce,* U.S. Senate, 85th Congress, 1st Session on S. 1488 (1957).

——— *Study of Vessel Transfer, Trade-in, and Reserve Fleet Policies, Hearings before the Subcommittee on Merchant Marine and Fisheries,* House of Representatives, 85th Congress, 1st Session, Pts. 1 and 2 (1957).

——— *Study of Trade out and Build Activities of Onassis Companies, Hearings before the Special Subcommittee on Merchant Marine and Fisheries,* House of Representatives, 85th Congress, 2d Session (1958).

——— *Conventions on the Law of the Sea, Hearing before the Commit-*

tee on Foreign Relations, U.S. Senate, 86th Congress, 2d Session on Executives J,K,L,M,N (1960).

United States Department of Commerce, *Merchant Shipping Statistics Through 1958* (1959).

United States Department of State, *Papers Relating to the Foreign Relations of the United States:* [1874] (1874); [1885] (1886); [1909] (1914); [1916] (Supplement) (1929); [1928] vol. I (1942); [1929] vol. I (1946).

——— *Treaties in Force: A List of Treaties and other International Agreements of the United States in Force on January 1, 1960* (1960).

——— "U.S. and West European Nations Discuss Shipping Problems," *Department of State Bulletin* 41:10 (July 6, 1959, No. 1045).

Van Eik, J., "Apercue de la législation néerlandaise récente sur la nationalité des navires," *Revue de Droit International et de Législation Comparée* 2:583 (1870).

Van Panhuys, H. F., *The Role of Nationality in International Law* (1959).

Van Zijst, W. A., *De nationaliteit van Schepen beschouwd uit een internationaalrechtelijk oogpunt* (1897).

Verdross, Alfred, *Völkerrecht* (4th rev. ed. 1959).

Vereshchetin, V. S., *Svoboda sudokhodstva v otkrytom more* (Moscow, 1958).

Verzijl, J. H. W., "The United Nations Conference on the Law of the Sea, Geneva 1958 (II)," *Nederlands Tijdschrift voor Internationaal Recht* 6:115 (1959).

[Viet-Nam], Ordonnance du 2 Août 1956, *Le Droit Maritime Français,* 8:376 (1956).

Visscher, Charles de, "Observations sur effectivité en droit international public," *Revue Générale du Droit International Public* (3rd series, vol. 29) 62:601 (1958).

Vluchten of Vlechten, "De registratie van schepen onder goedkope vlag," *Marineblad* 68:60 (1958, no. 1).

Walker, Herman, Jr., "Modern Treaties of Friendship, Commerce and Navigation," *Minnesota Law Review* 42:805 (1958).

——— "Provisions on Companies in United States Commercial Treaties," *American Journal of International Law* 50:373 (1956).

Watts, A. D., "Florio, Nazionalità della nave e legge della bandiera," [review] *International and Comparative Law Quarterly* 7:399 (1958).

——— "The Protection of Merchant Ships," *British Yearbook of International Law* 33:52 (1957).

Westlake, John, *International Law,* vol. I (1910).
——— "The Muscat Dhows," *Law Quarterly Review* 23:83 (1907).
Wharton, Francis, *A Digest of the International Law of the United States,* vol. III, (1888).
Williamson, J. A., *The Ocean in English History* (1941).
Wilson, G. G., *International Law* (3d ed. 1939).
——— "Taking Over and Return of Dutch Vessels 1918–1919," *American Journal of International Law* 24:694 (1930).
Wolff, Martin, *Private International Law* (1950).

Table of Cases Cited

Index

Bei Fragen zur Produktsicherheit wenden Sie sich bitte an:
If you have any questions regarding product safety,
please contact:

Walter de Gruyter GmbH
Genthiner Straße 13
10785 Berlin
productsafety@degruyterbrill.com